DEVELOPING

DEVELOPING YOUR SPEAKING VOICE

DEVELOPING YOUR SPEAKING VOICE

BY *Harrison M. Karr*, **PH. D.**

Associate Professor of Speech, University of California, Los Angeles

HARPER & BROTHERS Publishers New York

✳ Contents

✳ Preface

Developing Your Speaking Voice is the outgrowth of some twenty years of teaching and research in the field of the speaking voice. It is designed as a text for beginning college classes which stress the effective use of the voice. It presents a developmental program for "average" students who seek to improve their voices for everyday speech as well as for public performances, including corrective exercises for such common voice faults as huskiness, nasality, and other undesirable tonal qualities, as well as monotony and bad tone placement.

The book's appeal to the student will probably rest primarily upon its simple straightforward style, which results from the author's conviction that necessary factual information about anatomy, physiology, and physics—the essential scientific knowledge—need not be obscure, confusing, or frustrating to non-scientific students; on the contrary it may be made understandable and interesting. Voice students need to know some of the basic facts about how the voice functions, enough to provide an intelligent approach to their program of voice improvement, and to prevent wrong or harmful practices.

Perhaps the distinguishing feature of this book is its constant effort to motivate the student to *want* to improve his voice, without which all drill exercises are fruitless. Facts about the voice and exercises for the voice are presented so that the student understands why he should follow a certain program, and what he may hope to gain from it. Too often students get the impression that the mere doing of so many drills will effect major changes. Exercises in themselves may or may not be effective, depending largely upon the student's understanding of why he is doing them, his desire to do them, and his belief that they will achieve results. These three are the heart of motivation, and they play an important part in the plan of development of the entire book.

A departure from tradition is the transposition of the order of the chapters on *breathing* and *tone production*. Instead of presenting the study of breath control first, as is customary, the author has treated tone production first, for a most important reason. Too many students, in their first eager zeal to hold a big supply of breath, develop considerable tenseness around the throat. When the student is first made aware of the proper method of tone production and learns how easily and relaxedly a good tone is made, he is more likely to develop good breath control.

For convenience of study, the book is divided into two main parts: *Producing the Voice* and *Using the Voice*. In a sense, Part I might be considered the scientific phase of voice study, for in this section is placed whatever information about anatomy, physiology, and physical science is essential to an effective course in voice training. Part II might be called the artistic phase of voice study, for in it are considered ways and means of using the speaking voice with artistic skill.

Much thought has gone into choosing the practice selections. An effort has been made to include passages which not only help to accomplish the purpose of the exercise, but are interesting and enjoyable, and make some contribution to the student's appreciation of literature. It is sincerely hoped that they will add materially to the usefulness and enjoyableness of the book.

ACKNOWLEDGMENTS

It is not possible to name specifically everyone who has given assistance, directly or indirectly, in the preparation of this book. Certain colleagues and other friends, however, have contributed so generously of their time and talents that I wish to acknowledge my deep indebtedness:

To the late Dean Ray K. Immel of the University of Southern California, Professor Wesley Lewis of the University of California, Los Angeles, and Professor Emeritus Dwight E. Watkins of the University of California, Berkeley, for their advice on the overall plan of the book; to Professor John Moncur of the University of California, Los Angeles, for invaluable aid in the chapters on articulation and pronunciation; to Dr. Joel J. Pressman, otolaryngologist, of the University of California, Los Angeles, Medical School, for expert guidance in the chapters dealing with voice physiology; to Dean Franklin Rolfe of the University of California, Los Angeles, for pertinent suggestions regarding rhythm; to Professor Norman Watson of the University of California, Los Angeles, for unfailing help and advice in the sections dealing with sound; to Mrs. Lucille Innes for illustrative drawings, Figs. 1, 3, 4, 5, 6, 9, 10, 11, 12, and 14; and to Miss Jacqueline Tobian for Figs. 2, 13, and 15.

HARRISON M. KARR

January, 1953

DEVELOPING YOUR SPEAKING VOICE

✳ *Voices*

Now I make a leaf of Voices—for I have found nothing mightier
    than they are,
And I have found that no word spoken, but is beautiful, in its
    place.

O what is it in me that makes me tremble so at voices?
Surely, whoever speaks to me in the right voice, him or her I
    shall follow,
As the water follows the moon, silently, with fluid steps, any-
    where around the globe.
All waits for the right voices;

Where is the practis'd and perfect organ? Where is the develop'd
    Soul?
For I see every word utter'd thence has deeper, sweeter, new
    sounds, impossible on less terms.

I see brains and lips closed—tympans and temples unstruck,
Until that comes which has the quality to strike and to unclose,
Until that comes which has the quality to bring forth what lies
    slumbering, forever ready, in all words.
                   —WALT WHITMAN, *Leaves of Grass*

1 ✻ You and Your Voice

When the motion-picture industry, along in the 1920's, quite suddenly changed from silent pictures to "talkies," a veritable havoc was created. Prominent screen actors awoke to find themselves in imminent danger of being pushed from their glamorous thrones, their fabulous salaries about to take wing and fly away, their public adulation likely to give place to a cold and cheerless oblivion.

Why this cataclysm? Simply because these actors' voices did not measure up to the rest of their personalities. Fans discovered that handsome heroes and beautiful heroines did not always have handsome or beautiful voices. It was a shocking disillusionment to find some of their idols equipped with voices that trembled, rasped, squeaked, or broke.

To their credit, by following programs of study and hard work, most of these actors succeeded in improving their voices sufficiently to effect the transition from silent to talking pictures.

There is significance in this incident—not only for motion-picture actors but for every person who hopes to develop his personality to the maximum—for two reasons:

1. People judge others, in part at least, by the sound of their voices.
2. Voices can be improved by attention and effort.

Let us examine these two statements in more detail.

People Are Judged by Their Voices

That your voice can "sabotage" your personality is not hard to demonstrate. A few examples from common experience will make this clear.

A stranger calls us on the telephone. It doesn't take us long to make up our minds whether or not we like the person at the other end of the wire, just from the quality of his voice and the way he uses it.

We hear a group talking in the next room, hidden from view. Instinctively we form a favorable or unfavorable impression of certain members of the group. Some we would like to have for friends; some—well, we just wouldn't. The sound of their voices has won or repelled us.

Even a dog detects the changes of quality in his master's voice and wags his tail or slinks away in response. How much more do human beings respond to these subtle factors of voice quality!

Radio and television admittedly are wonderful instruments; and one of their most attractive features, in the minds of many of us, is the dials which enable us to turn them off at will. Let a monotonous, droning voice assail our ears and we are usually not slow in clicking the dial.

On the other hand, these instruments also bring us voices that attract and hold us. One has but to mention the mellow tones of Lowell Thomas, the hearty good fellowship of Arthur Godfrey, the charm of Helen Hayes, the friendliness of Bing Crosby. You, personally, may not admire all these voices, but each does have qualities which cause millions of people to listen to it.

A person's voice is a badge of his personal traits. Some voices bespeak languor, others abounding vitality; some churlishness, others friendliness; some slovenliness, others exactness and precision. In each voice we discern—or think we discern (which amounts to the same thing so far as our estimate of the individual is concerned)—the key to the personality of the possessor. Just to hear certain voices is sufficient to brand their owners as pompous "stuffed shirts," while other voices as definitely suggest mastery, strength, and leadership.

Frequently these influences are so subtle that we scarcely realize them, much less analyze their nature. But they are none the less real. Fortunate indeed is the person whose vocal quality creates a favorable impression; and, conversely, greatly to be pitied is the one whose tones irritate or repulse.

The voice should match the rest of the personality. Imagine the following hypothetical examples of extreme mismatching of voice and other personality attributes:

1. An elderly gentleman of cultured appearance and digni-fied manner, but speaking in the hard, guttural tones of a gangster.

2. A beautiful and glamorous debutante talking with the "nosey" whine of a street waif.

3. A rugged outdoorsman gushing in the namby-pamby tones of an effeminate male millinery salesman.

Thus to create imaginatively a few of these personality misfits helps us to realize how unconsciously we come to expect the voice to harmonize with the rest of the personality. It also may serve to convince us individually of the desirability of striving to develop the kind of voice that goes with the type of person-ality we want for ourselves—a voice which will be an asset and not a liability.

It is gratifying to know that such striving produces results.

Voices Can Be Improved

Some people take the attitude, "Well, it's the voice I was born with; guess I'll have to put up with it."

Nonsense! You weren't born with any voice—just the equip-ment for making voice. True, nature is somewhat more gener-ous in the equipment she gives to some than to others. But few indeed are so ill treated by nature that they lack the mechanism for making acceptable voice if they learn to use it properly.

Demosthenes, who is generally recognized as one of the greatest speakers of all time, started out with defective articulation and a voice "weak and ill-managed." To correct these faults, he shouted against the roar of the ocean waves and struggled for pure articulation with the self-imposed handicap of a mouth full of pebbles. To hold himself to his rigid schedule of exercises, he lived for months in a cave; he shaved one side of his face and left the other side unshaved in order to avoid the temptation of returning to the comforts of civilization.

Henry Ward Beecher, the noted preacher and antislavery orator of Civil War days, made frequent public acknowledgment of the debt he owed to voice instruction and drills. A typical example is his reference to the way he and his brother in their boyhood utilized the woods back of their home to "make the night and even the day hideous, . . . exploding all the vowels from the bottom to the top of our voices," thus developing a "flexible instrument that accommodated itself readily to every kind of thought and every shade of meaning."

Beecher's enthusiasm for voice drill becomes more understandable when we learn what difficulties he had to overcome:

I had from childhood a thickness of speech arising from a large palate, so that when a boy I used to be laughed at for talking as if I had pudding in my mouth. When I went to Amherst I was fortunate in passing into the hands of John Lovell, a teacher of elocution, and a better teacher for my purpose I cannot conceive. His system consisted in drill, or the thorough practice of inflexions by the voice, and articulation. Sometime I was a whole hour practising my voice on a word—like "justice."[1]

Booker T. Washington, the great Negro leader and speaker, bears similar witness to the value of voice training:

Whatever ability I may have as a public speaker I owe in a measure to Miss Lord [a teacher at Hampton Institute]. When she found

[1] S. Scoville, *Biography of Henry Ward Beecher*, Webster & Co., 1888, p. 95.

out that I had some inclination in this direction she gave me private lessons in the matter of breathing, emphasis, and articulation. The debating societies at Hampton were a constant source of delight to me. These were held on Saturday evening; and during my whole life at Hampton, I do not recall that I missed a single meeting.[2]

Wendell Phillips added to unsurpassed natural endowments of grace and charm the most thorough training in the arts of speech. He says of Dr. Jonathan Barber, one-time instructor at Harvard, "Whatever I have acquired in the art of improving my voice, I owe to his suggestions and lessons."

A more recent example is found in the achievement of England's great war leader, Winston Churchill. This man, who so mastered the art of speech that he was able to rally and inspire a spiritually beaten nation, who used the magic of words to arouse his people to withstand the seemingly over-whelming force of Hitler's conquering hordes, who, as Edward R. Murrow, well-known news commentator, says, "mobilized the English language and made it fight"—this man, who has been called the greatest speaker in the world today, in youth was bedeviled with a stutter and a lisp. Determination and perseverance enabled him to conquer his handicaps. And to this day—such is his faith in drill and hard work—he prepares all his speeches carefully, painstakingly, testing different phrases aloud, then rehearsing them in toto before his wife.

Another inspiring example of voice improvement through training and effort is provided by the experience of Mrs. Franklin D. Roosevelt. In her syndicated news column, My Day, she mentions listening to a transcription of one of her speeches (a procedure highly recommended for every student of voice and speech). Mrs. Roosevelt states: "It is a curious sensation, sitting critically listening to yourself and realizing how un-utterably slow and dull you sound. . . . It is good for the soul to have an experience like this, but somewhat discouraging."[3] Even before this, however, Mrs. Roosevelt had been working

[2] Booker T. Washington, Up from Slavery, Page & Co., 1901, p. 67.
[3] Hollywood Citizen News, May 2, 1940.

on her voice and speech. *Life* for March 13, 1939, carried a full two-page spread showing pictures of her taking a voice lesson.

To conclude this consideration of the benefits to be derived from conscious attention to our voices, we perhaps cannot do better than to heed the words of one of America's most gifted actresses, Katharine Cornell. She has this to say about voice training: "A celebrated actress once said that beautiful speech is *not a gift but an achievement*. This is a very important thing for young people to remember, whether they are thinking of going into public life or not."[4]

Who Needs Voice Training?

It is obvious that persons in public life need good voices. Consider for a moment members of a few of the professions most prominently in the public eye.

Actors Have Special Need of Expressive Voices

An incident in the author's boyhood exemplifies this fact. As a high-school student he went with a group of classmates to a neighboring town to see the noted Polish actress, Madame Helena Modjeska, in the Shakespearian play, *Macbeth*. In the famous sleepwalking scene when Lady Macbeth descended the darkened stairs, wringing her hands in an effort to wash away the imaginary blood of the murdered King Duncan, and accompanied the wringing with heart-rending groans, "Oh," "Oh-h," "Oh-h-h"—this last a long, shuddering, sobbing sigh that seemed to be drawn from the depths of her agonized soul— little cold-footed mice seemed to run up and down that young observer's spine and over his scalp, pulling at the roots of his hair. So vivid was the impression, so deep the imprint upon his consciousness, that to this day the author has little trouble in calling up and reliving the experience at will. Here, indeed, was a voice with the magic power to make a character live and

---

[4] From a letter to the author, quoted by permission. Italics are the author's.

breathe and have being. Lacking some of this power, an actor must be content to be ranked as a second-rater, or worse.

In the comparatively new medium, television, the actor's voice is no less important. As we watch a televised drama, if we take time to analyze our reactions we can readily detect how much our liking or disliking of an actor depends upon his voice.

In the case of the radio actor, since we do not see him at all, we probably should not say that his voice is "an important aspect of his personality," but rather, "his voice *is* his personality."

Public Speakers Are Handicapped Without Good Voices

The public speaker needs a voice which can be heard, a voice which carries conviction, a voice which suggests sincerity, a voice which does not irritate or antagonize hearers.

A glimpse at the pages of history discloses the importance of voice in the equipment of great speakers of the past.

The ability of Demosthenes and Cicero to influence their audiences was testimony to the power and effectiveness of their voices, for most of their speaking was done to huge outdoor assemblages where powerful voice was an absolute necessity. William Pitt's voice was described as "possessing spirit-stirring notes which were perfectly irresistible"; Gladstone's as "singularly pure, clear, resonant, strong, vibrant, and silvery"; Daniel Webster's as having great "beauty and power"; Henry Clay's as "indescribably melodious." It was said of Wendell Phillips that "mobs could not resist the magic of his voice"; and the poet Lowell said of Ralph Waldo Emerson, "There is a kind of undertow in that rich baritone of his that sweeps our minds from their foothold into deeper waters with a drift we cannot and would not resist."

To come a little closer to our own times, no small element in the late Senator Beveridge's charm as a speaker was the pure, bell-like quality of his voice. Part of the equipment which made

William Jennings Bryan so remarkably effective on the platform was the purity and clarity of his magnificent voice. Senator Robert La Follette, Sr., possessed round, full, melodious tones that compelled attention and stirred emotional responses in the huge audiences which came to hear him. These three probably were the most popular speakers in the early part of this century, and all of them owed their appeal in no small measure to their superior voices.

But we do not need to look back beyond our own time for convincing proof. Right now the world is trying to recover from a war in which the influence of the spoken word was dramatically demonstrated. To an amazing degree, the might of Hitler and Mussolini came from their ability to dominate and command huge audiences. If we forget for a moment our abhorrence of their misguided and evil objectives, we cannot escape the realization that the personal magnetism which enabled these men to acquire dictatorial powers and eventually to lead their nations into a devastating war was largely the magnetism of powerful speech personalities.

Fortunately for the cause of democracy, some of the leaders of the Allies were endowed with speaking skill equally outstanding. The oratorical prowess of England's great prime minister was discussed in another connection earlier in this chapter. In our own country, history probably affords no better example of the effectiveness of a good voice in furthering a speaker's prestige and influence than that evidenced in the career of our late President, Franklin Delano Roosevelt. The warm, friendly, human quality in his tones, the note of confident and assured leadership, the direct, personal, conversational style of his "fireside chats," proved well-nigh irresistible to millions upon millions of people. Recognized as the master of all radio speakers of his day, it was often said of him that, were he deprived of his office, any radio network in the land would be overjoyed to hire him.

The political advantage which Roosevelt derived from his

superb voice was especially evident in the campaign of 1940. Wendell Willkie, Roosevelt's Republican opponent, waged a vigorous and resourceful campaign. And Willkie's dynamic progressivism and virile personality made him a formidable opponent. But his diction was bad (for example, "Amurica" for "America") and his voice was a little harsh, a little raspy, and rather poorly adapted to the radio. It seemed particularly unappealing when contrasted with the friendly, intimate, yet dignified tones of Roosevelt. Impartial observers attributed no small share of Roosevelt's success in the campaign to his matchless voice.

To be sure, good voice is not the only factor of importance in public speaking. The often-heard slogan, "It doesn't matter what you say; it's how you say it that counts," if taken literally, is unmitigated nonsense. What you say matters very, very much. When you substitute fine-sounding phrases or mellifluous tones for ideas, you become ridiculous and, what is worse, you cast a shadow of ill repute upon all training in voice and speech. It is this type of substitution which prompted Christopher Morley to say: "The unluckiest insolvent in the world is the man whose expenditures of speech are too great for his income of ideas." George Bernard Shaw described this type of individual as "a man who talks splendidly and has nothing to say." Without a content of ideas, oratory becomes but a cheap display of verbal technique and a provocation to ridicule.

The best delivery and voice are those which do not attract attention to themselves, but which, like a well-lighted plate glass window, put the merchandise in the most favorable light.

A good voice will not make a good speaker. It will not put the thoughts into his head. It will, however, add enormously to the conviction and persuasiveness of such ideas as he has. Given its proper place as an auxiliary to ideas and not a substitute for them, the expressive voice can and will be of inestimable advantage to the speaker.

Voice Training Is Important for Everyone

Potential actors and public speakers usually realize their need and try to overcome their shortcomings. Not so with many of us. In spite of its obvious importance, how little attention the average person gives to voice development! And that is strange, for all of us strive to make good impressions. We have to; otherwise we shall be left behind in the competitive struggle. We sacrifice to obtain an education, we dress as attractively as we can, we cultivate a smile and a pleasant manner. Why? Is it not to increase our influence over our fellows? To make a good impression? But we are prone to neglect one of the factors of most intimate and vital concern to the personality— the development of a pleasing voice.

Good voice is not simply an *adornment* for the personality, something to be hung on the person like a necklace. It is a factor with genuine bread-and-butter significance. Persons whose voices are displeasing are severely handicapped in their occupational pursuits. Teachers, salesmen, receptionists, demonstrators, managers, foremen—all whose occupational success depends upon their influence over others—to a considerable degree can measure their success or failure by the kind of voice they have.

Neither is good voice just a matter for dress-up occasions. It is a vital part of our day-by-day living. Millions of persons do not write their thoughts on paper oftener than a few times a year, but they engage in talk many times a day. Most people, in fact, speak a vast number of times for every time that they write. And the *way* they speak is about the most dependable advertisement of their cultural classification.

America is gradually becoming voice-conscious. The great number of articles on the speaking voice in the popular magazines attest the growing public interest in the subject. It is significant of the spirit of the time when a "charm" expert like John Robert Powers writes in his syndicated column,

Secrets of Charm, "Every woman can have a pleasing and impressive voice. It is an asset of charm that cannot be overrated; many women have been sought after merely because of the sound of their voices over the telephone."[5] Mr. Powers once urged beauty-conscious young ladies not to neglect their voices: "Peacocks are pretty—until they sound off."[6]

Recent influences in this direction have been the radio and television. All America is now able to hear good voices. As we turn the dial we hear one announcer after another, and we are coming to note those voices which please and those which do not. And this growing public discrimination is resulting in increasing selectivity among radio and television stations, for they are now choosing their announcers with considerable care.

Another influence in this same direction is the movies. When a good film appears, the public turns out by the millions to see and *hear* it. People from the farm, the factory, the crossroad village; cosmopolites, college students, and society matrons—all hear voices that are cultured and pleasing. They hear men with virile yet refined tones; they hear women with voices that are ever "soft, gentle, and low."

These factors are gradually reflecting themselves in the voices of the public at large. The change, however, is slow. Speech is a habit function, and there is probably no habit more difficult to change than our speech. It takes conscious attention and persistent effort to overcome bad habits. But slowly the transformation is taking place. Already the marks of an educated man include a pleasing voice and its proper use.

Voice Faults, Great and Small

Defective speech may be defined as speech which (1) calls attention to itself, (2) interferes with communication, and (3) is conducive to the individual's social or psychological maladjustment. It is readily apparent that there are various stages

[5] Los Angeles *Times,* August 4, 1950.
[6] *Ibid.,* October 20, 1950.

of these conditions, all the way from a slight deviation from normal to the most extreme abormalities, and that the differences often are matters of degree rather than of nature. Nevertheless, for convenience and efficiency in treatment, voice faults may be classified roughly into *major* and *minor* defects. And although the line of demarcation is not always clear cut, especially in the case of certain psychological disorders, it is desirable for us at this time to look briefly at these two general classifications. It is vitally important that the student recognize the proper field of study—and the limitations—of a course in voice improvement designed for the average, "normal" person.

Major Speech Defects

Certain speech disorders deviate so markedly from normal patterns of speech that they cannot be treated effectively in a textbook on general voice improvement. Some of these are organic in nature—for example, cleft palate, an abnormally high and narrow palatal arch, excessive jaw protrusion or recession, abnormally large tonsils or adenoids, tongue-tie, growths on the vocal cords, paralyzed vocal cords, and extreme muscular incoördination. These conditions require the services of a physician, surgeon, or dentist. Then, too, there are psychological disorders such as hysterical aphonia (loss of voice) and stuttering. Such conditions require the services of a trained speech therapist. The instruction in this book cannot alleviate major disorders resulting from either physiological or psychological causes. The student suffering from such defects should not waste his time on the drills and exercises set down here; little or no good will come from them—indeed, actual harm may result. He should by all means seek help from the properly trained specialist.

However, to any sufferer from one of these major afflictions who may read this discussion, the author hastens to say that he most certainly does not intend to discourage you from attempting to improve your voice. Far from it. Nothing should induce you to reconcile yourself to a lifetime of inarticulateness. It may be that your handicap will be the spur to drive you to achievement far above average. History records numerous cases of such "overcompensation" in many different fields.[7] But it is the part of wisdom first to get the help of competent medical specialists and speech correctionists to make sure that you do not engage in any exercises which may impede rather than promote your voice development.

MINOR VOICE DEFECTS

Voice defects which can be considered minor are many and varied in nature. Among them are hoarseness, harshness, nasality (too much nasal resonance), denasality (too little nasal resonance), stridency, and the types of voice quality called guttural, thin, flat, and infantile or juvenile. These "minor" defects take the form of the ear-piercing screech of excited children at play; the lifeless tones of the chronic invalid and the hypochondriac; the raucous, shudder-producing clacking of a certain type of extroverted salesman. Other defects, either in the way the tone is produced or in the way it is used after it is produced, include insincere or affected voices; voices pitched too high or too low; monotonous voices that run along as flat as the kitchen floor; voices that do not pause for phrasing; voices that die away on important words and leave the listener struggling to understand; voices that fill all potential rest periods with "uh's" and "ah's"; voices that lisp; voices that hiss and whistle; voices that pronounce words in a slovenly or provincial manner; and voices that fit the description given by the humorous writer, E. B. White, when he said that too many speakers "talk as if they had marshmallows for tonsils."

[7] A notable example of "overcompensation" recently made public is Supreme Court Justice William O. Douglas' stirring account of his struggle to overcome the effect of a childhood attack of infantile paralysis which left him with "pipe-stem legs," a struggle which resulted in a positive love for the most strenuous hiking and pack trips into the mountains. See W. O. Douglas, *Of Men and Mountains*, Harper & Brothers, 1950.

It should be understood that some of these conditions, even though we have classified them as minor speech and voice defects, may be so aggravated in nature or so persistent in duration that they should have attention from a trained medical authority or speech therapist. This is particularly true in the case of long-standing hoarseness. The student so afflicted should not delay in consulting a competent laryngologist. The condition may be the result of serious malformation or malfunctioning of the larynx, which would be made worse by voice exercises. Only after this condition has been corrected should voice exercises be undertaken.

But cases so serious in nature are infrequent. Most voice weaknesses, of both tone production and tone use, are the result of bad habits; comparatively few result specifically from defective speech mechanisms. The kinds of voice faults often encountered are illustrated by the following examples:

1. A young lady, just graduated from college and launched upon her first year of high-school teaching, encountered a group of obstreperous boys who made her life miserable by whispering and laughing. Her efforts to hold their attention resulted in a nervous and high-pitched voice. This had an unfavorable effect upon all the pupils and made them restless. The condition went from bad to worse until the young teacher was in imminent danger of an emotional crackup. Fortunately, an understanding and sympathetic principal came to her rescue in time, by appealing to the boys' better natures. At the same time he counseled the young teacher on how to approach the class with a more relaxed attitude and how to keep her voice pitched at a more restful level. The crisis was safely passed, and the teacher was saved from failure in her chosen career.

2. A husky young college freshman once had an unpleasant experience which threatened to leave him with a permanent affliction. During his adolescent voice-changing years, a misadventure had made people laugh at him, causing him great embarrassment. As a result he had become frightened of this strange new croaking voice that made him an object of ridicule.

He sought refuge in using the familiar high-pitched voice of his childhood, which he felt better able to control. By keeping tight enough rein on his throat muscles, he could use his pre-adolescent voice without danger of distressing breaks. The habit became fixed. He carried his "infantile" voice into young adulthood, the thin high tones contrasting ludicrously with his rugged physique. When, under tutelage, he overcame his fear complex and gradually let his tones drop until they reached their natural level, he made the surprising and gratifying discovery that he had a strong and rather pleasing baritone voice.

3. A middle-aged businessman talked in a voice which had become perpetually husky and displeasing. He was convinced that the trouble resulted from an injury to his speech mechanism received during an unskillful tonsil operation. Careful medical examination disclosed, however, that there was no physiological reason for the huskiness. It was thought that possibly he might have placed a strain upon the vocal cords by trying to talk too soon after the operation, while the whole throat area, including the vocal cords, was still inflamed and "raw." Also, on his disclosure that he had a hard-of-hearing wife, it was concluded that the chief cause of his difficulty lay in his constantly forcing his voice in an effort to be heard by his partially deafened wife. Successful therapy was provided in the form of rest and relaxation, until the vocal cords had a chance to recover their natural resiliency and to function normally.

The student who is interested in reading further along this line will find abundant literature. Two examples of the types of articles available are Williamson's report of an experiment with persons who had chronically hoarse voices,[8] and Moses' report of research on the relation of voice defects to personality development.[9]

Among most students, however, voice faults are less glaring

[8] Arleigh B. Williamson, "Diagonsis and Treatment of Seventy-Two Cases of Hoarse Voices," *Quarterly Journal of Speech*, April, 1945, pp. 189-202.

[9] Paul J. Moses, "Social Adjustment and the Voice," *ibid.*, December, 1941, pp. 532-537.

than those indicated above, and corrective measures are less dramatic in result. In perhaps the majority of persons the chief fault is that their voices are just ordinary, that they are simply dull.

Goals of Voice Training

The specific object of this book is to offer suggestions which will enable the conscientious student to develop a voice which has certain characteristics. It should be: (1) *Expressive,* capable of portraying shades of meaning, free from monotony. (2) *Vital,* big and strong enough to suggest strength of personality. (3) *Articulate,* characterized by easy distinctness of utterance. (4) *Pleasant,* tonal quality which attracts rather than repels. (5) *Free from affectation,* for vocal ostentation is as objectionable as any other kind of exhibitionism, and one of the most appealing qualities any voice can have is forthright sincerity. (6) *Possessed of personality,* personality appropriate to the person's age and sex; not merely a "pretty" voice, but a voice with character.

On the negative side, the aim should be to overcome detrimental traits, particularly the light futile tones and the shrill piercing tones frequently associated with female voices, and the harsh and muffled tones common to male voices.

Sound voice training is not an attempt to "change" voices. Only a ventriloquist like Edgar Bergen with his Charlie McCarthy should change his voice. Every person has a natural voice quality, determined by his physical structure and the size and shape of his voice mechanism. Any attempt to make it over into something different may result in disaster. The aim should be not to change but to develop—to train the natural qualities.

PATIENCE IS NECESSARY

In all speech and voice work, patience is essential. Wrong habits that have persisted for a dozen years cannot be corrected in a dozen days. It takes time to build properly. All that can be accomplished in the few weeks devoted to a voice course is to make a start in the right direction. The conscientious student should be satisfied if he can note the beginnings of improvement in his own speech habits and chart a course for his future development. But remember! *The voice can be trained.* The speaking voice as well as the singing voice will respond to guidance. The voice can be developed, just as any other part of the body can be developed, through proper exercise and attention to the laws of hygiene. Nearly every man and woman may have a pleasing and expressive voice. It depends wholly upon the intelligence and perseverance of the person setting out to acquire it.

Should the Student Listen to His Own Voice?

The answer is that he *must* listen to his voice; otherwise there can be no improvement. Many teachers have said: "The minute I can get a pupil to hear his own voice, improvement begins." Some voice students are fearful that this critical listening to themselves may have undesirable side effects, but no great hazard should be involved if the student makes a clear distinction between drill sessions and actual speaking occasions. In drill sessions the conscientious student will use every device at his command to help him to hear himself, including recordings of his voice, the practice of cupping his hand back of his ears, and intense concentrated attention. On the other hand, when conversing with others he should avoid any tendency to listen critically to his own tones; the chances are that if half his attention is directed toward listening to his own voice, three-fourths of his auditor's attention will be directed there too. Note how this situation is paralleled in other fields. The musician makes such a distinction between practice periods and public performances. The *accomplished* musician is able so to lose himself in the interpretation of his selection that he does not give conscious attention to the technique of his finger movements. Proficient golfers, tennis players, and sprinters have

quite different attitudes toward techniques when they are
drilling to perfect certain strokes or strides than when they
are engaged in actual competition. With the use of the voice,
as with these other skills, drill has to be continued until new
habits are established and an unconscious carry-over into life
situations results. Practice has to be so consistent and so long
continued that the improvement becomes second nature.

A Voice May Be "Too Beautiful"

If a speaking voice sounds as if it were seeking to be admired
for its own sake, like a lovely painting on the wall, it may be
said to be "too beautiful." It is better for a voice to have
strength and character than to have "perfection." A too perfect
voice may easily attract attention to itself and thus interfere
with the auditor's getting the flow of thought.

If audiences take pleasure in a speaking voice, it should be
an unconscious pleasure that leaves their minds free to consider
the thoughts being presented. If the voice has beauty, it should
be a subtle harmony that steals into their consciousness and
unlocks barriers, so that ideas may have easier entrance. It
should not be a quality that prompts people to say, "My, what
a lovely voice." Such a tone is a distraction, and therefore
undesirable.

Even the greatest voices are not perfect. Henry Lee Smith,
WOR's speech expert, once described what he considered the
perfect public speaking voice—a composite of qualities found
in leading speakers and actors:

> Franklin D. Roosevelt—diction, showmanship, fluency,
>   timing.
> Raymond Swing—authority.
> Winston Churchill—dramatic force.
> Helen Hayes—charm.
> Maurice Evans—resonant tone.
> Will Rogers—informality, warmth.
> Walter Winchell—punch.[10]

[10] *Word Study,* October, 1941, G. & C. Merriam Co.

BE YOURSELF!

The most important thing about you should be your individual personality, the something that distinguishes you from all other people. Your voice is part of that personality. Don't try to trade it for somebody else's. To be liked and admired you must be real, sincere, natural. If you are always trying to imitate someone else, you will find it hard to be yourself. Develop your own best characteristics, and let your voice be the outward expression of your inner self.

SET YOUR GOAL HIGH

Do not be satisfied with mediocrity. Remember the tribute Mark Twain paid a leading speaker of his day. After listening to a lecture by Robert G. Ingersoll, he exclaimed, "Lord, what an organ is the human voice when played on by a master."

PROJECTS IN ANALYZING VOICE AND PERSONALITY

1. Go to a motion-picture show with the special purpose of listening to the actors' voices. Make mental notes of the way the voices contribute to the different characterizations. Try to analyze any special effects produced by either tonal quality or dramatic use of the voice. This project will be easier if you go to a picture you have previously seen. It is difficult to dissociate yourself from—and objectively analyze—a drama which is being unrolled before you for the first time.

2. Listen critically to the voices on one of the radio quiz programs. Note the difference between the confident, vital quiz master's voice and the timid weak voices of most of the contestants. Observe how even the nasal twang of Groucho Marx helps to create his zany radio personality as he "razzes" what he calls the "yahoos."

3. Study the speech delivery of a professor whose lectures you enjoy. and ask yourself how much and in what way his voice contributes to your liking of him. Do the same with one you do not enjoy.

4. Most important of all, make a voice record and listen objectively to your own voice. If no recording machine is available in your college, you can no doubt find a commercial recording studio (possibly in connection with a music store) in your vicinity; the cost will be small in comparison to the possible benefits. A six-inch record is long enough (a little over two minutes). As material for the recording you might read one of the shorter selections in this text; or, better still, read about a one-minute excerpt from one of these selections, using the other minute to talk extemporaneously. You may talk about the meaning of the selection you are about to read, or about yourself and your voice problems.

As you hear yourself as others hear you, possibly for the first time, you probably will be surprised—you may even be a little shocked. Upon first hearing his voice, Billy Rose the theatrical producer said: "That's an impostor. It sounds like a nail file rubbing a cheese grater."[11] It puts the voice to a pretty severe test to separate it from all the rest of the personality traits—the smile, the light of the eye, the physical animation—and ask it to carry the burden all alone. Few voices measure up to the challenge. But to brave this encounter with your own voice is the beginning of wisdom.

You may not even recognize your voice when you first hear it. Very few persons do. The most commonly heard expression on such occasions is, "Is that me?" Yes, it's you, all right. But save the voice record. We'll hope that the voice we hear from you after a period of training won't be quite the same.

[11] *This Week,* January 15, 1950, p. 8.

Part One PRODUCING THE VOICE

II * The Four Basic Phases of the Speech Process

Simply as a matter of general intelligence it is worth while for college students to know something about the way voices are produced. There is a vast amount of ignorance concerning the human voice. Persons otherwise fairly well educated sometimes display a surprising lack of understanding of the mechanism by which they are enabled to talk, ignorance even of where their voices come from, to say nothing of how to take care of the delicate mechanism and how to use it most efficiently.

Sometimes this lack of knowledge may be passed over merely as regrettable ignorance. Occasionally, however, the lack of information, or the possession of certain misinformation, may have unfortunate consequences. It is easy for ignorant persons to become victims of stupid or unscrupulous exploiters. Sometimes these exploiters masquerade as voice teachers, charging large fees for their harmful instruction.

In front of the writer is a treatise on voice instruction which illustrates the point. The pamphlet was distributed without charge as a good-will gesture by a large music store. Its teaching is so factually inaccurate as to be ludicrous if it were not for its great potential harm. Imagine, for example, the disastrous effect of trying to follow the author's insistent and often repeated instruction that you must form the vowels not in your mouth, but "back and on top of the uvula," the uvula being the small conical tip of the soft palate which, by looking into the mirror, you can see suspended from the back part of the roof of your mouth. This patent absurdity is typical of the instruction presented by the "voice teacher" who wrote the pamphlet.

Students of voice obviously need to understand the basic facts of tone and speech production, facts which have been established by scientific research. They need this knowledge early in their voice training to insure that they will get started along the right lines.

The present chapter, giving a concise general statement of these known facts, serves as an introduction to the more detailed analysis presented in the succeeding chapters of Part I.

Before proceeding further, however, in this brief statement of the four basic processes of voice, it is desirable to pause a minute and consider sound in general. To gain even a rudimentary understanding of the process of human speech, we should know something about how our voices resemble other types of sound.

Factors Common to All Sound-Producing Instruments

Every sound-making device must have two elements: (1) some sort of motive power, which we call the *motor*; and (2) something that will vibrate, which we call the *vibrator*. Vibration is necessary, for sound *is* vibration. To the above two elements is almost always added a third, something that will amplify, or resonate, the sound. This is the *resonator*.

In a violin, the motor is the bow, the vibrator the strings, and the resonator the violin box. In the clarinet and the saxophone, the motor is the breath stream, the vibrator a reed in the mouthpiece, and the resonator the whole instrument. One of the simplest sounds is that produced by letting air escape through the small neck of a toy balloon. The outward rush of air under pressure constitutes the motor and the walls of the balloon neck are the vibrator; such resonation as there is comes from the balloon as a whole acting as a resonator. On this last principle, greatly refined, are based such musical instruments as the trumpet, the trombone, and the pipe organ.

The Human Speech Organism

In the human organism, the expelled breath stream is the motor, the larynx is the vibrator, and the cavities of the throat and head are the chief resonators. In addition to these three there is a fourth factor not found in other sound-making devices, except for a few birds and beasts which can be trained to imitate it. This is the articulator, or, more properly, the articulators, for there are several structures which aid in this process.

Let us recapitulate the four phases of speech production in the human organism.

1. *Respiration.* All speech sounds in the normal voice are based upon breath exhaled from the lungs. Controlled exhalation, which is essential to good voice, is accomplished by the action of certain muscles upon the lungs. The nature of this muscular action, together with instruction on how to develop control of the muscles, is discussed in Chapter V.

2. *Phonation.* The exhaled breath stream passes through the larynx, popularly called the voice box. Contained within the larynx are the vocal cords, which are made to vibrate by the stream of air passing between them. These vibrations set up sound waves which pass outward through the air. This process of creating sound waves in the larynx is called phonation, or tone production. Chapters III and IV explain the action of the larynx in creating tone, and present exercises for producing tone most efficiently.

3. *Resonation.* The sound waves carried from the larynx into the throat, mouth, and nose of the speaker are resonated (intensified and enriched) into the normal speaking voice. Effective use of the prin-

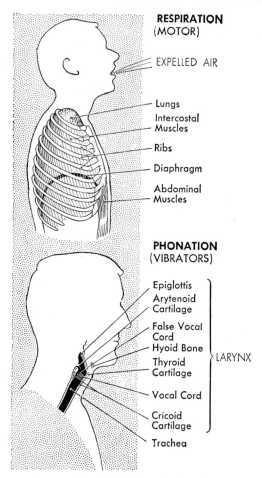

FIG. 1.   The four phases of the speech process—
respiration, phonation.

ciples which produce good vocal resonance is considered in Chapters
VI and VII.

4. *Articulation.* Through manipulating the mouth, tongue, lips,
teeth, soft palate, and other organs of articulation, tone is modified
into articulate speech. Chapters VIII and IX develop this phase of
the speech process.

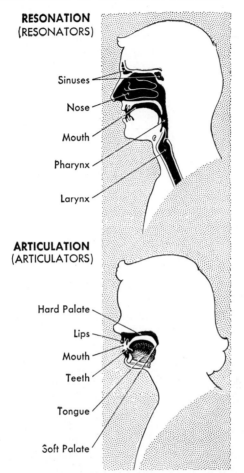

RESONATION
(RESONATORS)

Sinuses
Nose
Mouth
Pharynx
Larynx

ARTICULATION
(ARTICULATORS)

Hard Palate
Lips
Mouth
Teeth
Tongue
Soft Palate

FIG. 1. The four phases of the speech process—
resonation, articulation.

Although, for convenience in study, we separate these activities and consider them one at a time, in actual speech, respiration, phonation, resonation, and articulation are all aspects of a continuous process. The drawings in Fig. 1 show graphically the four aspects of speech. All the structures labeled in these drawings play important roles in the creation of speech sounds.

III ✳ Phonation:
How the Voice Box Works

To understand the development of the voice, some knowledge of the physiological processes involved is desirable, if not absolutely necessary. However, for the purposes of this text, a detailed treatment of the physiology of the vocal mechanism and of the physics of sound is not necessary. Our aim is to present only such information as is essential for a sound program of voice improvement. The present chapter is concerned chiefly with the functioning of the larynx.

Although this basic information is presented as simply as possible, it should be borne in mind that the act of speaking is not simple; it is an extremely complicated process. In childhood we learn to make speech sounds through imitation, and these sounds come to be so much a part of us that we take them for granted. Actually, however, the making of even the simplest vocal tone is a highly involved and complicated process requiring the coördinated action of many nerves, muscles, and other parts of the human organism. With all the fine adjustments required, it is not strange that occasionally the mechanism gets "out of kilter."

The Larynx
The most important part of the speech mechanism is the larynx, for it is here that the tone is produced. Recent scientific

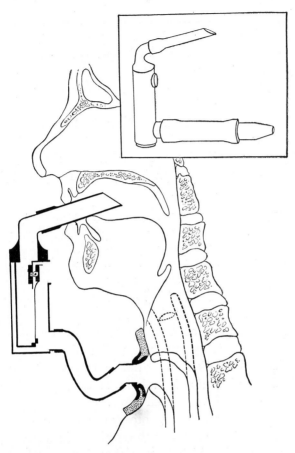

FIG. 2. Diagram of a reed type of artificial larynx in use, with one end of the larynx assembly connected to the throat of the speaker and the other end held in the mouth. The inset shows the outside appearance of the larynx. (After illustrations in *Artificial Larynx No. 2 Type,* by permission of the Western Electric Company.)

investigation, including extensive motion-picture studies of the action which takes place inside the larynx, reveals the extremely complicated process involved in tone production. Perhaps the following indirect approach may help to make clear the main features of that process.

THE ARTIFICIAL LARYNX

To gain some understanding of how the larynx functions, let us first look at a simplified type of speech mechanism, called an artificial larynx, which was created to take the place of vocal cords in persons who through injury or surgery have lost the use of the natural cords.[1]

The artificial larynx is a small round container, not much larger than a man's finger, which encloses a metal reed (see Fig. 2). When a blast of air rushes through the rubber tube and strikes the reed, the reed is set into vibration. This vibration makes a low buzzing sound, resembling the squawk of an anemic duck. When this sound is carried, by means of another small rubber tube, from the larynx to the speaker's mouth, an amazing phenomenon occurs: the weak humming sound is amplified into a strong tone not unlike that of the natural human voice. The speaker molds this tone into articulate speech by manipulating his mouth and throat exactly as if the tone were coming from his own vocal cords.

In the operation called tracheotomy (removal of the trachea), the patient's windpipe is made to terminate in a silver tube in the throat, through which he breathes. For speech, the tube of the artificial larynx is attached directly to the silver tube, thereby enabling the patient to utilize his own breath stream for motivating the reed.

This artificial larynx has made life pleasanter for hundreds of persons who otherwise would have been deprived of the

[1] It usually is possible for the interested student to observe an artificial larynx in operation, by getting in touch with the public relations department of the telephone company in any large city. In such demonstrations, the "breath stream" is provided by a small bellows held under the demonstrator's arm.

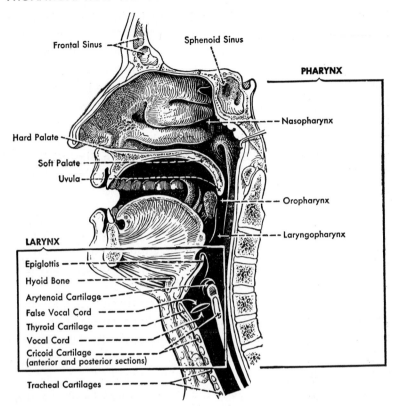

Frontal Sinus

Sphenoid Sinus

PHARYNX

Nasopharynx

Hard Palate

Soft Palate

Uvula

Oropharynx

Laryngopharynx

LARYNX

Epiglottis

Hyoid Bone

Arytenoid Cartilage

False Vocal Cord

Thyroid Cartilage

Vocal Cord

Cricoid Cartilage
(anterior and posterior sections)

Tracheal Cartilages

FIG. 3. Diagrammatic median section of the head and throat, showing the position of the human larynx in relation to the nose, mouth, trachea, and the three divisions of the pharynx—the nasopharynx, the oropharynx, and the laryngopharynx. (Modified from Millard and King, *Human Anatomy and Physiology*, by permission of W. B. Saunders Company.)

joys and satisfactions which come from communication by speech. However, while it is a remarkable device, in comparison to the normal speaking voice it is notably deficient. The tone is flat and unvaried in pitch; it has none of the interesting inflectional changes of the natural voice; it lacks the shading and "coloring" of which the natural voice is capable; it does not respond to thought and emotion.

The Human Larynx

Compared to its manufactured substitute, the human larynx is infinitely complex, but the basic principle is essentially the same. The larynx is a boxlike arrangement of cartilages and muscles located at the upper end of the trachea, or windpipe, as illustrated in Fig. 3. A front view is shown in Fig. 4. Like the artificial larynx, it houses a vibrator that is activated by the outgoing breath stream.

Framework of the Larynx. The "skeleton" of the larynx is composed of cartilages rigid enough to hold the trachea open when we want to breathe, but flexible enough to permit various minor adjustments when we want to speak or swallow. The chief of these cartilages are the following:

1. *The cricoid cartilage* is a circular cartilage which serves as the base of the larynx. It is ringlike in shape, similar to a signet ring, and located just above the top ring of the trachea. The enlarged, or signet portion of the ring, is at the back. The name comes from a Greek word meaning "finger ring."

2. *The thyroid cartilage* is the large cartilage at the front of the larynx, directly above the cricoid cartilage. It is composed of two plates joined together at about a 90-degree angle to form what we call the Adam's apple. The name "thyroid" comes from a Greek word meaning "shield," and this cartilage rather closely resembles a shield. The plates do not join in the back. The anterior or front ends of the vocal cords are attached to the inner surface of this cartilage at the point where the two plates are joined.

3. *The arytenoid cartilages* are two upright cartilages above the back part (the signet portion) of the cricoid. They are like little pyramids. To them are attached the posterior ends of the vocal cords. It is of the greatest significance in tone production

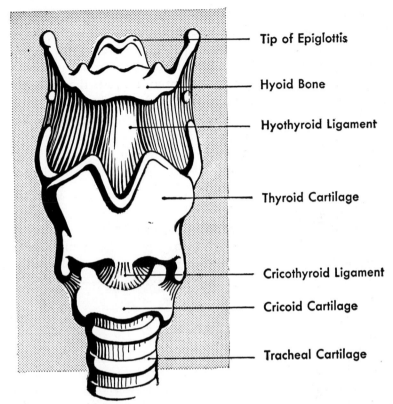

Tip of Epiglottis

Hyoid Bone

Hyothyroid Ligament

Thyroid Cartilage

Cricothyroid Ligament

Cricoid Cartilage

Tracheal Cartilage

FIG. 4.   Front view of the larynx, showing its cartilaginous frame-work and the ligaments which connect the various parts together and to other structures.

that these cartilages are movable. They can be moved toward and away from each other, and they can be made to rotate upon their bases. When they rotate inward, they bring the vocal cords together so that tone can be made. When they rotate outward, they pull them apart to permit free and unobstructed breathing. (See Fig. 5.)

Muscles Which Control the Larynx.   The larynx has two main sets of muscles, the intrinsic and extrinsic. The *extrinsic*

include various muscles which hold the larynx in place by
attaching it above to the jawbone or mandible, the hyoid or
tongue bone, and the styloid processes (projections of the
temporal bone), and at the bottom to the sternum or breastbone. The "ex" of the word "extrinsic" suggests that only one
end of these muscles is attached to the larynx and the other

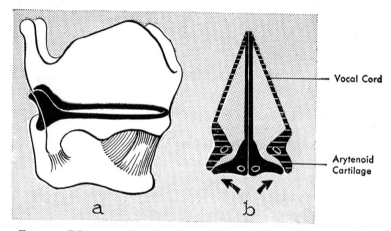

Vocal Cord

Arytenoid
Cartilage

a   b

FIG. 5.   Diagrams showing the position of the arytenoid cartilages
and their action in tensing and relaxing the vocal cords. a, Side
view of the larynx, showing (solid black) the arytenoids attached
to the posterior end of the vocal cords; b, schematic representation
of the pivotal action of the arytenoids in drawing the cords together
for tone production (solid black) and drawing them apart for
breathing (crosshatched portion).

end is attached to some outside "anchor." These muscles not
only hold the larynx in place, but as various ones contract they
lift and tilt the larynx in swallowing and in making certain
high-pitched tones. You can readily feel this action by placing
your fingers lightly upon your Adam's apple as you swallow.
The *intrinsic* muscles are attached at both ends to the larynx
itself. They bring the vocal cords together and tense and relax
the cords.

Varied Functions of the Larynx. The larynx is a structure having several uses, only one of which is the making of vocal tone. Others of its functions are much more fundamental to the sustaining of life. One of its major responsibilities is to serve as a valve which opens the trachea when we want to breathe and closes it when we want to swallow food or liquid. The *vocal folds* or cords supply part of this valvular action. Situated about midway between the top and bottom of the larynx, they serve as the lower tier of shelflike valves employed in shutting off the windpipe. Just above them are two other folds of tissue called *false vocal cords*. These also can come together and help to close off the windpipe when occasion demands. The protective function of the larynx is aided still further by the contraction of the extrinsic muscles during swallowing, so that the top of the larynx is lifted and pressed against the back of the tongue, thus effectively blocking the laryngeal opening so that (normally) food and liquid do not enter.

Another function of the larynx is to help retain the breath by aiding the strong action of the abdominal or chest muscles. For lifting or striking, or for any strong abdominal exertion, this closure of the trachea is essential. You can feel this valvular action by clenching your fists and straining in an imaginary lifting act; the closure of the larynx is apparent. Similar closure occurs in sneezing and coughing. This valvular action may become a serious hindrance to the effective production of tone if permitted to interfere with the free vibration of the vocal cords during phonation. Ways of eliminating such interference are discussed in the next chapter.

The Vocal Bands

So far as tone production is concerned, the essential feature of the larynx is that within its walls are folds of elastic tissue which can be drawn together toward a median line. When the two folds, or bands, or lips (cords, they are usually called—an inept name because they are not at all like pieces of string) are thus brought together, or approximated, the air pressure from below sets them into vibration. It is this vibration which becomes sound. An idea of how the vocal cords perform (we continue to use the term because of its wide acceptance) can be gained by watching a somewhat analogous action at the front of the mouth: Stand in front of a mirror, bring the lips lightly together, blow vigorously between them. The flutter of the lips is a little like the oscillation of the vocal cords, except that the latter vibrate much faster.

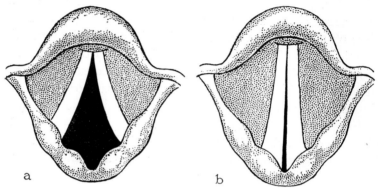

FIG. 6.   The vocal cords from above. *a,* The cords separated for deep breathing; *b,* approximated for tone production. (After Homans.)

In normal breathing, the vocal cords are relaxed and lie close to the inner walls of the larynx. They are some distance apart at the back, but always together at the front; this produces a triangular opening between them. This opening is called the *glottis.* When the impulse to speak occurs certain intrinsic muscles bring the arytenoids together and rotate them inward, thus bringing the cords together and closing the glottis; at the same time other intrinsic muscles stretch the cords tight. In this taut condition they can be vibrated to produce tone, the motive power for the vibrating being provided by the exhaled breath stream. (See Fig. 6.)

The vibrations set up by the action of the vocal cords are transmitted to the air surrounding the cords and, after being resonated (i.e., enlarged, strengthened) in the resonating chambers of the throat and head, move outward in the form of sound waves, as indicated in Fig. 7.

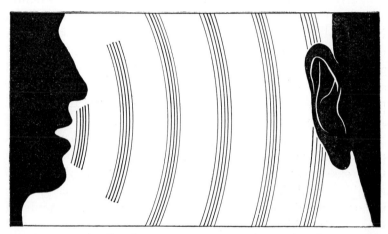

FIG. 7. How vibration patterns are set in motion by a person speaking and are carried through the air in the form of wave impulses. On striking the ear, these impulses stimulate complicated nerve reactions which we interpret as sound. (Modified from the film *Sound Waves and Their Sources*, courtesy of Encyclopædia Britannica Films, Inc.)

The sound waves travel through the air until they reach our ears, and we identify them as human vocal tones. This process will be described more fully in the chapter on the nature of sound.

PITCH

Pitch (i.e., the highness or lowness of the tone) is determined by the number of vibrations of the vocal cords per second. In general, the faster the rate of vibration, the higher the pitch;

and conversely, the slower the rate of vibration, the lower the pitch.

Two factors are involved in determining the rate of vibration: (1) the structure of the larynx, including the length, thickness, and density of the vocal cords, and (2) the degree of tenseness of the cords while the tone is being made.

The length and thickness of the cords vary greatly among individuals, and largely determine whether one is to be a tenor or a baritone, a soprano or an alto. They vary from ⅜ to ⅞ of an inch in length, according to the age, sex, and general physical structure of the individual. Women's voices are normally higher pitched than men's because their vocal cords are thinner and shorter (roughly three-quarters as long).

Shorter cords also explain why, like women, boys have higher-pitched voices than men. And they offer a partial explanation of the croaks and squeaks which often accompany a boy's attempts to talk around the 13th or 14th year. There is a period here when his vocal cords nearly double in length in a couple of years. This suddenly changed structure is hard to manage; and before he learns to control the new mechanism, unexpected and astonishing breaks in pitch cause him untold embarrassment.

The tenseness of the cords also helps to determine pitch; for, with a given length, a tense cord will vibrate faster than a less tense one. Tenseness varies not only among different individuals, but within the same individual according to his changing thoughts and moods. That is, a person's vocal cords are capable of great variety in length and tenseness. This change is accomplished by certain of the intrinsic muscles when stimulated by nerve impulses from the central nervous system.

To raise the pitch, the cords are drawn closer together and stretched tighter. This process of stretching and tensing the cords can be continued to produce higher and higher tones. It is apparent that in this process two types of muscular action come into conflict: Tensing the cords tends to make them vibrate faster, but lengthening them tends to make them vibrate slower. Nature takes care of this discrepancy by another action of the intrinsic muscles, sometimes called *damping*. That is, by the action of certain intrinsic muscles, portions of the cords are brought together so firmly that they cannot vibrate, and only a part of the tensed cords is permitted to function. In the highest pitches, vibration is confined to only a short section at the anterior end of the cords. This action is similar to that of a violin string. To raise the pitch of a tone, the violinist places his finger on the string and blanks out a portion of it so that only a segment is permitted to vibrate.

Each time the rate of vibration is doubled, the pitch of the tone is raised one octave. For example, if a vibrating body gives off a tone whose pitch is bass C, it is vibrating at the rate of 128 vibrations a second; if the rate of vibration is doubled (256 vibrations a second), the tone produced will be middle C.

Thus we see that the interesting and colorful changes of pitch in the human voice are the result of a complicated process of adjustment in the tone-producing mechanism. To appreciate how really marvelous it is, one has but to compare the agreeable fluctuations of the human voice with the flat, monotonous tone of the artificial larynx.

Loudness

Loudness or volume is determined by two factors: (1) amplitude of vibration, and (2) resonance. In determining the volume of sound, it is not the rate but the *extent* of the vibrations which is the controlling factor. The more extensive the swing of the vocal cords, the louder the sound. The degree of force with which the breath stream strikes the cords is the chief factor in determining the extent of their swing. Resonance is discussed in a later chapter.

Tone Quality

Voice quality, or timbre, is still another factor that is influenced and largely controlled by the vibration of the cords. Resonance also plays an important part in determining quality, but at this point we are considering only the manner in which the tone is initiated. In this respect, the vibration of the cords is basically important.

Tones have individual qualities which distinguish them from each other. When we listen to an orchestra tuning up, we have little difficulty in identifying the tones of many of the different instruments, even though they are all playing the same key. The full round tone of the bass viol is quite different from the thinner tone of the violin, and the rich full tone of the organ contrasts markedly with the piping tone of the fife or piccolo. The same difference is apparent, though to a lesser degree, in the quality of the voices of different persons. It is not difficult to distinguish individual voice quality among our friends and acquaintances.

Quality depends upon the *kind* of vibration which reaches the ear. Most sounds are complex, because the vibrating body that gives off the sound vibrates not only as a whole but in parts. The violin or the piano string, for example, vibrates both as a whole and also in segments. The vibration of the entire string gives off what we call the fundamental tone. The segmental vibrations give off the overtones, or partials. If these overtones bear a harmonious relationship to the fundamental, the sound is agreeable and we call it a pleasant tone. If there is no harmonious relationship—as in striking a sheet of tin or dropping a book on the floor—we call it noise. Richer tones have more harmonious overtones.

In the human voice, if there are many harmonious overtones and if there is effective use of *resonance*, the quality is full and melodious. Ways of achieving this type of voice quality are discussed in the next chapter.

IV ✳ Phonation:
Developing Good Voice Quality

Tone production should be easy. A good vocal tone is made with little effort in and around the larynx. (For big and strong tones there *is* vigorous muscular action in another part of the body, as will be explained when we take up the study of controlled breathing.) The best voices come from larynxes which are most free from strain. Developing pleasing and effective voice quality is a virtual impossibility so long as there is strain in the muscles of the larynx.

Relaxation
The first step in tone production—first in the order of time, and probably first in the order of importance—is to learn how to relax.

For the great mass of normal human beings, those not afflicted with some physiological defect which requires medical or surgical attention, the remedy for most vocal inadequacies begins with the simple prescription—*relax*. This letting down of tension—the breaking up of vocal strain—is the starting point for all improvement. Little can be done for the voice student until he learns how to relax.

The voice cannot be forced. It is like a headstrong child who yields to gentle measures of restraint and guidance but resents coercion. When harshly driven, the voice breaks, quavers, or grows harsh and unresponsive. Sometimes, when forced too far, it quits altogether. On the other hand, when gently guided within the realm of its natural capabilities, it responds tractably.

A multitude of common voice ailments may be directly charged to strain: harshness, hoarseness, huskiness, breathiness, shrillness, high "pinched" tone, "flat" tone, and many others. The "apologetic cough"—the little hacking sound some speakers make—is often the result of nervous tension.

The "glottal stop," sometimes called "glottal catch" or "glottal shock" (a momentary block of the vocal bands often followed by a strident, harsh explosion of tone), the student can easily recognize in his own speech by uttering with exaggerated force and tension such ejaculations as *gr-r-r-r, caw-caw, quack-quack.* Used ill advisedly, this type of ejaculatory speech may not only produce unpleasant tonal effects, but also result in injury to the vocal mechanism.

"Speaker's sore throat" is usually the result of speaking under chronic conditions of strained muscles in the throat and jaw; the membranes of the larynx have finally become inflamed and swollen. The only corrective for such a condition is rest, with no speaking at all, sometimes for considerable periods, followed by a regime of easy, relaxed speaking after the manner outlined here.

Naturally it should not be assumed that strain is the sole cause of such conditions; we must recognize that other factors may be at work. In the case of breathiness, for example, it may be that some maladjustment other than mere tenseness is disrupting the delicate coördination necessary between breath control and phonation. Possibly the cords have not been brought close enough together to utilize the escaping breath, resulting in a half-whispered tone suggestive of extreme exhaustion. Or the breathiness may be the result of a derangement of functions of a more serious nature, such as roughness on the edges of the cords which prevents them from occluding properly. These rough spots may be calluses or "corns" or, as they are sometimes called, "singer's nodes" or "vocal nodules." Or the condition may be the consequence of persistent sinusitis, or other infectious disease affecting the vocal mechanism. In these latter cases, relaxation or even prolonged vocal rest may not—probably will not—be sufficient. The student should consult a laryngologist. The fault may be purely functional, in which case he will be relieved of worry and can concentrate upon vocal exercises for improvement. If the condition is pathological, the pathologist will know what steps to take.

At any rate, breathiness is caused by breath escaping between the vocal cords in greater quantity than is needed to vibrate the cords. The corrective does not lie in pinching the throat, but in establishing a state of "tonicity," which means using enough energy to approximate the cords properly, and no more.

On the whole, when no pathological condition exists, the student may safely and profitably assume that most of his faults of phonation are associated with excessive tension.

The young speaker, especially, should recognize that when his voice is harsh or high pitched from too much tenseness, his hearers are adversely affected. If his voice and manner show strain, the audience will respond in kind. By overcoming the constricted tones in his voice, he can help to place his hearers in a receptive frame of mind.

The antithesis of strained voices can be noted by listening to the radio or television. Turn the dial to an announcer whose voice pleases you with its roundness and fullness, or find a radio or television play in which the actors seem to be using their voices easily, without stagy affectation; then listen. It does not take a trained ear to detect the freedom from strain, the easy, effortless tones.

Physiological Basis of Strained Tone

Physiologically, this is what happens when the extrinsic muscles are unnecessarily tense: Upon contracting, these "swallowing muscles" lift the larynx and press it against the base of the tongue to protect the opening to the trachea from the admission of food. In this position, no tone at all is possible; the act of swallowing effectively cuts off vocal tone. Similarly, partial contraction of the extrinsic muscles will partially constrict the area, thus adding an element of effort to the production of tone. At the same time, the contraction of the muscles of the false vocal cords brings these cords together to aid in protecting the trachea. It is possible for the false vocal cords to be so closely approximated that they completely close the glottis (the opening between the cords), thus effectively blanketing the vocal cords. Partial contraction of these false cords will partially close the glottis and partially restrict the functioning of the true vocal cords. Furthermore, some of this tension is likely to be transmitted to other muscles in adjacent areas, notably the soft palate, which has the function of shutting off the passage into the nasopharynx. If this passage is closed by tension, the tone is prevented from gaining the rich resonance imparted by the nasal resonating chamber. Similarly, tightening the muscles of the chin and back part of the tongue prevents correct action of the pitch mechanism, so that abnormally high-pitched tone is likely to result. One of the chief purposes of vocal training is to eliminate all this unnecessary tension.

THE EXTRINSIC MUSCLES MUST BE RELAXED

The vocal cords themselves cannot be directly controlled by an act of will. They function automatically in response to our thoughts and feelings, if they are not restrained by interference from muscles which surround them. This potential interference, as has just been pointed out, comes from the contraction of the extrinsic muscles, which can be controlled and trained. Since the condition of these muscles—i.e., whether or not they are in a condition of tensed rigidity—has a direct bearing upon the state of the vocal cords themselves, it becomes of paramount importance that we learn to control them. Without such control, voice training is fruitless.

The extrinsic muscles, it will be recalled, connect the larynx, above, to the jaw, the hyoid bone, and the styloid processes, for the purpose of holding the larynx in place and lifting it during swallowing. It is possible to feel the tightening of these muscles by placing the hand on the throat during swallowing. It is likewise possible to learn to feel when the muscles are comfortably relaxed.

Throat and jaw stiffness, i.e., tension in these extrinsic muscles, interferes with the free, unhampered swing of the vocal cords. It dampens a portion of the cords, so that the functioning portion has to work much harder. The result is strain, soreness, and possibly permanent incapacity. Also, it should be remembered that when the contraction of the false vocal cords cuts off part of the tone, the part usually cut off is the fundamental tone—the part produced by the functioning of the whole cord. This leaves only the shorter segments of the cords free to vibrate; consequently the voice becomes higher pitched.

Tone Production Automatically Controlled

One of the most important things to remember about the making of tone is that the process is automatic. When you want to speak, you do not have to manipulate your vocal cords by an act of will. You do not have to say to them, "Snap together now; I want to make a tone." All you have to do is think what you want to say, and the two little cartilages at the back of the larynx to which the cords are attached (the arytenoids) automatically swing around together and bring the cords into proper position.

The cords also act automatically to control pitch. In the normal speaking voice, the tension of the cords is constantly fluctuating in response to the speaker's thoughts and feelings. That is what makes the pleasant little steps and slides of pitch. It is what keeps us from having a flat monopitch, and gives emphasis and fine shades of meaning to our words. How boresome it would be if we had to exert an act of will every time we wanted to tense or slacken the cords in order to change our pitch! One of the worst features of the artificial larynx described in the last chapter is that the voice it produces has to stay on one dead level of pitch.

It is extremely fortunate for us that the vocal cords do not need to be volitionally manipulated. In fact, with a normal voice, the less attention paid to them during the making of tone, the better.

Fortunately, also, the vocal cords do not do exhaustive work. If they are free from the strain of unnecessary constriction of surrounding muscles, they should not get tired. A speaker or singer who produces his tones properly can use his voice hours upon end without causing strain or producing sore throat.

RELAXATION IS OFTEN DIFFICULT TO ACHIEVE

Relaxation is not easy. The noise, the hurry, the strain of our competitive living are all against it. People who play golf and have tried to hit the ball by a relaxed and coördinated effort instead of brute strength, know something of the difficulty of relaxing the body. But golfers know that until they do achieve this harmonious bodily state they must be satisfied to be golfing "dubs."

It is sometimes difficult for emotional speakers to make a clear distinction between forceful speaking on the one hand and throat constriction on the other. But this distinction they must make if they would use their voices properly. They may acquire volume in time; but, like the golfer who has learned how to make long drives through perfect physical coördination, involving a lot of relaxation in muscles not needed to execute the drive, speakers must learn that volume comes from coördination of controlled breath stream, relaxed throat, and effective use of the resonating chambers. Continued use of a constricted and strained throat in a misguided effort to gain volume not only will result in poor tones, but may result in great damage to the speech mechanism.

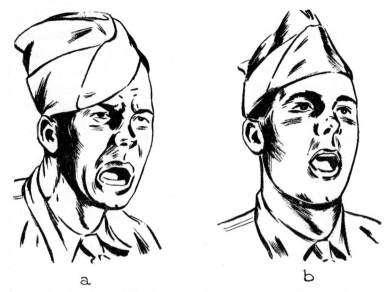

a   b

FIG. 8. Strain and relaxation in speech, as illustrated in an officers' training manual, *Command Voice*. In *a*, the face and neck muscles show excessive strain. In *b*, these areas are free from unnecessary tension, indicating that the officer is getting his vocal power from his breathing muscles. With respect to the second picture the manual states: "No sign of strain is evident. Commands from this man will be clear, understood and definite, as against the jumbled garbled sound of the [first] specimen. . . . Excess physical exertion has no place in giving commands properly." (Courtesy Quartermaster School, Fort Lee, Virginia.)

Unfortunately, you may be so accustomed to your own voice that you do not recognize its stiffness. You may have to experiment for some time before you are able to distinguish between tensed and relaxed throat and jaw. If for years your tones have been produced by sheer force and ignorance, it will not be easy to change. If you are such a person, the following advice is important: Take it easy!

Easy does it. Begin easily. Do not expect a big voice at the start. Your tones under this system will probably be small and weak at first. And in the early stages of practice they should remain that way, at least for the first few weeks. Strength and volume will come in time, through proper breath control and efficient use of resonance. Do not try to get a strong, vibrant tone all at once. Lay a firm foundation in right methods, and build slowly thereon. Nothing but harm can come from trying to force the process. Be patient.

In learning how to relax we are taking the first steps toward not only an improved method of tone-making, but an improved way of living. Better judgment, clearer thinking, calmer spirit, improved poise—all these should and will come to him who learns to combat nervous tensions.

To the student who has long been a victim of inner conflicts which have resulted in extreme muscular tensions, the author recommends reading one or more of the helpful books which have been written on this subject. Among the well-known and trustworthy writers in this field are the medical authority, Dr. Edmund Jacobson,[1] and the neuropsychiatrist, Dr. David H. Fink.[2]

As these writers point out, one of the difficulties we experience in achieving the desired state of relaxation comes from the fact that muscles *have* to contract (i.e., shorten their fibers) in order to perform their functions. Walking, jumping throwing, breathing, all involve the tensing of muscles. It is obvious that there cannot be *complete* relaxation in all the muscles of the speech mechanism during speech, for if there were, no tone would be produced. What is needed, of course, is the desired degree of relaxation, or, as it is sometimes called, a state of tonicity in the muscles. Jacobson uses the term "differential relaxation" to indicate that there should be "a minimum of tension in the muscles required for an act along with the

[1] Edmund Jacobson, *Progressive Relaxation,* University of Chicago Press, rev. ed., 1938; *You Must Relax,* McGraw-Hill Book Company, rev. ed., 1948.
[2] David Harold Fink, *Release from Nervous Tensions,* Simon & Schuster, 1943.

relaxation of other muscles." Only those muscles are used which are needed for the performance of the act, and there is no *excess* tension even in them. Much time is taken in these books, and many approaches are used, in trying to help the person recognize when his muscles are unduly tense. Jacobson calls this the development of "muscle sense."

Testing for Muscular Relaxation. Test for yourself the effect of extreme contraction of the extrinsic muscles upon tone production, and also the effect of conscious and deliberate release of tensions. First, start a sentence but swallow in the middle of it and note how the tone is cut off; next, whisper a sentence (remember that the whisper is a friction noise which does not involve the vibration of the vocal cords) and note the effect expended in whispering; next, say a sentence in a strained voice with the muscles of the throat and jaw highly tensed, and note the muscular effort in the throat as you make the tone; next, speak a sentence in your normal voice, making careful note of the degree of tension in your throat and jaw; and finally, consciously and deliberately relax your throat and jaw and speak a sentence in an easy, quiet tone. In the last phase of the experiment, you will undoubtedly observe a lowered pitch and a fuller and rounder tone. Sentences such as the following might be used:

1. (*Whispering*) "This is the whispered tone. I see that I am expend-ing a great deal of effort to make a small amount of sound."
2. (*Strained tone*) "This is a high-pitched, strained tone. When I talk like this, the vocal cords are not functioning properly."
3. (*Normal tone*) "This is the way I usually talk. Possibly I am putting more strain into it than is necessary."
4. (*Relaxed, easy tone*) "This is a relaxed, easy tone. I am trying to let the vocal cords vibrate fully and freely."

Basic Considerations Concerning Exercises in Phonation

There are certain fundamental principles pertaining to tone production which, if we understand them thoroughly, will help to make practice sessions more profitable.

DAILY DRILL PROGRAM

A now-and-then approach to voice drills will do you little good. As the aspiring young vocalist practices hour after hour, day after day, week in and week out, and as the aspiring young athlete perfects his skill by a regimen of daily practice, so you must establish a set of drill habits and cling to them for a considerable period before you will begin to notice results.

It is not meant that you necessarily have to do the exercises in this chapter; they are intended to be suggestive rather than restrictive. The important thing is that you understand the principles underlying the specific exercises; then perhaps you can make up others better suited to your own needs. Try the various exercises, find some that appeal to you and seem to meet your needs, or devise some for yourself that are based upon the same principles, and then incorporate them into a daily practice program. The benefit will come to you, not from doing many exercises a few times, but from doing a few exercises many times.

VOICE IN SPEECH AND SONG

In the exercises that follow (both in this and in succeeding chapters), you will find some suggested by prominent singers. Practically everything in this book pertaining to the speaking voice applies just as truly to the singing voice, and vice versa. Tone should be produced in the same manner for both speaking and singing. The identical mechanism is employed and the mechanism should function in identical fashion.

Certain skeptical ones may say, "I know a fellow who sings beautifully but talks like a foghorn." And most of us know persons who reverse the process. Moreover, we may know someone who sings beautifully but speaks with a painful stutter, or someone who speaks engagingly in conversation but is inarticulate over the telephone or on the public platform. The difference does not lie in a different mechanism, but in different emotional states connected with the two situations. All that can be said is that the person uses his mechanism well for one activity and badly for the other. In the case of the distinction between speech and song, however, there is also a difference in pitch control. Song notes usually are more sustained in pitch than are speech notes. The singer, most of the time, *steps* from one sustained note to another. The speaker, on the other hand, *glides* from note to note, his voice constantly changing in small inflections up and down the scale.

Since this parallel between tone production in speech and in song may be a new thought to some students, and therefore possibly a little startling, we might consider a few statements by famous singers and singing teachers.

Pacchierotti, a noted singer of the eighteenth century, once said, "He who knows how to speak and to breathe, knows how to sing."[3] Dr. P. Mario Marafioti, Caruso's medical and vocal adviser, went even further: "Singing, in its very essence, is merely speaking in musical rhythm; hence, no correct singing can exist without a correctly produced speaking voice."[4] This interesting theme is further developed in Chapter XII.

Because speech and song are produced in identical fashion, the exercises in this chapter are of equal value to speakers and singers, provided that the speaker remembers always that *he is exercising his tones to make them more responsive to his thoughts and feelings, not so that they will be admired for their beauty.*

RIGHT MENTAL ATTITUDE

So close and intimate is the relationship between mind and body, between what we *think* and what we *do,* that this whole program of phonation exercises is largely dependent upon cultivating the right state of mind. This means that while we are

[3] Quoted in W. A. Aiken, *The Voice,* Longmans, Green & Co., 1920, p. 12.
[4] P. Mario Marafioti, *Caruso's Method of Voice Production,* Appleton-Century-Crofts, 1922, p. 115.

trying to develop a condition of relaxed tonicity in the speech mechanism, we need at the same time to try to develop a state of relaxed calmness of spirit.

As preparation for phonation exercises, listen to quiet, soothing musical recordings. Listen to relaxing musical programs on the radio—if you can find programs moderately free from blaring commercials. Listen to birds' songs. Listen to a mother crooning to her baby. Read gentle, serene poetry. Read it to yourself as mental preparation for the phonation exercises, and read it aloud as part of the exercises. Think restful, relaxing thoughts, using mental imagery to help you. Visualize a quiet green pasture with sheep grazing peacefully or resting in the cool shade of wide-spreading trees; think of an eagle soaring gracefully in the high blue sky; imagine a peaceful valley cradled in the arms of majestic mountains; picture yourself reclining lazily in the warm summer sun beside some clear stream that murmurs soothingly to you. You can find these places in spirit, if not in body. And cultivating this state of inner tranquillity (stopping short, of course, of going to sleep) will do much to help you acquire the relaxed, easy tones you aspire to.

Exercises Do Accomplish Results!

Exercises have worked for others; they will work for you. Listen, for instance, to the words of Estelle Taylor, the actress: "My teacher made me work to relax the muscles of my throat, to adjust my tones to the proper place, to let the voice come out as if it belonged to me. . . . I used to go after my parts, take hold of them and play them hard. Now I let my parts take hold of me. I have learned not to force the voice. The same applies to the part."[5]

The popular Bing Crosby, whose voice, it is claimed, is heard by more people than any other voice in the world's history,

[5] Quoted by Muriel Babcock, "Voice Lowering Modern Vogue," Los Angeles *Times,* March 3, 1931.

adds his testimony to the value of relaxation as an aid to tone production: "To make a good stroke in golf a person has to concentrate upon what he is doing, but at the same time he has to keep relaxed. So it is in singing, a person needs to be sincere but free from strain. There is no conflict between being earnest, and at the same time being relaxed."[6]

EXERCISES

In several of the following exercises the first step is to tense the muscles. Understand that the tensing does not aid in the relaxing but in developing your "muscle sense." The tensing phase of the exercises is put there solely to help you cultivate a sensitivity to muscular tension as contrasted with muscular release. Once you have developed this sensitivity, discontinue the tensing step of the exercises. Work toward the time when you can begin the exercises in as relaxed a condition as possible, and then progress from that point to greater and greater relaxation. Continue the tensing phase of the exercises only until you learn what *not to do.*

Group I. Exercises for Total Bodily Relaxation

1. Stand erect with your body tense. Make your legs and the trunk of your body rigid. Tense your abdominal muscles. Raise your shoulders and pull them back in an exaggerated military posture. Tense your neck muscles. Hold your head stiff, with your eyes staring straight ahead. Hold your body thus at rigid "Attention!" for a few seconds.

   Now let go. Relax all over, to the point where you have barely enough "starch" in your muscles to keep you erect. Your neck muscles, your shoulders, your abdominal muscles—let them all sag.

2. Sit tensely in a straight chair. Hold the upper part of your body "stiff as a ramrod." Tense the muscles of the upper part of your legs, the lower part, your feet. Sit straight and stiff all over. Tense! More tense! Grip your hands, clench your teeth, scowl!

---

[6] In a personal letter to the author; quoted by permission.

Hold yourself thus until your muscles begin to quiver in the exertion.

Now slump! Let go! Think of a cat stretching, then curling up to snooze before a warm fire. Sigh contentedly, and let those tired muscles relax.

3. Stand erect, with arms outstretched. Tense the arms clear to the tips of your extended fingers. Feel the strength of steel in your sinews.

Now let them drop. Simply release all tension and let them drop! At the same time let your shoulders sag. Let the whole arms, fingers and all, hang like dead, heavy weights at your sides.

4. Take the same position as in Exercise 3, with arms, hands and fingers outstretched in tensed rigidity. On the count of "One!" release the fingers and let them dangle from your hands. On "Two!" relax the hands and let them dangle from your wrists. On "Three!" let your forearms drop and dangle from your elbows. On "Four!" let the whole arms drop and hang at your side.

5. Stand erect, with the whole body tense. From this standing position, slowly bend forward at the waist. Let the whole upper part of your body become limp as a rag and hang from your hips. Relax the muscles in the back of your neck so that your head sags lifelessly. Swing your trunk, head, and arms slowly back and forth, letting the fingers dangle close to the floor.

Repeat these exercises several times, until you can feel the clear distinction between tensed and relaxed muscles.

Group II. Exercises for Relaxation of Throat and Jaw

1. Stand erect. Tense your jaw and neck muscles! More tense! And more tense still! Pull them tighter and tighter, until they stand out like whipcords under your skin. Feel, with your hand, the hard rigidity in your entire neck region.

Now begin slowly to relax. Release the tension a little more, and more, and more. When your neck and jaw feel as limp and flabby as a strip of uncooked bacon, go on and relax still more.

Keep striving for a deeper and deeper state of relaxation. This condition will be realized only progressively, by cultivation.

2. Tense your jaw and neck as in the preceding exercise. Slowly pull the jaw to one side and then the other. Have the muscles so taut that the action seems like the movement of a stiff-jointed mechanical doll.

   Now let everything go. Let your head drop forward. Lazily roll it to the left, to the right. Now let it roll all the way, to the left, back, right, forward. Repeat slowly—very slowly. Be sure to let the mouth drop open when the head is back; otherwise there will be strain about the jaw. Permit the head to roll freely, with just as little muscular propulsion as possible.

3. Let the head drop forward. Then shake it back and forth, permitting the jaw to swing loosely. The jaw should flop back and forth almost as if it were unhinged.

4. Start a yawn. Just at the beginning of it there should be a feeling of release of tension around the jaw. Keeping this relaxed feeling, but not completing the yawn, shake the head again, letting the jaw wag freely.

5. Touch the tips of the fingers lightly to the forehead. Draw them slowly and lightly down the face and off the chin. Let each muscle of the face relax completely as the fingers pass lightly over it. Smooth out with a gentle touch the lines of the forehead, the crow's-feet around the eyes, the lines at the mouth corners. Let the jaw sag. The object is to let the face look as imbecilic as possible, devoid of all expression.

6. Slowly massage the muscles of the neck and jaw. Gently manipulate the jaw until it seems to swing loosely on its hinges.

7. The following set of exercises was suggested to the author by G. Marston Haddock, formerly principal of Leeds College of Music and School of Acting for Northern England, and himself a recognized concert singer. The exercises will serve as a review of

the principles in Groups I and II, and as an introduction to the phonation exercises in Group III.

"Bend from the waist, allowing the hands and arms to hang freely downward. Start to shake vigorously, the hands, arms, shoulders, fingers. Shake them all loose and gradually come to an upright position still shaking.

"Lie flat on the back, preferably on a mattress. Allow the body to become a dead weight. Lift one hand; let it fall. Lift the arm and allow it to fall back a dead weight, not trying to stop its fall at all. Do this with the arms, legs, and head. Lift the body from the waist and let it fall back again (this is where the mattress is useful!).

"Let the head fall forward on the chest, relax the neck muscles and roll it round and round, making sure that there is no place where there is temporary constriction or the muscles bunch. When this is accomplished, continue the roll but start to speak quietly, saying anything, but keeping the loose roll the entire time. This prevents so much of that stiffness which people immediately jump into when they start to speak.

"Practice letting the jaw fall open the width of two fingers. Again and again. (I practiced this for four months and it freed my voice for me.) Get the sensation of letting it fall back and down and not outwards and down. Don't let it drop out of joint."

Group III. Exercises in Easy, Effortless Phonation

1. Review the exercises for relaxing the throat and jaw. Do this in every practice period, until you are sure you have the complete release from tension which is so essential for good tone production.

2. Yawn, and at the same time enjoy a good relaxing stretch. Now prepare for a second yawn. While the throat and jaw muscles are all relaxed, instead of yawning, say "one." Repeat several times. Do it easily. Avoid all strain. If you have difficulty in yawning, let the jaw begin to sag, at the same time touching the lips lightly together. This will usually induce a yawn. In these early phonation exercises, do not try to breathe deeply. Just ordinary breathing is best at this stage.

3. Another way to induce the desired relaxation of throat muscles preparatory to phonation is to "drink" from an imaginary glass of water. Prepare thus, and then quietly and effortlessly say *oh, ah, mah.*

4. After inducing relaxation in the "swallowing muscles" until you are sure that they will not interfere with the free swing of the vocal cords, sigh softly on the easily vocalized tone "lah." Repeat slowly, over and over, being sure to let the jaw drop open as you make the tone. If you have the least trouble in letting the jaw drop, refer to Exercise 7 on page 55. In many cases this opening of the mouth (always by relaxing the muscles, never by forcibly and muscularly opening it) is the one thing needed to improve the tone.

5. Another way to achieve this needed openness of throat and mouth is to repeat the syllable "blah" over and over again. *Chant* it up and down the scale. This exercise is reported to be one of Lawrence Tibbett's favorites.

6. The late Alois Havrilla, a winner of the Radio Diction Medal of the American Academy of Arts and Letters, reported to the author some of the methods used by his voice teacher, Percy Rector Stephens: "In breath control or diction, Stephens uses direct or indirect suggestion adroitly. His first lessons are spent in making his pupil relax completely physically, sometimes by lying flat, sometimes by bouncing a large ball while walking and speaking—anything to take the pupil's mind off 'voice production.' This accomplished, he starts with a series of grunts and groans, employing the whole body as a resonator. These groans and grunts resolve into 'yay, yay, yay,' 'yeee,' etc.; according to *individual* needs of resonating and diction. So each pupil develops his *own* voice, instead of forcing sounds like somebody else. It is difficult to put this on paper, but the unconventional beginnings give a freedom of mind and control of body and complete release from tension which is so essential for good tone production."[7]

[7] Quoted by permission.

7. Now try to develop smoothness of tone. Stand easily and comfortably erect. Inhale through the mouth as if about to yawn. Form the lips for producing the sound *lah,* and begin on a singing tone, striving for softness and smoothness. Sing the syllable at different pitch levels, keeping always within your easy range; do not strain for high or low tones.

8. Practice for "roundness" in the tone, thus:
   Exhale easily while saying (or singing) on a sustained pitch the tone *hoh,* up and down the scale. The shape of the mouth cavity and lips for this tone suggests the quality of voice desired —roundness and fullness.
   Say the following lines slowly and easily, aiming the tone toward the ridge at the top of the upper teeth:
   Gold! Gold! Gold! Gold!
   The road was a ribbon of moonlight.
   The road to Rome is rugged, rough, and round.

9. Next, try to project the tone:
   On various pitch levels, say the vowel *oo,* as in the word *loot.* Easy! Easy! Don't force the tone. The form of the lips will help you "place" the tone. (Trained singers and actors know that a loud voice is not necessary to send the tone to the back of a large room. The feat is accomplished largely by placing the tone out front where it belongs.)
   Put an "h" before the vowels and say them on different levels of pitch, thus: hā hē hī hō hū. Project the tone, i.e., direct it out of the front of the mouth. Think of focusing the tone about a foot or so in front of your lips. Hold your hand out there to help you gain the concept. Remember—slow and easy; don't "push" the tone.

10. An exercise to test your tone control is this:
   Make the sound *hoh* on any easy sustained pitch. Begin very softly; then, as effortlessly as possible, and very gradually, increase to considerable volume; then gradually let the tone fade away into the softest possible note. Repeat on *boo* and *bah,* always using a mono-pitch.

11. This exercise will give a convincing demonstration of the difference between effective and ineffective phonation:

First *whisper* the following stanza of poetry, trying to make yourself heard across the room but keeping to a pure whisper. Note how quickly the breath is exhausted:

> Out of the night that covers me,
> Black as the Pit from pole to pole,
> I thank whatever gods may be
> For my unconquerable soul.

Now, talking easily and without any vocal strain, but aiming the tone out of the front of the mouth, repeat the same stanza and note how little breath is used.

SELECTIONS FOR PRACTICE IN EASY TONE PRODUCTION

Here, as well as in succeeding chapters, more poems than prose selections are suggested for practice. This is because of the abundance of round, full vowels in poetry. The beauty of our language lies chiefly in its vowels. Consonants serve the purpose of breaking up the flowing sound of the vowels to give meaning to the sounds. But in these exercises in tone production we are chiefly concerned with quality of the tone; therefore poetry serves our purpose best. The few prose selections included are poetical in their imagery, emotional content, and phonetic arrangement.

However—and this is important—just because you are dealing with poetry, do not let your voice sound affected or artificial. Keep your voice quiet but not "mushy." Avoid the oversoft, unnaturally hushed tones which affect some voices just as soon as they begin the interpretation of poetry. That breathy and unsubstantial voice quality is an offense to honest, forthright people and should be shunned. Your voice should have "body," even though it is quiet. It will have body if you permit the vocal cords to function as they should. Keep your voice relaxed, and your tones easy, unstrained, and natural.

1.
> So let the mind, with care o'erwrought,
> Float down the tranquil tides of thought:
> Calm visions of unending years
> Beyond this little moment's fears.
> —Edward Rowland Sill

2.   Weep not, think not, but rest!
                     The stars in silence roll;
                  On the world's mother breast,
                     Be still and sleep, my soul!
                          —EDWARD ROWLAND SILL

3.   The ocean old,
                     Centuries old,
                  Strong as youth, and as uncontrolled,
                  Paces restless to and fro,
                  Up and down the sands of gold.

                  His beating heart is not at rest;
                  And far and wide,
                  With ceaseless flow,
                  His beard of snow
                  Heaves with the heaving of his breast.
                          —HENRY W. LONGFELLOW

4.   They are slaves who fear to speak
                  For the fallen and the weak;
                  They are slaves who will not choose
                  Hatred, scoffing, and abuse,
                  Rather than in silence shrink
                  From the truth they needs must think;
                  They are slaves who dare not be
                  In the right with two or three.
                          —JAMES RUSSELL LOWELL

5.   Lord God of Hosts, be with us yet,
                  Lest we forget—lest we forget!
                          —RUDYARD KIPLING

6. The most beautiful thing we can experience is the mysterious.
   It is the source of all true art and science. He to whom this
   emotion is a stranger, who can no longer pause to wonder and
   stand rapt in awe, is as good as dead.
                          —ALBERT EINSTEIN

7.   O, lonely tomb in Moab's land,
        O, dark Beth-peor's hill,
    Speak to these curious hearts of ours,
        And bid them to be still.
    God hath His mysteries of Grace—
        Ways that we cannot tell;
    He hides them deep, like the secret sleep
        Of him he loves so well.
                    —MRS. CECIL FRANCES ALEXANDER

8. Roll on, thou deep and dark blue Ocean—roll!
    Ten thousand fleets sweep over thee in vain;
    Man marks the earth with ruin—his control
    Stops with the shore;—upon the watery plain
    The wrecks are all thy deed, nor doth remain
    A shadow of man's ravage, save his own,
    When, for a moment, like a drop of rain,
    He sinks into thy depths with bubbling groan,
    Without a grave, unknelled, uncoffined, and unknown.
                    —GEORGE GORDON, LORD BYRON

9.   The curfew tolls the knell of parting day,
        The lowing herd winds slowly o'er the lea,
    The plowman homeward plods his weary way
        And leaves the world to darkness and to me.

    Now fades the glimmering landscape on the sight,
        And all the air a solemn stillness holds,
    Save where the beetle wheels his droning flight,
        And drowsy tinklings lull the distant folds;

    Save that from yonder ivy-mantled tower
        The moping owl does to the moon complain
    Of such as, wandering near her secret bower,
        Molest her ancient solitary reign.
                    —THOMAS GRAY

10. With malice toward none; with charity for all; with firmness
    in the right, as God gives us to see the right, let us strive on to

finish the work we are in; to bind up the Nation's wounds; to
care for him who shall have borne the battle, and for his widow,
and his orphan—to do all which may achieve and cherish a just
and lasting peace among ourselves, and with all nations.

—ABRAHAM LINCOLN

11. Young gentlemen, young gentlemen . . . do not let yourselves
be discouraged by a deprecating and barren skepticism, do not
let yourselves be discouraged by the sadness of certain hours
which pass over nations. Live in the serene peace of laboratories
and libraries. Say to yourselves first: What have I done for my
instruction? and, as you gradually advance, What have I done
for my country? until the time comes when you may have the
immense happiness of thinking that you have contributed in
some way to the progress and good of humanity.

—LOUIS PASTEUR

12.   SONG

When I am dead, my dearest,
    Sing no sad songs for me;
Plant thou no roses at my head,
    Nor shady cypress tree;
Be the green grass above me
    With showers and dewdrops wet;
And if thou wilt, remember,
    And if thou wilt, forget.

I shall not see the shadows,
    I shall not feel the rain;
I shall not hear the nightingale
    Sing on as if in pain;
And dreaming through the twilight
    That doth not rise nor set,
Haply I may remember,
    And haply may forget.

—CHRISTINA ROSSETTI

13. There is sweet music here that softer falls
Than petals from blown roses on the grass,
Or night-dews on still waters between walls
Of shadowy granite, in a gleaming pass;
Music that gentlier on the spirit lies,
Than tired eyelids upon tired eyes;
Music that brings sweet sleep down from the blissful skies.
Here are cool mosses deep,
And through the moss the ivies creep,
And in the stream the long-leaved flowers weep,
And from the craggy ledge the poppy hangs in sleep.
—ALFRED, LORD TENNYSON

14. I met a traveller from an antique land
Who said: "Two vast and trunkless legs of stone
Stand in the desert. Near them, on the sand,
Half sunk, a shattered visage lies, whose frown,
And wrinkled lip, and sneer of cold command,
Tell that its sculptor well those passions read
Which yet survive, stamped on these lifeless things,
The hand that mocked them, and the heart that fed;
And on the pedestal these words appear:
'My name is Ozymandias, king of kings;
Look on my works, ye Mighty, and despair!'
Nothing beside remains. Round the decay
Of that colossal wreck, boundless and bare,
The lone and level sands stretch far away."
—PERCY BYSSHE SHELLEY

15. SWEET AND LOW

Sweet and low, sweet and low,
Wind of the western sea,
Low, low, breathe and blow,
Wind of the western sea!
Over the rolling waters go,
Come from the dying moon, and blow,
Blow him again to me;
While my little one, while my pretty one, sleeps.

Sleep and rest, sleep and rest,
   Father will come to thee soon;
Rest, rest, on mother's breast,
   Father will come to thee soon;
Father will come to his babe in the nest,
Silver sails all out of the west
   Under the silver moon;
Sleep, my little one, sleep, my pretty one, sleep.
                   —ALFRED, LORD TENNYSON

16.   A RED, RED ROSE

O my Luve's like a red, red rose
   That's newly sprung in June:
O my Luve's like the melodie
   That's sweetly played in tune.

As fair art thou, my bonnie lass,
   So deep in luve am I;
And I will luve thee still, my dear,
   Till a' the seas gang dry.

Till a' the seas gang dry, my dear,
   And the rocks melt wi' the sun;
I will luve thee still, my dear,
   While the sands o' life shall run.

And fare thee weel, my only Luve!
   And fare thee weel awhile!
And I will come again, my Luve,
   Tho' it were ten thousand mile.
                   —ROBERT BURNS

17.   TO SLEEP

A flock of sheep that leisurely pass by,
One after one; the sound of rain, and bees
Murmuring; the fall of rivers, winds and seas,
Smooth fields, white sheets of water, and pure sky;
I've thought of all by turns, and yet do lie
Sleepless! and soon the small birds' melodies

Must hear, first uttered from my orchard trees,
And the first cuckoo's melancholy cry.
Even thus last night, and two nights more, I lay,
And could not win thee, Sleep! by any stealth:
So do not let me wear tonight away:
Without Thee what is all the morning's wealth?
Come, blessed barrier between day and day,
Dear mother of fresh thoughts and joyous health!
                    —WILLIAM WORDSWORTH

18.   Here, where the world is quiet;
                Here, where all trouble seems
             Dead winds' and spent waves' riot
                In doubtful dreams of dreams;
             I watch the green field growing
             For reaping folk and sowing,
             For harvest-time and mowing,
                A sleepy world of streams.

             I am tired of tears and laughter,
                And men that laugh and weep,
             Of what may come hereafter
                For men that sow to reap;
             I am weary of days and hours,
             Blown buds of barren flowers,
             Desires and dreams and powers,
                And everything but sleep.
                    —ALGERNON CHARLES SWINBURNE

19.   PSALM XXIII

The Lord is my shepherd; I shall not want.
He maketh me to lie down in green pastures:
He leadeth me beside the still waters.
He restoreth my soul: He leadeth me in the paths of
    righteousness for his name's sake.
Yea, though I walk through the valley of the shadow of death,
    I will fear no evil: for thou art with me; thy rod and thy staff
    they comfort me.

Thou preparest a table before me in the presence of mine enemies: thou anointest my head with oil; my cup runneth over.

Surely goodness and mercy shall follow me all the days of my life: and I will dwell in the house of the Lord for ever.

20.   PSALM XXIV

The earth is the Lord's, and the fulness thereof; the world, and they that dwell therein.

For he hath founded it upon the seas, and established it upon the floods.

Who shall ascend into the hill of the Lord? or who shall stand in his holy place?

He that hath clean hands, and a pure heart; who hath not lifted up his soul unto vanity, nor sworn deceitfully.

He shall receive the blessing from the Lord, and righteousness from the God of his salvation.

This is the generation of them that seek him, that seek thy face, O Jacob.

Lift up your heads, O ye gates; and be ye lift up, ye everlasting doors; and the King of Glory shall come in.

Who is this King of glory? The Lord strong and mighty, the Lord mighty in battle.

Lift up your heads, O ye gates; even lift them up, ye everlasting doors; and the King of glory shall come in.

Who is this King of glory? The Lord of hosts, he is the King of glory.

21.   Yon rising Moon that looks for us again—
          How oft hereafter will she wax and wane;
          How oft hereafter rising look for us
          Through this same Garden—and for *one* in vain!

          And when like her, O Sákí, you shall pass
          Among the Guests Star-scattered on the Grass,
          And in your joyous errand reach the spot
          Where I made One—turn down an empty Glass!
                              —EDWARD FITZGERALD

22.   SONNET 29

When, in disgrace with fortune and men's eyes,
I all alone beweep my outcast state,
And trouble deaf heaven with my bootless cries,
And look upon myself and curse my fate,
Wishing me like to one more rich in hope,
Featured like him, like him with friends possessed,
Desiring this man's art and that man's scope,
With what I most enjoy contented least;
Yet in these thoughts myself almost despising—
Haply I think on thee; and then my state,
Like to the lark at break of day arising
From sullen earth, sings hymns at heaven's gate;
    For thy sweet love remembered such wealth brings
    That then I scorn to change my state with kings.
                                        —SHAKESPEARE

23.   DOVER BEACH

The sea is calm tonight,
The tide is full, the moon lies fair
Upon the straits,—on the French coast the light
Gleams and is gone; the cliffs of England stand,
Glimmering and vast, out in the tranquil bay.
Come to the window, sweet is the night air!
Only, from the long line of spray
Where the sea meets the moon-blanched land,
Listen! you hear the grating roar
Of pebbles which the waves draw back, and fling,
At their return, up the high strand,
Begin, and cease, and then again begin,
With tremulous cadence slow, and bring
The eternal note of sadness in.

Sophocles, long ago,
Heard it on the Aegean, and it brought
Into his mind the turbid ebb and flow

Of human misery; we
Find also in the sound a thought,
Hearing it by this distant northern sea.

The Sea of Faith
Was once, too, at the full, and round earth's shore
Lay like the folds of a bright girdle furled.
But now I only hear
Its melancholy, long, withdrawing roar,
Retreating, to the breath
Of the night-wind, down the vast edges drear
And naked shingles of the world.

Ah, love, let us be true
To one another! for the world, which seems
To lie before us like a land of dreams,
So various, so beautiful, so new,
Hath really neither joy, nor love, nor light,
Nor certitude, nor peace, nor help for pain;
And we are here as on a darkling plain,
Swept with confused alarms of struggle and flight,
Where ignorant armies clash by night.

—MATTHEW ARNOLD

24.   THE DAFFODILS

I wandered lonely as a cloud
That floats on high o'er vales and hills,
When all at once I saw a crowd,
A host, of golden daffodils,
Beside the lake, beneath the trees,
Fluttering and dancing in the breeze.

Continuous as the stars that shine
And twinkle on the milky way,
They stretched in never-ending line
Along the margin of a bay:
Ten thousand saw I at a glance,
Tossing their heads in sprightly dance.

The waves beside them danced, but they
Outdid the sparkling waves in glee—
A poet could not but be gay
In such a jocund company.
I gazed—and gazed—but little thought
What wealth the show to me had brought.

For oft when on my couch I lie
In vacant or in pensive mood,
They flash upon that inward eye
Which is the bliss of solitude,
And then my heart with pleasure fills,
And dances with the daffodils.

—WILLIAM WORDSWORTH

25. In this world of incessant and feverish activity men have little time to think, much less to consider ideals and objectives. Yet how are we to act even in the present unless we know which way we are going and what our objectives are? It is only in the peaceful atmosphere of a University that these basic problems can be adequately considered. It is only when young men and women who are in the University to-day, and on whom the burden of life's problems will fall tomorrow, learn to have clear objectives and standards of values that there is hope for the next generation.[8]

—PANDIT JAWAHARLAL NEHRU

[8] From "The Pursuit of Peace," *Vital Speeches*, November 1, 1949.

V ✳ Respiration:
Controlled Breathing

Now that we have considered how to make the tone, we are ready to study how to control and strengthen the tone. It is obvious that if we work for relaxation and ease in the throat, we must look elsewhere for power and control. That elsewhere is in the breathing apparatus; the basis for building a strong, vital, and responsive vocal instrument lies in developing breath control.

Since it is the exhaled breath stream that activates the vocal cords and thus initiates tone, it is the muscles of exhalation that are of primary importance in developing control. That is, power and control in *initiating* the tone come from well-developed muscles of exhalation. In the final analysis the type of voice that a person has depends largely upon the kind of tone that is initiated; and that, in turn, is dependent upon the free swing of the vocal cords, and the controlled breath stream which activates them.

For initiating the tone properly, what we seek is:

1. *Ease* in phonation.
2. *Strength* and *control* in exhalation.

Or, to state the same thing in terms of musculature, what we must work for is:

1. Relaxation of the muscles of the throat and jaw.
2. Strong, flexible, and controlled muscles of the abdomen.

70

But before taking up a detailed study of how this improved control of exhalation is to be achieved, let us turn aside for a moment and give our attention to breathing in general.

Breathing for Health

Breathing is so fundamental a life process that it is practically synonymous with life itself. When breathing ends, life ends. And probably there is a good deal of truth in the proverb which has come to us from ancient India: "He who only half breathes, only half lives."

The close relationship between good breathing and abounding good health has long been recognized. Innumerable persons have spoken and written of the manner in which breathing exercises have contributed to the building up of their physiques and their general health. Not only voice teachers, physical training experts, and athletes have given this testimony; in nearly every business and profession can be found persons of vigorous and contagious vitality who attribute no small part of their well-being to a sustained program of breathing exercises.

So important is this radiant good health in the equipment of the singer, speaker, and actor that no particular urging should be necessary to induce young aspirants in these fields to avail themselves of every possible means of building strong and healthy bodies, one of the means being regular and conscientious breathing exercises.

But young people of today are skeptical—perhaps justifiably so—of the moralizings of their elders. If you are skeptical of the efficacy of deep breathing, here is an experiment to try. You can perform it in your home and it needs no special equipment. It is simply this: The next time you feel listless, fatigued, or "blue," take a series of deep breaths of pure, fresh air; then observe the results. See the dullness and languor give place to vitality. Deep breathing is a specific for depression of spirit. Speeding up the flow of blood through the blood vessels, bringing fresh oxygen to depleted cells, it sends new spirit coursing through the body.

Perhaps you have noticed how shyness, fear, and stage fright influence your breathing. If these emotional conditions are at all extreme, breathing is likely to become short and jerky. As the rhythm of breathing becomes disintegrated, fear emotions are intensified. The effect is cumulative. A corrective of this condition can be inaugurated by reversing the process, i.e., by deliberately controlling the rate of breathing. You can do this. You are so constituted that by an act of will you can, within limits, take over the control of breathing and regulate it to suit your wishes. Reëstablish the rhythmic process. Breathe slowly and regularly. Force yourself to slow up; make the inhalation and the exhalation conform to a steady, slow, rhythmic pattern. Almost certainly some of the fear complex will disappear. At the very least, you can make it less noticeable.

Improper eating habits, lack of exercise, poor posture, and constant inhaling of impure city air have all contributed to the inadequacies of our breathing. Sedentary living has affected us all. Instead of running, leaping, climbing, swimming, as did our less "civilized" ancestors, we sit cramped before desks or slouched in overstuffed chairs. For coarse natural foods we have substituted refined delicacies which we eliminate with the aid of purgatives. Correct breathing will do something toward compensating for these unnatural habits. Physiologically, the oxygen breathed into the lungs, and from there disseminated through the blood stream, affects the chemistry of the blood, nerve currents to the brain, the pulse rate, and digestion. Good breathing improves posture by expanding the chest and pushing back the shoulders. It calms "nerves." Doctors recommend it for health; physical training experts recommend it for posture; beauty experts recommend it for the complexion; and psychologists recommend it for stage fright. In truth, proper breathing has a wholesome effect upon body, mind, and spirit.

To these recommendations the author wishes to add his own conviction: If you will honestly and sincerely follow the breathing exercises outlined in this chapter, if you will spend a certain amount of time on them every day, and keep at the routine until it is an established habit, you will bless the day that you started voice training. Not only will your voice be improved, but your general health and buoyancy of spirit will receive a real uplift.

How We Breathe

Briefly stated, breathing is a biological process by which we inhale air through the nose or mouth into the lungs. There some of the oxygen from the fresh air is exchanged for the waste product, carbon dioxide, which is exhaled.

Ordinarily the act of breathing is automatic. That is, it functions like the heartbeat, without conscious attention on our part. When the oxygen in the blood stream becomes depleted, a message automatically goes out from the respiratory centers of the nervous system to the muscles which control breathing, and a new breath cycle is initiated. Usually we breathe in and out, the complete cycle, about fifteen or twenty times a minute. However, as was stated previously, at any time the conscious will can take over and control the rate of breathing. We can speed up from fifteen or twenty respirations a minute to twice that many, or we can slow down to five or six, or we can stop altogether and hold the breath for a few seconds —even up to two minutes or more if we are trained for it. And we can break up the cycle; that is, whereas we ordinarily take about the same amount of time on the inhalation and the exhalation, we can, if we wish, breathe in slowly and exhale quickly, or we can do the reverse. This last fact has a vital bearing upon tone production. Since tone is produced by the exhaled breath, the ability to control the rate of exhalation becomes of paramount importance, as will be explained later.

MECHANICS OF BREATHING

The breathing apparatus consists principally of (1) the air passages leading to the lungs, (2) the lungs themselves, (3) the chest cavity in which they are located, (4) the muscles which control the bringing of air into the lungs, and (5) those which force the air out again.

The air is drawn into the lungs through the nose or mouth, through the glottis of the larynx, thence into the trachea. The trachea divides into the right and left bronchial tubes. These in turn divide and subdivide into smaller and smaller tubes called bronchioles. Each bronchiole ends in numerous minute air sacs, which are porous and elastic. Embedded in the thin walls of these air sacs are tiny blood vessels, or capillaries. Through these thin walls oxygen is exchanged for carbon dioxide. The bronchial tubes, air sacs, and blood vessels, together with their connective tissue, constitute the *lungs*. The chest cavity in which the lungs are housed is surrounded by the rib cage, or *thorax*.

The lungs nearly fill the chest cavity, being large, spongy, and cone-shaped. Their broad bases rest upon the diaphragm, and their narrow, rounded tops extend above the first rib.

Contrary to popular opinion, we do not breathe with the lungs. The lungs themselves are largely passive. More than anything else they resemble large sponges. In function they are reservoirs for holding air in storage. The lungs are acted upon by outside muscle systems which perform the act of breathing.

THE MUSCLES WHICH CONTROL BREATHING

Inhalation. The *diaphragm* is one of the principal muscles of inhalation. It is a broad, leaflike sheet of muscle and fiber, attached at the sides and back to the ribs and spinal column, and in front to the breastbone. Extending transversely across the body, the diaphragm is a partition separating the heart and lungs from the digestive system (it has been facetiously described as separating the victuals from the vitals). In its relaxed state it is highly arched and dome-shaped. When a nerve impulse comes to it, indicating the need for a fresh supply of oxygen, the diaphragm contracts and is drawn down so that it is much less convex. This downward pressure flattens out the viscera and causes the abdominal walls to protrude. Thus during inspiration we can feel bulging at the front and sides of our abdomen.

At the same time that the diaphragm contracts and pulls downward, the muscles of the chest (principally the intercostals) contract and lift the rib cage (principally the lower ribs).

This double action enlarges the chest cavity and thereby reduces the air pressure in the little air sacs of the lungs, creating a low-pressure area. Air rushes in to equalize the pressure. This constitutes inhalation.

Exhalation. The relaxing of the diaphragm causes it to resume its normal highly convex position, and the relaxing of the chest muscles causes the ribs to settle back. Thus the chest cavity is reduced in volume, pressure is put upon the tiny air sacs, and exhalation takes place.

This is the cycle of breathing for normal life functions. A little later we shall consider certain changes that take place, particularly in exhalation, in speaking and singing.

A fair idea of the process of breathing may be obtained by observing the action of a laboratory device known as Hering's apparatus (Fig. 9). This consists of a wide-mouthed glass bottle with a sheet of rubber stretched across the bottom in place of the glass; to it is attached a ring by which the sheet may be pulled down. From the cork of the bottle is suspended a tube which divides into two branches, to each of which a rubber bag is attached.

In a in Fig. 9, the rubber bags hang deflated in an airtight cavity. In b, the rubber sheet has been pulled downward, thus increasing the volume of the bottle. The air pressure in the bottle is thereby decreased, creating a low-pressure area. Because of the greater pressure of the atmosphere outside, air rushes in through the tube to equalize the pressure, and the rubber bags are inflated.

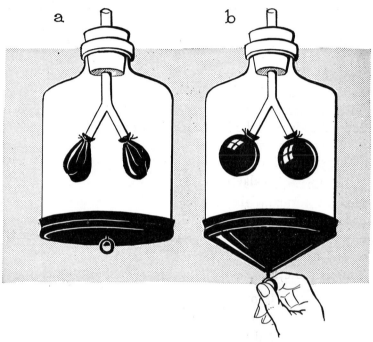

FIG. 9.   Hering's apparatus illustrating the breathing process.

If the rubber sheet is allowed to return to its normal position, the process is reversed—the volume of the bottle is decreased, pressure within the bottle is correspondingly increased, air is forced from the bags, and they again become deflated.

This is roughly comparable to the process of human breathing. The neck of the bottle may be compared to the human throat, the walls to the rib cage which houses the lungs, the rubber bags to the lungs, and the sheet of rubber to the muscles (particularly the diaphragm) which stimulate inhalation and exhalation.

There are, to be sure, differences between Hering's apparatus and the human breathing mechanism which should be noted. (1) The ribs, being less rigid than the bottle walls, can and do move slightly; (2) the lungs, unlike the rubber bags, fill the

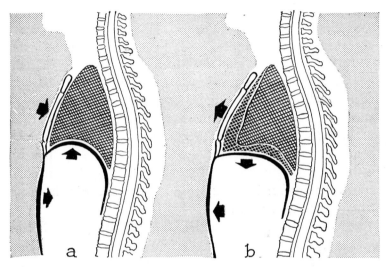

FIG. 10. The position of the diaphragm, lungs, abdomen, and chest in breathing. *a*, Exhalation; note decreased chest size, relaxed dome-shaped diaphragm, and taut indrawn abdominal wall. *b*, Inhalation; note increased chest size, contracted and flattened diaphragm, and relaxed and distended abdominal wall.

chest cavity; (3) instead of consisting of a single bag, each lung consists of great clusters of tiny sacs; (4) the diaphragm, being a muscle is not pulled down by an outside force, but descends by its own contraction; and (5) instead of changing from a flat to a concave position, it changes from its normal domelike position to one slightly less arched.

The schematic drawing in Fig. 10 shows changes in the

position of the diaphragm and the abdominal walls in inhalation and exhalation.

Breathing for Speaking and Singing

To provide the controlled breath stream necessary for tone production, the passive breathing carried on for normal life processes, just described, is not adequate. Control must be active and precise. This is true to some extent in inhalation, but much more so in exhalation.

In inhalation control is necessary because we have to be able to take in air quickly and inconspicuously in order that the flow of speech will not be interrupted or the tone impaired by inadequate breath. Trained speakers and singers learn to replenish their supply of breath by small inconspicuous "catch breaths" between phrases, so that they never appear run down or out of breath. Likewise, they learn to breathe through the open mouth during the act of speaking or singing, instead of through the nose, as is desirable in normal quiet breathing and during breathing exercises.

But it is during exhalation that the need for control is most important, since merely relaxing the diaphragm and chest muscles would fall far short of meeting the demands of speaking and singing. Precise control of the muscles of exhalation is essential to provide for the full, round, and frequently modulated tones which characterize the efficient speaking voice.

When a nerve impulse starts a controlled exhalation for tone production, the abdominal muscles contract, pull the walls of the abdomen in, and by pressure upon the viscera force the diaphragm upward. Thus air is forced out of the lungs under pressure.

The abdominal muscles can be trained to provide perfect control of the exhaled breath stream. It is to the development of this type of control that Lawrence Tibbett refers when he says:

You can't sing powerfully throughout a performance unless you have a diaphragm like a heavyweight wrestler's. On tour I always carry a folding rowing machine with me, and every morning in my room I row—it seems to me—from New York to Albany.[1]

Many people commonly refer to this mid-section breathing simply as *diaphragmatic breathing*. To be more exact, the term should be *diaphragmatic-abdominal-muscle breathing*, to cover both inhalation (diaphragmatic action) and exhalation (abdominal muscle action). However, as is the case with the inexactly named vocal cords, we shall continue to use the half-true term *diaphragmatic breathing* rather than attempt to change a name which has become deeply intrenched. Terminology is not of paramount importance so long as we understand the process of controlled breathing.

For this type of strong controlled muscular action singers train long years. This is what they mean when they talk of "adequate support" for the tone. To this type of control much singing instruction is devoted.

Control of the abdominal muscles promotes easy, relaxed speech or song, free from strain. It provides power to make big, powerful tones or light, lyric tones, as occasion demands, without pushing and pinching the tones. It provides breath for holding the tone—a necessary adjunct of colorful speech and song. It provides breath control for proper phrasing, long or short as the meaning requires. And, most important, it makes possible the buoyant, "floating" tones which are the first requisite of good vocalization.

Probably the majority of singers and actors would agree with the popular actress, Cornelia Otis Skinner, when she says: "My own difficulties, when they arise, are always connected with breathing. Deep regular breathing will force you to better posture, keep your voice under control, and give an appearance

---

[1] Lawrence Tibbett, "Story of My Life," *American Magazine,* September, 1933, p. 80.

—outwardly at least—of calmness. Tension of the throat can be obviated by correct breathing."[2]

Mistaken Notions About Deep Breathing

Often, when a teacher first asks a beginning voice class to take a deep breath, from different sections of the room come loud heavings of air drawn forcibly through dilated nostrils, accompanied by raised shoulders, protruding chests, and pulled-in waist lines. Entirely wrong! Trained speakers and singers who have learned breath control go through no such manifestations. Athletes do not ordinarily breathe with heaving shoulders. Watch a dog panting after exertion. The heaving is discernible not in an expanding and contracting chest, but in the soft portion of the trunk below the ribs, the abdomen. Or watch a baby, preferably a sleeping one, to see correct breathing.

Note that the inhalation in such cases is accompanied not by an indrawn waistline, but by an expanded waistline. The shoulders do not rise with the inhalation; rather you see only a gentle lifting of the lower ribs, and a settling back of these ribs during exhalation.

Chest breathing, often accompanied by lifted shoulders, has been taught by military men—probably because a big high-lifted chest seems to contribute to a military posture. Likewise swimmers sometimes develop abnormally large upper chests, caused by their method of gulping breath in the fraction of a second when the mouth is out of the water between swimming strokes. They need a fresh and abundant supply of oxygen quickly, but not the controlled exhalation needed for speaking and singing.

The amazing vitality of many actors and singers who give exhausting performances night after night, often to an advanced age, testifies to the value of good breathing. Likewise, the ability of the trained singer to hold a high, strong note for a

[2] From a letter to the author; quoted by permission.

period that seems like minutes, comes not from using the hard, inflexible chest and shoulders, but rather from using the highly flexible, well-disciplined abdominal muscles. This flexibility and amenability to control will be amply demonstrated in the exercises which follow.

FIXING RIGHT HABITS

If the author could sit down with you and have a quiet friendly chat regarding the way to use the exercises which follow, that would be an ideal situation. But lacking the opportunity for this direct contact, he is going to do the next best thing: Talk to you just as directly and informally as cold type will permit, and give some advice which he hopes you will see fit to take. It pertains to habits.

We hear a lot about the bad habits of personal indulgence in one form or another, and of how they bind us until we become their helpless slaves—even as the sleeping Gulliver became the helpless victim of the Lilliputians, when they bound him with one thread after another, until upon waking he found himself unable to move. But habits can be, and are tremendously beneficial. They are the greatest time and energy savers in our whole make-up. Suppose for example, in putting on your shoes in the morning, that you had to go through all the mental and physical effort that you did as a child when first learning to put them on. Or suppose walking—simply taking a step—were as difficult as learning to take your first step. Watch a young couple teaching their baby to walk, and note their—and his— exultation when he succeeds in balancing himself alone and taking that first single step, and you will realize what a real achievement it is. But now you walk, skip, run, jump with no conscious attention to the act at all; and while you are putting on your shoes you are thinking about almost anything *except* what you are doing. What is the difference? Simply habit! Good habit! Habit that frees your mind so that you can settle the affairs of state, if you are so inclined, while you perform acts that once were the acme of physical difficulty.

The point is simply this: If these breathing exercises are to do any good, it will be because you turn them into good habits. It will be because you make out a schedule for yourself and budget your time. No one can do that for you. It's up to you.

Breathing Exercises

In the exercises which follow, correct posture is essential to prevent the fixation of bad habits. Stand erect, but not rigid; chest up, shoulders relaxed. Be sure there is no strain in the throat. Let the principal action come from the diaphragm and the abdomen. Keep the body relaxed and at ease. Move the head and arms enough to be sure they are flexible.

All the exercises in this chapter are for developing vocal control through correct breathing. *They are not instructions on how to breathe when on the platform.* When you are actually speaking, breathing must be automatic. Good habits, once established, will continue to function at all times.

Usually the speaker should not be conscious of his breathing when speaking. There are two exceptions to this rule: (1) Just before starting to speak publicly, breathing is likely to be shallow and jerky because of nervousness; correct this by deliberate, slow, rhythmical breathing which has a steadying effect upon the nerves. (2) During speaking, if you notice yourself becoming nervous, with voice high-pitched and fast, stop, breathe slowly, then resume more deliberately.

But so far as possible, when actually before an audience lose yourself in your ideas and forget about breathing. Use the exercises in this chapter as drills for homework, and keep working on them until they have become fixed habits. The perfection of art in breathing is to breathe so naturally, so unobtrusively, that none of your listeners will be conscious of either your breath or your lack of breath.

EXERCISES

General Breathing Exercises for Health

First be sure that you are breathing correctly. Frequently beginners find that they are devoid of any noticeable reaction around the waist or, as sometimes happens, that the reaction is the opposite of that outlined above. The reason is that they are doing their breathing with the upper chest. Such breathing, while it may provide adequate oxygen to sustain life, is not likely to give the fine control desirable for speaking and singing. To insure that you are breathing correctly, the following procedure is suggested:

1. Lie flat on your back, placing the hands over the abdomen. Breathe regularly and easily, but deeply. In this position it is difficult for the shoulders to move and it is more likely that the diaphragm and abdominal muscles will function properly. The hands should rise noticeably with the intake of breath and fall with exhalation.

   Now, standing easily erect, try to keep the movement in the same center it was in while you were lying down. Place the hands over the waist at the sides, above the hipbones and below the ribs, fingers toward the front and thumbs to the back. Inhale deeply but easily. See if you can detect an expansion all along the waistline. You should feel a distinct pressure under your hands with the intake of breath—the pressure that comes from the diaphragm contracting and pressing down upon the intestines, which in turn push out the walls of the abdomen.

   Repeat this exercise over and over until you are sure that the activity is the same when you are standing as it is when you are lying down.

2. When the correct method of breathing is ascertained, begin to prolong the breaths. Count (silently) 1, 2, 3, 4 on one inhalation, and the same on the exhalation. Keep it rhythmical. Gradually extend the time for each respiration until you are taking only three or four breaths to a minute. This exercise can be practiced while walking, riding, or resting. When walking you can synchronize the counts with your steps.

3. Practice holding the breath. Begin by retaining it only 15 seconds. Within a few weeks the breath can be held a minute and a half or two minutes without harmful results.

4. Breathing exercises can be combined profitably with general physical exercises.

   Stand erect with the arms hanging at sides. Rise on the toes, while raising the arms and touching the hands together above the head. At the same time, and in perfect coördination with the physical action, draw in a deep breath. With the beginning of exhalation let the arms fall gently to the sides and the weight settle back upon the balls of the feet. Repeat five or six times.

   Standing easily erect, stretch the hands in front of the body, the backs of the hands touching. Inhale gently, and at the same time slowly swing the arms as nearly straight back as is possible without bending forward; touch the hands in back of the body. Exhale and bring the hands forward. Repeat.

   Exhale slowly as you bend forward from the hips until the hands nearly touch the floor. Relax torso, arms, hands, and neck. Rotate the trunk on the hips; allow the head and arms to dangle lifelessly. When completely relaxed, begin to inhale from the waistline up. As you feel the expansion along the waist, allow the body to rise in response to the pressure. Slowly come to the erect position, with the sensation that you are packing the breath in around the waistline, and from there upward.

5. Draw in a full breath with five gasps through the mouth. With the first three the expansion should be noticed exclusively below the ribs; with the last two the upper chest should be filled to capacity. Exhale in a slow, steady hiss. Reverse the process, i.e., inhale in a slow steady inhalation; exhale on five puffs.

6. A good exercise for developing the diaphragm and abdominal muscles is laughing. Its efficacy as a health measure has long been recognized. Massaging the intestines and expelling used air from the lungs, it is a better tonic than most that come in bottles. Good comedians are doctors' worst competitors. There is more than a witticism in the sentence, "He who laughs—lasts."

7. If you are too shy or "refined" to laugh loudly, heartily, and boisterously, the following exercise is a good substitute: Close your lips and laugh noiselessly. As you do so, place your hands over your waist and note the diaphragm and abdominal muscles at work.

8. With the hands over the abdomen, pant vigorously through the open mouth. Note the quick response of the diaphragm and abdominal muscles, with the rapid changes from inhalation to exhalation.

9. Lie on your back as in the first part of Exercise 1. This time, however, you will work not just to locate the center of breathing in the diaphragm and abdominal muscles, but to strengthen those muscles. Place a pile of five or six ordinary-sized books on your abdomen. Now raise the books with your inhalation. See that there is a perceptible but gradual rise with the intake of breath, and a correspondingly gradual fall with the exhalation. (If you happened to see the motion picture, *One Night of Love,* starring the late Metropolitan Opera singer, Grace Moore, you probably will recall an amusing scene in which her voice teacher made her do this exercise over and over and over again—to her intense disgust, for she wanted to get to singing, not waste time "training to be a book-lifter.")

10. Start each day right by standing before an open window and doing deep breathing exercises for at least three minutes. As you do so, maintain a good standing position, erect but not tense. Do not strain. Be particularly sure that there is no undue tenseness about the throat and jaw.

Exercises Coördinating Breathing with Phonation

In the following exercises, the first consideration is not the amount of breath inhaled or exhaled, but its efficient and economical use. Try to use just enough breath to set the vocal cords into vibration, and no more; that way you will avoid a breathy tone.

The voice needs plenty of breath in a free flowing stream; in this respect it is like any of the musical wind instruments. As time goes on and you continue the breathing exercises, you will develop an abundant supply. But at this point you must be more concerned about how the breath stream is used than about how much breath is used. Be sure that all the exhaled breath is applied to the production of tone.

1. On an easy exhalation, make the simple grunting sounds *uh, uh, uh* and *u-u-h, u-u-h, u-u-h.* Vary the sounds with *yah, yah, yah.* Don't try for volume or force. Just engage in some easy, quiet grunts, seeing how effortlessly the sounds can be made.

2. Review the exercises in Chapter III, showing the difference between a well-made tone (that is, with just enough breath used to vibrate the vocal cords, letting them do the work of making the tone) and a tone that is poorly made (that is, with breath permitted to escape "around the tone").

3. Imagine a ship passing, possibly two or three hundred yards out at sea. Cup your hands and shout to it, but in a pure whisper: *Ship ahoy! Ship ahoy!* Note how your breath supply was exhausted and how your throat was strained in the effort.

   Now, shout to the ship again. Only this time use a vocal tone. Don't strain! Get the force from your abdominal muscles, and keep your throat open and relaxed. Notice the difference in the amount of volume achieved. Note that you can repeat the phrase over and over on the same breath, whereas in the whispered shout you probably used all your breath on one phrase.

4. Place your hands on your sides, below your ribs, as described earlier. Draw in a breath. Easy now—not too much. Don't strain. With your throat open like a funnel make the tone *a-a-a-h.* Hold it as long as you can. Did you feel the muscles of your abdomen contracting? Do you see how those muscles function to supply the stream of controlled breath to support the tone? (Along toward the end of this exercise, your tone probably will not be good; it may be quavery and rough. This is purely a demonstration exercise. In actual tone production, you should not hold the tone after it begins to be rough.)

5. To open the throat and at the same time draw in an adequate supply of breath, imagine you are drinking fresh air as you would fresh, clear mountain water. Now, with the throat still open, exhale on the tone *a-a-h*. Repeat the tone five times on the one breath, all on the same mono-pitch.

6. Repeat the preceding exercise, this time giving a little force to the tones. Hit them with a stroke of the abdominal muscles—be sure, though, that you put no strain upon the throat. Keep your hands on your sides to observe the action of the strong abdominal muscles. In a sharp, staccato tone, say *hā, hē, hī, hō, hū*.
Give the sharp command, *Forward march!* then count *one, two, three, four!*

7. Use the abdominal muscles to project strong sentences, such as:

Boomlay, boomlay, boomlay, BOOM!

A roaring, epic, rag-time tune.

Fe, fi, fo, fum;
I smell the blood of an Englishman.

All aboard! All aboard!

Hi, ammunition-mules and Gunga-Din.

Boom, steal the pygmies,
Boom, kill the Arabs,
Boom, kill the white men,
Hoo, Hoo, Hoo.

Lord God of Hosts, be with us yet,
Lest we forget—lest we forget!

8. Hold a lighted candle or match three or four inches in front of the lips. Sing up and down the scale, at first softly, then with gradually increased volume. Try to keep the light from being blown out—as far as possible from even flickering. If the tones are well produced and the breath stream well controlled, flickering will be reduced to a minimum. If you prefer, this exercise may be done with speech instead of song notes.

9. Assume a good standing position, with chest up but not rigid; abdomen flat but not tense; shoulders, neck, and jaw relaxed. Inhale deeply through the open mouth, and gently begin to say the alphabet. When you reach the end of it, begin over again without taking additional breath. Say the alphabet as many times as you can on one breath, without permitting your chest to cave in. Be sure that the speaking is accompanied by a gradual contracting and drawing in of the abdomen. At first you may not be able to say the alphabet more than twice on one breath; but if you practice regularly five or ten minutes a day, at the end of a few weeks you should easily say it six or eight times, as your diaphragm and abdominal muscles gain strength and control.

Exercises Combining Phrasing and Breathing

Several factors affect the length of the phrases we use in speaking; most of them will be discussed in a later chapter. But one of the important considerations that helps to determine the length of the phrases is the speaker's need for breath. This factor should receive our attention at this time.

In talking we do not normally take a long breath and keep on talking until all the breath is exhausted. Rather, we break up our sentences into phrases, taking little sips of breath between the phrases. For a speaker to use long, continuous sentences, without breaks for breathing, is extremely exhausting both to him and to his listeners.

1. Look, for a minute, at Lincoln's well-known sentence:

> Fourscore and seven years ago, our fathers brought forth on this continent a new nation, conceived in liberty, and dedicated to the proposition that all men are created equal.

It would be possible, of course, to say this sentence in two phrases, pausing for breath only at the comma in the middle of the sentence. But this would not be wise, either for getting full meaning from the sentence, or for securing a good, well-supported tone. The speaker does not have to follow the phrasing that is indicated by the punctuation of the written page. He can make his own phrasing. There are a dozen different ways the above

sentence can be phrased. Try some of them, and at many of
the pauses for phrasing draw in a little sip of breath to keep
your supply replenished. Try this way, for example:

> Fourscore and seven years ago / our fathers brought forth
> on this continent / a new nation / conceived in liberty / and
> dedicated to the proposition / that all men / are created equal.

Now imagine you are talking to a huge audience (in general, the
larger the audience the shorter the phrases—partly because of
the bigger voice used by the speaker and his consequent need of
more breath) and try this phrasing:

> Fourscore / and seven / years / ago / our fathers / brought
> forth / on this continent / a new nation / conceived / in
> liberty / and dedicated / to the proposition / that all men /
> are created / equal.

2. Try different-length phrases, with quick intakes of breath interspersed, on the following sentence by Walter Lippmann:

> At a time when the world needs above all other things the
> activity of generous imaginations and the creative leadership
> of planning and inventive minds, our thinking is shriveled
> with panic.

3. Do the same with the following sentence by Theodore Roosevelt.

> No people on earth have more cause to be thankful than ours,
> and this is said reverently, in no spirit of boastfulness in our
> own strength, but with gratitude to the Giver of Good, who
> has blessed us with the conditions which have enabled us to
> achieve so large a measure of well-being and of happiness.

4. Try different-length phrases, with little inhalations interspersed,
on the following quatrain from *Omar Khayyám*. Remember, you
do not have to pause at the end of every line; good phrasing
often demands that you do not pause at the end of certain lines.

> The Worldly Hope men set their Hearts upon
> Turns Ashes—or it prospers; and anon,
> Like Snow upon the Desert's dusty Face,
> Lighting a little hour or two—is gone.

SELECTIONS FOR PRACTICE

The following selections—calm, forceful, light, heavy, prose, poetry—are designed not only to meet various tastes, but to afford practice in (1) coördinating breath control with phonation, (2) coördinating breath control with phrasing, and (3) providing support for the tone in both quiet and forceful types of readings.

1. There's a barrel-organ carolling across a golden street
    In the City as the sun sinks low;
   And the music's not immortal; but the world has made it sweet
    And fulfilled it with the sunset glow;
   And it pulses through the pleasures of the City and the pain
    That surround the singing organ like a large eternal light;
   And they've given it a glory and a part to play again
    In the Symphony that rules the day and night.

   —ALFRED NOYES[3]

2. As a fond mother, when the day is o'er,
    Leads by the hand her little child to bed,
    Half willing, half reluctant to be led,
    And leave his broken playthings on the floor,
   Still gazing at them through the open door,
    Nor wholly reassured and comforted
    By promises of others in their stead,
    Which, though more splendid, may not please him more;
   So Nature deals with us, and takes away
    Our playthings one by one, and by the hand
    Leads us to rest so gently, that we go
   Scarce knowing if we wish to go or stay,
    Being too full of sleep to understand
    How far the unknown transcends the what we know.

   —HENRY W. LONGFELLOW

[3] Reprinted by permission of the publishers, J. B. Lippincott Company, from *Collected Poems in One Volume* by Alfred Noyes. Copyright, 1906, 1934, 1947, by Alfred Noyes.

3.   REMEMBER

Remember me when I am gone away,
    Gone far away into the silent land;
  When you can no more hold me by the hand,
Nor I half turn to go, yet turning stay.
Remember me when no more, day by day,
    You tell me of our future that you planned:
    Only remember me; you understand
It will be late to counsel then or pray.
Yet if you should forget me for a while
    And afterwards remember, do not grieve:
    For if the darkness and corruption leave
    A vestige of the thoughts that once I had,
Better by far you should forget and smile
    Than that you should remember and be sad.

                    —CHRISTINA ROSSETTI

4. ROMEO: But, soft! what light through yonder window breaks?
It is the east, and Juliet is the sun!—
Arise, fair sun, and kill the envious moon,
Who is already sick and pale with grief,
That thou her maid art far more fair than she:
Be not her maid, since she is envious;
Her vestal livery is but sick and green,
And none but fools do wear it; cast it off.—
It is my lady; O, it is my love!
O, that she knew she were!—
She speaks, yet she says nothing: what of that?
Her eye discourses, I will answer it.—
I am too bold, 'tis not to me she speaks:
Two of the fairest stars in all the heaven,
Having some business, do entreat her eyes
To twinkle in their spheres till they return.
What if her eyes were there, they in her head?
The brightness of her cheek would shame those stars,
As daylight doth a lamp; her eyes in heaven
Would through the airy region stream so bright

That birds would sing, and think it were not night.—
See how she leans her cheek upon her hand!
O, that I were a glove upon that hand,
That I might touch that cheek!

—SHAKESPEARE

5.
    O wind, that is so strong and cold,
    O blower, are you young or old?
    Are you a beast of field and tree,
    Or just a stronger child than me?
        O wind, a-blowing all day long,
        O wind, that sings so loud a song!

    I saw the different things you did,
    But always you yourself you hid,
    I felt you push, I heard you call,
    I could not see yourself at all—
        O wind, a-blowing all day long,
        O wind, that sings so loud a song!

—ROBERT LOUIS STEVENSON

6.   MACBETH. If it were done when 'tis done, then 'twere well
    It were done quickly. If the assassination
    Could trammel up the consequence, and catch
    With his surcease success; that but this blow
    Might be the be-all and the end-all here,
    But here, upon this bank and shoal of time,
    We'd jump the life to come. But in these cases
    We still have judgment here; that we but teach
    Bloody instructions, which, being taught, return
    To plague the inventor: this even-handed justice
    Commends the ingredients of our poison'd chalice
    To our own lips. He's here in double trust;
    First, as I am his kinsman and his subject,
    Strong both against the deed; then, as his host,
    Who should against his murderer shut the door,
    Not bear the knife myself. Besides, this Duncan
    Hath borne his faculties so meek, hath been
    So clear in his great office, that his virtues

Will plead like angels, trumpet-tongu'd, against
The deep damnation of his taking-off;
And pity, like a naked new-born babe,
Striding the blast, or heaven's cherubim, hors'd
Upon the sightless couriers of the air,
Shall blow the horrid deed in every eye,
That tears shall drown the wind. I have no spur
To prick the sides of my intent, but only
Vaulting ambition.

—SHAKESPEARE

7.   AMERICA THE BEAUTIFUL

O beautiful for spacious skies,
   For amber waves of grain,
For purple mountain majesties
   Above the fruited plain!
      America! America!
   God shed His grace on thee,
And crown thy good with brotherhood
   From sea to shining sea!

O beautiful for pilgrim feet,
   Whose stern, impassioned stress
A thoroughfare for freedom beat
   Across the wilderness!
      America! America!
   God mend thine every flaw,
Confirm thy soul in self-control,
   Thy liberty in law!

O beautiful for patriot dream
   That sees beyond the years
Thine alabaster cities gleam
   Undimmed by human tears!
      America! America!
   God shed His grace on thee,
And crown thy good with brotherhood
   From sea to shining sea!

—KATHARINE LEE BATES

8.   IF I WERE A ONE-LEGGED PIRATE

If I were a one-legged pirate
Ga-lumping around on a peg,
I'd flourish my pistol and fire it,
Then, sure as my right wooden leg,
I'd buy me a three-decker galleon
With cannon to port and to lee,
And wearing the king's medallion,
I'd head for the tropical sea!
Roaring a rough Ha-Ha, Ha-Ho,
Roving the routes of old,
Over the billows we would go,
Sweeping the seas for Gold;
Plying the lane
Of the Spanish Main,
For Gold!
    Gold!
        Gold!

—ANONYMOUS

9   Farewell, a long farewell, to all my greatness!
This is the state of man: To-day he puts forth
The tender leaves of hope, to-morrow blossoms,
And bears his blushing honors thick upon him:
The third day comes a frost, a killing frost;
And—when he thinks, good easy man, full surely
His greatness is aripening—nips his root;
And then he falls as I do. I have ventured,—
Like little wanton boys that swim on bladders,—
This many summers, in a sea of glory,
But far beyond my depth: my high-blown pride
At length broke under me, and now has left me
Weary and old with service, to the mercy
Of a rude stream that must forever hide me.

—SHAKESPEARE

10.   O God of battles! steel my soldiers' hearts;
Possess them not with fear; take from them now
The sense of reckoning, if the opposed numbers
Pluck their hearts from them. Not to-day, O Lord,
O, not to-day, think not upon the fault
My father made in compassing the crown!
I Richard's body have interred new;
And on it have bestow'd more contrite tears
Than from it issued forced drops of blood:
Five hundred poor I have in yearly pay,
Who twice a-day their wither'd hands hold up
Toward heaven, to pardon blood; and I have built
Two chantries, where the sad and solemn priests
Sing still for Richard's soul. More will I do;
Though all that I can do is nothing worth,
Since that my penitence comes after all,
Imploring pardon.

—SHAKESPEARE

11.   HOME-THOUGHTS, FROM ABROAD

Oh, to be in England
Now that April's there,
And whoever wakes in England
Sees, some morning, unaware,
That the lowest boughs and the brush-wood sheaf
Round the elm-tree bole are in tiny leaf,
While the chaffinch sings on the orchard bough
In England—now!

And after April, when May follows,
And the white-throat builds, and all the swallows!
Hark, where my blossomed pear-tree in the hedge
Leans to the field and scatters on the clover
Blossoms and dewdrops—at the bent spray's edge—
That's the wise thrush: he sings each song twice over,
Lest you should think he never could recapture
The first fine careless rapture!

And, though the fields look rough with hoary dew,
All will be gay when noontide wakes anew
The buttercups, the little children's dower—
Far brighter than this gaudy melon-flower!
—ROBERT BROWNING

12.   Half a league, half a league,
Half a league onward,
All in the valley of Death
Rode the six hundred.
"Forward the light Brigade!
Charge for the guns!" he said;
Into the valley of Death
Rode the six hundred.
—ALFRED, LORD TENNYSON

13. Sink or swim, live or die, survive or perish, I give my hand and my heart to this vote. It is true, indeed, that in the beginning we aimed not at independence. But there's a divinity that shapes our ends. The injustice of England has driven us to arms; and, blinded to her own interests . . . she has obstinately persisted, till independence is now within our grasp. We have but to reach forth to it, and it is ours. Why, then, should we defer the declaration? Is any man so weak as now to hope for a reconciliation with England, which shall leave either safety to the country and its liberties, or safety to his own life and his own honor? Are not you, sir, who sit in that chair—is not he, our venerable colleague near you—are you not both already the proscribed and predestined objects of punishment and of vengeance?
—DANIEL WEBSTER[4]

14. The struggle for peace, which is the major crisis of our generation, is a struggle for men's minds rather than for their emotions. It is a struggle for human decency rather than for human debauchery. It involves an appeal to reason. Peace can be won

[4] From Daniel Webster's speech *Adams and Jefferson*. This excerpt is called *The Supposed Speech of John Adams*.

and maintained only if we can convince the American people and freedom-loving people elsewhere in the world that rules of reason, procedures of international justice, relinquishment of many selfish interests must be substituted in the thinking of people everywhere for the emotional nationalism that still dominates the world in spite of all our laudatory efforts to set up a system of international justice by way of the United Nations.

We need to face the fact that we will not see the sunrise of peace this year or next, but unless we see at least some of those early hour rays of a dawn of peace in the near future, mankind may awaken only to die in the pitch blackness of war.

This country of ours was founded primarily upon the basic democratic principle that the spiritual value of the individual citizen is the very core of self-government. One cannot read the Constitution nor the Declaration of Independence nor the great debates out of which was born this Republic without recognizing the fact that our founding fathers believed that a society of free people must rest upon a devotion to the spiritual value of the individual person. They considered that the primary purpose of a democratic form of government was to protect the dignity of the individual.

—SENATOR WAYNE MORSE[5]

15. There is plenty of room for difference of opinion as to how this or that should be done. There is room for views strongly held, and wisely debated. There is room for criticism. But there is also room for a final consensus of opinion. We must work toward consensus of opinion; we must broaden the area of agreement so that the Congress and the Executive—both parties of the Congress and the Executive—will view every problem and deal with every problem as part of the total problem.

What makes this possible is a common loyalty to our democratic institutions.

—DEAN ACHESON[6]

[5] From "The Rise or Sunset of Peace," *Vital Speeches*, May 1, 1950.
[6] From "Consensus Vital," *Ibid.*, May 15, 1950.

16. Today, by the grace of God, we stand a free and prosperous nation with greater possibilities for the future than any people have ever had before in the history of the world. . . .

Our aim for a peaceful, democratic world of free peoples will be achieved in the long run, not by force of arms, but by an appeal to the minds and hearts of men. . . .

In the world today, we are confronted with the danger that the rising demand of people everywhere for freedom and the better life may be corrupted and betrayed by the false promises of Communism. In its ruthless struggle for power, Communism seizes upon our imperfections, and takes advantage of the delays and setbacks which the democratic nations experience in their effort to secure a better life for their citizens.

This challenge to us is more than a military challenge. It is a challenge to the honesty of our profession of the democratic faith; it is a challenge to the efficiency and stability of our economic system; it is a challenge to our willingness to work with other peoples for world peace and world prosperity. For my part, I welcome the challenge.

—HARRY S. TRUMAN

17. To myself, mountains are the beginning and the end of all natural scenery; in them, and in the forms of inferior landscape that lead to them, my affections are wholly bound up; and though I can look with happy admiration at the lowland flowers, and woods, and open skies, the happiness is tranquil and cold, like that of examining detached flowers in a conservatory, or reading a pleasant book; and if the scenery be resolutely level, insisting upon the declaration of its own flatness in all the detail of it . . . it appears to me like a prison, and I cannot long endure it. But the slightest rise and fall in the road —a mossy bank at the side of a crag of chalk, with brambles at its brow, overhanging it, a ripple over three or four stones in the stream by the bridge, above all, a wild bit of ferny ground under a fir or two, looking as if, possibly, one might see a hill if one got to the other side of the trees—will instantly give me intense delight, because the shadow, or the hope, of the hills is in them.

—JOHN RUSKIN

18. Mr. Vyshinsky, with the customary arrogance, not of himself but of his propaganda machine, once more told us airily and emphatically, when he was referring to the so-called Peace Congresses, that Soviet Russia marches with banners streaming at the head of six hundred million ordinary people throughout the world, who believe confidently that Soviet Russia is the leader, and the only leader, of the peace movement. This is an interesting assertion upon which Mr. Vyshinsky might let us have a little arithmetic. Presumably this alleged army of six hundred million people will, and do, show their sympathy for the foreign policy of Soviet Russia by taking advantage of every election to cast their votes for the candidates who support that policy. Where then are these six hundred million? It is a little difficult to discern their electoral success. It cannot be that they are to be found in Norway where the Communist party have just lost all their seats. It cannot be in Austria where they polled only 10% of the votes. It cannot be in Sweden, it cannot be in Switzerland, it cannot be in Italy, it cannot be in the State of New York, and it cannot be in Great Britain—if I am to judge from the recent municipal results. Indeed, I would go so far as to say that whenever free elections have been recently held the results have shown that the great sympathy and admiration built up among the free peoples by the resistance of the Russian peoples to the Nazi attack, which was reflected to some degree in the free elections held in 1945 and 1946, has disappeared. It has perished not because these free peoples have forgotten the valour of the Russian people. It has perished because these free peoples have been distressed and bewildered by the statements of the representatives of the Soviet regime as they have displayed themselves at international conferences and in the Soviet press. This is an exasperating and a mournful tragedy—that so few men could have, by their ambitions, their arrogance or their stupidity, destroyed such a power for peace as the admiration and the sympathy which free men had for the people of Soviet Russia. . . .

"Go back" we plead with Mr. Vyshinsky "to tell the Soviet Government that they and they alone are cutting off their people from the sympathy of the world. Go back to tell them that the conscience of the world is revolted by the mechanical cynicism of the Soviet regime. Go back to tell them that they may for this moment, for this year or for that, prevail in their hideous and ignoble purposes, against this patriot man, this little country or that territory, but that the peoples of the world are on the march. Not on the march to battle against the Soviet Union but on the march against creeds outworn, against outmoded nineteenth century conceptions, which separate us, nation from nation and continent from continent. Free mankind is on the march against separatism, against the idea that any nation, however mighty, can live for itself. Against all threats to their peace, to their possession of freedom, of mind as well as of body.

—HECTOR MCNEIL, M.P.[7]

[7] From "Saboteurs of Peace," speech delivered in the Political and Security Committee of the United Nations General Assembly, Lake Success, N. Y., November 16, 1949. Reprinted from *Vital Speeches,* December 1, 1949.

VI * The Nature of Sound

Of the four phases of the speech process—respiration, phonation, resonation, and articulation—thus far we have considered only the first two. We are now ready to proceed to the third phase, resonation. Before this extremely important characteristic of voice can be studied, however, it is necessary to understand something about sound in general.

An old question goes something like this: If a meteor were to fall in the midst of a desert, far from any person or animal, would there be any sound? The answer depends upon whether the person answering is a physicist or a psychologist—in other words, whether we base our judgment on objective or subjective evidence. From the objective point of view, sound is vibration of a certain type passing through some medium such as air; from the subjective point of view, there is no sound unless the vibrations reach an ear, are carried to the brain, and are there interpreted as sound.

Physically, sound originates as follows: Some vibrating body, such as the moving tine of a tuning fork or a plucked or stroked violin string, sets the surrounding air into vibration. When a vibrating body moves in a given direction, it compresses the layer of air in front of it. This compression is transmitted to the next layer of air, and to the next, and the next, and so on. The process is somewhat analogous to the way a row of dominoes behaves if you set the dominoes on end and then push the first one in the row. As the first one falls, it knocks over the next one, and so on down the line.

As the wave of condensed air moves outward, it is followed by a wave of rarefied air caused by the backward swing of the vibrating body. Thus the vibrations are propagated as alternate layers of condensed and rarefied air. These waves have often been compared to the ripples which move across the surface of a pond when a pebble is dropped into it. The particles of water do not travel to the edge of the pond. If they did, the water would pile up on the shore, leaving a hollow in the center of the pond. The water particles simply oscillate up and down in a circular pattern. The ripples pass over the surface of the water. So it is with sound waves. The air particles move but a minute distance each way. They do not travel with the sound. If they did, when we hear a sound we would feel a blast of air strike our ears along with the sound. As with the waves over the water, the sound waves travel *through* the air.

Sound waves cannot exist in a vacuum; there has to be some medium through which the vibrations can transmit their energy. A common method by which physicists demonstrate this fact is by means of a large airtight glass bottle containing a buzzer which can be electrically activated. The bottle is equipped with a valve by which most of the air can be extracted, leaving a partial vacuum. If the buzzer is activated while the air is out of the bottle, the buzzer can be seen to oscillate vigorously, but no sound is forthcoming. If air is replaced in the bottle, the buzzing of the bell is instantly audible.

Sound waves travel through different mediums at different but constant speeds. Through air at ordinary temperatures the speed is approximately 1100 feet a second; through sea water it is about 5000 feet a second;[1] through steel rails, about 16,000

---

[1] An invention developed during World War II is based upon this knowledge of the rate of sound through sea water. It is a sound system which makes possible the location of air and ship survivors at sea. The device is called the *Sofar*, from the initials of the phrase *Sound Fixing and Ranging.* The survivors drop a certain type of depth bomb which explodes between 3000 and 4000 feet below the ocean's surface. Station operators on shore, by means of certain sensitive instruments, plus a knowledge of the rate at which sound travels, can plot the position of the explosive. They have been able to determine the location to within one square mile of survivors 2000 miles away.

feet a second. Fortunately all the different vibration frequencies travel through a given medium at the same speed. If this were not so, the distortion which would accompany the music of a distant band, for instance, would make the sound almost unendurable.

The rate at which sound waves travel is slow compared to the speed of light waves. This difference is made manifest by observing a drummer who is some distance away; when he strikes the drum you see the stroke long before you hear the report. The same difference exists in the case of radio waves (which travel at approximately the speed of light). If, for instance, a microphone is placed near a speaker in a large auditorium, a radio listener in London or Tokio can hear the words before people in the rear of the auditorium hear them.[2]

Characteristics Common to All Types of Sound

Three basic characteristics of sound are *frequency, intensity,* and *tone structure.* A fourth factor, although not precisely an element of the tone itself, is nevertheless closely associated with it; this is the *duration* of the tone. Subjectively, these four usually are called, respectively, *pitch, loudness* (or *force* or *volume*), *quality* (or *timbre*), and *time* (or *rate*).

FREQUENCY

The frequency of a sound is the number of vibrations per second associated with it. Frequency largely determines what we subjectively interpret as *pitch* (i.e., highness or lowness of the sound). Intensity and tone structure also have secondary effects on pitch. The effect of intensity on pitch is demonstrated by the action of the whistle on a peanut roasting machine. When the pressure of the steam—i.e., the *motor* for the tone—is increased, not only is the tone louder, it is also higher pitched.

---

[2] Similarly, radio waves sent out by radar equipment have traveled to the moon and back in about $2\frac{1}{2}$ seconds.

But primarily it is frequency—the number of vibrations a second—which determines our sensation of pitch.

The human ear is capable of hearing only sounds with frequencies within certain limits. The frequency of the lowest tone we can hear is about 20 vibrations a second. This is a deep rumble, like the lowest note on the pipe organ. At the upper extreme, about 20,000 vibrations a second is the frequency of the highest note we can hear. This is a thin piping whistle. Naturally, these limits vary somewhat with different individuals; but in general, below and above these extremes we cannot identify vibrations as sound. Whistles are made with frequencies above the range of human hearing, but audible to dogs. A recent scientific experiment discloses that bats employ high-pitched cries, far above human audibility—up to 120,000 vibrations a second—as "sonar devices." By listening for the reflected sound, they avoid collision with objects in their line of flight.

The fundamental frequency[3] of the human voice ranges from about 65 vibrations a second, a very low bass tone, to about 1200 vibrations a second, a high soprano note. The usual fundamental frequency of the male speaking voice is from 100 to 150 vibrations a second; of the female speaking voice, from 200 to 300 vibrations a second, or about one octave higher than the male voice. As this suggests, every time the vibration rate is doubled the frequency level is raised one octave; thus middle C (concert pitch) has a vibration rate of 264 a second, C an octave above a rate of 528, and so on.

INTENSITY

The intensity of a sound is the primary characteristic upon which is based our sensation of *loudness.* Frequency and tone structure also have some effect on loudness, but they are of

---

[3] To refresh your mind regarding the difference between *fundamental* and *overtones,* reread the section on tone quality in Chapter III. Further discussion of this subject appears later in the present chapter, in the section on tone structure.

secondary importance. Intensity depends upon the amplitude of the vibrations—that is, upon the extent of the swing of the vibrating body—plus resonance. Note the difference: the main determining factor in pitch is the *number* of vibrations a second, whereas in loudness it is the *extent* or *amplitude* of the swing. In other words, if the vibrating body swings through a wider arc, the resulting sound wave strikes the ear with a sensation of greater intensity or loudness. (See Fig. 11.)

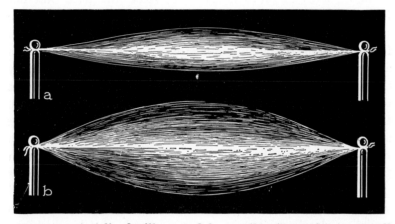

Fig. 11. Amplitude illustrated by a vibrating string. *a*, Small amplitude; *b*, large amplitude. This roughly parallels vocal cord action in increasing or decreasing the loudness of the tone.

The term *force* is sometimes used as a synonym for intensity or loudness. There is some logic in this interchange of terms, because ordinarily to produce louder tones we increase the pressure of the breath stream against the vocal cords. In the strictest sense, however, the terms are not synonymous, for added pressure does not necessarily produce louder tones. Much depends upon the degree of efficiency with which the vocal cords utilize the pressure of the breath stream. If the cords are in a state of relaxed tonicity so that they can vibrate freely (and if resonance is also used effectively), the tones will be louder.

But if the vocal cords are so tense and poorly occluded that unused breath is allowed to slip past them, and a breathy tone results, these tones may actually have less intensity rather than more. The term *force*, as applied to speaking, has other implications. It is likely to include the total emotional state of the speaker, as suggested by the expression "He is a forceful speaker."

Another word sometimes employed to suggest degrees of vocal intensity is *volume*. But here again the terms are not identical in meaning. Physicists and sound engineers measure sound intensity in terms of *decibels*, and in reporting their findings to the lay public sometimes use the word *loudness* as a synonym to express the *sensation of intensity* received by the human ear. But they shun the term *volume* as being subject to too many different interpretations by different individuals. In general, *volume* is the name we give to sounds we think of as "full," such as the low notes of the pipe organ and the rumble of distant thunder. We do not apply it to the thin piping notes of the fife or piccolo. This sensation of volume is quite apart from mere loudness, for volume may be associated with soft, quiet tones as well as with loud tones. Volume is probably closely related in our minds with sounds which are compounded of many overtones. This concept will be made clearer as we come to understand more fully the nature of a complex tone.

Tone Structure

Tone structure is the objective basis upon which we form our judgment of *quality* or *timbre*. In Chapter III we discussed the nature of fundamentals and overtones, and how they are produced. We also learned something about how the sound wave is made up of several simple waves blended together into a complex wave. It is now desirable for us to make a little more thorough analysis of the nature of this "tone complex."

We recall that sound always originates in some vibrating

body. The vibrating agent may be a violin string that has been stroked by a violin bow; or a piano string that has been struck by the action of a pianist's fingers on the piano keys; or the membrane of a drum that has been struck by a drumstick; or a reed (as in the saxophone and the mouth organ) which has been activated by a stream of air being blown over it; or the telephone receiver activated by the fluctuation of an electric current.

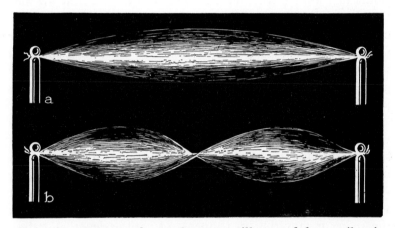

Fig. 12. Simple and complex tones illustrated by a vibrating string. In *a*, the string is oscillating as a whole in a simple pattern; in *b* it is oscillating in two separate segments. It is possible for a string or other vibrating body to vibrate as a whole and in many segments at the same time. Roughly this parallels the action of the vocal cords in creating fundamental and overtones.

These sound waves are nearly always complex, because the vibrating body nearly always vibrates in a complex pattern (Fig. 12). Therefore, when these tones reach the ear and are interpreted as sound, the sound is complex. But it is possible to imagine a simple tone; and in the physics laboratory, under controlled conditions, it is possible to produce a simple tone which the physicist would call a "pure" tone. Such a tone results when the vibrating body fluctuates in what the physicist calls "simple harmonic motion." If we imagine a pendulum swinging in a series of cycles (a cycle being the complete swing of the pendulum in both directions and back to the point of origin) in a straight line instead of in a curved arc, we shall have a picture of simple harmonic motion. If the swing of the pendulum were speeded up to the range of audibility, i.e., roughly to a rate of from 20 to 20,000 vibrations a second, the resultant sound wave would be simple (called a *sine* wave by the physicist) and would be represented graphically by a simple curved line. But in actual life conditions, sound waves are seldom of this nature. Nearly always they are compounded of several simple waves; and sometimes the waves are exceedingly complex, being a blend of a great many waves of various proportions.

As suggested previously, this concept is best understood if we think of a violin string. When the string is plucked, or stroked, it vibrates as a whole: this vibration is called the fundamental tone. Because this fundamental tone is always stronger (has greater intensity) than any of its overtones, it is this tone which we identify as the pitch of the tone. But at the same time the string is vibrating in segments of various lengths—halves, thirds, fourths, etc. These segmental vibrations are called partials, and their resultant tones are called overtones. Such a complex wave would be represented graphically not by a simple curve, but by a line whose major undulations would be altered by a great many minor deviations, as shown in Fig. 13.

A simple sound wave, like that represented by *a* in Fig. 13, would be unpleasant to the ear, or at the very least it would be decidedly uninteresting. A close approximation to this simple sound is the squeal that sometimes emanates from a poorly tuned radio. On the other hand, the combination of a number of these simple sounds having various degrees of frequency and intensity may create the beautiful tones that delight us in music and in certain human voices; or it may result in a hodge-

podge which our ears interpret as unpleasant noise, the difference being whether the combination is a blending of harmonious overtones with the fundamental, as in the artistic blending of the various instruments of an orchestra, or merely a
haphazard association of unassimilable elements. One purpose

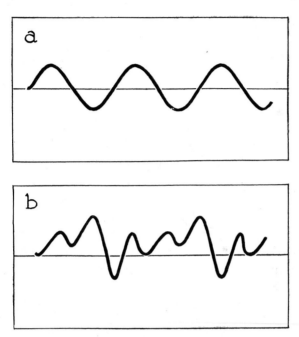

FIG. 13. The difference between a simple sound wave and a
complex sound wave as recorded by an oscillograph. *a*, A sine wave,
representing a simple tone—the fundamental only; *b*, a complex
tone consisting of fundamental and overtones.

in taking a voice course is to learn to distinguish between these
two with respect to our own voices.

We should remember that the term *quality* refers to vocal
tones which are either pleasant or unpleasant—in other words,
to both good and poor voice quality. Judgment of quality is
extremely subjective in nature; it depends upon the background

and experience of the person forming it. This variability is illustrated by the reactions of different persons to the same orchestra, especially to certain "hot" bands; sounds that are pleasant to many young people are disagreeable noises to many of their elders. Because of this difference in judgment, the terminology used in describing different sounds is not always constant or definitive. In general, however, *tone* refers to sounds in which the overtones bear a harmonious relationship to the fundamental, and *noise* or *dissonance* refers to sounds in which there is no such harmonious relationship between fundamental and overtones.

DURATION

Duration refers to the length of time the sound lasts. In speech, duration of tones, coupled with length of pauses between tones, determines the rate of speaking.

Visible Speech

These component elements of sound which we have been discussing are given practical application in a recent invention by the Bell Telephone Laboratories. It is a machine which enables the totally deaf to "hear" speech by looking at vibrations on a screen. A trained reader of this "visible speech" not only can recognize the words spoken, but also can tell whether the voice is bass or tenor, detect dialect peculiarities, and determine a good deal about the voice quality of the speaker.

The four primary objective characteristics of sound—frequency, intensity, tone structure, and duration—all appear in the spectograms produced by this machine. Each word has its own pattern that exhibits all these elements on the screen.

In the not too-distant future it may be possible for the voice pupil to study pictures of his own voice and note the number and intensity of overtones, the strength of the fundamental tone, and other pertinent factors. He may then compare these with pictures of the tones made by the best models speaking or singing the same words. The possibilities of the invention are great.[4]

How One Person "Hears" Speech

Helen Keller, that remarkable woman who, though totally deaf and blind, is able to converse fluently on the most erudite subjects, has learned to *feel* the vibrations of sound. By placing one finger on a nostril, one on the lips, and one on the larynx of the speaker, she is able to "hear." In the larynx she feels the vibrations of the vocal cords; in the lips she detects the different types of vowels and consonants which depend upon lip action; and in the nose she recognizes the sounds which depend primarily upon nasal resonance.

You may gain some idea of the manner in which Miss Keller "hears" sound through her fingers by noting in your own throat the difference between voiced and unvoiced consonants. Place your fingers lightly upon your Adam's apple while you utter the sounds of the letters listed below, and note that the sounds in the column at the left cause no vibration beneath your fingers, while those in the right-hand column cause a perceptible vibration. In all other respects except this voicing, the paired consonants are identical.

Unvoiced Consonants	Voiced Consonants
f	v
k	g
p	b
s	z
sh	zh
t	d
th (thin)	th (thou)

With these basic characteristics of sound in mind, we should be able better to understand the nature of resonance.

[4] The limitations of this text do not permit a more extensive discussion of this interesting scientific development. But the student may, if he desires, make further investigation for himself. Thoroughgoing scientific analyses are presented by Ralph K. Potter in *Science* for November 9, 1945 (pp. 463-470), under the title "Visible Patterns of Sound," and in *Visible Speech* by Ralph K. Potter, George A. Kopp, and Harriet C. Green (D. Van Nostrand Company, 1947). More popular discussions of the subject will be found in "Pictures in Speech," *Life,* November 26, 1945, pp. 91-94, and "Visible Speech," *Time,* November 19, 1945, p. 50.

VII ✳ Developing Effective Vocal Resonance

Resonance has several times been mentioned as an element of the speaking voice. Indeed, wherever and whenever voice is discussed, resonance is one of the terms most often used. We hear expressions like: "He has a fine, resonant voice" or "His voice lacks resonance."

In spite of the frequent allusions to resonance, however, there is little general understanding of what resonance is. If you were to ask the average person to define the term, he probably would have a good deal of difficulty. And reference to the dictionary isn't too helpful. *The American College Dictionary*, for example, gives several definitions among which is this one: "The amplification of vocal tone by the bones of the head and upper chest and by the air cavities of the pharynx, mouth, and nasal passages."

To gain any true comprehension of the nature of resonance, a much more detailed explanation is necessary, especially for the voice student, because some understanding of the nature of resonance, as well as knowledge of how to use it in his own voice, is a fundamental part of his training.

All musical instruments (and practically all sound-producing instruments of every description) have resonators. All band and orchestral instruments, for example, have either sounding boards, or air columns in pipes, tubes, or metal chambers, which take up the weak tones initiated by the vibrating body and through a system of interactions enlarge and strengthen the tones into the melodious tones we hear.

In the animal world extreme examples of resonance are the bull's deep, vibrant, and powerful tones which travel so far and so fearsomely, and the guinea hen's sharp raucous tones which demonstrate forceful if not beautiful resonance. Resonance is the phenomenon by which a bullfrog, a little animal less than eight inches long, can boom forth a tone which will carry a mile or more across a quiet lake.[1] Resonance plays a significant role in creating the magnificent tones which come from the strings of a Stradivarius in the hands of a Fritz Kreisler; those same strings, *if suspended in the air*, even if bowed by the same master artist, would make scarcely any audible sound at all. Resonance is the phenomenon which causes the little squeaks of the vibrated reed in the artificial larynx (see page 29) to emerge from the mouth of the user as a respectable representation of the human voice. Resonance is one of the most important attributes of the voice of such a speaker as the late William Jennings Bryan, of whom George Ade, a prominent writer and newspaper reporter of Bryan's day, said, "I didn't believe one word of that 'Cross of Gold' oratorical paroxysm, but it gave me the goose pimples just the same."[2]

A few simple experiments will give some idea of the way resonance operates.

1. Tap the cheeks sharply with an ordinary lead pencil, at the same time forming the lips into various shapes. Note that much of the time the blow of the pencil makes a dull thud, but with certain shapes of the mouth the sound is much louder.

2. The jew's-harp gives a better demonstration of resonance. Set it into vibration while it is held in the hand, and the tone will be scarcely audible. But bring the vibrating instrument to

---

[1] An interesting article on how the frog achieves its resonance by means of its "expandable" throat appeared in *National Geographic Magazine,* April, 1950.

[2] Fred C. Kelly, *George Ade,* The Bobbs-Merrill Company, 1947, p. 129.

the mouth and hold it between the lips, and a considerable volume will be achieved. Note too that the quality of the sound changes materially in response to the changing shapes of the mouth, even though neither the method nor the force of striking is changed at all.

3. Some interesting experiments can be performed with a tuning fork:

a. Hold the vibrating fork in front of the open mouth, and note how the faint, almost inaudible sound is strengthened.

b. Hold the end of the vibrating fork against a table and note how the sound is immediately amplified.

c. Hold the vibrating fork over an empty tumbler. The chances are that you will get little if any amplification of the sound. Now begin to pour water into the tumbler. When the water approaches a certain level, the sound gradually increases to a full-bodied tone. But if you keep on pouring, it begins to fade, and ultimately dies almost completely away. The reason for this phenomenon is that when the air chamber above the water is of the right or "optimum" size the vibrations from the tuning fork are picked up and amplified; this will be explained later.

Types of Sound Amplification

There are three ways in which sound is built up: (1) reverberation, (2) forced or sounding board amplification, and (3) free resonance.

Reverberation

Reverberation is the type of amplification which occurs when you shout in a canyon and the sounds come echoing back to you reflected from the walls of the canyon; or when you talk loudly in an empty room that has bare, smooth walls. The sounds are literally bounced off the walls and concentrated in a certain direction, so that they strike the ear with great intensity. A contrast to this phenomenon is observed when you talk in a room whose walls are hung with heavy draperies and whose floor is covered with a thick rug. Because of the absorption of many of the sound vibrations by the soft coverings, the voice is hushed, and echoes are practically eliminated.

FORCED OR SOUNDING BOARD AMPLIFICATION

Forced or sounding board amplification occurs when a solid body takes up vibrations that impinge upon it. In the experiment with the tuning fork, when the butt of the fork was held against the table, the entire table acted as a sounding board, vibrating in harmony with the vibrations of the fork.

FREE RESONANCE

Free resonance is a bit more involved and difficult to understand, but it is by far the most important factor in building up and enriching the human voice. Briefly stated, the principle is this: Every column of air, such as that confined in a violin box, a pipe organ tube, or the human mouth, has one or more natural vibration rates, depending upon its size and shape. When vibration frequencies are presented which exactly conform to one of the air column's natural frequencies, the whole column of air is set into *sympathetic vibration*, and the tones are reinforced and amplified. This is the type of amplification obtained in the experiment with the tuning fork and the glass of water.

This principle may be likened to the pushing of a child's swing. If the pushes are applied at the right instant, the amplitude and energy of the swing are easily increased. If, however, the pushes are not well timed, the effort is partly neutralized, and much harder pushes are required to accomplish the same result. In a properly adjusted resonating chamber, incoming vibrations are timed perfectly with the natural vibration rate of the air column in the chamber, and the tone is built up. The entering sound waves set the larger column of air into vibration, thus reinforcing the original vibration and consequently reinforcing the tone.

Note that while the resonators just mentioned—the pipe organ, the violin, and the human mouth—are of the air-column type, and consequently exemplify free resonance, they have some essentially different features. Pipe organ resonators, for example, consist of several sets of pipes of varied shapes and sizes. Some of the pipes are of the proportions of a pencil, and resonate only the highest overtones. Some are more the size of tree trunks, and resonate the fundamental and lowest overtones. Also, some of the pipes have large openings and some have small openings (this difference was illustrated in tapping the cheek with a pencil while changing the size of the mouth opening). Some have closed ends and others have open ends. This variation provides resonance not only for tones of different frequencies, but also for tones of different *kinds,* i.e., tones of different vibration patterns. Because of the great variety of pipes in this largest and most complicated of all musical instruments, a skilled organist, by manipulating the different keyboards, can make tones as low as the rumble of distant cannon, in fact so low that sometimes it is difficult to tell whether we hear them or feel them as pulsations in the air; he can make tones as high as the whistle of wind through a crack in the window; and he can make tones to represent almost all the instruments in an orchestra, singly or in combination.

A much simpler instrument, similar to the pipe organ in that it uses pipes for resonators, is the marimba. The playing board of this instrument consists of a number of strips of wood of various sizes, which, when struck by small hammers in the hands of the musician, emit musical sounds. Beneath the strips of wood hang the resonators, a series of metal tubes graded in length and diameter to correspond to the strips of wood.

The essential resonance feature of both the marimba and the pipe organ is that they have "tuned" pipes for resonators, each one designed to resonate only certain tones.

The violin resonator is fixed in size and shape, and there is only the one air chamber. Therefore this column of air can respond only to a limited number of tones. However, in the violin, free resonance is supplemented by the sounding board type of resonance. Through the bridge and the attachments at the ends of the strings, vibrations are transmitted directly from the strings to the body of the violin, and thus the whole violin becomes a sounding board. These vibrations can be felt by placing the fingers on any part of the violin box or its neck while the instrument is being played. But the column of air within the violin box does much to provide the rich fullness of the lower tones.

Human resonators likewise use some forced amplification of the sounding board type, as does the violin; but far more important is free resonance. With human resonators also, another significant fact is that the shape and size of the resonators are not fixed and static, as in the pipe organ and the violin, but highly flexible. The importance of this fact will be explained in the next section.

Resonance in the Human Voice

Free resonance in the human voice is provided principally by three cavities: the pharynx (the chamber back of the nose and mouth and above the larynx), the nasal chambers, and the mouth (see Fig. 3.) As already stated, the factor of greatest importance about these cavities is their marvelous adjustability. They can be lengthened or shortened, made wider or narrower, made to have soft or hard walls, and can even be shut off entirely, so that one, two, or all three of them can be used to resonate different sounds. This adaptability is utilized in human speech not only to resonate tones with a great variety of qualities and pitches, but also to form the different sounds of our spoken language—the vowels, consonants, and diphthongs.

To make clear just how this principle works with our own

voices in forming the various sounds of our speech, try the following experiments:

1. Make an easy tone—for example, $\overline{oo}$ as in *food*—and prolong it. On this steady sustained tone change the shape of the mouth and lips, and note that there are material changes in the sound. In fact, entirely different vowel sounds are produced—a simple demonstration of the fact that the various vowels are the result of different resonance combinations.

2. Make the following vowel sounds in succession: $\overline{oo}$ as in *food, ō* as in *cold, ạ* as in *awful, ä* as in *father, ă* as in *fat.* Say them on one breath in a sustained mono-pitch: $\overline{oo}$, *ō, ạ, ä, ă.* Repeat them several times. Observe that the $\overline{oo}$ sound is made back in the pharynx (the chamber back of the mouth), the *ō* in the full, well-rounded mouth, the *ạ* with the mouth a little wider open, the *ä* farther forward and with the mouth opened still wider, and the *ă* far forward in the well-opened mouth. Reversing the order of the vowels (*ă, ä, ạ, ō,* $\overline{oo}$) will help to make the process obvious.

As suggested earlier, these resonators probably are aided to some extent by the sounding board effect of the teeth, hard palate, and skull. But these bony structures are of only secondary importance in resonance. Bone, at best, is not the most efficient sounding board material, for it is too porous to function well in this respect. And bone overlaid with flesh is even less efficient. Nevertheless, the advice given by voice teachers to direct the tone toward the upper teeth ridge is *psychologically* very good advice indeed. Directing the tone thus forward tends to get it out in front where it belongs, and helps to prevent the muffled quality which develops when tones are held back in the mouth.

Likewise, it is sometimes thought that the walls of the larynx itself and the chest cavity with its enclosing rib cage play an important role in vocal resonance. Certainly it is true that a person can feel vibration in these areas by touching his fingers to his larynx during tone production, or to his chest while speaking or singing some of his lower tones. It is likely that the larynx, and the trachea leading to it, function to some degree as resonators; also that the bony structures of the head and chest add their bit through forced resonance. Indeed it is quite possible that the whole body may have some function as a sounding board for certain tones. Research, however, has not been able to measure the amount of resonance from these areas, and the opinion among the majority of research students is that their contribution is negligible in comparison with that of the chief resonating chambers, the cavities above the larynx in the head and throat.

Whether or not a cavity amplifies a given tone depends upon several factors, among them *the size of the cavity, its shape, the nature of its walls,* and *the size of its openings.* With these facts in mind, consider the great flexibility of the cavities of the head and throat. The pharynx can be lengthened or shortened at its lower extremity by raising or lowering the larynx. (You can observe this action by placing your fingers upon your larynx and swallowing.) The pharynx may also be lengthened or shortened at its upper extremity by raising or lowering the soft palate. The nose, while not so flexible as either the pharynx or the mouth, is still capable of some adjustment through the dilation and contraction of the nostrils. The mouth, with its hinged jaw at the bottom, its mobile lips at the front, its contractible throat muscles at the back, and its extremely pliant tongue in the middle, is most adjustable of all. And all these cavities are capable of additional adjustment through changes in the nature of their walls. Tensed muscles in the walls of these areas will do much to change the surface from soft to hard, and will affect the tone accordingly; too tense a wall will produce strident, harsh, metallic tones. Taken together, these cavities are capable of almost limitless adjustment which enables them selectively to pick up, amplify, and enrich the various nuances of our infinitely varied speech.

When all the resonating chambers function together harmoniously, supported by such aid as may be given by the sounding board effect of the various parts of the body, the tone comes forth as an amplified and melodious whole. It is this harmonious integration which voice teachers call "pure" tone. As a pleasing shade of color may be compounded of a harmonious blending of many fundamental colors, so "pure" tone is a perfect blend of various elements of resonance. The voice teacher uses this term "pure tone" in a different sense than does the physicist, to whom a "pure" tone is a fundamental tone without any overtones.

The fact that resonating chambers vary so greatly in size and shape in different individuals is a major factor in providing what we call "voice personality." And the fact that these chambers are capable of such flexible adjustment within an individual, according to his changing moods and thoughts, helps greatly in making the human voice by all odds the most marvelous of all sound-producing instruments.

One other fact should be borne in mind. Resonating chambers do not originate tone; they merely pick up and amplify, selectively, sounds which come to them from some other source. Hence we see the importance of the free, unhampered swing of the vocal cords in creating a rich fundamental tone and many overtones, so that the resonating chambers can have something to work on.

To appreciate more fully the manner in which the mouth, the pharynx, and the nose function as resonators, it is desirable to analyze the action of each of them a little more fully.

The Mouth as a Resonator

As stated earlier, of all the instruments of resonation, the most flexible and adaptable for amplifying different speech sounds is the mouth. It is bounded at the front by the lips (which can be adjusted to make openings all the way from zero to the diameter of a tennis ball, or larger, as some of our comedians demonstrate); below, by the tongue (which is capable of changing its shape by lengthening, shortening, thickening, pointing, and assuming various shapes in its tip, blade, or dorsum, so that it can alter the size of the mouth materially, and its shape almost without limit); at the back, by the soft palate and the wall of the pharynx (which are capable of extensive adjustment, in either position or degree of tenseness, or both); and above, by the hard palate (the only one of the four boundaries incapable of adjustment).

When we take up the study of vowels and consonants, we will analyze more fully the action of the tongue, lips, and other instruments of articulation in the formation of individual sounds.

THE PHARYNX AS A RESONATOR

The pharynx is the large cavity which extends from the top of the larynx up to and including the cavity back of the nostrils. For purposes of study and analysis the pharynx is divided into three sections: the laryngopharynx (the part of the pharynx just above the larynx), the oropharynx (the part of the pharynx back of the mouth), and the nasopharynx (the part of the pharynx back of the nose). Taken as a whole, the pharynx has almost as many adjustment possibilities as the mouth. These adjustments are controlled in part by the action of the muscles embedded in the walls of the pharynx, the extrinsic muscles of the larynx, the velum (soft palate), and the tongue.

The *laryngopharynx*, as already noted, is extremely flexible. By the upward and downward movement of the larynx, plus the contracting and relaxing of the constrictor muscles at the top, the diameter and length of the laryngopharynx can be, and are, adjusted easily and speedily to pick up and amplify different overtones. Thus it performs a most important function in producing both the different vowels and voiced consonants and the subtle differences in individual voices.

The *oropharynx* can function in a sort of paired action with the laryngopharynx, or with the mouth, or with the nasopharynx, or with all three at once. This remarkable adjustability gives this chamber great selectivity as a creator of fine shades of resonance.

The *nasopharynx* can be shut off completely from the mouth and other sections of the pharynx by the action of the soft palate; or it can become an integral part of the mouth and all the other parts of the pharynx; or it can function in conjunction with the mouth cavity but with the frontal opening of the mouth completely closed. This latter condition occurs in humming and in forming the sound of *m* (*me, mine, home*) and *n* (*no, nine, hundred*), except that in the latter sound the tip of the tongue partially shuts off the frontal opening of the mouth. In forming the sound *ng* (*singing, ringing*) the dorsum of the tongue presses against the soft palate, which is lowered to aid in the process of blocking off the mouth and sending the sound out through the nose.

THE SINUSES

The part played by the sinuses as resonators is not known. The sinuses are small openings branching off from the nasal cavity, which give us considerable discomfort at times under the general heading of "sinus trouble." Some authorities claim that the openings to these small cavities are too small to admit air waves for resonation; others hold that they perform a vital function in resonating the higher overtones of the voice. Empirically it would seem that they do play a part, for certainly when the sensitive mucous membranes which line their walls become irritated and inflamed, and the sinuses become filled with mucus, voice quality is impaired. However, we cannot rule out the possibility that the voice impairment is the result of associated factors. For example, when the sinuses become infected, the inflammation is likely to spread to surrounding areas, for all the walls of the pharynx and larynx are lined with sensitive mucous membranes. Thus large areas of the pharyngeal cavities may be partially blocked off. Also, exudations from the sinuses, in the form of infected mucus, may drop down even onto the vocal cords themselves, causing the inflammation known as laryngitis. With all these potentialities, further research, and possibly more precise instruments of measurement, are necessary to determine just what function is performed by the sinuses as resonating chambers. At any rate, the question of possible resonance in the sinuses is of comparatively minor importance in relation to the phenomenon of nasal resonance, for it is in the nasopharynx itself that the chief function of nasal resonation is performed. This whole matter of nasal resonance is so important that it deserves special consideration.

NASAL RESONANCE

Fig. 14 shows how the soft palate acts to open and close the nasopharyngeal cavity. The solid black shows the soft palate tensed and elevated, pressing against the wall of the pharynx. In this position the "door" between the nasopharynx and the oropharynx is closed, permitting very little of the sound to enter the nasopharynx for resonation. The dotted lines show the soft palate relaxed and lowered, thus opening the passageway and permitting the tone to enter freely into, and be resonated by, the nasal cavity. This passage between the soft palate and the wall of the pharynx is open widest on the sounds *m*, *n*, and *ng*, these being distinctly nasal sounds. This is why, when we have head colds which partially block off our nasal chambers, our voices sound so peculiar on words like *human*, *mine*, and *spring*.

It has been claimed by some that except for these three sounds there should be no nasal resonance in English speech. In certain other languages, notably French, several of the vowels are distinctly nasalized. X-ray photography has shown, however, that in making vowels immediately before or immediately after nasal consonants the passage is partially open; thus we may be sure that there is some degree of nasal resonance on the vowels in such words as *home, stone, man,* and *can.* This is true of practically all speakers, whether or not they are considered to have "nasal" voices. The reason, of course, is that the soft palate begins to relax in preparation for the *n* in such words as *can,* and remains partially relaxed and open after the formation of the nasalized consonant in such words as *mouth.* There

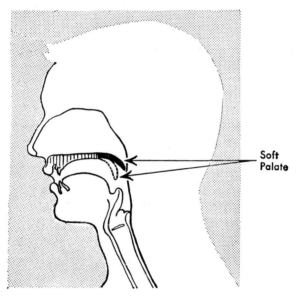

Soft Palate

FIG. 14. Diagram of the action of the soft palate
in controlling resonance.

is, therefore, more nasal resonance in the average voice on the *a* in *man* than on the same vowel in *cab.* Also, it is quite possible that some of the vibrations from the mouth pass directly through the thin membranes of the hard palate into the nasopharynx, and thus give a certain degree of nasal resonation to other speech sounds.

Although there is a difference of opinion among research students and voice teachers as to the amount of nasal resonance desirable on the various vowels and voiced consonants in our language, the majority of voice teachers agree that most of us have far too little nasal resonance in our voices. This belief is supported by the way our tones become muffled and lifeless when head colds inflame the lining of the nasopharynx, and partially clog the cavities with excess mucus. The full rich tones of our best Negro singers are attributable in no small measure to the wide nostrils and voluminous nasal cavities with which they are endowed.

The methods used by singing teachers seem to substantiate the need for more nasal resonance. Most of these teachers employ exercises to "tie the vowels onto the nasalized consonants," exercises like the one favored by the late John Smallman, one-time director of the Los Angeles Oratorio Society. He employed a lilting phrase which he had his pupils sing over and over again, using syllables like *neen, neen, neen; nain, nain, nain;* and *maim, maim, maim.*

Prominent singers and actors realize the importance of this type of resonance. Nasal resonance is what Cornelia Otis Skinner is striving for when she says: "I hum a lot, until my head seems to reverberate like a bell."[3] One prominent concert baritone of our day utilizes the ten or fifteen minutes immediately preceding one of his concerts in walking back and forth just off stage, humming, and at the same time tapping his ample nose with his finger.

The author joins with these teachers and noted performers of the stage and concert platform in recommending humming exercises, in the firm conviction that they will help to impart the quality which is sometimes called the "ping" in the voice, they will help overcome any tendency to dead and lifeless tones.

Try a little experiment. Begin to hum a vigorous but not a forced tone with your lips closed. If your nose is free from obstruction caused by a cold or a foreign growth, the tone should be vibrant and ringing. Now suddenly pinch the nostrils

[3] In a letter to the author; quoted by permission.

closed with your fingers. You will observe that the tone ceases
instantly. This indicates that this tone comes through the nose;
and this tone has a desirable quality which many voices lack,
the quality often called brilliance.

We should not, of course, lose sight of the fact that there
can be too much nasal resonance; also, that there can be the
wrong kind of nasal resonance. Some undesirable kinds will be
discussed later in this chapter. But in general, it can safely be
said that there is little danger of acquiring too much nasal
resonance if the throat and jaw are kept relaxed. The harsh,
metallic nasal tone which is so objectionable is almost invariably associated with a rigid jaw and a mouth only partially
opened.

Furthermore, in these exercises as in all other phases of voice
development, ear training is essential. To repeat the recommendations made earlier, the student should make frequent
records and listen to his voice objectively. He should also strive
to hear his own voice during his practice sessions. And, in addition, it is always better if he can have the counsel of a competent instructor and sympathetic and coöperative classmates.

Types of Voice Quality

For a century or more it has been customary for voice
teachers to designate various types of voice quality by certain
rather universally accepted names. Specifically these are: *aspirate, falsetto, guttural, nasal, normal, oral, orotund,* and
pectoral. Of late years the tendency has been for some voice
teachers and writers of voice texts to discard all such attempts
to classify types of quality, on the grounds that such classification is too arbitrary and too mechanical an approach to the
study of voice. Nevertheless, many students of voice still believe
that these classifications provide a convenient method of an-
alyzing different kinds of resonance, and that for the student
to know and recognize them by name does not necessarily induce a mechanical approach to his voice problems.

*Most of these qualities are stage devices rather than essential equipment for the ordinary person who merely wants a pleasant and expressive voice to meet his everyday needs. It is true, nevertheless, that these devices, if used judiciously and in artistic moderation, may be useful to anyone who undertakes to interpret pieces of literature orally, and to anyone who simply likes to indulge in a bit of impersonation in telling his anecdotes and stories. Often they are the best available means of producing comedy effects. But that is not the chief reason for their inclusion in this text. The reason they appear here is that many of these qualities are objectionable as part of the everyday speaking voice. It is hoped that by knowing precisely how the different qualities are made, the student of speech may be able to eliminate the undesirable ones from his own voice.

ASPIRATE QUALITY

The aspirate quality is a half-whisper that is lacking in tonal quality. It is a breathy sound, getting little aid from the vocal cords. Its amplification comes principally from friction against the walls of the mouth and throat. Actors use this device for whispering stage secrets. It suggests mystery, fear, extreme agitation.

Sh-sh-sh! Don't make a sound! There's something white over there that looks like a ghost!

> But hush! hark! a deep sound strikes like a
> rising knell!
> Did ye not hear it?—No; 'twas but the wind,
> Or the car rattling o'er the stony streets.

FALSETTO QUALITY

Falsetto is a light, high tone produced by the vibration of only a small segment of the vocal cords. It is resonated far back in the mouth, really in the dome of the pharynx. It is the tone heard in the "breaking voice" of adolescent boys. In adults, it is higher than the normal pitch. Some tenors resort to it when they attempt to reach notes above their natural range. It also is heard in the quavery voice of old age and illness. One sometimes hears it in the artificial tones of poorly executed Punch and Judy shows. As a stage device it is used to suggest artificiality and effeminacy.

> . . . His big manly voice,
> Turning again toward childish treble, pipes
> And whistles in his sound.

> The weird sisters, hand in hand,
> Posters of the sea and land,
> Thus do go about, about;
> Thrice to thine, and thrice to mine.
> And thrice again, to make up nine.

GUTTURAL QUALITY

The guttural quality is a throaty, often harsh quality, made familiar to movie-goers by Pop-Eye. It seems to get its resonance chiefly in the walls of the larynx and the laryngopharynx. It suggests anger, hate, toughness, rowdyism, "hard-boiledness." Some individuals mistakenly believe that it denotes strength.

An undesirable kind of guttural quality is employed by certain men who have potentially excellent voices. Their voices are held deep in their throats where they apparently attempt to do their articulating. The deep rumbles evidently please the inner ears of the speakers.

A certain amount of guttural quality would be helpful in interpreting the following lines:

Gr-r-r-r-r, how I hate him!

> You limpin' lump o' brick-dust, Gunga Din!
> . . . Water, get it! . . .
> You squidgy-nosed old idol, Gunga Din!

NASAL QUALITY

The term *nasal*, as it was used in older classifications, frequently connoted an undesirable quality. Nowadays the word more commonly used in this connection is "nasality." *Nasality*, as it is employed today, has very wide application. It means too much, and too little, and various and sundry kinds of poorly used nasal resonance. Too much nasal resonance (sometimes called *positive nasality*) is produced when the jaw is held rigid, the mouth opened only in a tiny slit, and the voice forced out through the nose. Emerson accused New Englanders of having this kind of nasality because the climate is so cold they hate to open their mouths. "Hillbillies" use it; so do whiny children. And many radio and stage comedians (notably Fred Allen) use it for comedy effects.

Too little nasal resonance, or *negative nasality*, or *denasality*, occurs when, from either a nose-clogging cold or a too-tense soft palate, the tone is not permitted to enter the nasal cavity to be resonated. This results in a dull and characterless type of voice.

Still another type of nasality results when a lazy soft palate permits too great a body of tone to surge into the nasopharynx —a tone which has no adequate means of egress because the nostrils are too small to let all the sound out. The confined vibrations create something akin to eddies in the nasal chambers, and result in a sort of smothered resonance which is decidedly unpleasant. You can demonstrate this type of resonance for yourself by making the sound *m*, *n*, or *ng* and interrupting the tone by closing off part of your nostrils with your fingers. By experimenting with various-sized nasal openings you will learn the full effect of this "blind alley" type of resonance. A pathological condition which exemplifies this type of resonance in extreme form—and whose treatment is outside the province of this text—is cleft palate.

Now, Paul, don't you do that.

I have a bad cold in my head. (Pinch your nostrils closed with your fingers to get the desired effect.)

> Yet the ear distinctly tells
> In the jangling
> And the wrangling,
> How the danger sinks and swells—
> By the sinking or the swelling in the anger of the bells.

Observe the difference between the above examples of nasality and the desirable nasal resonance called for in the following lines:

Room for the leper, room.

The road was a ribbon of moonlight, over the purple moor.

Many men are made miserable through money madness.

> Medicine men on the medicine drum,
> Beating out the rhythm with a steady thrum.

NORMAL QUALITY

Every voice has its own personality. It is this personality, this something which distinguishes it from every other voice, that we call normal voice quality. It is as distinctive as the shapes of noses and mouths and the different complexions of various faces. Some time ago the author walked by a house where a radio or record player was playing loud enough for him to hear the voice but not distinguish the words of the speaker. It was no trouble whatever to recognize it as the voice of the late President Roosevelt. Partly it was the inflections—a positive, decisive downward slide at the end of every sentence along with plenty of pleasant variations between; partly it was the deliberate rate, with interesting pauses for emphasis; but chiefly it was the unmistakable quality.

Normal quality is usually described in such terms as warm,

friendly, colorful, grating, dull. We repeat that the statement sometimes offered as an apology for an atrocious quality, "It's the voice I was born with," is not true. You weren't born with any voice—merely with the mechanism for voice! The way you use it is a learned activity. Vocal equipment, of course, does vary and in a sense is responsible for our voice quality. It does place definite limitations upon us. But nature on the whole is quite generous. She equips us well. Nearly everyone has the mechanism to make pleasant tones. Our normal voices are the voices we have developed through imitation and habit; it is hardly fair to blame nature for them.

Oral Quality

Oral quality is a light, weak tone, often called *infantile*. It has some of the characteristics of the falsetto tone but is less resonant and generally lower in pitch. Such resonance as it has comes from the open and soft-walled mouth; it has little of the deep pharyngeal or ringing nasal resonance. Tones that are unnaturally hushed might be called oral. Librarians and undertakers seem especially prone to this type of quality, because of the vocal restraints imposed upon them. Conversely, you are not likely to hear much of this quality around stockyards and steel mills. It suggests weakness, tiredness, and extreme repression, as well as old age and tranquillity. Often, as a stage device, it is used to portray a weak personality.

We were drifting on a calm, unruffled sea.

> Is "old dog" my reward? Most true, I have
>   lost my teeth in your service. . . .

> Though I look old, yet I am strong and lusty;
> For in my youth I never did apply
> Hot and rebellious liquors in my blood, . . .
> Therefore my age is as a lusty winter,
> Frosty, but kindly. . . .

Dear Master, I can go no further: O, I die for food! Here lie I down, and measure out my grave. Farewell, kind master.

An excellent example of oral quality is contained in the diatribe by Cassius (page 148), especially in the lines in which he shows his contempt for Caesar by burlesquing Caesar's voice.

OROTUND QUALITY

An orotund quality is a full, round quality. It uses all types of resonance, and uses them efficiently to make strong, melodious tone. It is the quality used by public speakers before large audiences, especially when they are dealing with noble or elevated sentiments. Such speech is usually slow, measured, and inclined to be ponderous. When used in deep sincerity, it is extremely effective. But when used in mock sincerity, it suggests pomposity.[4] Sentences like the following are well adapted to its use:

The road to Rome is rugged, rough and round.

Oh, Thou that rollest above, round as the shield of our fathers, Whence are thy beams, Oh Sun, thy everlasting light?

The ocean old, centuries old; strong as life and as uncontrolled.

Rouse ye, men of Athens!

Lift up your head, oh ye gates; and be ye lift up,
Ye everlasting doors; and the King of Glory shall come in.

PECTORAL QUALITY

The pectoral is a quality which seems to come from the chest. Actually the tone is resonated low in the laryngopharynx and in the larynx, as is the guttural. In this tone, however, the walls of the cavities are relaxed, whereas in the guttural they are tensed. It is a deep, "hollow" tone, appropriate for ghosts and spooks. Occasionally it is mistakenly used by ministers at funerals. It is well called a sepulchral voice.

[4] For an amusing experiment, switch the oral and orotund qualities, i.e. use oral quality on the orotund practice lines, and vice versa.

I am thy father's spirit—
Doomed for a certain time to walk the night;
And, for the day, confined to fast in fires,
Till the foul crimes done in my day of nature,
Are burnt and purged away.

> Mumbo-Jumbo will hoo-doo you,
> Mumbo-Jumbo will hoo-doo you,
> Mumbo-Jumbo will hoo-doo you.

You understand, of course, that these types of voice quality are not set off from each other as fields of potatoes are fenced off from fields of beans. They mingle and blend in all sorts of combinations according to the speaker's individual voice characteristics and his varying moods. The shadings from one general classification to another, the changing degrees of intensity within each classification, the various permutations are almost infinite. You perhaps will recognize varying degrees of these types of voice quality in some of your friends, if not in your own voice. Furthermore, you no doubt will observe, if you have not already done so, that the more expressive voices instinctively veer from one to another of these qualities in telling stories and recounting anecdotes.

The daily press recently reported the selection, by a national organization, of the "10 outstanding voices in the world." You may recognize some of the qualities we have been discussing in this list. Note, however, that some of them are not so much qualities of tone as they are personality characteristics, as for example Leo Durocher's "explosive" voice.

Here is the selection of outstanding voices: Winston Churchill, "most theatrical"; Dean Acheson, "suavest"; Emperor Hirohito, "most effeminate"; radio's Ben Grauer, "most authoritative"; Sir Stafford Cripps, "most paradoxical"; Leo Durocher, "most explosive"; radio's Dan Seymour, "friendliest"; John L. Lewis, "most pugnacious"; actress Lauren Bacall, "sexiest"; and the United Nations' Trygve Lie, "sincerest."

Conscious Manipulation of the Resonators Seldom Necessary

The fact that you now have acquainted yourselves with the physiological processes by which certain kinds of resonance are achieved does not mean that from now on you are to manipulate the resonators mechanically. Fortunately, in cases where there is no functional derangement and no long-standing pernicious habits, nature will take care of the manipulation of the resonance chambers automatically. Conscious adjustment is neither necessary nor desirable. The only conscious coöperation required is sufficient relaxation of the throat, jaw, and face to permit the necessary muscular adjustment. When a fault is to be corrected, however, or when a change in resonance is deliberately sought, experimentation and practice are necessary to master the new adjustments. Many of the exercises which follow will aid in this experimentation. Ideally, however, thought and emotion should automatically bring about the proper adjustments to produce the best tone for the occasion.

EXERCISES

Remember that voice exercises are not to be said over once or twice and then forgotten, but to be gone over day after day, week in and week out.

1. Hum with the lips closed. Feel the nose and lips vibrating. Touch the fingers lightly to the bridge of the nose and feel the vibrations.

2. Set the whole mask of the face vibrating on the hummed *m-m-m-m,* then open the lips and let the sound out on *ē,* as *m-m-m-m-m-ēē.* Do the same with the hummed *n,* as *n-n-n-n-n-n-ēē.* Repeat on different levels of pitch. Dam up the vowels and hold them back until the mask is vibrating freely.

3. Repeat with *m-m-m-m-m-ōō, n-n-n-n-n-ōō, m-m-m-m-m-ah.* and *n-n-n-n-ah.*

4. Form a funnel with the hands in front of the lips, and repeat the above exercise, sending the tones ringing across the room.

5. To gain a clear sensation of the tensing and relaxing action of the soft palate discussed earlier in the chapter, experiment with the combined *t* and *n* sounds, as in the words *ton, tune, tone.* Note that preceding the explosive *t* sound the soft palate is tensed, but relaxes to let the *n* sound through the nose. Hold the tensed position of the soft palate for a few seconds to be sure that you get the sensation of tenseness, then quickly relax the soft palate and let the *n* sound come surging through the nose.

6. Experiment with the difference between tensed and relaxed jaw in achieving desirable nasal resonance.

   First tense your partially opened jaw—tense! Note what happens to the tongue. Feel it bunch up against the soft palate. Now speak a sentence—for example, "Just listen to this 'nosey' tone." Observe how the tone is *forced* out through the nose. Newsboys sometimes develop this hard, metallic, far-carrying tone to a high degree; and many persons talk (and some even sing) with too much of this quality in their tones.

   In contrast to the above exercise, experiment with a relaxed jaw, as follows: Begin a yawn. Feel the tongue flatten out in the floor of the mouth. You can see this action by looking in a mirror during the exercise. At the same time place your fingers lightly upon your Adam's apple and feel the larynx being drawn downward. Observe how this action of the tongue and larynx elongates and enlarges the pharynx, making of it a rounder, more efficient resonance chamber. In this relaxed position, utter on a slow, steady mono-pitch the vowel sounds *oh, ah, aw.*

7. After you have achieved the clear and definite sensation of relaxation in soft palate and jaw described in Exercises 5 and 6, repeat Exercises 1-4. Sing them or speak them over, and over, and over again. Make them part of your daily exercise program.

8. Sing the tone ōō as in *boot* on different pitch levels, pursing the lips and protruding them well forward. Make a sort of funnel out of them. Send the tone out to some imaginary person at a distance. Don't permit the lips to get stiff or rigid; keep them flexible.

9. On a level, sustained pitch, say: *Hung-e-e-e, Hung-e-e-e.* Repeat over and over on different pitch levels. Vary the exercise with *Hung-ah-o-e-e, Hung-ah-o-e-e.* Look in a mirror and note how the dorsum of the tongue blocks off the mouth passage during the *ng* sound, and is pulled smartly away from the soft palate to emit the vowels through the mouth.

10. Pronounce the following words in a sustained resonant tone: *sing, king, wing, ring, swing, fling, bing.*

11. Say the following lines first as if you had a severe cold in your head, stopping up the nasal chambers; then say them again, letting the nasalized consonants and the vowels next to them come ringing vibrantly through the nose. Note the difference in your voice quality.

> The wind was a torrent of darkness among the gusty trees,
> The moon was a ghostly galleon tossed upon cloudy seas,
> The road was a ribbon of moonlight over the purple moor,
> And the highwayman came riding—
> Riding—riding—
> The highwayman came riding, up to the old inn-door.
>
> —ALFRED NOYES[5]

12. Practice the following phrases and sentences. Give them plenty of nasal "ping," but at the same time keep the throat and jaw relaxed in order to insure the proper mixture of pharyngeal resonance in the tone:
    1. Military might is not always right.
    2. Nine hundred and ninety-nine.

[5] Reprinted by permission of the publishers, J. B. Lippincott Company, from *Collected Poems in One Volume* by Alfred Noyes. Copyright, 1906, 1934, 1947, by Alfred Noyes.

3. A sweet melody flooded the morning air.
4. The song was sung, while incense hung heavy in the room.
5. We be merry men; merry men are we.
6. One thousand men marching.
7. No, no, I can never do it.
8. I am no more than a morsel of meat.
9. Nothing is so unnecessary as nagging.
10. Make way for the Monarch.
11. The gong goes bong. Bong goes the gong.
12. Bennie had a penny; Bennie had a penny.
13. Any many any many any many any many any many.
14. Anna ate a banana; Anna ate a banana.
15. I would never lay down my arms, *never,* NEVER, NEVER.
16. We are the dreamers of dreams.
17. Give me men to match my mountains.
18.   Memory room is an attic room
       Where never a mop and seldom a broom
       Disturbs the dust and the cobwebs there.

SELECTIONS FOR PRACTICE

1. The following selections should help you to place the tone forward in the mouth and achieve some of the quality called brilliance.

1.   She left the web, she left the loom,
       She made three paces through the room,
       She saw the water-lily bloom,
       She saw the helmet and the plume. . . .
                           —ALFRED, LORD TENNYSON

2.   Clear and cool, clear and cool,
     By laughing shallow and dreaming pool;
     Cool and clear, cool and clear,
     By shining shingle and foaming weir;
     Under the crag where the ouzel sings,
     And the ivied wall where the church bell rings . . .
                           —CHARLES KINGSLEY

3. I am the daughter of earth and water,
    And the nursling of the sky;
I pass through the pores of the ocean and shores;
    I change, but I cannot die.
For after the rain, when with never a stain
    The pavilion of heaven is bare,
And the winds and sunbeams with their convex
      gleams
    Build up the blue dome of air,
I silently laugh at my own cenotaph,
    And out of the caverns of rain,
Like a child from the womb, like a ghost from the
      tomb,
    I arise and unbuild it again.

               —PERCY BYSSHE SHELLEY

4.   My heart leaps up when I behold
      A rainbow in the sky:
    So was it when my life began;
    So is it now I am a man;
    So be it when I shall grow old,
      Or let me die!
    The Child is father of the Man;
    And I could wish my days to be
    Bound each to each by natural piety.

               —WILLIAM WORDSWORTH

5.   We are the music-makers,
      And we are the dreamers of dreams,
    Wandering by lone sea-breakers,
      And sitting by desolate streams—
    World-losers and world-forsakers,
      On whom the pale moon gleams—
    Yet we are the movers and shakers
      Of the world forever, it seems.

With wonderful deathless ditties
We build up the world's great cities,
  And out of a fabulous story
  We fashion an empire's glory;
One man with a dream, at pleasure,
  Shall go forth and conquer a crown;
And three with a new song's measure
  Can trample a kingdom down.
                    —ARTHUR O'SHAUGHNESSY

6.   Oh, joyous boon! oh, mad delight;
        Oh, sun and moon! oh, day and night!
          Rejoice, rejoice with me!
        Proclaim our joy, ye birds above—
        Ye brooklets, murmur forth our love,
          In choral ecstasy:
        Oh, joyous boon!
          Oh, mad delight!
        Oh, sun and moon!
          Oh, day and night!
        Ye birds, and brooks, and fruitful trees,
        With choral joy delight the breeze—
          Rejoice, rejoice with me![6]
                    —W. S. GILBERT

7.   Gold! Gold! Gold! Gold!
     Bright and yellow, hard and cold,
     Molten, graven, hammered, and rolled;
     Hard to get and heavy to hold;
     Hoarded, bartered, bought and sold,
     Stolen, borrowed, squandered, doled:
     Spurned by the young, but hugged by the old
     To the very verge of the church-yard mould;
     Gold! Gold! Gold! Gold!
     Good or bad a thousand-fold!
       How widely its agencies vary—
       To save—to ruin—to curse—to bless—

---

[6] This and subsequent excerpts from the poems of W. S. Gilbert are taken from *The Complete Plays of Gilbert and Sullivan*, Random House, Inc.

As even its minted coins express,
Now stamped with the image of good Queen Bess,
And now of a Bloody Mary.

—THOMAS HOOD

8.   Hear the sledges with the bells—
         Silver bells!
What a world of merriment their melody foretells!
How they tinkle, tinkle, tinkle,
         In the icy air of night!
         While the stars that oversprinkle
         All the heavens, seem to twinkle
              With a crystalline delight;
         Keeping time, time, time,
         In a sort of Runic rhyme,
To the tintinnabulation that so musically wells
         From the bells. . . .

Hear the mellow wedding bells—
         Golden bells!
What a world of happiness their harmony foretells!
         Through the balmy air of night
         How they ring out their delight!—
              From the molten-golden notes,
                   And all in tune,
              What a liquid ditty floats
To the turtle-dove that listens, while she gloats
         On the moon!

—EDGAR ALLAN POE

9.   THE CONGO[7]

Fat black bucks in a wine barrel room,
Barrel-house kings, with feet unstable,
Sagged and reeled and pounded on the table,
Pounded on the table,
Beat an empty barrel with the handle of a broom,
Hard as they were able,

[7] From Vachel Lindsay, *Collected Poems,* copyright 1931 by The Macmillan Company, and with The Macmillan Company's permission.

Boom, boom, BOOM,
With a silk umbrella and the handle of a broom,
Boomlay, boomlay, boomlay, BOOM.
THEN I had religion, THEN I had a vision.
I could not turn from their revel in derision.
THEN I SAW THE CONGO, CREEPING
    THROUGH THE BLACK,
CUTTING THROUGH THE FOREST WITH
    A GOLDEN TRACK.
Then along that riverbank
A thousand miles
Tattooed cannibals danced in files;
Then I heard the boom of the blood-lust song
And a thigh-bone beating on a tin-pan gong.
And "BLOOD" screamed the whistles and the
    fifes of the warriors,
"BLOOD" screamed the skull-faced, lean
    witch-doctors,
"Whirl ye the deadly voo-doo rattle.
Harry the uplands,
Steal all the cattle,
Rattle-rattle, rattle-rattle,
Bing!
Boomlay, boomlay, boomlay, BOOM,"
A roaring, epic, rag-time tune
From the mouth of the Congo
To the Mountains of the Moon.
Death is an Elephant,
Torch-eyed and horrible,
Foam-flanked and terrible.
BOOM, steal the pygmies,
BOOM, kill the Arabs,
BOOM, kill the white men,
HOO, HOO, HOO.
Listen to the yell of Leopold's ghost
Burning in Hell for his hand-maimed host
Hear how the demons chuckle and yell
Cutting his hands off, down in Hell.
Listen to the creepy proclamation,

Blown through the lairs of the forest-nation,
Blown past the white-ants' hill of clay,
Blown past the marsh where the butterflies play:—
"Be careful what you do,
Or Mumbo-Jumbo, God of the Congo,
And all of the other
Gods of the Congo,
Mumbo-Jumbo will hoo-doo you,
Mumbo-Jumbo will hoo-doo you,
Mumbo-Jumbo will hoo-doo you."

—VACHEL LINDSAY

2. The following group of selections, in serious mood and elevated sentiment, calls for full rich tones. In reading the selections, however, be sure that you avoid pomposity. Above all, whether or not you get the big round tones you desire, be sincere. And remember, your best chance of getting those round tones is through relaxing the throat and jaw and getting vocal strength from your abdominal muscles.

1. I was born an American; I live an American; I shall die an American; and I intend to perform the duties incumbent upon me in that character to the end of my career. I mean to do this with absolute disregard of personal consequences. What are the personal consequences? What is the individual man, with all the good or evil that may betide him, in comparison with the good or evil which may befall a great country, and in the midst of great transactions which concern that country's fate? Let the consequences be what they will, I am careless. No man can suffer too much, and no man can fall too soon, if he suffer or if he fall in the defense of the liberties and constitution of his country.

—DANIEL WEBSTER

2. Thou, too, sail on, O Ship of State!
Sail on, O Union, strong and great!
Humanity with all its fears,
With all the hopes of future years,

Is hanging breathless on thy fate!
We know what Master laid thy keel,
What Workmen wrought thy ribs of steel,
Who made each mast, and sail, and rope,
What anvils rang, what hammers beat,
In what a forge and what a heat
Were shaped the anchors of thy hope!
Fear not each sudden sound and shock,
'T is of the wave and not the rock;
'T is but the flapping of the sail,
And not a rent made by the gale!
In spite of rock and tempest's roar,
In spite of false lights on the shore,
Sail on, nor fear to breast the sea!
Our hearts, our hopes, are all with thee,
Our hearts, our hopes, our prayers, our tears,
Our faith triumphant o'er our fears,
Are all with thee,—are all with thee!
—HENRY W. LONGFELLOW

3. O Thou vast Ocean! ever sounding sea!
Thou vast symbol of drear immensity!
Thou thing that windest round the solid world,
Like a huge animal, which, downward hurled
From the black clouds, lies weltering alone,
Lashing and writhing till its strength is gone.
Thy voice is like the thunder, and thy sleep
Is as a giant's slumber, loud and deep.
—BRYAN WALLER PROCTER

4. We are engaged in the most difficult of all arts—the art of
living together in a free society. It is comfortable, if slothful,
to live without responsibility. Responsibility is exacting and
painful. Democracy involves hardship—the hardship of the
unceasing responsibility of every citizen. Where the entire
people do not take a continuous and considered part in public
life, there can be no democracy in any meaningful sense of

the term. Democracy is always a beckoning goal, not a safe harbor. For freedom is an unremitting endeavor, never a final achievement. That is why no office in the land is more important than that of being a citizen.

—JUSTICE FELIX FRANKFURTER

5.   THE FLAG[8]

I am not the flag, not at all. I am but its shadow.
I am whatever you make me, nothing more.
I am your belief in yourself, your dream of what a
    people may become.
I am all that you hope to be, and have the courage to
    try for.
I am song and fear, struggle and panic, and ennobling
    hope.
I am the day's work of the weakest man, and the
    largest dream of the most daring.
I am the Constitution and the Courts, statutes and
    statute makers, soldier and dreadnaught, drayman
    and street sweep, cook, counselor and clerk.
I am the battle of yesterday, and the mistake of
    tomorrow.

*   *   *

I am no more than what you believe me to be and I
    am all that you believe I can be.
I am all that you make me, nothing more.
I swing before your eyes as a bright gleam of color,
    a symbol of yourself, the pictured suggestion of
    that big thing which makes this nation. My stars
    and my stripes are your dream and your labors.
    They are bright with cheer, brilliant with courage,
    firm with faith, because you have made them so
    out of your hearts. For you are the makers of the
    flag and it is well that you glory in the making.

—FRANKLIN K. LANE

[8] From *Freedom and Union*, December, 1949.

3. The following selections offer opportunity for experimentation
with various types of resonance. Pay special attention to considerations such as these: (1) In Cunningham's sea poem when
the "old salt" shows his contempt for the "fair one" who wishes
for a soft and gentle breeze, make a clear distinction between
the sailor's mimicry and his natural voice; (2) in Hunt's delightful childish fantasy about Cupid be sure you do not use a sledge-
hammer to do a job best done with a tack hammer; (3) in the
old poem by Saxe, the humor intended by having Echo twist the
sound of certain words ever so slightly but enough to give them
an entirely different meaning, is best achieved by making your
voice sound as much as possible like an echo on the appropriate
lines; and (4) most important of all, be sure that you do not
strain your voice in your effort to achieve any of these resonance
effects.

1.   THE BEE AND THE FLOWER

       The bee buzz'd up in the heat.
       "I am faint for your honey, my sweet."
       The flower said "Take it, my dear,
       For now is the spring of the year.
         So come, come!"
           "Hum!"
       And the bee buzz'd down from the heat.

       And the bee buzz'd up in the cold
       When the flower was wither'd and old.
       "Have you still any honey, my dear?"
       She said "It's the fall of the year,
         But come, come!"
           "Hum!"
       And the bee buzz'd off in the cold.
               —ALFRED, LORD TENNYSON

2.   FOREBODING[9]

Zoom, zoom, zoom!
That is the sound of the surf,
As the great green waves rush up the shore
With a murderous, thundering, ominous roar;
And leave drowned dead things by my door.
Zoom, zoom, zoom!
Sh-wsh-wsh! Sh-wsh-wsh! Sh-wsh-wsh!
That is the sound of the tow
As it slips and slithers along the sands
Like terrible, groping, formless hands,
That drag at my beach house where it stands.
Sh-wsh-wsh! Sh-wsh-wsh! Sh-wsh-wsh!
Ee-oh-i-oo! Ee-oh-i-oo! Ee-oh-i-oo!
That is the sound of the wind.
It wails like a banshee adrift in space.
It threatens to scatter my driftwood place.
It splashes the sand like spite in my face.
Ee-oh-i-oo! Ee-oh-i-oo! Ee-oh-i-oo!
Surf?
Tow?
Or the wind?
Which of the three will it be?
The surf, will it bludgeon and beat me dead?
Or the tow drag me down to the ocean bed?
Or the wind wail a dirge above my head?
Zoom!
Sh-wsh-wsh!
Ee-oh-i-oo!

—DON BLANDING

[9] Reprinted by permission of Dodd, Mead & Company from *Vagabond's House* by Don Blanding. Copyright 1928 by Don Blanding.

3.   A WET SHEET AND A FLOWING SEA

A wet sheet and a flowing sea,
  A wind that follows fast
And fills the white and rustling sail
  And bends the gallant mast;
And bends the gallant mast, my boys,
  While like the eagle free
Away the good ship flies, and leaves
  Old England on the lee.

O for a soft and gentle wind!
  I heard a fair one cry;
But give to me the snoring breeze
  And white waves heaving high;
And white waves heaving high, my lads,
  The good ship tight and free—
The world of waters is our home
  And merry men are we.

There's tempest in yon hornéd moon,
  And lightning in yon cloud;
But hark the music, mariners!
  The wind is piping loud,
The wind is piping loud, my boys,
  The lightning flashes free—
While the hollow oak our palace is,
  Our heritage the sea.
                              —ALLAN CUNNINGHAM

4.   CUPID SWALLOWED

T'other day, as I was twining
Roses for a crown to dine in,
What, of all things, midst the heap,
Should I light on, fast asleep,
But the little desperate elf—
The tiny traitor—Love, himself!
By the wings I pinched him up

Like a bee, and in a cup
Of my wine, I plunged and sank him;
And what d'ye think I did?—I drank him!
Faith, I thought him dead. Not he!
There he lives with tenfold glee,
And now this moment, with his wings,
I feel him tickling my heart-strings.

—LEIGH HUNT

5. For once, upon a raw and gusty day,
The troubled Tiber chafing with her shores,
Cæsar said to me, "Dar'st thou, Cassius, now
Leap in with me into this angry flood,
And swim to yonder point?" Upon the word,
Accoutred as I was, I plunged in
And bade him follow; so indeed he did.
The torrent roar'd, and we did buffet it
With lusty sinews, throwing it aside
And stemming it with hearts of controversy;
But ere we could arrive the point propos'd,
Cæsar cried, "Help me, Cassius, or I sink!"
I, as Æneas, our great ancestor,
Did from the flames of Troy upon his shoulder
The old Anchises bear, so from the waves of Tiber
Did I the tired Cæsar. And this man
Is now become a god, and Cassius is
A wretched creature, and must bend his body
If Cæsar carelessly but nod on him.
He had a fever when he was in Spain,
And when the fit was on him, I did mark
How he did shake—'tis true, this god did shake,
His coward lips did from their colour fly,
And that same eye whose bend doth awe the world
Did lose his lustre; I did hear him groan.
Ay, and that tongue of his that bade the Romans
Mark him and write his speeches in their books,
Alas, it cried, "Give me some drink, Titinius,"
As a sick girl. Ye gods, it doth amaze me

A man of such a feeble temper should
So get the start of the majestic world
And bear the palm alone.

—SHAKESPEARE, *Julius Caesar*

6.   ECHO

I asked of Echo, t'other day
  (Whose words are often few and funny)
What to a novice she could say
  Of courtship, love and matrimony.
  Quoth Echo plainly,—"Matter-o'-money!"

Whom should I marry? Should it be
  A dashing damsel, gay and pert,
A pattern of inconstancy;
  Or selfish, mercenary flirt?
  Quoth Echo sharply,—"Nary flirt!"

What if, aweary of the strife
  That long has lured the dear deceiver,
She promise to amend her life,
  And sin no more; can I believe her?
  Quoth Echo, very promptly,—"Leave her!"

But if some maiden with a heart
  On me should venture to bestow it,
Pray, should I act the wiser part
  To take the treasure or forego it?
  Quoth Echo, with decision,—"Go it!"

What if, in spite of her disdain,
  I find my heart entwined about
With Cupid's dear delicious chain
  So closely that I can't get out?
  Quoth Echo, laughingly,—"Get out!"

But if some maid with beauty blest,
   As pure and fair as Heaven can make her,
Will share my labor and my rest
    Till envious Death shall overtake her?
    Quoth Echo (SOTTO VOCE),—"Take her!"

                   —JOHN G. SAXE

7. FIRST WITCH: Round about the cauldron go;
   In the poison'd entrails throw.
   Toad, that under cold stone
   Days and nights has thirty-one
   Swelt'red venom sleeping got,
   Boil thou first i' the charmed pot.
  ALL: Double, double, toil and trouble;
   Fire burn and cauldron bubble.
SECOND WITCH: Fillet of a fenny snake,
   In the cauldron boil and bake;
   Eye of newt and toe of frog,
   Wool of bat and tongue of dog,
   Adder's fork and blind-worm's sting,
   Lizard's leg and howlet's wing,
   For a charm of powerful trouble,
   Like a hell-broth boil and bubble.
  ALL: Double, double, toil and trouble;
   Fire burn and cauldron bubble.

                   —SHAKESPEARE

VIII * Articulation: Speaking Distinctly

Consonant Sounds Analyzed

The importance of uttering words so that they are easily understood has always been recognized, but never more than today, when radio and television have made mass communication possible. Careless speech is one of our most irritating habits. Slurring, mouthing, and mumbling, unpleasant enough in ordinary conversation, are unpardonable in all forms of public address. No one who.is not willing to pay the price necessary to achieve distinct utterance has a right to appear before an audience.

With most people who garble their words, the fault is simply a matter of habit, which can be overcome by a little serious attention and conscious effort continuously applied. But whatever the cause, and however severe the malady, it must be overcome by anyone who aspires to success in any field involving communication with others.

Your hearers must hear what you say, and they must hear without strain. There is no surer way to lose the interest of an auditor than to cause him to miss key words. In this matter of easy audibility articulation is more important than volume. Good actors are able to speak in quiet, modulated tones and still be understood with perfect clarity. Indeed, certain scenes of our best plays would completely lose their effectiveness if such tones were not possible on the stage. Speakers likewise would lose some of their most telling effects if they could not be heard with distinctness when speaking quietly.

Rupert Hughes, prominent author and popular after-dinner speaker, writes about his deafness: "In conversation I find that I can hear people who articulate plainly even if they speak softly; but many people have so little control that when I say, 'Louder, please!' they swallow their voices more and more." He also offers an interesting explanation of a phenomenon often noted in hard-of-hearing persons. They are frequently accused of failing to hear the things they are supposed to hear, while being almost sure to hear bits of conversation which they were not intended to hear. His explanation is: "In ordinary conversation, few people make any effort to focus their tones or articulate distinctly. We just wobble our lips and let the words spill. But when we want to convey a confidential remark to someone, we point the tone and speak with great distinctness. That is why a stage whisper carries so far. So, when you are trying to slip a message past a deaf person, you do the very thing he has given up imploring you to· do; you speak distinctly."[1]

Before we get into the discussion of articulation, let us lay down one principle of basic importance: *Articulation should not be ostentatious.* No one should be made aware of the fact that we are striving to be precise in our speech. The desired goal is speech that is clear, distinct, and easy—free from lazy mouthing of words that sound as if the mouth were full of hot potatoes, and equally free from that exaggerated niceness which attracts attention to itself and is variously called "pedantic precision," "elocutionary exaggeration," or "elegant English."

How can we overcome long habits of careless speaking? How can we be sure that we are speaking clearly, distinctly, and accurately? First of all, if you wish to be sure that you are using

[1] Rupert Hughes, "New Ears for Old," *Liberty Magazine*, January 26, 1935.

the English language as it should be used, you must know what the sounds of English are. To that end, the International Phonetic Alphabet (IPA) is an indispensable tool.

Reasons for Studying the Phonetic Alphabet

There are several good reasons why the student of voice and diction should familiarize himself with the International Phonetic Alphabet. Among them are the following:

1. Since most modern works on diction (e.g., the National Broadcasting Company's book of instructions to its announcers[2]) employ this alphabet, diction students are handicapped if they do not know phonetic transcription.

2. To approach the study of voice and diction in this scientifically accurate way helps the student to hear the sounds more accurately; hence it is an aid to the ear training which is so essential to the improvement of diction.

3. It helps to overcome the bewildering confusion in English spelling, because the IPA provides just one symbol for each sound in the language.

4. This set of symbols helps to make clear the distinction between sounds when they stand alone and when they appear in connected speech. This distinction is a material aid in avoiding both slovenly and overprecise speech.

SPELLING AND DICTION

The lack of consistency between the way our words are spelled and the way they are pronounced is illustrated by noting the silent and therefore unnecessary letters in such common words as *gnaw, gnat, thumb, debt, palm, salmon, though, through,* and so on. And note the difference in the pronunciation of the italicized letters in such word groups as ar*ch*—ar*ch*itect and *g*esture—*g*arter—rou*g*e.

Observe the numerous ways some common English sounds

[2] James F. Bender, *N.B.C. Handbook of Pronunciation.* Thomas Y. Crowell Company, 1943.

may be spelled. For example, the italicized letters in the following words illustrate variant spellings of the sound *i* as in *ice*: *i*re, h*eigh*t, h*igh*, t*ie*, *ai*sle, *aye*, *eye*, m*y*, b*uy*, and l*ye*. Similarly, the sound of *a* as in *ale* is spelled in many ways: *a*te, r*ai*n, g*ao*l, g*au*ge, r*ay*, st*ea*k, v*ei*l, ob*ey*, and f*ete*. And note some of the spellings for the *k* sound: *k*ite, hi*ck*, *c*at, *ch*orus, *q*uilt, and *kh*aki. Note also some of the various sounds which may be given to a single letter, for example the *i* in *mice, it, pique, Sioux, sirloin;* the *a* in *ate, art, at, all, dare, alone;* and the *e* in *he, ebb, sergeant* (note both the first and last *e*), *sedan, fete,* and *there.*

Daniel Jones, head of the Department of Phonetics at the University of London, has been reported as illustrating the absurdities of our spelling by claiming that the word *fish* could be spelled *ghoti* and still be pronounced *fish,* simply by taking the *gh* from *cough,* the *o* from *women,* and the *ti* from any word ending in *tion* such as *tuition.*

It is not strange that children find so much difficulty in learning to spell, nor that foreigners as well as persons from different parts of our own country can consult the same dictionary and get quite different concepts of the way a given word should be pronounced.

The International Phonetic Alphabet

In contrast to this perplexing muddle of sounds and symbols, the International Phonetic Alphabet is an attempt to give to each symbol a definite and precise pronunciation—one sound and only one sound for each symbol.[3] The phonetic alphabet is thus much more accurate and definitive than any system of

[3] Actually this goal never has been and never can be fully achieved, because of the minute differences in pronouncing a given sound in various letter combinations. For example, the long *a* sound in *name* differs from the long *a* sound in *ate.* Careful listening will disclose that in the word *name* the sound *a* is influenced to some degree by the nasal [m] and [n] sounds which precede and follow it, while in the word *ate* the [t] which follows tends to bring the *a* farther forward in the mouth and gives it a slightly different sound. However, these differences are minute.

diacritical marks, the code of dots and bars which dictionary editors use to indicate pronunciation. And when the phonetic alphabet is used not only as an aid to ear training but also as a guide to the study of the muscular adjustments of the articulatory organs, it can become a highly valuable tool to the student of diction. With it, he can take a word apart and really see what it is made of. He should even be able to pronounce with reasonable correctness unfamiliar foreign words written in phonetic script, for the symbols are the same for all languages, with certain additions necessary for sounds peculiar to each language.

And, an important point, the student can become familiar with the meaning of the symbols—only some forty in number, representing all the sounds in American speech—by a few hours of concentrated study.

Following is a list of the phonetic symbols as adapted from the introduction to *The American College Dictionary*,[4] and as they will be used in this book.

The Consonants

Although the old and often-quoted maxim, "Take care of the consonants and the vowels will take care of themselves," is an exaggeration, most articulation problems, so far as they relate to distinctness, are associated with the consonants. Problems related to correct pronunciation and good tone quality are more often concerned with the vowels, but not so with distinct articulation. Being understood is the attribute of the speaker who takes care of his consonants. Much more movement of the jaw, tongue, and lips is required for articulating consonants than vowels.

CONSONANTS DISTINGUISHED FROM VOWELS

If you utter the vowel sounds [u-o-ɔ-a-æ] on a continuous exhalation while looking into the mirror, you will observe that

---

[4] *The American College Dictionary*, Text Edition, Harper & Brothers, 1948.

CHART OF PHONETIC SYMBOLS
Consonants

Phonetic Symbol	Key Word	Phonetic Transcription	Various Spellings	Examples
[p]	*p*et	[pɛt]	p, pp	pen, stopper
[b]	*b*et	[bɛt]	b, bb	bed, hobby
[t]	*t*ip	[tɪp]	ed, ght, t, th, tt	talked, bought, toe, thyme, bottom
[d]	*d*id	[dɪd]	d, dd, ed	do, ladder, pulled
[k]	*c*at	[kæt]	c, cc, cch, ch, ck, cq, cque, cu, k, qu	car, account, bacchanal, character, back, acquaint, sacque, biscuit, kill, liquor
[g]	*g*ive	[gɪv]	g, gg, gh, gu, gue	give, egg, ghost, guard, demagogue
[h]	*h*at	[hæt]	h, wh	hit, who
[f]	*f*ill	[fɪl]	f, ff, gh, ph	feed, muffin, tough, physics
[v]	*v*ery	['vɛrɪ]	f, ph, v, vv	of, Stephen, visit, flivver
[θ]	*th*in	[θɪn]	th	thin
[ð]	*th*is	[ðɪs]	th, the	then, bathe
[s]	*s*ea	[si]	c, ce, s, sc, sch, ss	city, mice, see, scene, schism, loss
[z]	*z*oo	[zu]	s, sc, ss, x, z, zz	has, discern, scissors, Xerxes, zone, dazzle
[ʃ]	*sh*ow	[ʃou]	ce, ch, ci, psh, s, sch, sci, se, sh, si, ss, ssi, ti	ocean, machine, special, pshaw, sugar, schist, conscience, nauseous, ship, mansion, tissue, mission, mention
[ʒ]	mea*s*ure	['mɛʒər]	g, s, si, z, zi	garage, measure, division, azure, brazier
[tʃ]	*ch*ief	[tʃif]	ch, tch, te, ti, tu	chief, catch, righteous, question, natural
[dʒ]	*j*u*dg*e	['dʒʌdʒ]	ch, d, dg, dge, di, g, gg, j	Greenwich, graduate, judgment, bridge, soldier, magic, exaggerate, just
[m]	*m*an	[mæn]	chm, gm, lm, m, mb, mm, mn	drachm, paradigm, calm, more, limb, hammer, hymn
[n]	*n*ow	[nau]	gn, kn, n, nn, pn	gnat, knife, not, runner, pneumatic
[ŋ]	goi*ng*	['gouɪŋ]	n, ng, ngue	pink, ring, tongue
[l]	*l*et	[lɛt]	l, ll	live, call
[r]	*r*un	[rʌn]	r, rh, rr	red, rhythm, carrot
[j]	*y*es	[jɛs]	g, i, j, y	lorgnette, union, hallelujah, yet
[w]	*w*ord	[wɝd]	o, u, w	choir, quiet, well

CHART OF PHONETIC SYMBOLS

Vowels

Phonetic Symbol	Key Word	Phonetic Transcription	Various Spellings	Examples
i]	s*ee*	[si]	ae, ay, e, ea, ee, ei, eo, ey, i, ie, oe	Caesar, quay, equal, team, see, deceive, people, key, machine, field, amoeba
ɪ]	*i*f	[ɪf]	e, ee, i, ie, o, u, ui, ʋ	England, been, if, sieve, women, busy, build, hymn
e]	*a*te	[et]	a, ai, ao, au, ay, ea, eh, ei, ey	ate, rain, gaol, gauge, ray, steak, eh, veil, obey
ɛ]	b*e*t	[bɛt]	a, ae, ai, ay, e, ea, ei, eo, ie, oe, u	any, aesthetic, said, says, ebb, leather, heifer, leopard, friend, foetid, bury
æ]	s*a*t	[sæt]	a, ai	hat, plaid
a]⁵	*a*sk	[ask]	a	
u]	wh*o*	[hu]	eu, ew, o, oe, oo, ou, u, ue, ui	maneuver, grew, move, canoe, ooze, troupe, rule, flue, fruit
ʊ]	c*ou*ld	[kʊd]	o, oo, ou, u	wolf, look, should, pull
o]⁶	*o*mit	[o'mɪt]	o	
ɔ]	*a*ll	[ɔl]	a, ah, al, au, aw, o, oa, ou	tall, Utah, talk, fault, raw, order, broad, fought
ɒ]⁷	st*o*p	[stɒp]	a, o	wander, box
ɑ]	f*a*ther	['fɑðɚ]	a, e, ea	father, sergeant, hearth
ɝ], [ɜ]⁸	b*ir*d	[bɝd] [bɜd]	er, ear, ir, or, our, ur, yr	term, learn, thirst, worm, courage, hurt, myrtle
ɚ]⁹	ev*er*	['ɛvɚ] ['ɛvə]	ar, er, ir, or, our, ur, yr	liar, father, elixir, labor, labour, augur, martyr
ə]⁹	*a*bove	[ə'bʌv]	a, ai, e, ei, eo, i, ia, o, oi, ou, u	alone, mountain, system, mullein, dungeon, easily, parliament, gallop, porpoise, curious, circus
ʌ]	b*u*t	[bʌt]	o, oe, oo, ou, u	son, does, flood, couple, cup

⁵ This vowel appears primarily in Eastern Standard speech.

⁶ Except in unstressed syllables, as in *obey, omit*, this sound in English is usually a diphthong. See [ou].

⁷ Dialectal differences occur on this vowel. In General American speech [ɑ] is frequently substituted for [ɒ].

⁸ General American speech differs from both Eastern Standard and Southern Standard on this vowel, as will be explained in the next chapter under the discussion of vowels.

⁹ These symbols are used primarily in unstressed syllables.

CHART OF PHONETIC SYMBOLS

DIPHTHONGS

Phonetic Symbol	Key Word	Phonetic Transcription	Various Spellings	Examples
[aɪ]	b*y*	[baɪ]	ai, ay, ei, ey, i, ie, uy, y, ye	aisle, aye, height, eye, ice, tie, buy, sky, lye
[ɔɪ]	b*oy*	[bɔɪ]	oi, oy	oil, toy
[au]	n*ow*	[nau]	ou, ough, ow	out, bough, brow
[eɪ][10]	l*ay*	[leɪ]	a, ai, ao, au, ay, ea, eh, ei, ey	ate, rain, gaol, gauge, ray, steak, eh, veil, obey
[ou][10]	*o*ld	[ould]	au, eau, eo, ew, o, oa, oe, oh, oo, ou, ow	hautboy, beau, yeoman, sew, note, road, toe, oh, brooch, soul, flow
[ju][10]	b*eau*ty	['bjutɪ]	eau, eu, eue, ew, ieu, iew, u, ue, ui, yu, yew, you	beauty, feud, queue, few, adieu, view, use, cue, suit, yule, yew, you

: Indicates prolongation of the vowel which it follows.
ı When placed beneath a consonant, indicates that the consonant is used syllabically, i.e., to form a syllable without an accompanying vowel.
ˈ When placed above and to the left of a syllable, indicates that this syllable is to receive primary accent.
ˌ When placed to the left and below the syllable, indicates secondary accent.
[ʔ] Symbol used to indicate the glottal stop.

---

at all times the mouth is partly open so that the tone is relatively unobstructed. Now utter on a continuous breath the consonants [p-t-s-d-g], and you will see that each of the sounds either partly or completely checks the flow of the outgoing breath stream. That is essentially the difference between vowels and consonants. In vowels the mouth is open and the flow of sound relatively unobstructed, whereas in consonants the flow of sound is restricted or temporarily stopped. The accompanying chart comparing vowels and consonants will further clarify some of their chief differences.

[10] Listed as diphthongs by some authorities; see the next chapter for further discussion.

COMPARISON OF VOWELS AND CONSONANTS

Vowels	Consonants
1. Vowels are sonorous speech sounds and are relatively open and unobstructed.	1. Consonants, on the whole, are less sonorous, have more noise elements, and are generally more obstructed than are vowels.
2. Vowels make possible good carrying power for the voice.	2. Consonants have less phonetic power and in many instances detract from good voice quality.
3. Vowels, with few exceptions, have little specific meaning in themselves.	3. Consonants are chiefly responsible for clearness in diction; they are the chief agent for making words understandable.
4. Vowels depend upon certain pitch and resonance characteristics as well as duration for their identification.	4. Consonants depend upon specific movements of the articulators (i.e., tongue, lips, jaw, and soft palate) for their identity.
5. All vowels are voiced, except in whispering.	5. Many consonants are unvoiced.

CLASSIFICATION OF CONSONANTS

For convenience of study, consonants are classified in various ways, depending upon physical characteristics of the sounds or on manner of articulation.

Perhaps the simplest and most clear-cut of these classifications is based on whether they are voiced or voiceless. In many instances, for each adjustment of the articulators we have two different sounds. The following pairs demonstrate this point: [p-b], [t-d], [k-g], [f-v], [ʃ-ʒ]. In each pair the second sound is differentiated from the first only in that the vocal folds are brought together and the breath stream is voiced. In order to demonstrate this difference, place your finger on your larynx during the production of [f], holding it for a few seconds; then without interrupting the steady flow of breath, bring your vocal folds together, the added vibration of the vocal folds changes the [f] to [v]. Note, however, that all consonants are not paired in this manner.

A second classification, popular in the study of phonetics, is based on the arrangement of consonants according to their physical characteristics: (1) *plosives* [p, b, t, d, k, and g]; (2)

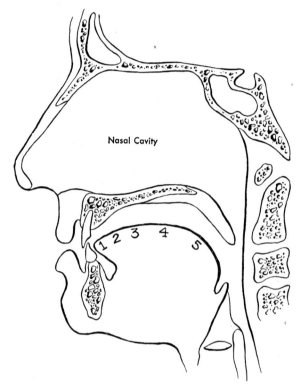

Fig. 15. The articulatory mechanism, showing the different parts of the tongue. 1, tip; 2, blade; 3, front; 4, middle; 5, back.

fricatives [f, v, θ, ð, s, z, ʃ, ʒ, and h]; *nasals* [m, n, and ŋ]; (4) *glides* [l, r, j, and w]; and (5) *consonant combinations* [tʃ and dʒ].

A third classification is based upon the placement of tongue, lips, jaw, and palate during the production of the sounds: (1) *labial* [p, b, m, and w]; (2) *labiodental* [f and v]; (3) *lingua-dental* [θ and ð]; (4) *lingua-alveolar* [t, d, n, l, s, and z]; (5) *lingua-palatal* [ʃ, ʒ, r, and j]; (6) *linqua-velar* [k, g, and ŋ]; and (7) *glottal* [h]. Fig. 15 shows the articulatory mechanism.

We should think of these classifications not as being mutually exclusive, but rather as being interrelated and sometimes over-lapping. They should, however, aid the student in gaining a better understanding of the sounds. The accompanying chart shows the interrelationship of the three classifications.

CONSONANT CLASSIFICATION CHART
(vs = voiceless; v = voiced)

	Bilabial		Labio-Dental		Lingua-Dental		Lingua-Alveolar		Lingua-Palatal		Lingua-Velar		Glottal	
	vs	v	vs	v	vs	v	vs	v	vs	v	vs	v	vs	v
Plosives	p	b					t	d			k	g		
Fricatives			f	v	θ	ð	s	z	ʃ	ʒ			h	
Nasals		m						n				ŋ		
Glides		w						l		r j				
Consonant combina-tions[a]										tʃ dʒ				

a Sometimes called affricates.

The Plosives

The plosives (or stops, as they are sometimes called) are a group of consonants formed by momentarily halting the outward passage of the breath stream, building up pressure, then suddenly releasing the breath in a little explosion.

THE CONSONANTS [p] AND [b]

[p] and [b] are called *lip, labial,* or *bilabial plosives.* They are made by stopping the breath stream at the firmly closed lips, at the same time elevating the soft palate so that no breath escapes through the nose, then suddenly opening the lips and releasing the impounded breath stream with a perceptible explosion. [p] is voiceless, and [b] is voiced.

FAULTS AND DANGERS

1. The labial plosives, when well articulated, give crispness and precision to the speech; they also help to place the succeed-

ing vowel sounds well forward in the mouth and give them clarity. Carelessly articulated, they give a slovenly quality to the speech. Few consonant sounds so quickly label the lazy speaker as poorly articulated [p] and [b] sounds. Speakers with stiff and lazy lips often have no complete closure, and therefore no clear-cut small explosior. of sound. The result is an indefinite mumbling.

2. In common with the other plosives, weakness in articulation becomes especially evident when the [p] and [b] occur in conjunction with other consonants, as in *caps, cabs, flapjacks, abduction,* etc. In these cases one of the consonants is likely to be seriously slighted or even dropped entirely.

3. Foreigners sometimes substitute the voiceless [p] for the voiced [b]. Thus *tub* may become [tʌp], *shrub* may become [ʃrʌp], *slab* may become [slæp], etc.

EXERCISES

1. Repeat the following words over and over:

	Initial		Medial		Final
[p]					
pot	pretty	happy	sharply	hop	harp
power	proud	supper	nuptials	catnip	clasp
puff	plural	pamper	topmast	tulip	yelp
pan	principle	poppy	aptly	pulp	warp
political	plenty	pepper	capital	gap	sloop
[b]					
balm	bargain	table	substitute	cherub	diatribe
been	basket	sherbet	submarine	crib	probe
bill	bright	cabal	cabbage	rob	tribe
beat	blend	rabbit	cupboard	describe	drab
bet	brown	rubble	fabricate	bribe	absorb

2. Enunciate the following sentences clearly:
   1. Power politics involves principles that are apt to keep the world in suspense.
   2. Popcorn and peanuts are a happy combination.

3. Please pass the pepper, Peter.
4. Stopgap legislation may precipitate unhappy results.
5. Apparently the people at the pageant were pleased with the players.
6. The babbling brook broke its boundaries near the Arab tents.
7. The basket on the table was filled with cabbages.
8. The baby's bib is not on the table but in his crib.
9. His job was to probe for microbes.
10. Benjamin Franklin could not be bribed by foreign cabals.

3. Repeat several times words and syllables like the following:
   1. Pretty, pretty, pretty, pretty.
   2. Blue, blue, blue, blue.
   3. Bloppety, bloppety, bloppety, blop.

4. Work on the following lines of poetry and tongue twisters:
   1. I bubble into eddying bays,
      I babble on the pebbles.
   2. I sing of brooks, of blossoms, of birds, and bowers.
   3. Boots, boots, boots, boots,
      Moving up and down again!
   4. A tap at the pane, the quick sharp scratch
      And blue spurt of a lighted match.
   5. Fat, black bucks in a wine-barrel room . . .
      Beat an empty barrel with the handle of a broom . . .
      Boomlay, boomlay, boomlay, boom.
   6. Beat, beat, beat, beat,
      Beat upon the tom-toms.
   7. Baa, baa, black sheep, have you any wool?
   8. Peter Prangle, the prickly prangly pear picker,
      Picked a peck of prickly, prangly pears
      From the prickly, prangly pear trees on the pleasant prairies.
   9. Peter Piper, the pepper picker, picked a peck of pickled peppers. A peck of pickled peppers did Peter Piper, the pepper picker, pick. If Peter Piper, the pepper picker, picked a peck of pickled peppers, where is the peck of pickled peppers that Peter Piper, the pepper picker, picked?

10. Betty bought a bit of butter,
But, said she, "This butter's bitter.
If I put it in my batter, it will make my batter bitter."
So Betty bought a bit of better butter,
Put it in her batter and made her batter better.
11. Algy met a bear. The bear was bulgy. The bulge was Algy.
12. Two bootblacks, one white and one black, were standing at
the corner doing nothing, when the white bootblack agreed
to black the black bootblack's boots. The black bootblack
was willing to have his boots blacked by his fellow bootblack,
and the bootblack who had agreed to black the black bootblack's boots went to work.

THE CONSONANTS [t] AND [d]

[t] and [d] are called *postdental plosives*. They are made by
blocking the exhaled breath stream by the firm pressure of
the tip of the tongue against the upper teeth ridge, raising the
soft palate so that no breath can escape through the nose, then
quickly releasing the tongue tip and letting the breath escape
in a small explosion. [d] is voiced, [t] is unvoiced.

FAULTS AND DANGERS

1. If the tongue tip is allowed to fall too low, so that it rests
against the teeth rather than the teeth ridge, the sound resembles
a lisp. Thus *cat* [kæt] becomes *cath* [kæθ], *fate* [feɪt] becomes
faith [feɪθ], etc.

2. When either of these sounds occurs at the end of a word,
careless speakers may completely drop the sound. Thus *asked*
[æskt] becomes *ask* [æsk], *apt* [æpt] becomes *ap* [æp], etc.

3. The above danger becomes a special hazard when one of
these sounds follows another in successive words, as in *cold day*
[koʊld deɪ] and *sit down* [sɪt daʊn]; these phrases are likely
to sound like *col' day* [koʊldeɪ] and *si' down* [sɪdaʊn]. In correcting this fault, do not go to the opposite extreme and labor
out the two sounds with elaborate obviousness. Experiment

with the above two phrases and with others in the following exercises, trying to make the words distinct but not pedantic.

4. When one of these plosives is followed by [l], [m], [n], or [ŋ], one of two things may happen:

a. Being too difficult for a lazy speaker to bother with, it may simply be left out. Thus *little* ['lɪtl̩] may become *lil* [lɪl], and *middle* ['mɪdl̩] may become *mil* [mɪl].

b. The glottal stop may be substituted. Thus *bottle* ['batl̩] may become ['baʔl̩], and *battle* ['bætl̩] may become ['bæʔl̩].

5. In the difficult combination of sounds where [t] occurs between two [s] sounds, care and practice are often required to make these sounds distinct, so that *lists* [lɪsts] does not become [lɪs], and *chests* [tʃests] does not become *ches* [tʃɛs].

6. Some persons fail to realize that the *-ed* past tense of verbs is pronounced sometimes as [t] and sometimes as [d], depending upon whether it follows a voiced or an unvoiced sound. Following a voiced sound the *ed* is pronounced [d], and following an unvoiced sound it is pronounced [t]. For example, *clipped* is pronounced [klɪpt], *tabbed* is pronounced [tæbd], *tripped* is pronounced [trɪpt], and *cribbed* is pronounced [krɪbd].

7. One other fault, rare but still common enough to merit being mentioned, is the adding of a final [t] where it does not belong, on such words as *once* [wʌns] and *twice* [twaɪs], making them [wʌnst] and [twaɪst].

EXERCISES

1. Repeat the following words over and over:

		Initial	Medial		Final	
[t]						
tie	trip	bitter	butter	bucket	debt
time	trowel	quantity	pretty	pit	straight
taught	trite	patter	plenty	part	strident
tooth	trouble	little	turtle	sot	fright
team	trombone	battle	bestial	mat	boast

[d]

dimple	delve	peddle	madame	pod	shade
dentist	drown	saddle	pardon	pride	occurred
dare	drab	today	middle	afraid	bleed
dart	drought	Sunday	quandary	crowed	allude
dog	dress	haddock	hardy	deride	approved

2. Enunciate the following sentences clearly:
   1. Terry bit the tip of his tongue.
   2. The pitter-patter of the rain frightened the little children.
   3. The bestial act caused twenty-two thousand Hottentots to be held suspect.
   4. The strident tones of the soprano were apparent from the outset.
   5. The pretty little girl encountered trouble with her front teeth.
   6. Madame, afraid of the dentist, darted past his door.
   7. The hardy haddock defied the daring fisherman.
   8. Mad dogs go out in the noonday sun.
   9. On Sunday people drive out of the crowded city into the open fields.
   10. To meddle in somebody else's business is unpardonable.

3. Try the following paired words over in rapid succession, working for clear and distinct but easy articulation:

bold—bolt	had—hat	nod—not	paid—pate	heed—heat
cold—colt	cod—cot	found—fount	feed—feet	code—-coat
mold—molt	send—sent	pod—pot	wad—watt	road—rote

4. Repeat the following syllables rapidly several times:

[te, ti, taɪ, toʊ, *t*u].
[de, di, daɪ, doʊ, du].

5. Try words in the difficult [ts] combination:

hats—cats	clots—blots	shots—Scots	skates—mates
cents—rents	coats—floats	brutes—shoots	hates—rates

6. Distinguish between the [d] and [t] sounds in the following lines:

1. He hurdled the fence when he saw the machine hurtling toward him.
2. The cads threw stones at our cats.
3. The skipper nodded with satisfaction as his ship hit fifteen knots.

7. Work on the following tongue twisters and lines of poetry:

   1. A tree toad loved a she-toad
      That lived up in a tree.
      She was a three-toed she-toad.
      But a two-toed tree toad tried to win
      The she-toad's friendly nod,
      For the two-toed tree toad loved the ground
      That the three-toed she-toad trod.

   2. Amidst the mists and coldest frosts,
      With stoutest wrists and loudest boasts,
      He thrusts his fists against the posts,
      And still insists he sees the ghosts.

   3. And darest thou then
      To beard the lion in his den,
      The Douglas in his hall?

   4. Dust thou art, to dust returnest,
      Was not spoken of the soul.

   5. I dare do all that doth become a man;
      Who dares do more is none.

   6. Into the street the piper stept,
      Smiling first a little smile,
      As if he knew what magic slept,
      In his quiet pipe the while.

THE CONSONANTS [k] AND [g]

[k] and [g] are called *soft palate* (or *velar*) plosives. In forming them the back of the tongue is pressed firmly against the tensed soft palate to block the breath stream, and the com-

pressed air is then released in a small explosion by the quick withdrawal of the tongue. [g] is voiced, [k] is unvoiced.

FAULTS AND DANGERS

1. The chief danger here is a harsh, guttural quality caused by substituting, in some degree, the glottal plosive for the velar plosive, i.e., letting the action take place near the larynx instead of at the soft palate. Correction lies in keeping the back of the tongue arched toward the velum as far forward as the nature of these sounds permits.

2. A second danger arises in not making a tight enough closure and having insufficient breath pressure; the [k] and [g] in this case lose some of their plosive quality.

3. Care must be taken to prevent final [k] and [g] from being almost completely dropped, as frequently happens with all final plosives. In substandard speech, it is common for a speaker to weaken these final sounds until they are inaudible. Give full value to final [k] and [g] in the exercises below.

EXERCISES

1. Repeat the following words over and over:

Initial		Medial		Final	
[k]					
cat	crop	packed	occur	medic	music
caught	clean	uncle	accurate	static	lock
cure	crime	accompanist	oracle	peak	flick
culinary	crystal	plucked	acute	bleak	opaque
kine	clipper	instruct	anchor	pork	oblique
[g]					
gas	gravel	doggerel	plagued	peg	brig
get	gloom	dogma	flogged	pig	rag
gone	grimace	beggar	finger	hug	plague
gust	glean	bigger	figure	flag	agog
gain	grammar	buggy	trigger	cog	prig

2. Enunciate the following sentences clearly:

1. The music instructor could accompany his students as well as conduct the orchestra.
2. The crystal was packed carefully into a clean crate.
3. The cat cleaned her kittens with incredible care.
4. The oracle at Delphi could not always be considered accurate in forecasting world conditions.
5. Uncooked pork may cause trichinosis.
6. If gas gets scarce, the horse and buggy of bygone days may gain in popularity.
7. Goodness and greatness often go hand in hand.
8. The ghastly green light cast a ghostly shadow across the grass.
9. The Hungarian linguist could not conquer the English language.
10. The dog growled at the beggar.

3. Avoid guttural or glottal sounds in the following words and syllables. Keep them as "light" as possible and as far forward in the mouth as is consistent with proper articulation of the sounds. Repeat them many times in order to develop the desired kinesthetic sense.

1. [keɪ, ki, kaɪ, koʊ, ku].
2. [geɪ, gi, gaɪ, goʊ, gu].
3. *bag* [bæg], *flag* [flæg], *sag* [sæg].
4. *darken* ['dɑrkn̩], *garden* ['gɑrdn̩], *taken* ['teɪkn̩].
5. *carpet* ['kɑrpɪt], *market* ['mɑrkɪt], *sparklet* ['spɑrklɪt].

4. Articulate the following jingles carefully:

1.   The king was in the counting house,
        Counting out his money.

2.   Eight gray geese in a green field grazing;
        Gray were the geese and green was the grazing.

3.   There was a crooked man
        And he walked a crooked mile,
        He found a crooked sixpence
        Against a crooked stile.

5. The following selections afford excellent drill in the [k] and [g] sounds, as well as in many other consonant combinations.

1. "Lying Awake," p. 209.
2. " Jabberwocky," p. 206.

The Fricatives

Fricatives are made by narrowing the vocal openings in such a manner as to impinge upon the outgoing breath stream, causing various frictional noises to be created. They may be either voiced or voiceless.

THE CONSONANTS [f] AND [v]

[f] and [v] are *lip-teeth (labio-dental) fricatives.* To form these sounds, the lower lip and the upper teeth are brought into contact and the breath stream is forced audibly between them. [v] is voiced, [f] unvoiced.

FAULTS AND DANGERS

1. Sometimes insufficient force is used on the exhaled breath to make these sounds audible, with the result that a word like *five* [faɪv] becomes [faɪ] and *fifth* [fɪfθ] becomes [fɪθ].

2. If the lower lip is inactive so that it does not come in positive contact with the upper teeth, [f] and [v] become blurred and indistinct.

3. Many foreigners learning English confuse the voiced [v] with the unvoiced [f], so that *of* [ʌv] is pronounced [ʌf], *love* [lʌv] becomes [lʌf], etc. Careless speakers, not of foreign extraction, also occasionally fall into this error, as noted in such expressions as *have to* becoming [hæftʊ] instead of [hævtʊ].

EXERCISES

1. Repeat the following words over and over:

	Initial		Medial		Final
[f]					
tur	fun	awful	afraid	half	proof
finish	frank	draught	affluent	laugh	staff
foggy	face	gopher	baffle	rough	bluff
fen	fright	effect	different	enough	whiff
foam	philosophy	traffic	buffer	cuff	tough

	Initial	Medial		Final	
[v]					
vile	valuable	invincible	trivial	strive	perceive
vary	voracious	universal	revise	hive	suave
vanish	vulnerable	event	evident	save	twelve
vital	vest	uvula	alleviate	sleeve	retrieve
verse	vinegar	heaven	prevalent	love	brave

2. Enunciate the following sentences clearly:

1. The tough traffic officer felt that a fine of fifteen dollars was insufficient for the offense.
2. The gopher baffled the furious housewife.
3. Fred and Frank fought furiously over Florence.
4. The far-flung effects of Christian philosophy have never been fully explored.
5. He offered fifty-five dollars for finding his flea-bitten fox terrier.
6. The visible universe is trivial in comparison to the vast infinity of time and space.
7. The storm hovered over the village, obstructing the view of the visitor.
8. Vera and Eva vied for valedictorian honors.
9. Viking victories have been recorded in various verse forms by the medieval writers.
10. The uvular muscle of the velum has very nearly lost its function.

3. While articulating the following words, observe your lip action in a mirror, at the same time touching your larynx to determine whether or not the sound is voiced: *velvet* [ˈvɛlvɪt], *value* [ˈvælju], *vaudeville* [ˈvoudvɪl], *revolver* [rɪˈvɑlvɚ], *fife* [faɪf], *wife* [waɪf], *wives* [waɪvz], *life* [laɪf], *lives* [laɪvz], *self* [sɛlf], *selves* [sɛlvz], *shelf* [ʃɛlf], *shelves* [ʃɛlvz], *fain* [feɪn], *vain* [veɪn].

4. Work for both accuracy and ease on the following lines:

1. Fee, fi, fo, fum.
2. Fair is foul and foul is fair.
3. The fair breeze blew, the white foam flew,
   The furrow followed free.
4. False face must hide what false heart doth know.

5. Practice the following phrases:

off—of   waifs—waves
fifty—fifth   shuffle—shovel
fear—veer   fine vines
safe—saves   think over my offer

THE CONSONANTS [θ] AND [ð]

[θ] and [ð] are *lingua-dental fricatives*. They are made by lightly touching the tip of the tongue to the edge of the upper front teeth and forcing the breath stream between the teeth and the tip of the tongue. [ð] is voiced, [θ] unvoiced.

FAULTS AND DANGERS

1. Some persons fail to make a clear distinction between [θ] and [ð], often substituting one for the other. A word like *frothing* ['frɔθɪŋ] is likely to sound more like ['frɔðɪŋ], *oath* [ouθ] like [ouð].

2. Occasionally, people with foreign accents have difficulty in distinguishing between these two sounds and the [d] and [t]. Since the [θ] and [ð] do not appear in most other languages, it is necessary to teach these persons the proper positions for the sounds.

Bite the tip of your tongue lightly, retract the lower teeth and emit the breath stream between the tongue tip and the upper front teeth—and a properly placed [θ] should result. Another way of approximating this sound is to extend the tongue tip well beyond the upper front teeth, and emit the breath stream while keeping the tongue blade in contact with the upper front teeth. Now slowly retract the tongue until the tip reaches the upper front teeth. If the tongue is not too tense and the friction of the outgoing breath stream is sufficient, a good [θ] sound should result.

3. Faulty production of these sounds may often be attributed

either to carelessness in placement of the tongue or to poor muscular coördination.

EXERCISES

1. Repeat the following words over and over:

Initial		Medial		Final	
[θ]					
thin	three	catholic	pathology	width	myth
thick	thigh	healthy	ether	hearth	wreath
thought	thimble	birthday	atheist	mirth	teeth
thaw	thumb	method	ethical	wealth	mouth
thousand	theory	mythical	author	death	fifth
[ð]					
that	the	another	southern	soothe	tithe
this	thus	either	smoother	smooth	loathe
those	then	neither	whither	blithe	breathe
thou	thine	although	weather	clothe	bathe
there	though	mother	lather	teethe	sheathe

2. Enunciate the following sentences clearly:

1. Three thousand Christians thought death no threat to their faith.
2. The author may not have been wealthy, but he was ethical.
3. The youth spoke the truth concerning his pathological methods.
4. Thirty-three thugs hid in the thatched hut.
5. Through the thicket the stealthy panther crept.
6. Another Southerner seethed and writhed at the smothered legislation, but was loath to leave.
7. The blithe spirit then pointed to the sheathed sword.
8. This is the mother rather than the grandmother.
9. Although there may be those who tithe, there are those who are loath to do so.
10. My brother was not bothered with his teething, but the weather withered him.

3. Practice before the mirror to observe the tongue action on such words as *death, hearth, dearth, thud, thing, Thaddeus*, etc.

4. Distinguish between the voiced and unvoiced *th* ([ð] and [θ]) in the following word pairs:

thing—thou	thought—those	fifth—mouthed
thirst—that	thumb—wither	sixth—though
theater—there	twelfth—worthy	wealth—farthing

5. Carefully distinguish between the following paired words:

ether—either	cloth—clothe	moth—mother
south—southern	north—northern	breath—breathe

6. Work on the following tongue twisters and other passages:

1. The sea ceaseth and sufficeth us.
2. Theophilus Thistle, the successful thistle sifter, in sifting a sieve full of unsifted thistles, thrust three thousand thistles through the thick of his thumb. Now, if Theophilus Thistle, the successful thistle sifter, in sifting a sieve full of unsifted thistles, thrust three thousand thistles through the thick of his thumb, see that thou in sifting a sieve full of unsifted thistles, thrust not three thousand thistles through the thick of thy thumb. Success to the successful thistle sifter!
3. The wind bloweth where it listeth, and thou hearest the sound thereof, but canst not tell whence it cometh or whither it goeth.
4. Breathes there the man with soul so dead
   Who never to himself hath said:
   This is my own, my native land!
5. As feud-seeking foemen afore-time assailed thee, a thousand thanes to thee did I bring, heroes to help thee.

THE CONSONANTS [s] AND [z]

Probably, for the majority of people, the *postdental fricatives* [s] and [z] afford more difficulty than any of the other English sounds. The proper production of these sounds requires not only keen hearing, but an extremely delicate adjustment of the articulators. The sides of the tongue must be kept in contact (laterally) with the teeth, yet raised and grooved sufficiently to force the air along the mid-line of the tongue. The tip of the tongue must not come in contact with either the upper front teeth or the gum ridge, and the breath stream must be directed across the cutting edges of the teeth. A second method of producing this sound involves placing the tip of the tongue behind the lower front teeth, and arching, grooving, and bringing the tongue laterally into contact with the teeth, in much the same way as was described above. These two methods are known respectively as *up* and *down* techniques of tongue placement. [z] is voiced, [s] unvoiced.

Faults and Dangers

1. The *central lisp* (also called the *frontal* or *dental lisp*) is made by the substitution of [θ] for [s], and [ð] for [z]. This substitution results from allowing the tongue tip to touch the upper teeth as in the formation of [θ] or [ð]. The correction lies primarily in properly retracting the tongue tip and redirecting the breath stream between the slightly parted teeth. Test this on words like *sick* [sɪk], *snow* [snou], *Suzy* ['suzɪ], and the like.

2. The *lateral lisp* is caused by allowing the air to escape at the sides of the tongue over the bicuspids or canine teeth. Firm contact must be maintained between the sides of the tongue and the upper gum and teeth as far forward in the mouth as the canines to prevent this leakage.

3. One of the most common faults is overemphasis of [s] so that it is either too prominent or whistled. This can be corrected in various ways.

Perhaps the simplest means of correcting this fault is to reduce breath pressure or to reduce the duration of the sound itself. Don't breathe too heavily; don't force the sound. "Gently, brother, gently pray!"

Occasionally the whistle is caused by too wide an aperture between certain teeth, or poor occlusion of the upper and lower teeth, or some other condition which defies even the most skillful efforts at compensation. In such a case you will be wise to consult your dentist or orthodontist.[11]

4. Another common fault in the production of [s] and [z] is the occurrence of too high or too low frequency. The first condition results from having the tongue elevated too high, and the latter from having the tongue placed too low.

EXERCISES

1. Repeat the following words over and over:

Initial			Medial		Final
[s]					
sit	string	distinguish	Christmas	fuss	flecks
soothe	street	decimal	system	press	confess
sartorial	slide	dastardly	drastic	crass	address
saint	slope	absolute	dorsal	numerous	superstitious
settle	sweet	classify	destitute	gloss	across
[z]					
zone	zenith	lazy	amused	gaze	trees
zeal	Zion	prizes	scissor	goes	always
zip	zinc	razor	imposing	was	knives
zoo	zany	cousin	closet	choose	arise
zephyr	zero	museum	crazed	cruise	chives

2. Enunciate the following sentences clearly:

1. Saint Nicholas, the patron saint of the Christmas season, is synonymous with Santa Claus.
2. The sun rises in the east and sets in the west.
3. Our distinguished senator rose to his feet to address us.
4. Sulfur and molasses was used as a spring tonic.
5. The street lights glistened on the glossy pavement.
6. My cousin was amused by the zebras in the zoo.
7. Knives and razors should be used with caution.
8. Lazy, hazy days are dog days.

[11] In her book, *My Boss* (Scribner, 1949), Grace Tully, for many years secretary to the late President Franklin D. Roosevelt, revealed the little-known fact that he wore a bridge to eliminate a whistle caused by an opening between two of his lower front teeth.

9. I gazed at the imposing trees which lined the horizon.

10. A zany zephyr zipped through the trees.

3. Practice the following syllables repeatedly:

[seɪ, si, saɪ, soʊ, su];
[zeɪ, zi, zaɪ, zoʊ, zu].

4. Practice words which contain both [s] and [z], such as *signs, suppose, sausages, solos, business, saws,* etc.

5. Practice the following phrases:

1. Sit in solemn silence.
2. Short, sharp, shock.
3. Ships, many ships sailing.
4. Seasons of mists.
5. Steps of passing ghosts.
6. Silver shoes.
7. The assassin suddenly sallied.
8. Seas and shoals.

6. Say the following jingles and tongue twisters rapidly:

1. The sixth sheik's sixth sheep is sick.
2. Some shun sunshine; do you shun sunshine?
3. Sister Susie's sewing shirts for soldiers.
4. Esau saw the sheep and the sheep saw Esau.
5. Susan sells sea shells on the sea shore.
6. Six slim, slick, slender saplings.
7. Two twin-screw steel cruisers.

8.   Sing a song of sixpence
            A pocket full of rye
        Four and twenty blackbirds
            Baked in a pie.

9.   Swan swim over the sea;
        Swim, swan, swim.
        Swan swim back again;
        Well swam, swan.

10. To sit in solemn silence in a dull, dark dock,
    In a pestilential prison, with a life-long lock.
    Awaiting the sensation of a short, sharp shock,
    From a cheap and chippy chopper, on a big, black block.

7. Work on the following lines of poetry:

1.   Silver sails all out of the west
              Under the silver moon.

2. . . . Go not like a quarry-slave at night,
     Scourged to his dungeon, but sustained and soothed
     By an unfaltering trust.

3.   The setting sun, and music at the close,
          As the last taste of sweets, is sweetest last.

4.   Marching along, fifty-score strong,
          Great-hearted gentlemen, singing this song.

5.   Round the cape of a sudden came the sea,
     And the sun looked over the mountain's rim . . .

6.   Sleep is a reconciling,
          A rest that peace begets;
          Shall not the sun rise smiling
          When fair at even it sets?

7.   Hail to thee, blithe Spirit!
              Bird thou never wert,
          That from heaven, or near it
              Pourest thy full heart
          In profuse strains of unpremeditated art.

8.   My soul today
          Is far away,
          Sailing the Vesuvian Bay;
          My wingéd boat,
          A bird afloat,
          Swims round the purple peaks remote.

          Round purple peaks
          It sails and seeks
          Blue inlets, and their crystal creeks,
          Where high rocks throw,
          Through deeps below,
          A duplicated golden glow.

Oh, happy ship,
To rise and dip,
With the blue crystal at your lip!
Oh, happy crew,
My heart with you
Sails, and sails, and sings anew!
—THOMAS BUCHANAN READ

THE CONSONANTS [ʃ] AND [ʒ]

[ʃ] and [ʒ] are *lingua-palatal fricatives* and are articulated with the whole tongue drawn slightly farther back and lower than it is for the [s] and [z] sounds. Note also that the blade of the tongue is spread laterally, so that the breath emerges in a broad sheet rather than in a narrow stream. [ʒ] is voiced, [ʃ] unvoiced.

FAULTS AND DANGERS

1. Occasionally these sounds become defective when the tongue is allowed to rise too high toward the palate; the resultant [ʃ] and [ʒ] are too high in frequency, somewhat resembling the German *ich*. Lowering of the blade of the tongue and thorough ear training will eliminate this fault.

2. A second fault arises in allowing the tongue to be lowered and retracted to such an extent that too large a resonating chamber is formed in the front of the mouth. Particularly is this true when the [ʃ] sound follows a back vowel, as in *gauche* [gouʃ] and *emotion* [i'mouʃn̩]. This fault is often associated with lateral lisps.

EXERCISES

1. Repeat the following words over and over:

Initial		Medial		Final	
[ʃ]					
shell	shrimp	seashell	patience	crush	radish
shingle	shake	description	emotion	cash	finish
sharp	shadow	diction	bushel	wish	gauche
should	sheen	sachet	profession	fresh	fetish
shirk	shallow	direction	anxious	clash	astonish

	Initial		Medial	Final	
[ʒ]					
jabot	Gironde	usual	composure	mirage	prestige
genre	Gide	pleasure	illusion	barrage	beige
gendarme	Giraud	regime	collision	corsage	garage
Jeanne	Jacques	usurer	casual	sabotage	menage
d'Arc	Joffre	derision	occasion	rouge	persiflage

2. Enunciate the following sentences clearly:

1. She became anxious when sharks surrounded the ship.
2. The roof of the mansion was finished with shake shingles.
3. The shad is a fish, while the shrimp is a crustacean.
4. She shaded her shoulders with a mesh shawl.
5. The sun shone on the shabby shop windows.
6. The plans for invasion by the Hoosier division underwent revision.
7. The usurer made his decision of seizure with composure.
8. A mirage is a visionary illusion.
9. The beige jardiniere was stored in the garage.
10. Jacques, the jongleur, entertained the gendarme.

3. Compare and contrast the following word pairs:

shell—genre	fisher—azure
sharp—Jacques	emotion—regime
anxious—pleasure	sheen—rouge
precious—prestige	sachet—casual

4. Try the following tongue twister:

The Shah of Shay shouted short shrill shrieks, which shattered the shadowy night.

5. Work on the following passages:

1.   Better than all measures
     Of delightful sound,
     Better than all treasures
     That in books are found,
     Thy skill to poet were, thou scorner of the ground

2.   A flock of sheep that leisurely pass by,
     One after one; the sound of rain and bees

    Murmuring; the fall of rivers, winds and seas,
    Smooth fields, white sheets of water, and pure sky.

3.   Hush, ah, hush, the scythes are saying,
        Hush, and heed not, and fall asleep;
        Hush they say to the grasses swaying;
        Hush they sing to the clover deep!

4. We shall go on to the end, we shall fight in France, we shall fight on the seas and oceans, we shall fight with growing confidence and growing strength in the air, we shall defend our Island, whatever the cost may be. We shall fight on the beaches, we shall fight on the landing grounds, we shall fight in the fields and in the streets, we shall fight in the hills; we shall never surrender.

THE CONSONANT [h]

[h] may be classified as a *voiceless glottal fricative*. In making this sound the vocal cords are approximated sufficiently to restrict the outgoing breath stream, thus creating a fricative sound. However, the cords are not brought close enough together to create tone, hence the sound is voiceless. This sound occurs in the initial and medial positions of words only.

Faults and Dangers

Usually the [h] sound does not give Americans much trouble, except in the [hw] combination which will be discussed later. Care should be taken, however, to see that an excessive amount of air does not escape during the production of this sound.

EXERCISES

1. Repeat the following words over and over:

Initial		Medial	
how	health	behalf	behind
half	hint	behead	uphold
home	honey	cohort	perhaps
hello	hustle	rehearse	anyhow
hunt	hazard	inhale	overhead

2. Enunciate the following sentences clearly:

1. High heels have been called a hazard to good health.
2. Hundreds of tomahawks were held high as the hardy Mohawks hunted their prey.
3. Hydrogen and helium have to be handled with caution.
4. The hotel in the hollow has housed many historic figures.
5. His humility and heroism have held him in high repute.

3. Distinguish between the words in the following pairs:

oh—hoe	err—her	ate—hate	eat—heat
you—who	eye—high	ear—hear	ale—hale
awe—haw	at—hat	them—hem	it—hit

4. Practice the following jingles:

1. It ain't the 'eat that 'urts the 'orses 'oofs;
   It's the 'ammer, 'ammer, 'ammer on the 'ard 'ighway.

2. If to hoot and to toot a Hottentot tot
   Were taught by a Hottentot tutor,
   Should the tutor get hot if the Hottentot tot
   Should hoot and toot at the tutor?

5. Work on the following lines of poetry:

1. Sing, heigh ho, the holly!

2. Home is the sailor, home from the Sea,
   And the hunter home from the hill.

3. Tell me where is fancy bred,
   Or in the heart, or in the head?

4. That hour it was when heaven's first gift of sleep
   On weary hearts of men most sweetly steals.

The Glides

There are four glides in the English language: [r], [j], [w] and [l].[12] A glide may be described as a transitionary sound resulting from the movement of the articulators from one vowel

---

[12] [l] is sometimes classified by phoneticians as a lateral continuant. For purposes of convenience, the author has chosen to classify this sound as a glide.

position to another during continuous voicing. For example, prolong an [i:] sound; without stopping the vocalized breath stream, proceed quickly to an [ʌ] sound—the transitional sound should be [j]; do likewise with [u] and [ʌ], and [ɝ] and [ʌ]—the resultant sounds should approximate [w] and [r].[13] Such a demonstration also illustrates the vowel-like nature of these sounds; it is not without reason that some authorities look upon the glides as semivowels. All glides are voiced.

THE CONSONANT [r]

[r] may be classified as a *voiced lingua-palatal glide.* The tip of the tongue is curled slightly back toward the hard palate and glides quickly to whatever sound happens to follow it; this process is reversed whenever any other sound precedes the [r]. Actually, the [r] sound varies in resonance characteristics, depending upon what phonetic elements happen to surround it. There has been a great deal of controversy concerning the history and nature of this sound, but it is recognized that the pronunciation of the [r] sound varies greatly, not only among different speakers, but also among different dialectal regions.

In sections of the East and the South, the [r] sound following a vowel is either greatly softened or omitted altogether. For example, *fear* [fir] may become [fiə], *poor* [pur] may become [puə], *harbor* ['harbɚ] may become ['ha:bə], *start* [start] may become [sta:t], etc. The student of diction should use as his standard the pronunciation of the best speakers in his section of the country.

FAULTS AND DANGERS

1. Very often an individual will curl (retroflex) the tip of his tongue backward excessively (at the same time tensing the

---

[13] Much of the identity of these sounds depends upon the speed of movement of the articulators from one position to another; for if the movement is not made with speed and precision, the resultant sound loses much of its identifiable character.

tongue), which gives rise to a rather hard, unpleasant tone. This is especially true of certain sections of the country where General American is the regional dialect.

2. As was mentioned earlier, sluggish tongue movements do much to destroy the identifiable characteristics of the glides, particularly the [r]. In this case, drill in precision and speed is indicated.

3. Various other distortions, substitutions, and omissions are possible on the [r] sound. For example, trilled [r], uvular [r], and no [r] whatsoever are typical of certain types of foreign accent. Various physiological and pathological conditions also may seriously impair the proper production of [r]. In such cases the student will do well to seek the services of a competent physician or speech correctionist.

EXERCISES

1. Repeat the following words over and over:

Initial		Medial		Final	
rat	radio	America	sparse	mother	monster
ripe	religion	Africa	around	clear	fodder
rogue	region	bury	arid	pier	floor
run	ruminate	barn	variety	creator	veneer
read	rodent	sparrow	pardon	patter	sheer

2. Enunciate the following sentences clearly:

1. America, South America, Africa, Asia, Europe, and Australia present a variety of flora and fauna.
2. The pitter-patter of the rain on the roof interferes with our radio reception.
3. To rid the barnyard of the variety of rodents that frequent it is a major undertaking.
4. Arid regions of the Rockies are sparsely settled.
5. Reading the newspaper every morning is a religion with our father.

3. Drill repeatedly on the following phrases:

round room	rapid reading	drowsily dreaming
rough road	round robin	brightly burnished
rare recipe	recently married	rarely reciting
red rose	merrily rolling	wearily running

4. Speak these lines with distinctness:

1. Rubber baby buggy bumper.
2. Around the rugged rock the ragged rascal ran.
3. Rude Rupert raucously ate round red apples.

5. Work on the following selections:

1.
When a merry maiden marries,
Sorrow goes and pleasure tarries;
Every sound becomes a song.
All is right and nothing's wrong.

2.
Over hill, over dale,
Through brush, through brier,
Over park, over pale,
Through flood, through fire,
I do wander everywhere.

3.
Drip, drip, the rain comes falling,
Rain in the woods, rain on the sea;
Even the little waves, beaten, come crawling,
As if to find shelter here with me.

4.
Our purses shall be proud, our garments poor,
For 'tis the mind that makes the body rich;
And as the sun breaks through the darkest clouds,
So honor peereth in the meanest habit.

5.
Once upon a midnight dreary, while I pondered, weak and
weary,
Over many a quaint and curious volume of forgotten lore—
While I nodded, nearly napping, suddenly there came a
tapping,
As of someone gently rapping, rapping at my chamber door,

" 'Tis some visitor," I muttered, "tapping at my chamber
    door—
Only this and nothing more."

6.   The rainbow comes and goes,
        And lovely is the rose,
        The moon doth with delight
    Look round her when the heavens are bare;
        Waters on a starry night
        Are beautiful and fair;
        The sunshine is a glorious birth;
        But yet I know, where'er I go,
        That there hath pass'd away a glory from the earth.

THE CONSONANT [j]

[j] is often described as a *voiced lingua-palatal glide*; however, some writers prefer to call it a *palatal semivowel*. To form
[j] the tongue starts from a position approximating that for the
vowel [i], then moves quickly to the position of a following
vowel. To demonstrate this sound prolong an [i:] for a few
seconds, then move quickly to the vowel [u]; the result should
be the word *you* [ju]. The [j] sound occurs only in initial and
medial positions.

Faults and Dangers

As a general rule, the formation of [j] presents no great problem to most speakers. However, two tendencies with regard to
its use should be noted:

1. There is a growing tendency, even among careful speakers,
to eliminate [j] in favor of a more intermediate sound in certain
words. For instance, *due* [dju] is rapidly changing to [dɪu] or
even [du]. Usage is the law and rule of speech; hence the student
of diction should be guided by the most acceptable standard of
his dialectal area for guidance in this problem.

2. Too frequently [j] is intruded where it does not belong, as
in such words as *coupon* ['k(j)upɑn], *column* ['kɑl(j)əm], *escalator*
['ɛsk(j)əleɪtɚ], *percolator* ['pɝk(j)əleɪtɚ], *similar* ['sɪm(j)əlɚ], and
tremendous [trɪ'mɛnd(j)əs].

EXERCISES

1. Repeat the following words over and over:

Initial		Medial	
yam	yeast	accuse	bunion
year	yesterday	million	familiar
yoke	yellow	onion	canyon
yet	yarn	beyond	civilian
youth	yacht	companion	senior

2. Enunciate the following sentences clearly:
   1. My youthful companion gazed beyond the vineyards to the yachts and yawls anchored in the Yellow Sea.
   2. Yes, he yearned for his yesterday's youth.
   3. The yams and onions in our yard are valueless.
   4. A million Brazilians yelled, "Hallelujah."
   5. My senior companion yelped when York's yak stepped on his bunions.

THE CONSONANT [w]; THE COMBINATION [hw][14]

[w] is a *bilabial glide*. It is produced by forming the lips for [u] and moving quickly to the position of the following vowel. To illustrate this process, prolong [u:] for a few seconds, then move rapidly to [i:]; the product should be a clearly articulated *we*. Inasmuch as [hw] is a combination of [h] and [w], no detailed description will be given. Suffice it to say that this sound unit is produced by making a glottal fricative approach to [w].

FAULTS AND DANGERS

1. As is common with the other bilabial consonants, people with stiff or lazy lips articulate [w] and [hw] poorly.

2. Perhaps the most common fault with the combination sound [hw] is that some individuals have difficulty in articulating the glottal fricative approach, and fall into error by com-

---

[14] [hw] is often described by phoneticians as voiceless [w], and is represented by the symbol [ʍ].

pletely omitting [h]. Thus *why* [hwaɪ] becomes [waɪ], *which* [hwɪtʃ] becomes [wɪtʃ], *wheel* [hwil] becomes [wil], etc. This fault may cause complications in meaning, because the only distinguishing characteristic of many word pairs is the glottal fricative approach to [w]. The following word pairs illustrate this point: wail—whale, wear—where, witch—which.

3. As is true of [r] and [j], [w] very often loses much of its character if the glide is not made with speed and definiteness.

EXERCISES

1. Repeat the following words over and over:

	Initial	Medial	
[w]			
we	window	beware	aware
wash	weather	anyone	sway
wit	worship	reward	dwell
watch	wealth	away	unworthy
one	wonder	dwarf	swear
[hw]			
where	whistle	meanwhile	anywhere
what	whether	somewhat	overwhelm
which	when	somewhere	awhile
whip	whet	nowhere	bobwhite
while	whirl	elsewhere	everywhere

2. Enunciate the following sentences clearly:
   1. Warren washed the windows as William watched.
   2. Twelve bewitched dwarfs were walking in our woods.
   3. To woo is not always to win.
   4. Onward the stalwart wagons wended their way to the West.
   5. The weary wanderer waded through the billowy waters.
   6. Why whip or whack a horse when a "whoa" serves better?
   7. The whippet whined and whimpered when the bobwhite whistled.
   8. We were somewhat overwhelmed when the whale whirled and whizzed by the pier.

9. While Mr. Wherry whispered to the whippoorwill, Grandpa chortled in his whiskers.

10. When the millwheel refused to whirl, the wheat remained unground.

3. Distinguish between the words in the following pairs:

were—whir	wear—where	woe—whoa
wet—whet	wight—white	way—whey
wail—whale	wine—whine	weather—whether
witch—which	wetted—whetted	wot—what

4. Work on the following lines:

1.
     To the gull's way, and the whale's way
     Where the wind's like a whetted knife.

2.
     Water, water, everywhere.

3.
     But whether we meet or whether we part
     (For our ways are past our knowing),
     A pledge from the heart to its fellow heart
     On the ways we all are going!

4.
     Into this Universe, and *Why* not knowing
     Nor *Whence*, like Water willy-nilly flowing;
     And out of it, as Wind along the Waste,
     I know not *Whither*, willy-nilly blowing.

     What, without asking, hither hurried *Whence?*
     And, without asking, *Whither* hurried hence!
     Oh, many a Cup of this forbidden Wine
     Must drown the memory of that insolence!

                   —FITZGERALD

THE CONSONANT [l]

[l] is a *voiced glide* of extreme variability. It is often called a *lateral continuant* because the breath stream is emitted over the sides of the tongue. The tongue serves a purpose much as does a boulder in the middle of a stream that divides the current. The tip of the tongue touches the gum ridge, forming a

barrier which directs the breath stream out of the mouth over the sides of the tongue. While [l] is being made, the tongue holds its position against the gum ridge; but when you get ready to make the next sound, the tongue is pulled sharply away.

In certain combinations this sound has practically the value of a vowel; some phoneticians classify it as one of the vowel-like consonants, along with the other glides and the nasals. The vowel-like nature of [l] is especially noticeable when it is syllabicated, as in battle ['bætl] and saddle ['sædl].

FAULTS AND DANGERS

1. As with many other sounds, there is a tendency to pronounce this sound too far back in the mouth. There are, to be sure, some differences in the position of the tongue, depending upon the type of vowel preceding or following the [l] sound; an example is the difference between *fell* and *full*. The second of these sounds is sometimes called the "dark" [l] in contrast to the "light" [l] in the first word. The real danger comes in permitting all the [l] sounds to become "dark." In extreme cases this tendency results in what is called "retroflex" or "inverted" [l]. This undesirable pronunciation is indicated in dialect by spelling "wul" for "well," etc.

2. It is not uncommon to hear someone substitute [w] for [l]; in such cases, a word like *line* [laɪn] becomes [waɪn], *look* [lʊk] becomes [wʊk], and *low* [loʊ] becomes [woʊ]. The [w] sound is formed principally with the lips, whereas in making the [l] the tongue is more active.

3. Very often [l] is omitted altogether, as is common in such words as *William, million,* and *civilian,* which may become ['wɪjəm], ['mɪjən], and [sɪ'vɪjən].

EXERCISES

1. Repeat the following words over and over:

	Initial		Medial		Final
lady	laboratory	silence	silence	animal	broil
lest	lawyer	mild	highland	frail	appall
love	lantern	million	truly	trial	pile
lusty	languish	slash	pallor	conceal	swell
lure	ladder	clear	violence	bail	churl

2. Enunciate the following sentences clearly:

   1. A million lanterns lighted the landscape.
   2. A violent gale swept every hill and dale of the island.
   3. Swallows, larks, and quail all love our laurel tree.
   4. My lady loves lavender, silks, and old lace.
   5. Molly fell pell-mell into the well, and Willy laughed and laughed.

3. Practice with special care articulating the [l] sound in such combinations as the following: *scalp, Billy, yellow, silt, pall, kettle, fiddle, grilling, milk,* etc.

4. Observe a friend repeating the syllable, *la—la—la—la—la—la—la.* Have him say it both fast and slow. Watch the action of his tongue as he produces this sound combination. Study your own tongue action in a mirror as you make the sound. You may thus be able to detect whether or not you are making the [l] correctly. Study your tongue action as you pronounce the words *will* [wɪl], *willing* ['wɪlɪŋ], *William* ['wɪljəm], *Llewellyn* [lʊ'ɛlɪn], *Lewis* ['luɪs], *linoleum* [lɪ'nolɪəm], *lanolin* ['lænəlɪn], and *Lilliputians* [lɪlə'pjuʃənz].

5. Practice the following lines:

   1. Sail on! Sail on! Sail on and on!
   2. Alone, alone, all, all alone.
   3. The curfew tolls the knell of parting day,
      The lowing herd winds slowly o'er the lea.
   4. Why so pale and wan, fond lover?
      Prithee, why so pale?
    Will, when looking well can't move her,
      Looking ill prevail?

5. Across wide lotus-ponds of light,
   I marked a giant fire-fly's flight.
6. He loves but lightly who his love can tell.
7. Roll on, thou deep and dark blue Ocean, roll.

The Nasals
THE CONSONANTS [m], [n], AND [ŋ]

The nasals are made by blocking the flow of air out of the mouth and emitting it through the nasal passages. In all of these sounds the soft palate is lowered so that the voiced breath stream is directed through the nasal passages. The place and type of interference in the mouth vary with each of the three nasal consonants.

[m] is a *voiced bilabial nasal.* It is made by closing the lips as for the [b] sound. However, instead of the sound being temporarily blocked as in [b], the soft palate is lowered and the sound permitted to flow through the nasal passages.

[n] is a *voiced postdental nasal.* Although the tongue is pressed against the gum ridge as for [d], the soft palate is lowered, and the sound directed through the nose.

[ŋ], a *lingua-velar nasal,* is the *ng* sound in such words as *long, fling,* and the like. It is made by arching the back of the tongue against the soft palate, relaxing the velum, and directing the voiced breath stream through the nasal passages.

FAULTS AND DANGERS

Many of the faults of this category have already been discussed in the section on nasal resonance in Chapter VII. Several additional matters, however, deserve special mention at this time.

1. Care should be taken to avoid substituting [n] for [ŋ]. Careless speakers often are guilty of saying *runnin'* ['rʌnɪn] for ['rʌnɪŋ], *catchin'* ['kætʃɪn] for ['kætʃɪŋ], etc.

2. At the other extreme is the fault sometimes found in the speech of some foreigners as well as in that of some native-born

Americans. This is the tendency to add the [g] sound after the [ŋ] when it does not belong there. Thus *singer* [ˈsɪŋɚ] becomes [ˈsɪŋgɚ], *longing* [ˈlɔŋɪŋ] becomes [ˈlɔŋgɪŋ]; *Long Island* [lɔŋˈaɪlənd] becomes [lɔŋˈgaɪlənd].

3. Occasionally this is reversed and words that should be pronounced [ŋg] are pronounced simply [ŋ]. Thus *finger* [ˈfɪŋgɚ] becomes [ˈfɪŋɚ], etc.

4. It is a matter of interest that when our nasal passages are congested, as in severe head colds, our [m], [n], and [ŋ] consonants sound more like their cognates [b], [d], and [g]. Thus *my nose is running* [maɪ ˈnoʊz ɪz ˈrʌnɪŋ] becomes [baɪ ˈdoʊz ɪz ˈrʌdɪg]. Any obstruction of the nasal passages can give rise to denasality or typical "cold-in-the-head" speech.

EXERCISES

1. Repeat the following words over and over:

	Initial		Medial		Final
[m]					
mar	music	compose	common	swim	broom
men	maternal	companion	dramatic	same	perform
meet	marriage	summer	comely	palm	thumb
most	mourn	remember	tumult	dream	hymn
mill	mood	element	tamper	dome	tomb
[n]					
none	north	land	sound	cane	blown
know	near	many	pony	pain	wine
nest	neck	manic	stand	fine	vain
gnat	knit	penny	under	brown	plan
nine	pneumatic	funny	month	lane	coin
[ŋ]					
		longingly	hanger	young	tongue
		donkey	ringlet	hung	going
		jenny	wringer	bang	racing
		length	songster	song	playing
		strength	youngster	king	bring

2. Enunciate the following sentences clearly:

1. The music's mournful lament marred our homecoming.
2. Many middle-aged men were employed for the summer harvest.
3. Ham, yams, jam, and pumpkin pies made our Monday meeting a memorable occasion.
4. Many men prefer feminine companionship to masculine.
5. Hymns were hummed by the assembled multitudes at the Tomb of the Unknown Soldier.
6. The new minister warned the congregation against nurturing sinful thoughts.
7. Nine funny gnomes danced in the shining moonlight.
8. An open-minded discussion contributes to an acquisition of knowledge.
9. Ned's grandfather warned the neighbors never to frequent his manor on the plantation.
10. Man learns, but nature knows.
11. The Anglo-Saxons conquered the English long ago.
12. The young ringleader of the gang was hanged for killing the distinguished congressman.
13. The youngster was angry when the buzzing bee stung his tongue.
14. The hungry throng stormed the stronghold of the king.
15. Rowing, hiking, and swimming gave him outstanding strength.

3. Distinguish between the [ŋ] sounds in the following pairs of words:

song—finger	winged—wrangle	clanging—shingle
singer—linger	cling—languor	sting—wrangle
singing—longer	clinging—jungle	stinging—pringle
long—English	king—mingle	ring—hungry
longing—wink	kingly—single	ringing—language
wing—bank	clang—bungle	bring—angry

4. After carefully distinguishing between the two types of sounds above, practice the following lines diligently:

1. Ding-dong, ding-dong, ding-dong, ding.
2. Twinkle, twinkle, little star.
3. Drink, pretty creature, drink.
4. The song was sung.
5. Song is the language of the heart.

6. Out in the green fields grazing.
7. Grow old along with me.
8. Dreaming dreams of the long ago.
9. His shining morning face.
10. The moving finger writes.
11. A stream murmuring beside its green banks.
12. Hear the jingling and the jangling of the bells.
13. The night light glimmering through the groaning trees.

The Consonant Combinations
[tʃ] AND [dʒ]

The combinations [tʃ] and [dʒ] are sometimes called affricates by phoneticians (a fricative that is begun from a closed position). Each of these combinations has a double symbol because it is in reality two sounds blended into one. Note, however, that they are truly blended, for in forming either of them you do not completely finish one sound and then begin the other; rather, you merge the two, thus: The breath stream is stopped on the first part of the blend [t] or [d], held momentarily, then released directly into the second part of the sound unit, [ʃ] or [ʒ]. Since each element of these sound units has already been discussed in detail, further elaboration here is unnecessary. [dʒ] is voiced, [tʃ] unvoiced.

It will be observed that something approaching this merger occurs in several other consonant combinations, as in [st] in *first*, [pt] in *apt*, etc. However, the combinations [tʃ] and [dʒ] occur so frequently in our language and are so definitely merged that phoneticians use special symbols to represent them.

FAULTS AND DANGERS

For faults and dangers relating to these sounds, refer to the treatment given [t], [d], [ʃ], and [ʒ] earlier in this chapter.

EXERCISES

1. Repeat the following words over and over:

Initial	Medial	Final
[tʃ]					
church	chief	butcher	concerto	hatch	lunch
chose	chatter	satchel	hatchet	batch	beach
chair	chest	teacher	lecture	speech	catch
chuckle	cherry	question	exchange	march	such
churn	chop	escutcheon	merchant	pitch	scratch
[dʒ]					
joy	gentle	pigeon	magic	badge	gage
jolly	journey	majestic	manager	hedge	serge
gem	judge	object	fragile	orange	huge
jewel	jest	engine	agile	sage	image
jail	genius	badger	wager	language	strange

2. Enunciate the following sentences clearly:

1. Charlie chuckled while chopping chips from Churchill's cherry tree.
2. The pitcher chided the churlish catcher for changing his signals.
3. The teacher lectured on the nature and virtues of cello concertos.
4. Chicle is used chiefly in the manufacture of chewing gum.
5. The Chinese chieftain chastised Ching for leaving chopsticks in Chang's chop suey.
6. John and Jerry jumped with joy when their geology major was approved.
7. The jaunty major wagered his gems and jewels that the judge would not jail Jerome.
8. He emerged from college an educated gentleman but not a genius.
9. The geranium on the ridge bloomed earlier than the gentian in the gorge.
10. Midge's fudge became a hodgepodge when George added sage and orange to her batter.

3. Practice [tʃ] combinations in such words as:

chalk—clinch	change—flinch	chase—search
chink—cinch	charge—watch	chicken—birch
champion—winch	choice—scratch	choose—spinach

4. Practice the [dʒ] combination in such words as:

jam—charge	ginger—fidget	gesture—cage
jungle—smudge	Jasper—midget	joint—conjure
general—fudge	joke—Bridget	Jack—budget

5. Distinguish clearly between the following pairs of sounds:

match—magic	such—smudge
catch—cage	choose—refuge
cheer—jeer	choice—rejoice
choke—joke	breeches—bridges
chest—jest	punch—plunge
chill—jill	puncheon—dungeon
chunk—junk	lunch—sludge
chive—jive	bunch—budge

6. Read the following lines distinctly:

1. Cheerfulness and chastity are golden charms in woman.
2. Charge! Chester, Charge!
3. Jealousy is an awkward homage which inferiority renders to rage.
4. Jack and Jill went up the hill.
5. The damage had been done by the badger.

General Suggestions Regarding Articulation

Now that we have studied the individual consonants and are fairly sure that we are forming them correctly—or at least know how to form them correctly—the important thing is to practice various consonant combinations until we can articulate clearly, distinctly, and in that apparently easy manner which characterizes the effective speaker. For many of us this means the establishment of a new set of habits. Most of us habitually speak well enough to be understood most of the time—well, anyway, part of the time, especially with a few proddings of the "What-did-you-say?" type. But this is a far cry from that perfection of articulation which makes words stand out with crystal clearness, the type of diction we hear from top-flight speakers, actors, and singers. Many of us have little reason to be proud of our diction in everyday conversation.

Lincoln once made a remark which might well be applied to articulation. With reference to simplicity of style, he said that it had been his lifetime ambition to speak not so that everyone could understand, but so simply that no one could misunderstand. The serious diction student should strive for just that: such superior enunciation that no one—not even the partially deaf person in the group—can help but hear without effort.

In most cases this superior diction is not so much a matter of knowing as of doing. We do not do as well as we know how. To do well all the time, we have to practice until good habits are fixed. As Fredric March, motion-picture actor noted for his fine diction, once wrote the author: "It is a human failing to be careless in speech. The price of good diction is constant effort. . . . We must practice so diligently against this proneness to be sloppy in our speech, that correct diction becomes second nature."[15]

World War II gave new emphasis to the need for good articulation. Military leaders place great stress on it in the training of officers. In actual combat the fate of fighting men may depend upon their officers' ability to enunciate so that there is no possibility of misunderstanding. A humorous illustration of this very real danger was reported in the *Saturday Evening Post*:

A soldier on observation duty at one of our military outposts in Italy during the last war reported by phone to his regimental commander that he saw an Italian crawling up the forward slope of Hill Five-Seven-One. After a while the colonel called back:

"Has that enemy battalion dispersed yet?"

"Battalion!" groaned the lieutenant. "Sir, the report was *I*-talian, not *bat*-talion."[16]

[15] Quoted by permission.
[16] December 15, 1945.

Below are a few general suggestions for building a new set of desirable habits:

1. *Projection of voice is more important than great volume.* A speaker may have the volume of an old-time train announcer —and be just as inarticulate. The need is to get the words out on the lips. Do not try to articulate with the gargling muscles in your throat. As you speak the following practice lines, imagine you are popping ping-pong balls out of your mouth and bouncing them off the back wall.

Repeat this phrase rapidly and distinctly:

> *toy boat, toy boat, toy boat, toy boat.*

Project this sentence:

When William went west where Walter was working, we wished we were where we could watch him.

2. *We can learn a great deal about good articulation by listening to good speech models.* Records of good speeches are available at most record stores. Listen to them attentively; then compare recordings of your own voice.

3. *Much poor articulation results from the deeply ingrained habit of too rapid speech.* Drilling on the exercises in the section on rate (p. 381) should help to establish new habits of more deliberate, more meaningful, and hence clearer speech.

4. *Manipulation of the lips by the fingers will help to overcome long habits of rigidity in the muscles around the mouth.* Pull your lips out *gently,* stretch them this way and that way; massage them a bit. Gently massage the jaw muscles. Observe the tenseness of the muscles in a "fixed" smile, and the flabbiness of the muscles in lazy, lax lips. Counteract both these conditions by frequent but short sessions of muscle manipulation.

Some people, in an effort to speak distinctly, draw their lips back rigidly from their teeth in a manner which not only is unaesthetic to see, but is far from conducive to good tone quality and easy articulation. The lips must be relaxed, flexible, and not rigid.

5. *Exercises of your own devising may help to make your tongue more flexible and responsive,* such as running the tongue rapidly in and out of the mouth, pointing it toward one of the ears, then toward the other, etc.

As a demonstration of the importance of an agile tongue in good articulation, try the following experiment: Draw the tongue back toward the throat and let it lie there, thick and clumsy. Then say some sentence like "All the world's a stage, . . ." Note the thick mushy tones. Now extend the tongue forward until its tip just touches the inside of the lower teeth; try to feel a lightness and flexibility in the tongue as you say the same sentence; note the clear-cut precise articulation. From this simple exercise a lesson may be learned: In speech, keep the tongue well forward, not, of course, extending between the teeth, but lightly touching the inside of the teeth, and actively ready for use. Develop a kinesthetic sense in the tongue. *Feel* how it functions when words are well articulated.

6. Another frequent cause of poor articulation is suggested by a few lines in Shakespeare's *As You Like It.* After piling a series of rapid-fire questions one upon another, Rosalind says breathlessly, "Answer me in a word." Celia replies, "You must borrow me Gargantua's mouth first: 'tis a word too great for any mouth of this age."

Too many persons do not have—or do not use—mouths big enough to carve out the words. They try to squeeze words out of stingy little slits between their teeth.

But we must not leave this recommendation without qualification. Occasionally—in possibly about one person in a hundred —we find one who opens his mouth *too* wide, who talks with a "rubber mouth." The effeminate man and the "effusive" woman are sometimes afflicted with this fault. Their great need is to practice "aiming" their words (see 1 above).

On the whole, for most students the great need is to open the mouth wider. Watch the mouths of professional speakers and actors who speak with genuine distinctness; then stand in front of the mirror and watch your own mouth as you talk normally. And when you have observed the difference, practice opening your mouth r-e-a-l w-i-d-e, *à la* Gargantua, or at any rate *à la* Joe E. Brown.

EXERCISES

1. Listen to a group of fellow students "batting the breeze." Below are a few of the phrases you may hear, together with translations into Standard American. Speak them first as the mutilated spellings try to indicate, then say them in good American speech. Avoid being pedantic.

[nɛn]	n'nen	and then
[tɔl]	'tall	at all
[dʒu]	d'ju	did you?
[doʊntʃə'noʊ]	donchuno	don't you know?
[frʌs]	f'rus	for us
[fr'ɪnstənts]	f'instance	for instance
[gwaʊt]	g'wout	go out
['hiz'aʊt]	he'zout	he is out
['aɪm'gʊnə]	I'm gona	I am going to
[zæ'tʃu]	zat chew	is that you?
[zæt'soʊ]	zat so	is that so?
[mʊrn]	mor'n	more than
[kʊrs]	'course	of course
['sæftɚ'nun]	'safternoon	this afternoon
[s'mɔrnɪn]	'smornin'	this morning
[wɪli'goʊ]	wil'ego	will he go?
[wɝsə'nɛvɚ]	worse'never	worse than ever
[jɔl]	y'all	you all
[hoʊl'ɑn]	hol'on	hold on
[dʒit]	'jeat	did you eat?
[nɔ'dʒu]	naw; d'u	no; did you?

2. Speak the following rather tricky phrases distinctly, without being too obvious in your effort to do so:

1. An ice house, *not* a nice house.
2. The summer school, *not* the summer's cool.
3. Your two eyes, *not* you're too wise.

4. Five minutes to eight, *not* five minutes to wait.

5. Give me some ice, *not* give me some mice.

6. His acts, *not* his axe.

7. Red's pies, *not* red spies.

3. Whispering exercises can be of enormous aid in learning to direct words "out front" (not, to be sure, in developing tonal quality). A whisper, to be meaningful at a distance, requires exceptionally clear-cut articulation. Imagine a friend across the room to whom you whisper the italicized lines in the Shakespearian selections below. (In stage performances these lines are given in a stage whisper.)

1.   SIR TOBY LAYS A PLOT

(As MALVOLIO *enters, talking to himself,* SIR TOBY BELCH, SIR ANDREW AGUECHEEK, *and* FABIAN *are partially hidden behind a hedge, whispering.)*

MAL.   She uses me with a more exalted respect than any one else that follows her. What should I think on't?

SIR TO.   *Here's an overweening rogue!*

FAB.   *O, peace! Contemplation makes a rare turkey-cock of him: how he jets under his advanced plumes!*

SIR AND.   *'Slight, I could so beat the rogue!*

SIR TO.   *Peace, I say.*

MAL.   To be Count Malvolio!

SIR TO.   *Ah, rogue!*

SIR AND.   *Pistol him, pistol him.*

SIR TO.   *Peace, peace!*

MAL.   There is example for't: the lady of the Strachy married the yeoman of the wardrobe.

SIR AND.   *Fie on him, Jezebel!*

FAB.   *O, peace! now he's deeply in; look how imagination blows him.*

MAL.   Having been three months married to her, sitting in my state,—

SIR TO.   *O, for a stone-bow, to hit him in the eye!*

MAL.   Calling my officers about me, in my branched velvet gown; having come from a day-bed, where I have left Olivia sleeping,—

SIR TO. *Fire and brimstone!*

FAB. *O, peace, peace!*

MAL. And then to have the humour of state: and after a demure travel of regard, telling them I know my place, as I would they should do theirs, to ask for my kinsman Toby,—

SIR TO. *Bolts and shackles!*

FAB. *O, peace, peace, peace! now, now.*

MAL. Seven of my people, with an obedient start, make out for him. I frown the while; and perchance wind up my watch, or play with my—some rich jewel. Toby approaches; curt'sies there to me,—

SIR TO. *Shall this fellow live?*

FAB. *Though our silence be drawn from us by th' ears, yet peace!*

MAL. I extend my hand to him thus, quenching my familiar smile with an austere regard of control,—

SIR TO. *And does not Toby take you a blow o' the lips then?*

MAL. Saying, 'Cousin Toby, my fortunes having cast me on your niece, give me this prerogative of speech,—

SIR TO. *What, what?*

MAL. 'You must amend your drunkenness.'

SIR TO. *Out, scab!*

—SHAKESPEARE

2. LADY MACBETH WALKS IN HER SLEEP

(As LADY MACBETH *descends the stairs, holding a lighted candle, the* DOCTOR *and the* GENTLEWOMAN *are standing to one side, whispering.)*

GENT. *Lo you! here she comes. This is her very guise; and, upon my life, fast asleep. Observe her; stand close.*

DOCTOR. *How came she by that light?*

GENT. *Why, it stood by her: she has light by her continually; 'tis her command.*

DOCTOR. *You see, her eyes are open.*

GENT. *Ay, but their sense is shut.*

DOCTOR. *What is it she does now? Look, how she rubs her hands.*

GENT. *It is an accustomed action with her, to seem thus washing her hands. I have known her continue in this a quarter of an hour.*

LADY M.   Yet here's a spot.

DOCTOR.   *Hark! she speaks. I will set down what comes from her, to satisfy my remembrance the more strongly.*

LADY M.   Out, damned spot! out, I say! One, two: why, then 'tis time to do't. Hell is murky! Fie, my lord, fie! a soldier, and afeard? What need we fear who knows it, when none can call our power to account? Yet who would have thought the old man to have had so much blood in him?

DOCTOR.   *Do you mark that?*

LADY M.   The thane of Fife had a wife; where is she now? What! will these hands ne'er be clean? No more o' that, my lord, no more o' that: you mar all with this starting.

DOCTOR.   *Go to, go to; you have known what you should not.*

GENT.   *She has spoke what she should not, I am sure of that: heaven knows what she has known.*

LADY M.   Here's the smell of the blood still: all the perfumes of Arabia will not sweeten this little hand. Oh! oh! oh!

DOCTOR.   *What a sigh is there! The heart is sorely charged.*

GENT.   *I would not have such a heart in my bosom for the dignity of the whole body.*

DOCTOR.   *Well, well, well.*

GENT.   *Pray God it be, sir.*

DOCTOR.   *This disease is beyond my practice: yet I have known those which have walked in their sleep who have died holily in their beds.*

LADY M.   Wash your hands, put on your night-gown; look not so pale. I tell you yet again, Banquo's buried; he cannot come out on's grave.

DOCTOR.   *Even so?*

LADY M.   To bed, to bed: there's knocking at the gate. Come, come, come, come, give me your hand. What's done cannot be undone. To bed, to bed, to bed.   *(Exit.)*

—SHAKESPEARE

SELECTIONS FOR PRACTICE

1.   Once more; speak clearly, if you speak at all.
     Carve every word before you let it fall;
     Don't, like a lecturer or dramatic star,

Try over hard to roll the British "R";
Do put your accents in the proper spot;
Don't—let me beg you, don't say "How," for "What?"
And, when you stick on conversation's burrs,
Don't strew your pathway with those dreadful urs.
—OLIVER WENDELL HOLMES

2. We live in deeds, not words; in thoughts, not breaths;
In feelings, not in figures on a dial.
We should count time by heart-throbs. He most lives
Who thinks most, feels the noblest, acts the best.
—PHILIP JAMES BAILEY

3.   My good blade carves the casques of men,
               My tough lance thrusteth sure,
          My strength is as the strength of ten,
               Because my heart is pure.
          The shattering trumpet shrilleth high,
               The hard brands shiver on the steel,
          The splinter'd spear-shafts crack and fly,
               The horse and rider reel:
          They reel, they roll in clanging lists,
               And when the tide of combat stands,
          Perfume and flowers fall in showers,
               That lightly rain from ladies' hands.
—ALFRED, LORD TENNYSON

4. I am the very model of a modern Major General,
I've information vegetable, animal, and mineral;
I know the kings of England, and I quote the fights historical,
From Marathon to Waterloo, in order categorical;
I'm very well acquainted, too, with matters mathematical,
I understand equations, both the simple and quadratical,
About binomial theorem I'm teeming with a lot of news,
With many cheerful facts about the square of the hypotenuse.
—W. S. GILBERT

5.   HAMLET TO THE PLAYERS

Speak the Speech, I pray you, as I pronounced it to you, trip-
pingly on the tongue; but if you mouth it, as many of your
players do, I had as lief the town crier spoke my lines. Nor do
not saw the air too much with your hand, thus; but use all
gently: for in the very torrent, tempest, and, as I may say, whirl-
wind of your passion, you must acquire and beget a temperance
that may give it smoothness. Oh! it offends me to the soul to
hear a robustious periwig-pated fellow tear a passion to tatters,
to very rags, to split the ears of the groundlings, who, for the
most part, are capable of nothing but inexplicable dumb-shows
and noise: I would have such a fellow whipped for o'erdoing
Termagant; it out-herods Herod; pray you, avoid it.

Be not too tame, neither, but let your own discretion be your
tutor: suit the action to the word, the word to the action; with
this special observance, that you o'erstep not the modesty of
nature; for anything so overdone is from the purpose of playing, whose end, both at the first and now, was and is, to hold,
as 'twere, the mirror up to nature; to show virtue her own
feature, scorn her own image, and the very age and body of
the time his form and pressure. Now, this overdone, or come
tardy off, though it make the unskillful laugh, cannot but make
the judicious grieve; the censure of the which one must in your
allowance o'erweigh a whole theatre of others. Oh! there be
players that I have seen play, and heard others praise, and that
highly, not to speak it profanely, that neither having the accent
of Christians, nor the gait of Christian, pagan, nor man, have
so strutted and bellowed that I have thought some of nature's
journeymen had made men and not made them well, they
imitated humanity so abominably.

                                                   —SHAKESPEARE

6.   JABBERWOCKY

'Twas brillig, and the slithy toves
    Did gyre and gimble in the wabe;
All mimsy were the borogoves,
    And the mome raths outgrabe.

"Beware the Jabberwock, my son!
    The jaws that bite, the claws that catch!
Beware the Jubjub bird, and shun
    The frumious Bandersnatch!"

He took his vorpal sword in hand;
    Long time the manxome foe he sought—
So rested he by the Tumtum tree,
    And stood awhile in thought.

And as in uffish thought he stood,
    The Jabberwock, with eyes of flame,
Came whiffling through the tulgey wood,
    And burbled as it came!

One, two! One, two! And through and through
    The vorpal blade went snicker-snack!
He left it dead, and with its head
    He went galumphing back.

"And hast thou slain the Jabberwock?
    Come to my arms, my beamish boy!
O frabjous day! Callooh! Callay!"
    He chortled in his joy.

—Lewis Carroll

7.   IF YOU'RE ANXIOUS FOR TO SHINE[17]

If you're anxious for to shine in the high esthetic line as a
    man of culture rare,
You must get up all the germs of the transcendental terms, and
    plant them everywhere.
You must lie upon the daisies and discourse in novel phrases
    of your complicated state of mind,
The meaning doesn't matter if it's only idle chatter of a
    transcendental kind.
    And everyone will say,
    As you walk your mystic way,

[17] *The Complete Plays of Gilbert and Sullivan,* Modern Library edition,
Random House, Inc.

"If this young man expresses himself in terms too deep for *me*,
Why, what a very singularly deep young man this deep young
    man must be!"

Be eloquent in praise of the very dull old days which have
    long since passed away,
And convince 'em if you can, that the reign of good Queen
    Anne was Culture's palmiest day.
Of course, you will pooh-pooh whatever's fresh and new, and
    declare it's crude and mean;
For Art stopped short in the cultivated court of the Empress
    Josephine.
    And everyone will say,
    As you walk your mystic way,
"If that's not good enough for him which is good enough for
    me,
Why, what a very cultivated kind of youth this kind of youth
    must be!"

Then a sentimental passion of a vegetable fashion must excite
    your languid spleen,
An attachment *à la* Plato for a bashful young potato, or a
    not-too-French French bean!
Though the Philistines may jostle, you will rank as an apostle
    in the high esthetic band,
If you walk down Piccadilly, with a poppy or a lily in your
    medieval hand.
    And everyone will say,
    As you walk your flowery way,
"If he's content with a vegetable love which would certainly
    not suit *me*,
Why, what a particularly pure young man this pure young
    man must be!"

                          —W. S. GILBERT

8.   THE THROSTLE

"Summer is coming, summer is coming,
I know it, I know it, I know it.
Light again, leaf again, life again, love again!"
Yes, my wild little Poet.

Sing the new year in under the blue,
Last year you sang it as gladly.
"New, new, new, new!" Is it then *so* new
That you should carol so madly?

"Love again, song again, nest again, young again,"
Never a prophet so crazy!
And hardly a daisy as yet, little friend,
See, there is hardly a daisy.

"Here again, here, here, here, happy year!"
O warble unchidden, unbidden!
Summer is coming, is coming, my dear,
And all the winters are hidden.
                              —ALFRED, LORD TENNYSON

9.   LYING AWAKE[18]

When you're lying awake with a dismal headache, and repose
  is taboo'd by anxiety,
I conceive you may use any language you choose to indulge
  in, without impropriety;
For your brain is on fire—the bedclothes conspire of usual
  slumber to plunder you:
First your counterpane goes, and uncovers your toes, and your
  sheet slips demurely from under you;
Then the blanketing tickles—you feel like mixed pickles—
  so terribly sharp is the pricking,
And you're hot, and you're cross, and you tumble and toss
  till there's nothing 'twixt you and the ticking.
Then the bedclothes all creep to the ground in a heap, and
  you pick 'em all up in a tangle;
Next your pillow resigns and politely declines to remain at
  its usual angle!
Well, you get some repose in the form of a doze, with hot
  eye-balls and head ever aching,
But your slumbering teems with such horrible dreams that
  you'd very much better be waking.

                  .   .   .   .   .   .

18 *Ibid.*

You're a regular wreck, with a crick in your neck, and no
wonder you snore, for your head's on the floor, and you've
needles and pins from your soles to your shins, and your
flesh is a-creep, for your left leg's asleep, and you've cramp
in your toes, and a fly on your nose, and some fluff in your
lung, and a feverish tongue, and a thirst that's intense, and
a general sense that you haven't been sleeping in clover;
But the darkness has passed, and it's daylight at last, and the
night has been long—ditto ditto my song—and thank goodness they're both of them over!

—W. S. GILBERT

10.   PETER AND "SHE"
                              (A Student's Speech)

Last week after our talks, I was corrected on my enunciation,
so this week while in the process of trying to correct this bad
habit, I composed a little story of a boy and girl that I would
like to relate to you.

Once upon a time there lived in the San Fernando Valley
a boy by the name of Peter. Now Peter made his living by picking a peck of pickled peppers each day in the fields nearby.
However, during the day's work Peter always became quite
pickled himself.

One afternoon after picking his peck of pickled peppers and
becoming quite pickled, Peter wandered down to the beach of
Santa Monica, and here he met the girl in our story. Now for
the sake of simplicity let us call this girl "She." "She" sold sea
shells by the sea shore and by the continuous purchases by
Peter, the pickled pepper picker, from "She," who sold sea
shells by the sea shore, they became quite good friends.

As time went on this friendship blossomed into love, and
they were married and moved out to Peter's, the pickled pepper
picker's home in the valley where "She" got a job in the fields
picking pickled peppers.

Now every morning you see the two of them, "She," who
used to sell sea shells by the sea shore, and Peter the pickled
pepper picker, walking out to the fields to pick their peck of

pickled peppers, and every evening both of them pickled after a hard day of picking pickled peppers.

Now, fellow students, after you graduate and are seeking for a way of making your living, if some of you should chance to become pickled pepper pickers, please remember: while you are picking your daily peck of pickled peppers, don't become pickled, for there are already too many pickled people in this pickled old world today.

—RALPH McKENZIE

IX ✳ Articulation:
Pronouncing Words "Correctly"

Vowel Sounds Analyzed

To be sure of our pronunciation, accuracy on consonants is not enough. We need to know a number of things about vowels and diphthongs. Thus we should (1) know how the different vowels and diphthongs are made; (2) be able to hear fine shades of distinction between sounds; (3) be able to feel the difference kinesthetically in our articulatory organs; and (4) command a knowledge of the pronunciation symbols in the dictionary.

This chapter is designed to give help in these four respects. But before we begin the analysis of individual vowels and diphthongs, certain general principles deserve attention.

Standards of Pronunciation

The word *correctly* in the title of this chapter is put in quotation marks for a purpose—to indicate that the word must be qualified. One might perhaps refer to "proper" pronunciation, but *proper* has unfortunate implications; or "accurate," but *accurate* seems to apply more to the action of the articulatory organs than to the end result; or "acceptably," but that provokes the question, "Acceptable to whom?" The fact is that in our language there is no one standard of pronunciation which is "correct" to the exclusion of all other pronunciations; no one standard which is "proper," except to a comparatively few purists; no one standard which is "accurate" in the sense that it alone conforms to universal truth; no one standard which is "acceptable" to everyone. Each of these words may be used in one connection or another somewhere in this chapter, but each needs to be qualified and limited in its application. For example, when we say that a certain pronunciation is "acceptable," we mean that it is in good standing among persons of education and culture in our general area.

Even in England there are numerous standards of pronunciation—not just the difference between the speech of the Oxford graduate and the London cockney, but marked difference between the educated Londoner's speech and that of the educated citizen of Manchester or Leeds. Likewise in France, where the French Academy is exerting some autocracy in the direction of standardization, local differences still exist.

In the United States, in addition to many minor variations, there are three fairly well-defined standards: Eastern (frequently called New England), Southern, and General American (sometimes called Western).

Attempts have been made to standardize American pronunciation. Generally, those who advocate one standard point to the speech of the cultured New Englander (the Eastern) as the proper standard; and the fact that most of the early textbooks in phonetics were written either by Englishmen or by graduates of New England colleges has helped to advance the claims of those advocating the Eastern standard. But the great body of Americans in the Middle West and West, and even in parts of the East and South, insist that this is not the true American speech. And the weight of numbers (some 90 to 100 million) tends to support their contention. Also, the fact that three great influences on speech—talking pictures, radio, and television—lean definitely toward the General American, is working against the universal acceptance of the Eastern standard. It is true, of course, that the stage, still loyal to its English progenitor, clings more or less closely to an English, or at least an Eastern, standard. For that reason, students planning to make a career of the stage should become thoroughly conversant with Eastern pronunciation. This textbook, however, being written for the great body of average students, will use General American.

Much controversy has arisen over pronunciation, and differences of opinion have provided material for jibes and bantering. John Steinbeck, in *The Grapes of Wrath,* presents an amusing bit of conversation based upon this theme:

"I knowed you wasn't Oklahomy folks. You talk queer kinda— That ain't no blame, you understan'."
"Ever'body says words different," said Ivy. "Arkansas folks says 'em different, and Oklahomy folks says 'em different. And we seen a lady from Massachusetts, an' she said 'em differentest of all. Couldn' hardly make out what she was sayin'."

But sometimes the controversy grows bitter. In certain localities and among certain persons, to call attention to the differences is "fighting talk." Heywood Broun wrote, "A Georgian and a citizen of Massachusetts are set apart from each other not by vague recollections of the Civil War, but by the manner in which they tackle their consonants and vowels."[1]

It is not strange that some bitterness should be engendered. Few of us respond kindly to criticism, and fewer still can look on ridicule with equanimity. Manners, customs, clothes, and speech, if ours, are likely to appear to us as pretty much all right—at least we don't want them sneered at. And our pronunciation is closer to us, more intrinsically ours, than either customs or clothes. We guard it jealously from ridicule, and change it only with reluctance.

If it were conceivable that some dictator could wipe out all local differences and compel uniformity of pronunciation, it is doubtful whether he would be doing any service to American culture. To make the Southerner give up his soft modulation and slow drawl, to force the Westerner to relinquish all the in-

[1] Heywood Broun, *McCall's,* November, 1932.

dividualism of his vigorous speech, and to insist that the New Englander and the Middle Westerner compromise on their *r*'s and *a*'s would rob America of much of its color and one of its pleasantest heritages. It is doubtful if complete standardization of pronunciation would be any more tolerable to Americans than, say, complete standardization of dress.

But while too much standardization is undesirable, so likewise is too much variation. There is a band of variation beyond which individual differences may not go and still be considered cultured speech. None of the above discussion constitutes a valid argument either for slovenly pronunciation or for no standard at all. On the contrary, it is becoming increasingly important for every educated person to pronounce his words "acceptably" to the majority of cultured people. As we move further away from the pioneer stage of our national existence, more and more attention is paid to cultural values. Not only does social recognition frequently depend upon the careful use of words, but often business success is in a measure dependent upon it.

Everyone notices pronunciation. Even the uneducated are aware, often critically so, when words are pronounced in a manner to which they are not accustomed. And the educated are inclined to classify people in the social and intellectual scale by the way in which they pronounce words. The epitome of this attitude was expressed by Charles W. Eliot, the noted educator and long-time president of Harvard University, when he said, "I recognize but one mental acquisition as an essential part of the education of a lady or gentleman, namely, an accurate and refined use of the mother tongue." And the noted English author, Ruskin, went even further: "A false accent . . . is enough . . . to assign to a man a certain degree of inferior standing forever."

Possibly in some circles too much importance is attached to mere pronunciation; it becomes too convenient and too superficial a measuring stick for intellectual caliber. The fact remains, however, that mispronounced words are fearfully conspicuous and that educated people often consider pronunciation as the badge of culture. Consequently, it behooves everyone who desires to rate well with such people to see that his words are "correctly" pronounced.

Good Pronunciation

1. *Good pronunciation is not showy.* In general, that pronunciation is best which attracts least attention to itself. If a conversationalist, in recounting some thrilling or amusing anecdote, is greeted by such a remark as "My, what beautiful language you use," the language has been bad, because it has distracted the listener. In one respect language, pronunciation, and voice quality are alike. They should all be clear, pleasant, and *inconspicuous.* That pronunciation is best which has the least distractive elements, which gives least offense to cultured people, and—most important of all—which most effectively conveys thought and feeling.

2. *Good pronunciation is not overprecise.* Overniceness of pronunciation is as much to be avoided as carelessness. Labored precision is an offense to good taste. All must be done easily and naturally. The college president who puckers his lips meticulously and says "ev-e-ning" instead of "eve-ning" is pronouncing as improperly as the inebriate who says "shay" for "say."

3. *Good pronunciation is relatively free from local accent.* The late President Franklin D. Roosevelt showed wisdom in his pronunciation. While retaining some of the characteristics of Harvard speech, notably in his pronunciation of certain words such as "again," and in his broader *a's* and softer *r's,* still he tempered the extremes of local peculiarities so that few educated listeners in any part of the country took offense at his pronunciation.

In any nation-wide educational group, such as a meeting of the National Education Association, the speakers may disclose the identity of their homes by their speech, but peculiarities are seldom extreme. In cultured speech, rough edges are smoothed off and concessions are made. The Yankee twang, the extreme Southern drawl, and the Western "nosey" short *a's* are modified to conform to a cultured norm. This tendency is accelerated as the ears of every section are exposed to good models of speech via radio, movies, and television.

Possibly some day these forces, together with increased intersectional travel, will produce complete uniformity. The author, for one, hopes not.

CAUSES OF POOR PRONUNCIATION

Early Environment. Comparatively few of us have been reared in homes where good English was invariably spoken. To those who learned to pronounce words incorrectly in their youth, the habit clings tenaciously throughout the years; only by constant vigilance can these wrong pronunciations be overcome. Sometimes we know the correct form intellectually, but find it hard to practice what we know. Many of us who in childhood learned to say "chimley" for chimney, "mis-chie-vi-ous" for mischievous, or "bron-i-cal" for bronchial, find these mispronunciations slipping into our speech in unguarded moments, often to our great embarrassment. The person is as lucky as he is rare who has been reared in surroundings where words were always well pronounced. Like table manners, good pronunciation habits come easiest by means of almost unconscious observation and imitation.

Regional and Racial Influences. Another difficulty springs from regional peculiarities and racial backgrounds. The Texan and Oklahoman may say "daown" and "abaout." The New Englander may say "idear"; the Westerner, a nasalized "haf," "caf," and "laf," and so on.

Variation in Standards. Still another pronunciation difficulty arises from words for which there are two acceptable standards. In this class are such words as *either* ['aɪðɚ] or ['iðɚ], *neither* ['naɪðɚ] or ['niðɚ], *isolate* ['aɪsoleɪt] or ['ɪsoleɪt]. The best advice here is to employ the most common and accepted usage in your community. Good pronunciation is largely a matter of adapting oneself to the cultured element in the environment.

Acquiring Good Pronunciation Habits

Pronunciation difficulties can be overcome by care and attention, not attention only when the individual feels that his language is on exhibition before cultured people, but care at all times until right habits are fixed. As we have said repeatedly, good speech is a set of good habits so firmly established that they function in any and all situations.

For one who is desirous of establishing such habits the dictionary is indispensable. Too many voice and diction students seem not to realize this. In spite of the explanatory table in the front of most dictionaries, and the condensed pronunciation key at the bottom of every page, a surprising number of students lack any intimate knowledge of the meaning of these symbols.

To be sure, as was pointed out earlier, the dictionary has certain limitations in scientific analysis of speech sounds. Still it can be of enormous aid in acquainting us with what educated people are doing with any given sound. And, most important, for the majority of persons most of the time the dictionary is the only dependable pronunciation guide at hand.

In order to help you acquire something more than a passing acquaintance with the dictionary's system of diacritical marks and respellings, in the following analysis of each vowel or diphthong the dictionary pronunciation symbol is given along with the phonetic symbol.

The best advice that can be given you is: Get the dictionary habit. When you are not sure of a word, look it up. When you hear a word pronounced in some unaccustomed manner, look it up. When you encounter a word in your reading that you would like to add to your vocabulary, look it up. Have the dictionary always available. Learn the meaning of the pronunciation marks. *Use* the dictionary! Of course, it may be easier

to do what is commonly done, i.e., ask somebody how to pronounce the word; but the danger is that the person asked may
have no more exact knowledge than the questioner. The safe
rule is: Use the dictionary!

The Vowels

A vowel, as previously defined, is a speech sound in which
the outgoing breath stream meets practically no obstruction
from the articulatory organs. The distinctive nature of each
vowel is determined by the size, shape, and general nature (i.e.,
rigidity of the walls, size of the opening, etc.) of the resonance
chambers of the head and neck. This fact is easily demonstrated
as follows: If you begin uttering a vowel tone and on the
continuous tone change the size and shape of your mouth opening, you will note that the nature of the vowel changes. For
example, start with your lips pursed as for [u] as in *true* [tru],
then open them just a little, and the vowel will change to [o]
as in *old* [ould]; open them a little farther and the vowel will
change to [ɔ] as in *all* [ɔl], and so on. This change takes place
without affecting in the slightest the nature of the vocal cord
vibrations. Try it: [u-o-ɔ]. Reverse the procedure [ɔ-o-u].

The analysis of individual vowel sounds which follows will
show that instead of the five vowels traditionally recognized—
a, e, i, o, u—there are seventeen relatively "simple" or "pure"
vowels and six diphthongs. A "simple" or "pure" vowel is a
vowel sound in which the articulatory organs maintain a relatively fixed position during the uttering of the sound, as for
example the [i] sound in the word *eat* [it]. A diphthong on the
other hand, is a blend of two unlike vowels in the same syllable,
as for example the [au] sound in *now* [nau].

While it is recognized that minute differences (on-glides and
off-glides) occur that disturb the "purity" of the so-called
"simple" vowel sounds, for all practical purposes each may be
considered as one and only one sound.

Phoneme is a term sometimes used in connection with the study
of vowels. A phoneme is the name given to a group of very

closely related sounds—so closely related that to the ordinary ear they sound practically identical and are generally represented by the same symbol. The use of this word emphasizes the fact that no two persons make a given sound in exactly the same way, and also that the same person using the sound in different letter combinations—for example, [a] in *father* (['fɑðɚ) as contrasted with [ɑ] in *hearth* [hɑrθ]—will make the sound in a slightly different manner in the various combinations.

The seventeen single vowels follow.

THE SINGLE VOWELS

Phonetic Symbol	Diacritical Marking[2]	Key Word
[i]	ē	see [si]
[ɪ]	ĭ	pity ['pɪtɪ]
[e]	ā	rate [ret]
[ɛ]	ĕ	any ['ɛnɪ]
[æ]	ă	at [æt]
[a][3]	à	bath (baθ]
[u]	ōō	booth (buθ]
[ʊ]	ŏŏ	pull [pʊl]
[o]	ō	note [not]
[ɔ]	ô	jaw [dʒɔ]
[ɒ][4]	ŏ	stop [stɒp]
[ɑ]	ä	calm [kɑm]
[ɝ]	ûr	furcher ['fɝðɚ]
[ɜ][5]	ûr	further ['fɜðə]
[ɚ]	ər (ẽr)	ever ['ɛvɚ]
[ə]	ə	soda ['sodə]
[ʌ]	ŭ	above [ə'bʌv]

[2] Dictionaries differ in their systems of diacritical markings; in general the markings here follow those used in *The American College Dictionary* (ACD).

[3] Heard principally in Eastern speech; [a] is between [æ] and [ɑ].

[4] Heard chiefly in Eastern speech. In General American [o] is commonly used in place of [ɒ].

[5] Heard chiefly in parts of the East and South. Both [ɝ] and [ɜ] occur only in accented syllables; [ɚ] and [ə] occur only in unaccented syllables. (See discussion on p. 247 for further details.)

Vowel Diagram

Fig. 16 represents roughly the focal positions at which the different vowel sounds are formed, i.e., the point of greatest tension in the tongue. The lower line represents the lowest position of the tongue, and the upper line represents the roof of the mouth. The vowels at the left of the diagram are called *front vowels;* those at the right, *back vowels;* those near the top,

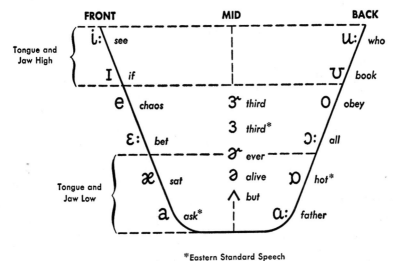

*Eastern Standard Speech

FIG. 16. The approximate focal positions at which the vowels are formed in the mouth.

high vowels; those near the bottom, *low vowels;* and those in the center *mid-vowels.* For example, [i] is a high, front vowel, and [ɔ] a low, back vowel.

THE VOWEL [i]

[i] is the vowel traditionally called long *e* (usual diacritical mark, *ē*). It is the highest of the front vowels. In forming this sound, the front of the tongue is tensed a little and raised close

to the hard palate behind the gum ridge. The slightly tensed lips are opened a little, and the sound issues through a comparatively narrow slit between them.

As the table on page 157 shows, [i] may be spelled in many different ways. Because [i] has the highest frequency of any of the vowel sounds, singing teachers use it a great deal to promote a bright, clear tone. Rightly used, it helps to produce the quality called brilliance.

FAULTS AND DANGERS

1. Since this vowel is formed with tongue and lips a little tense, there is danger that the tenseness may be extended to the muscles of the throat, thus interfering with a free, easy tone. It is important while making this sound to practice for relaxed throat to insure free swing of the vocal cords. Persons prone to talk "down in their throats" in thick, muffled tones should work with various combinations of [i].

2. In common with the other vowels which are prolonged (called long vowels), there is danger of adding what are known as on-glides or off-glides to [i]; these tend to destroy the purity and stability of the vowel. Thus, *he* [hi] may become [hɪi] (on-glide), or [hɪə] (off-glide).

EXERCISES

1. Repeat the following words over and over:

Initial		Medial		Final	
eel	Egypt	beat	steel	see	knee
each	Easter	keen	street	bee	spree
equal	eager	peel	treat	tree	key
ego	edict	deal	complete	flea	fee
easy	Edith	conceal	obese	agree	pea

2. Enunciate the following sentences clearly:

1. The beat of the hammer on the steel displeased the people in the street.

2. Easter would not be complete without Edith's being here to eat with me.

3. She tried to conceal her obesity.

4. Eva agreed to keep the key to the green cottage.

5. Maureen and Lee were eager to defeat Marie and me.

3. Repeat rapidly, in either singing or speaking tone, the syllable [mi-mi-mi-mi-mi]. Repeat this exercise again and again on various pitch levels, working for a bright, clear tone.

4. Watch your lips and tongue in a mirror as you speak the following pairs of words:

he—heed	tea—seat	beat—defeat
she—beat	sea—meat	creep—relief
be—feet	eat—repeat	leap—receive

5. In reading the following lines, form the [i] sound crisply and firmly, and with a pleasing resonance which seems to come from the front part of the mouth. By touching the fingers lightly to the nostrils or lips, you should be able to feel the vibration:

1. My Mary's asleep by thy murmuring stream,
    Flow gently, sweet Afton, disturb not her dream.

2. Sand-strewn caverns, cool and deep,
    Where the winds are all asleep;
    Where the spent lights quiver and gleam;
    Where the salt weed sways in the stream;
    Where the sea-beasts, ranged all round,
    Feed in the ooze of their pasture ground.

3. Over the ripening peach
    Buzzes the bee,
    Splash on the billowy beach
    Tumbles the sea.
    But the peach
    And the beach
    They are each
    Nothing to me.

4.   A rollicking band of pirates we,
                Who, tired of tossing on the sea,
                Are trying our hand at burglaree,
                With weapons grim and gory.

THE VOWEL [ɪ]

[ɪ] is commonly called short *i* (diacritical mark, ĭ). As indicated in the list of phonetic symbols (p. 157), it may be spelled in a variety of ways. In forming this vowel both tongue and lips are slightly more relaxed, the tongue is a little lower in the mouth, and the lips a little farther apart than for [i]. Also, the focal point of resonance is a bit farther back in the mouth, although [ɪ] is still definitely a *front vowel*. It is shorter in duration than [i].

FAULTS AND DANGERS

1. Persons who drawl their words are prone to give this sound an off-glide so that words like *it* [ɪt], *hit* [hɪt], and *fit* [fɪt] become [ɪət], [hɪət], [fɪət].

2. People who form their words too far back in the mouth frequently substitute [ə] for [ɪ], so that words like *smallest* ['smɔlɪst], *shortest* ['ʃɔrtɪst], *tallest* ['tɔlɪst], *biggest* ['bɪgɪst], *forfeit* ['fɔrfɪt], and *biscuit* ['bɪskɪt] sound more like ['smɔləst], ['ʃɔrtəst], ['tɔləst], ['bɪgəst], ['fɔrfət], ['bɪskət]. Notice that in all these examples the shift from [ɪ] to [ə] occurs in unstressed syllables; this is where the danger is most likely to occur, and therefore where it needs to be watched most closely.

3. Foreigners learning English are likely to substitute [i] for [ɪ], so that *it* sounds more like *eat* [it], etc. This fault is especially noticeable where the native language has no [ɪ] sound, as in French.

4. Some persons, striving to avoid the above faults and other similar ones, become overprecise and incorrectly employ a spelling pronunciation. Thus words like *goodness* ['gʊdnɪs], *badness* ['bædnɪs], *English* ['ɪŋglɪʃ], *been* [bɪn], *breeches*

['brɪtʃɪz], and *women* ['wɪmɪn] are pronounced as they are spelled, and consequently are said incorrectly according to accepted usage. There are many words in this class. The dictionary should be consulted to determine which words are pronounced as they are spelled and which are not. Here again the fault is most likely to occur in unstressed syllables.

EXERCISES

1. Repeat the following words over and over:

Initial		Medial		Final	
it	into	bit	pretty	city	dizzy
elapse	enigma	crib	familiar	family	Mary
efface	expend	admit	inhibition	ability	canopy
electron	expel	exit	responsible	apology	jalopy
Elyria	exhibit	knit	kinesthetic	any	elegy

2. Enunciate the following sentences clearly:

1. The responsibility for splitting the electron fell upon the university physicists.
2. The exhibition in the city was pretty, but was admittedly a fiasco.
3. Don't give any apologies for Mr. Whipple; his activities are invariably enigmatic.
4. The illiterate one in the family made millions as a financier.
5. Milly administered pills to Billy and William when they were ill.

3. Distinguish clearly between the [ɪ] and [i] sounds in the following pairs of words:

bit—beet	sin—seen
deem—dim	bean—bin
fit—feet	did—deed
peak—pick	reed—rid
pill—peal	hit—heat
seep—sip	meat—mit

4. Work for ease and sureness in distinguishing between [ɪ] and [i] in the following sentences:

1. The sheep were driven aboard the ship.
2. When the tide came in, the sea rose to our hips.
3. In the midst of the mist, we hit the reef.
4. I think it is queer to have tea at three.
5. We will begin by singing sonnet sixteen.

5. Work for good [ɪ] sounds in the following lines:

1.
>   Amidst the singing of the birds,
>   Amidst the buzzing of the bees.

2.
>   A little learning is a dangerous thing;
>   Drink deep, or taste not the Pierian spring.

3.
>   The Moving Finger writes; and having writ
>   Moves on: nor all your Piety nor Wit
>   Shall lure it back to cancel half a Line,
>   Nor all your Tears wash out a Word of it.

4.
>   Gaily tripping,
>   Lightly skipping,
>   Flock the maidens to the shipping.
>   Flags and guns and pennants dipping,
>   All the ladies love the shipping.

THE VOWEL [e] ([eɪ])

Because of the close relationship between the vowel [e] and the diphthong [eɪ], these two are considered together. The table on page 157 shows the many ways this sound may be spelled. This is the sound ordinarily called long *a* (diacritical mark, *ā*). In forming it, the mouth is open a little wider, and the tongue is a little flatter and more relaxed on the floor of the mouth than tor [ɪ]. If during its emission the mouth and tongue remain in one position, the sound is the single vowel [e]; but if these organs gradually change to the position for [ɪ], it becomes the diphthong [eɪ].

Some authorities do not list this sound as a single vowel at all, but treat it only as a diphthong. Most phoneticians, however, consider it to be both a vowel and a diphthong, depending upon various factors considered below.

There are, to be sure, great differences in the way this sound is made by different speakers, and this accounts in part for the disagreement among students of phonetics as to its classification. Therefore, in our analysis we speak only in general terms, allowing for normal variations in pronunciation.

In general, we may say that slow speakers are more likely to diphthongize the sound than are rapid speakers. The act of prolonging the sound [e] tends to give it an off-glide to the vowel [ɪ] thus creating the diphthong [eɪ]. Observe in a mirror the action of your mouth and tongue as you prolong the single vowel [e]. Note the strong tendency for the tongue to rise slightly and the lips to come a bit closer together.

In general, when used in stressed syllables [e] has a strong tendency to become a diphthong, as in *able* ['eɪbl̩], *fable* ['feɪbl̩], etc. Conversely, in unstressed syllables (particularly among rapid speakers) it is likely to be a single vowel, as in the unstressed syllable of *placate* ['pleɪket] and *waylay* [we'leɪ].

As a rule, when it occurs at the end of a word it is diphthongized, as in *may* [meɪ], *play* [pleɪ], *say* [seɪ], etc. Similarly when it comes before a voiced consonant it is likely to be diphthongized, as in *cable* ['keɪbl̩], *cradle* ['kreɪdl̩], *pain* [peɪn]. Conversely, before unvoiced consonants (again, especially in the case of rapid speakers) it is likely to be a single vowel, as in *cake* [kek], *chafe* [tʃef], *capable* ['kepəbl̩].

From the above analysis it will be observed that in most cases, in the speech of the majority of people, this sound is more often a diphthong than a single vowel.

FAULTS AND DANGERS

For most persons, no special difficulties are associated with the formation of the single vowel [e]. The following exercises are provided so that you may be sure that you are producing it correctly, and so that you may recognize the difference between the single vowel and the diphthong in your own speaking.

In forming the diphthong [eɪ] one danger deserves special attention. If drawled too much, the diphthong [eɪ] may become the triphthong [eɪə]. Such undesirable pronunciation may—and sometimes does—occur in a sentence like *She was so pale* [peɪəl] *I was afraid she might faint* [feɪənt].

EXERCISES

1. The words in this group often are pronounced with the single vowel, especially if they occur in an unstressed position in the sentence. Analyze them to find out why.

Initial	Medial
ate	hate
ape	faith
ache	freight
ace	station

2. The words in this group are likely to be pronounced as diphthongs. Why? Contrast them with the words above by saying one of those words, then one of the following words, thus: ate . . . aim, ape . . . ale, etc.

Initial	Medial	Final
aim	came	slay
ale	gave	pray
aid	same	portray
age	heinous	display

3. In working with the following words, be sure that the diphthong [eɪ] does not become the triphthong [eɪə].

say	maiden	maybe
claim	alien	angel
same	grade	fame
vain	blame	raindrop

4. Enunciate the following sentences clearly:

1. All day the rain maintained its same lame gait.
2. The capable mate blamed the sailor for aiding the alien to escape.

3. The nation's claim to fame lay in maintaining its great pace.
4. The playwright's "angel" aided the failing play to stay on Broadway.
5. The name of the maid who aided with the catering may be obtained by staying till after the fete.

5. Work on the following lines of poetry:

1.   Gather ye rosebuds while ye may,
          Old time is still aflying;
      And that same flower that blooms today,
          Tomorrow will be dying.

2.   For he who fights and runs away
       May live to fight another day;
       But he who is in battle slain
       Can never rise and fight again.[6]

3.   The glories of our blood and state
         Are shadows, not substantial things;
      There is no armor against fate;
         Death lays his icy hand on kings.

4.   Ere he alighted at Netherby gate,
       The bride had consented, the gallant came late. . . .
       So stately his form, and so lovely her face,
       That never a hall such a galliard did grace.

THE VOWEL [ɛ]

[ɛ] is the vowel called short *e* (diacritical mark, ĕ). Its varied spellings are shown in the chart on page 157.

In forming [ɛ] the front of the tongue is lower than for [e], and the mouth somewhat wider open; but resonance is still focused in the forward part of the mouth. Hence the vowel is considered a front vowel.

---

[6] Note that the rhyme calls for the British pronunciation of *again* [ə'gein].

Faults and Dangers

1. Careless speakers sometimes substitute [ɪ] for [ɛ], so that words like *get* [gɛt], *pen* [pɛn], and *hen* [hɛn] become [gɪt], [pɪn], [hɪn].

2. The substitution may be [e], so that words like *egg* [ɛg] and *beg* [bɛg] become [eɪg] and [beɪg].

3. Speakers who habitually drawl their words are prone to diphthongize this sound, changing [ɛ] to [ɛə]. Thus words like *said* [sɛd], *met* [mɛt], and *head* [hɛd] become [sɛəd], [mɛət] and [hɛəd].

EXERCISES

1. Repeat the following words over and over:

Initial		Medial	
ebb	exit	help	together
end	exude	whelp	forever
elk	exquisite	center	betting
edge	edible	never	penny
enter	engine	renter	whetting

2. Enunciate the following sentences clearly:

1. Let us not forget that our friends are our best investment.
2. Many forget to emphasize the direction of the breath stream in therapy for cleft palate speech.
3. The knell of the bell recalled unpleasant memories to the festive men.
4. The fretful guest then asked a question about the genuine feather bed.
5. He tested Fred with questions relative to Heaven and Hell.

3. Distinguish carefully between the words in the following groups:

> pen—pin—peek
> bet—bit—beet
> red—rid—reed
> set—sit—seat
> neck—nick—neat

4. Take care not to diphthongize the [ɛ] sound in the following words:

egg	led	pleasure
leg	fed	measure
beg	head	treasure
bell	there	twelve
fell	care	shelve

5. Work for ease and sureness in reading the following lines:

1.　　　The bell invites me.
　　　　Hear it not, Duncan, for it is a knell
　　　　That summons thee to heaven or to hell.

2.　　　Oh, young Lochinvar is come out of the west:
　　　　Through all the wide border his steed is the best.

3.　　　　　I do not love thee, Doctor Fell,
　　　　　The reason why I cannot tell;
　　　　　But this alone I know full well,
　　　　　I do not love thee, Dr. Fell.

THE VOWEL [æ]

[æ] is the symbol for the vowel called short *a* (diacritical mark, ă), as in *at*. To form it the front of the tongue is slightly elevated, although a little lower than for [ɛ]. Also the mouth is a little wider open than for [ɛ]. It is a low front vowel.

FAULTS AND DANGERS

1. Among careless speakers, substitutions for [æ] are common. Some of the more frequent substitutions are [ɛ], [ʌ], and [ɪ]. Thus, for example, *gather* ['gæðɚ] becomes ['gɛðɚ], *rather* ['ræðɚ] becomes ['rʌðɚ], and *can* [kæn] becomes [kɪn].

2. Nasalization of this sound is common, so that words like *ask* [æsk], *half* [hæf], *bath* [bæθ], *bag* [bæg], *lad* [læd], etc., take on a sharp nasal quality which is unpleasant to the ears of most persons. This fault is especially common in words in which the nasal consonants precede or follow the [æ], as in *can* [kæn], *man* [mæn], etc.

3. Often, in trying to avoid the above fault, poeple who are careful in their speech but untrained in phonetics go to the opposite extreme. They "broaden" their [æ] sounds into [ɒ]⁷ or [ɑ]. Thus, for example, *and* [ænd] *becomes* [ɒnd] and *hand* becomes [hɑnd]. This substitution is likely to sound affected. It is far wiser to learn to make the [æ] sound as it should be made, i.e., with the throat and jaw free and the soft palate raised.

EXERCISES

1. Repeat the following words over and over:

Initial		Medial	
at	abduct	ham	patter
add	angle	rang	brass
act	aspirin	jam	mantle
actor	attribute **(n.)**	fan	manner
atom	asterisk	mat	fraternize

2. Enunciate the following sentences clearly:

1. The ham actor had a hankering to play Falstaff.
2. Jams, yams, and hams are standard foods throughout the land.
3. The sand on the bank of the river was damp, and camping was hazardous.
4. The sacrilegious blasphemy of the crass blacksmith shattered dad's apathy.
5. The damsel was glad that the handsome young man asked for her hand.

3. Distinguish between the vowel sounds in the following word groups:

axe—egg—it	sat—set—sit
big—beg—bag	pit—pet—pat
bat—bet—bit	pan—pen—pin
mit—met—mat	dint—dense—dance

⁷ See pp. 236 and 234 for analysis of these vowels.

4. Repeat the following lines at your normal speaking rate, listening carefully for a clear distinction between [æ] and related vowel sounds.

   1. Nancy had a tame panda.
   2. Anna ate a ripe banana.
   3. Angus wrangles cattle on a famous ranch.
   4. Alfred tapped the glass with his cane.

5. Avoid diphthongizing the [æ] sound in the following lines:

   1. A black cat sat on the fence.
   2. They advanced through the pass.
   3. He ran from the tavern with his hat in his hand.
   4. The lad thanked his dad for the candy.

6. To avoid unpleasant nasality in the following words, articulate the [æ] sound well forward in the mouth, and keep the throat and jaw muscles relaxed:

ban	man	gnat	manna
can	mat	nab	banana
ran	mash	nag	manner
fan	mangle	nap	tanner

7. Work on the following verses:

   1.   His hair is crisp, and black, and long,
           His face is like the tan;
           His brow is wet with honest sweat,
           He earns whate'er he can.

   2.   Can storied urn or animated bust,
           Back to its mansion call the fleeting breath?
           Can honour's voice provoke the silent dust,
           Or flatt'ry soothe the dull cold ear of death?

THE VOWEL [a]

[a] (diacritical mark, *à*) occurs chiefly in Eastern Standard speech. It is formed just slightly farther back in the mouth, the tongue is slightly lower, and the mouth slightly wider open

than for [æ]. It lies midway between [æ] and [ɑ], the next vowel to be discussed.

Many phonetic authorities, including *The American College Dictionary,* do not recognize [a] as a separate vowel, except as it appears as the first element of the diphthongs [aɪ] and [aʊ]. They consider that this sound belongs either to the phoneme [æ] or to [ɑ], depending upon individual usage.

Because of its extremely limited use in General American speech, little more need be said about this sound, except the warnings which follow.

FAULTS AND DANGERS

1. For the average person it probably is wiser to make a clear distinction between [æ] words and [ɑ] words, and not try to draw the [a] line too fine.

2. For the limited number of people who endeavor to add the [a] sound to their speech, two special observations are in order: (a.) A reasonable degree of consistency is necessary. If you use [a] in *ask, grass, calf, laugh, bath,* and *craft,* you should not use [æ] in *France, advance, demand,* etc. (b.) It is a little ridiculous for a person to use the [a] sound (or even occasionally the broader [ɑ] sound) in words which are definitely in the [æ] phoneme, such as *and, hand, can, at, catch, flat, attic,* etc.

THE VOWEL [ɑ]

[ɑ] is the vowel sound in words like *palm* [pɑm], *calm* [kɑm], *arm* [ɑrm], etc. Its diacritical mark is ä. In forming this sound the tongue is flat and relaxed on the floor of the mouth, except for a very slight arching at the back; the lips are quite far apart and not rounded; the jaw is free from tension and the mouth is well opened. This vowel is the lowest of the back vowels.

FAULTS AND DANGERS

[ɑ] is one of the most easily made sounds in our language; it should present no special problems for the person who is able and willing to relax his throat and jaw and open his mouth. Because it is a relaxed, easy sound, it is greatly favored as a voice exercise by singing teachers. But if there is undue tension in the back part of the tongue, or if the lips are rounded, there is a tendency to substitute [ɔ] for [ɑ], thus making a word like *calm* [kɑm] sound more like [kɔm].[8]

EXERCISES

1. Repeat the following words over and over:

Initial		Medial		Final	
arm	argue	hearth	qualm	ah	pah
ark	ardent	cartoon	quality	rah	baa
alms	almond	father	rajah	shah	ma
army	artistic	garment	palmist	haha	yah
arbor	amen	bargain	balmy	fa	la

2. Enunciate the following sentences clearly:

1. The army bombarded the yards just before the Armistice.
2. Mama kept her almond tarts in a large jar.
3. The shepherd guarded his flock[9] from harm.
4. The parson's knowledge[9] of the Psalms was marvelous.
5. The artist argued that it would be stark melodrama for him to plead for alms.

3. To help obtain a kinesthetic sense of [ɑ], say these three vowel sounds repeatedly: [æ—ɑ—ɔ]. Reverse them [ɔ—ɑ—æ].

4. Use [æ], [ɑ], and [ɔ] in the following word groups:

at—art—ought
hat—ha—haw
fast—farm—forest
calf—calm—coffee
fat—father—fought
bat—balm—Boston

[8] Several exercises for achieving the desired relaxation of throat and jaw muscles to form [ɑ] will be found in Chapter IV.

[9] Note that *The American College Dictionary* gives [ɒ] as the preferred pronunciation for *flock* and *knowledge*; other authorities class these as [ɑ] words.

cat—calm—cost
damp—dark—daughter
lamb—lama—laundry
sand—psalm—saunter

5. Work on the following selections:

1.   There are maidens in Scotland more lovely by far,
       That would gladly be wed to the young Lochinvar.

2.   My spirit beats her mortal bars,
            As down dark tides the glory slides,
            And, star-like, mingles with the stars.

3.   To me more dear, congenial to my heart,
            One native charm than all the gloss of art.

4.   Twilight and evening bell,
            And after that the dark!
            And may there be no sadness of farewell
            When I embark.

THE VOWEL [ɒ]

[ɒ] is the vowel sound sometimes heard in words like *wander* ['wɒndɚ], *box* [bɒks], and *John* [dʒɒn]. Its diacritical mark is ŏ. It is spelled *a* and *o*, as in the above words; it may also be spelled *au* as in *laurel* and *aw* as in *Lawrence* (second dictionary pronunciations in both cases). In forming this sound the tongue is nearly flat in the mouth, but the back of it is raised slightly. The mouth is a little less rounded and the lips a little less tense than for [ɔ]. [ɒ] is a shorter, "crisper" sound than [ɔ]. As will be seen from the vowel diagram on page 221, it lies midway between [ɔ] and [ɑ].

This sound is heard more often in Eastern and Southern speech than in General American. Some authorities accord it no definite status in General American, holding that the normal variation between the two phonemes [ɔ] and [ɑ] is adequate. Other authorities, however, including *The American College Dictionary,* believe that [ɒ] not only deserves separate classifica-

tion but is the preferred pronunciation in many words, such
as the following:

Initial		Medial	
of	ocular	job	watch
on	oligarchy	hot	profit
odd	ominous	got	hospital
olive	oscillate	God	college
osprey	osculate	golf	column
omelet	Odyssey	flop	wander
Oliver	operatic	stop	progress
occupy	opposite	wash	prodigy

Since [ɒ] has something of an indefinite status throughout
much of our country, this textbook will not insist on adherence
to any one standard for the sound. However, if you live in a
section of the country where careful speakers give the sound
separate entity, you will do well to adjust your own speech to
the approved practice.

THE VOWEL [u] ([ju])

Because of the close relationship between the vowel [u] and
the consonant-vowel combination [ju],[10] these two are treated
together here. The single vowel [u] (diacritical mark, o͞o) is
found in the word *too* [tu]. Its varied spellings are shown on
the chart on page 157. As will be seen by glancing at the vowel
diagram on page 221, it is the highest of the back vowels. To
form it, the back of the tongue is raised close to the soft palate
and the slightly protruded lips are rounded into a small tense
circle.

The combined sound [ju] (diacritical mark, ū) is commonly

[10] It is not uncommon to see this consonant-vowel combination (or *vowel glide,*
as it is sometimes called) written phonetically as [ɪu] instead of [ju]. This difference need cause no confusion for the beginning diction student. The difference
between the two sounds is not great; in fact, in connected speech it is difficult to
distinguish between them. The [ɪu] variant may be used in the middle or at the
end of words; it is never used at the beginning. On the other hand, [ju] may be
used at the beginning, middle, or end.

known as long *u*, as found in the word *you* [ju]. This combined sound is made by gliding quickly from the consonant [j] (or the vowel [ɪ]) to the vowel [u] in the same syllable; this is the reason for calling it a *consonant-vowel glide* (or simply a *vowel glide* in the case of [ɪu]).

FAULTS AND DANGERS

1. In common with most of the other vowels, there is danger of drawing out the vowel [u] into the diphthong [uə], as in words like *croon* ['kruən], etc.; and of drawing the combined sound [ju] out into a sound resembling a triphthong [juə], possibly in such a sentence as *It's no use* [Its noʊ juəs].

2. Persons with lazy speech habits, and particularly people with lazy facial muscles, are likely to round their lips insufficiently, so that the vowel [u] sounds more like [ʊ], to be discussed next. Thus words like *spoon* [spun] and *soon* [sun] are likely to become [spʊn] and [sʊn].

3. For the average student, the greatest difficulty in relation to [u] and [ju] is when to use one and when to use the other. Particularly in words like *student*, *Tuesday*, *new*, and *tune*, he is sometimes in a quandary as to whether he should use [ju] or whether he may safely rely on [u], as the majority of Americans do. Although no useful purpose would be served in a beginning textbook by a detailed discussion of this somewhat controversial subject, a few generally accepted phonetic principles may help to clear up the confusion.

a. In general, the student may choose between [u] and [ju] when the sound follows [t], [d], and [n], in such words as *student* ['stjudn̩t], *duty* ['djutɪ], *new* [nju].

b. In general, when the sound follows [r], [s], [tʃ], and [l], it is pronounced [u]. The reasonableness of this principle becomes apparent when we note the difficulty of trying to pronounce [ju] in such words as *crew* [kru], *shoot* [ʃut], *choose* [tʃuz], and *flute* [flut].

c. In general, after [p], [b], [m], [f], [v], and [k], the sound is pronounced [ju], as in *pupil* ['pjupəl], *beauty* ['bjutı], *music* ['mjusɪk], *fuel* ['fjuəl], *view* [vju], and *cute* [kjut]. This rule, however, does not hold when the [u] sound is *spelled ou*, as in *pouf, boudoir, mousse, foulard.*

EXERCISES

1. Pronounce the following [u] words:

Initial		Medial		Final	
ooze	oubliette	rude	brood	blue	Sioux
oozy	ouzel	moon	group	shoe	through
oolong	Uhlan	loon	plume	threw	eschew
oorali	ulema	move	luminous	true	hoodoo
Ubangi	ulu	whose	trousseau	brew	kangaroo

2. Pronounce the following [ju] words:

Initial		Medial		Final	
U-boat	unite	mute	spume	cue	debut
utopian	unique	pupil	mule	hue	review
union	utility	pewter	futile	skew	imbue
eulogy	useless	amuse	putrid	mew	askew
ukulele	usury	mutation	immune	view	miscue

3. Take special care in distinguishing between the following pairs of words:

ooze—use	beauty—booty
too—few	buttes—boots
ruse—abuse	ewe—coo
snooze—accuse	dispute—troop
choose—refuse	youth—tooth
woo—view	

4. With respect to the following words, opinions and customs differ. Make your choice, based upon observation of the speech of educated persons with whom you associate; then try to maintain a reasonable degree of consistency.

new	student	multitude	introduce
due	assume	stupendous	tumult
tune	Tuesday	numerous	deuce
stupid	adieu	opportunity	neutral

5. Enunciate clearly the following sentences containing [u] words:

1. It is rumored that the Sioux are moving their troops at noon.
2. The fool's buffoonery ended when his spoon overthrew his soup.
3. The rooster was rudely crowing at noon.
4. The superstitious booby's belief in spooks was lampooned at school.
5. Lou's tooth was so loose that she couldn't eat her food.

6. Enunciate clearly the following sentences containing [ju] words:

1. Youth and beauty are lovely to view, but last only a few years.
2. Matthew was proud of his culinary acumen.
3. Our puny world is mutilated by futile disputes.
4. "Cute" pupils are not in good repute.
5. He called upon the muse of music to amuse us.

7. Enunciate clearly the following sentences containing [u] or [ju], but calling for consistency:

1. Please introduce me when you have the opportunity.
2. Don't be a stupid nuisance.
3. The tumult aroused the multitude.
4. The tuba can do things with tunes that the flute can't do.
5. Lucy seemed to deem it her duty to tell everything to Sue.

8. Practice the following selections:

1.
> Death will come when thou art dead,
>> Soon, too soon––
> Sleep will come when thou art fled;
> Of neither would I ask the boon
> I ask of thee, beloved Night—
> Swift be thine approaching flight,
>> Come soon, soon!

2.   We sail the ocean blue,
            And our saucy ship's a beauty;
            We're sober men and true,
            And attentive to our duty.

THE VOWEL [ʊ]

[ʊ] is the vowel sound found in the word *put* [pʊt] (diacritical mark, ŏŏ). In making this sound the lips are slightly less rounded and slightly less tense than in forming [u]. The back of the tongue is a bit lower in the mouth, though [ʊ] is also a high back vowel.

FAULTS AND DANGERS

1. The greatest danger with this vowel is in substituting it for [u], as just discussed. The exercises below will help to make this substitution clear. The corrective for most persons lies in cultivating flexible lips and tongue, and in practicing to distinguish clearly between the two sounds.

There is considerable difference of opinion regarding the preferred pronunciation of the following words. *The American College Dictionary*, for example, allows both sounds but prefers [u] for the words in the first column, and [ʊ] for those in the second.

root	hoop
roof	hoof
room	hooves
coop	soot
broom	bosom

2. Another fault is in weakening [ʊ] to [ʌ], as in the word *took* [tʊk], making it [tʌk]. This fault also occurs in such words as *should* [ˈʃʊd] and *could* [kʊd], making them [ˈʃəd] and [ˈkəd] when they should not be in a weak form, as in the sentence *Well, if you did that you SHOULD be ashamed* [. . . ju ʃəd bi . . . etc.].

EXERCISES

1. Pronounce the following [ʊ] words. This sound practically always occurs in the medial position.

Medial

book	look	stood	would	pull	wool
took	rook	cook	puss	bush	crook
forsook	shook	push	sugar	wooden	pudding
bull	foot	hook	could	bullet	fulfill
pullet	wood	should	put	Pullman	Buddha

2. Make a clear distinction between [ʊ] and [u] in the following paired words.

book—boot	wooed—would
look—loot	stool—stood
hook—hoot	crude—crook
shook—shoot	brood—brook
butcher—blucher	pooling—pulling

3. The following sentences contain both [ʊ] words and [u] words. Enunciate them clearly, and be sure that you make the distinction between the two sounds.

   1. Soon, soon, too soon!
   2. Some men seek good looks, others seek good cooks.
   3. The brook glimmered in the moonlight.
   4. She said she did not choose to cook the prunes.
   5. I understood that she took her poodle with her on her cruise.
   6. Cooper should have put the pullet in the coop.
   7. The cook made sugar cookies and pudding.
   8. She used worsted wool in making a hooked rug for her room.
   9. The woman knew that she was hoodwinked when she discovered that the Buddha was made of wood.
   10. The preacher took the Good Book from the pulpit and stood silently.

4. Practice the following selections:

   1.   No solemn sanctimonious face I pull.

   2.   My only books were women's looks.

3.   There is no friend so faithful as a good book,
        There is no worse robber than a bad book.

4.   "How," cried the Mayor, "d'ye think I'll brook
        Being worse treated than a cook?"

THE VOWEL [o] ([ou])

The vowel [o] and the diphthong [ou] will be treated together at this time. Both of these sounds are traditionally
referred to as long *o*, and the diacritical mark for both is ō.
Although this sound may be a single vowel, it is far more likely
in American speech to be diphthongized. As a simple vowel it
appears primarily in unaccented syllables, as in *obey* [o′beɪ],
hotel [ho′tɛl], *omit* [o′mɪt], and *rotund* [ro′tʌnd]; also in certain
accented syllables, particularly when it is followed by an unvoiced consonant, as in *ocean* [′oʃən] and motive [′motɪv].
When it occurs as a diphthong—this is far more common—it
forms a glide with [u], as in *go* [gou], *hoe* [hou], loath [louθ],
etc.

The simple vowel [o] is made by rounding the lips considerably more than for [u]. The lips also, as well as the blade of the
tongue, are somewhat more tense than in [u]. But the chief
point of distinction of the [o] is the definite rounding of the
lips into a circle, as suggested by the shape of the printed
symbol. It is a back vowel. The diphthong [ou] is formed by
gliding quickly from [o] to [u] in one continuous sound in the
same syllable.

Since [o] and [ou] are, like Shakespeare's justice, "in fair
round belly," they are much favored by poets and voice teachers.
In the exercises below you will find selections which help to
cultivate the fair round tones desired.

Faults and Dangers

1. There is no precise rule of procedure relative to the desirable degree of diphthongization of these two sounds. Variation
is normal and natural. The slow speaker inevitably will diph-

thongize them more than the rapid speaker. And such variation is not to be condemned, so long as it stays within the bounds of normalcy. However, as with [e, eɪ] and [u], [ju], the common practice is to use the diphthong [oʊ] in accented syllables and at the end of words, while in unaccented syllables and in accented syllables before unvoiced consonants it is often pronounced as a simple vowel [o].

2. If drawled too much this sound may become the triphthong [oʊə] as in the sentence *The poor dog was so old* [oʊəld] *his poor teeth couldn't hold* [hoʊəld] *the bone* [boʊən].

EXERCISES

1. Repeat the following words over and over:

Initial		Medial		Final	
old	opiate	soap	pony	low	pillow
oak	opaque	toad	poetic	grow	yellow
ode	O'Toole	road	lower	snow	mellow
obey	O'Reilly	hope	folder	cocoa	bureau
opal	O'Shanihan	shoal	boulder	hollow	potato

2. Enunciate the following sentences clearly:

1. "So long, old friend, so long"; he spoke emotionally.
2. The low tones of the oboe told the story in melody.
3. Most people know that Poe's poetry has moments of fine lyric quality.
4. The hobo's motto was "Follow the open road."
5. The boat came home so heavily loaded with potatoes and oats that it could scarcely keep afloat.

3. Practice the following selections:

1.   I know a bank where the wild thyme blows,
        Where oxlips and the nodding violet grows.

2.   A song to the oak, the brave old oak,
        Who hath ruled in the greenwood long.

3.   Now gold hath sway, we all obey,
        And a ruthless king is he.

4.   This hand, to tyrants ever sworn the foe,
            For freedom only deals the deadly blow.

5.   . . . If I should chance to fall below
            Demosthenes or Cicero,
            Don't view me with a critic's eye,
            But pass my imperfections by.
            Large streams from little fountains flow,
            Tall oaks from little acorns grow.

6.   Young Obadias,
                        David, Josias,—
                        All were pious.

7.   As unto the bow the cord is,
            So unto the man is woman;
            Though she bends him, she obeys him,
            Though she draws him, yet she follows:
            Useless each without the other.

8.   Banners yellow, glorious, golden,
                        On its roof did float and flow;
                        This, all this, was in the olden
                        Time, long ago.

THE VOWEL [ɔ]

[ɔ] is the vowel sound in words like raw [rɔ] and saw [sɔ]
(diacritical mark ô or a̤). In making this sound the tongue is
lower in the mouth than for [o]; also, the lips are wider apart
and projected farther forward than for [o]. Both the lips and
the tongue are somewhat tense. The sound is a low back vowel.

FAULTS AND DANGERS

Various substitutions are made for [ɔ], sometimes because of
regional customs and sometimes because of carelessness or ignorance. Among the more common substitutions are the following:

1. It is not uncommon for [ɔ] to be diphthongized into [ɔu],
changing the word *talk*, for example, to [tɔuk].

2. Occasionally the sound [ɑ] is substituted for [ɔ], as in a word like *auto*, which becomes [ɑtoʊ].

3. Regionally, sometimes an [r] is incorrectly added, as in *wash* [wɔrʃ].

4. In substandard speech, [æ] is sometimes substituted for [ɔ], as in a word like *gaunt*, which becomes [gænt].

EXERCISES

1. Repeat the following words over and over:

Initial		Medial		Final	
all	ought	cause	warm	saw	pshaw
awe	auction	sauce	lawn	raw	flaw
auto	awning	hawk	sought	jaw	gnaw
ordeal	autumn	caught	scrawl	law	claw
awful	author	falter	fortune	straw	withdraw

2. Enunciate the following sentences clearly:

1. All of the author's possessions were auctioned last autumn.
2. The hawk fought the dog over a piece of raw flesh.
3. The Shawnee squaws often wore shawls to keep them warm.
4. The outlaws fought the law all fall.
5. The cost of hauling the straw almost brought disaster to Paul.

FURTHER DRILL MATERIALS

Practice the exercises for the vowel [ɑ] on page 235; they contain word lists designed to aid you in distinguishing between [ɔ] words and words with the related sounds [ɒ] and [ɑ].

Practice the following selections:

1.
    Mourning when their leaders fall;
    Warriors carry the warrior's pall,
    And sorrow darkens hamlet and hall.

2.
    A song for our banner! The watchword recall
    Which gave the Republic her station:
    "United we stand, divided we fall!"
    It made and preserves us a nation!

3. Men use thought only as authority for their injustice, and employ speech only to conceal their thoughts.

4. Where law ends, tyranny begins.

THE VOWEL [ɝ] ([ɜ])

[ɝ] is the vowel sound in words like *fur* [fɝ], *earn* [ɝn], *fern* [fɝn], *world* [wɝld]; (the diacritical mark is *ûr*). [ɝ] represents this vowel sound as it is usually pronounced in General American speech. [ɜ] represents the sound as pronounced in parts of New England and the South, where people "drop their *r*'s."

[ɝ] is formed in various ways by different persons. Usually the tongue is slightly retracted, with the middle portion elevated a little, and the tip of it raised almost to the hard palate. Also, during the uttering of the sound the tip of the tongue is curled somewhat backward. This process is called *retroflexion* or *inversion*. The degree to which the tongue is inverted varies with different people. The lips are unrounded. The sound is a mid-vowel.

Both [ɝ] and its variant [ɜ] occur only in stressed syllables.

FAULTS AND DANGERS

1. Avoid retracting the tongue too much and curling the tip too far backward. This produces a "bucolic" type of speech which is undesirable. An extreme type of such speech, as burlesqued on the stage, is, "Wul' I'll be durned" [wʌl aɪl bi dɑrnd].

2. Occasionally a Westerner or Midwesterner with dramatic or "cultural" ambitions will go overboard in his effort to acquire what he considers eastern polish. In his haste to adopt the eastern pronunciation of this sound (phonetically represented by [ɜ]), he is likely to push the sound too far forward in his mouth, turning such words as *sir* [sɝ], bird [bɝd], etc., into something like [sɛ], [bɛd], etc. The impression he gives is not culture but affectation.

EXERCISES

1. Repeat the following words over and over:

Initial		Medial		Final	
earl	earth	dirt	swirl	fur	refer
earn	earnest	birth	third	her	deter
urn	urban	girt	shirt	stir	infer
urge	urchin	worth	perfect	blur	recur
early	earthly	mirth	burden	were	defer

2. Enunciate the following sentences clearly:

   1. Myrtle learned the first verse of the stirring song.
   2. Don't hurry, don't worry; learn to take your time.
   3. The colonel was irked when he heard that his shirts were dirty.
   4. The murder trial was adjourned pending further pertinent information.
   5. "Don't shirk work," chirped the bird to the turtle.

THE VOWEL [ɚ]

[ɚ] is the counterpart of [ɝ]. Whereas [ɝ] always occurs in stressed syllables, [ɚ] always occurs in unstressed syllables. Its diacritical mark is [ər] (or ẽr). Note its various spellings in the chart on page 157.

[ɚ] and [ɝ] are similar in position of the tongue and the unrounded shape of the lips, both being mid-vowels. But [ɚ] is much shorter in duration than [ɝ], and therefore weaker and less definite. The word murmur ['mɝmɚ] contains both sounds.

The vowel [ɚ] occurs only in General American speech. Persons using Eastern and Southern pronunciation substitute [ə], to be considered shortly.

The faults and dangers under [ɝ] apply with equal force to [ɚ].

EXERCISES

1. Repeat the following words over and over. Since it is always unstressed, [ɚ] forms the final syllable of many words in American speech.

ever	other	picture	further	alter	foster
never	actor	fixture	brother	debtor	poster
sever	humor	sister	mother	weather	roster
better	tumor	similar	leisure	fisher	taper
heifer	glamour	pillar	pleasure	measure	cater

2. Enunciate the following sentences clearly:

   1. The purser on the Clipper catered to the wealthier passengers.
   2. The dapper sailor thought his brother's humor odder than his own.
   3. Too much leisure and pleasure may adversely alter a worker's attitude.
   4. Greater numbers of red snappers than flounders are caught by fishermen in the harbor.
   5. The preacher married the actor and the glamour girl at the altar of the church.

3. Use Longfellow's "The Old Clock on the Stairs" (page 392) for practice in both [ɔ] and [ɝ].

THE VOWEL [ʌ]

[ʌ] is the vowel that is usually called short *u*, as in *up* [ʌp] (diacritical mark, ŭ). This vowel is easily made. In essence it is little more than an open-throated and open-jawed grunt. The jaw is relaxed, the mouth open, the lips unrounded, and the tongue lies at ease on the floor of the mouth. The sound is a mid-vowel.

Because of its ease of production, it offers no special difficulties to most persons. The following exercises will help to fix it in mind.

EXERCISES

1. Repeat the following words over and over:

Initial			Medial		
up	ugly	unload	but	wonder	much
upper	other	uncouth	bum	blunder	hungry
under	umpire	uncivil	won	brother	punish
usher	until	unreal	done	thunder	rough
uncle	unable	unless	chum	asunder	supper

2. Enunciate the following sentences clearly:

  1. The front sled bucked through the slushy snow.
  2. Some said the prisoners should be hung at sunset.
  3. The assumption that the budget for the structure had to be doubled was judged incorrect.
  4. Fuzzy-wuzzy was a bear; Fuzzy-wuzzy had no hair; Fuzzy-wuzzy wasn't fuzzy; was he?
  5. Once the grumpy umpire laughed at the funny bunch of players.

THE VOWEL [ə]

[ə] is the *neutral, indefinite,* or *schwa* vowel (diacritical mark, [ə][11]). It always occurs in unstressed syllables, as the first vowel sound in *alone* [ə'loun], *above* [ə'bʌv], etc., and as the last vowel in *sofa* ['soufə], *postman* ['poustmən], etc. Note its many spellings in the chart on page 157.

This vowel is the counterpart of [ʌ], discussed earlier. In forming [ə], like [ʌ] the tongue lies flat on the floor of the mouth, with the tip resting back of the lower front teeth; the jaw is relaxed, the mouth open, and the lips unrounded. The chief difference between [ʌ] and [ə] is that [ə] occurs only in unstressed syllables. Thus [ʌ] is both longer and stronger than [ə]. [ə] is one of the easiest, most relaxed sounds in our language; it is the lowest of the mid-vowels.

In natural, easy, unaffected speech, this vowel occurs more frequently than any other; in fact, it is the sound to which most vowels (with certain notable exceptions discussed below) have a natural tendency to revert in unstressed syllables. Also, it is the vowel sound substituted for [ɚ] in the speech of those who "drop their *r*'s."

Further analysis of the place of [ə] in connected speech appears in the discussion of stress on page 258.

---

[11] [ə] is the diacritical mark used by *The American College Dictionary,* the first college-level dictionary to use a single symbol for this variously spelled sound. In other dictionaries it may be marked ĕ, ŭ, ĭ, and in various other ways.

FAULTS AND DANGERS

1. In the discussion of strong and weak forms of words later in this chapter, it is pointed out that in continuous speech nothing but an impression of affectation can result when a person always tries to give unstressed vowel sounds their full pronunciation, or to give them the same value they have in stressed syllables. For example, it would be absurd to give the word *was* the same value in the following stressed and unstressed positions: "I *was* going until he said *he* was going." Because the first *was* is strongly stressed it would be pronounced [wɑz] or [wʌz], whereas the second one, being unstressed, would properly become [wəz]. Likewise, it is affected and academic to pronounce *professor* [pro'fɛsɔr], *debtor* [d'ɛtɔr], etc. The natural, unaffected, and "proper" pronunciation of these words in connected speech is [pro'fɛsɚ] and ['dɛtɚ]. And the unaffected pronunciation of *composition* is not [kɑmpo'zɪʃan] or even [kɑmpo'zɪʃən], but [kɑmpə'zɪʃən]; *moment* is not ['moʊmɛnt] but ['moʊmənt), etc.

2. Certain vowel sounds in American speech have resisted to some degree this general trend toward [ə], and retain much of their individuality even in unaccented syllables. This is especially true of the high front vowels like [i] and [ɪ], and the high back vowels like [u] and [ʊ]. For example, when the accented first syllable of *mystery* becomes unaccented in mysterious, we do not shift from [ɪ] to [ə]; all that occurs is a shortening of the [ɪ] sound. However, this [ɪ] sound does not always retain its individuality in unaccented syllables. For example, the "proper" pronunciation of *specimen* is ['spɛsəmən]. To be on safe ground in pronouncing such words, consult the dictionary for guidance, and at the same time cultivate ear training by listening to good speech models.

EXERCISES

1. Repeat the following words over and over. The [ə] sound is acceptable in the position indicated by italics.

Initial		Medial		Final	
*a*bout	*a*ttest	second*a*ry	port*a*ble	bo*a*	sod*a*
*a*round	*a*bbreviate	firm*a*ment	prom*i*nence	sof*a*	are*a*
*a*cquire	*a*nnounce	perm*a*nent	prom*o*ntory	comm*a*	Canad*a*
*a*djourn	*a*ffairs	spec*i*men	comp*o*sition	guerrill*a*	*A*merica

2. It is better, in the opinion of most careful speakers, not to go all the way to the neutral vowel in the italicized unaccented syllables in the following words. Consult the dictionary for the "acceptable" pronunciation.

*be*fore	short*est*
*be*lief	long*est*
*be*come	*mo*mentous
*de*cline	*Mo*ngolian
al*way*s	*ac*ceptable
prin*cess*	dis*pu*tatious

3. Enunciate the following sentences clearly:
   1. The area of Alabama is not comparable to the area of Montana.
   2. The quiet smile of the Mona Lisa has appealed to many.
   3. The notable explorer from America was found alive but alone in the jungle.
   4. The quality of the specimen of sedimentary rock was difficult to analyze.
   5. Civilian authority is more characteristic of domestic American life than is military authority.

The Diphthongs

As stated earlier, a diphthong is a compound vowel, i.e., two distinct vowels blended into one sound in the same syllable. Whereas a simple vowel is made by holding the articulatory organs in a relatively fixed position during its emission, the essential characteristic of a diphthong is the fact that during its emission the articulatory organs change position, causing the voice to glide from one vowel to another. This is clear, for example, in the [ɔɪ] sound in *oil* [ɔɪl] contrasted with the [i] sound in *each* [itʃ].

THE DIPHTHONGS

Phonetic Symbol	Diacritical Mark	Key Word
[aɪ]	ī	while [hwaɪl]
[aʊ]	ou	how [haʊ]
[ɔɪ]	oi	oil [ɔɪl]
[eɪ][12]	ā	obey [o′beɪ]
[oʊ][12]	ō	old [′oʊld]
[ju][13] (or [ɪu])	ū	beauty [′bjutɪ]

THE DIPHTHONG [aɪ]

[aɪ] is the so-called long *i* as heard in such words as *ride* [raɪd] and *hide* [haɪd] (diacritical mark, *ī*). It is not a simple vowel, as it has traditionally been considered to be, but a diphthong. Its various spellings are shown in the chart on page 157.

This sound is made by adjusting the articulatory organs for [a], then, while the sound is being emitted, quickly gliding to [ɪ]. As with all the diphthongs, the stronger emphasis is on the first element of the blend.

The first element of this diphthong is sometimes written [ɑ] instead of [a], so that it appears [ɑɪ] instead of [aɪ]. There is, without doubt, a normal variation from one to the other of these sounds even by careful speakers; and both pronunciations may therefore be considered entirely acceptable.

[12] Attention is once more directed to the fact that authorities differ as to whether [eɪ] and [oʊ] should be classed as diphthongs or as the simple vowels [e] and [o]. The author follows the practice of *The American College Dictionary* and other authorities in treating them in both categories. For analysis of these sounds, see pp. 226 and 243.

[13] Although [ju] is listed here with the diphthongs, since it is obviously more than a simple vowel, actually a more definitive name for it is *consonant-vowel combination*, and it is so designated on p. 237, where it is discussed. Note that [ju] is sometimes written [ɪu].

FAULTS AND DANGERS

1. Various sectional pronunciations do strange things to the [aɪ] diphthong, as for example the substitution of [ɑ] for the pronoun *I* by many Southerners. In certain sections of the South it is not uncommon for the off-glide [ɪ] part of the diphthong to be partially or even completely eliminated, and for the [a] to become a broad [ɑ]. We may hear such an expression as [ɑ du dɪ′klɛə] for *I do declare,* and [ɑm kəm′plitlɪ tɑd aʊt] for *I'm completely tired out.*

2. Various other substitutions, too many to enumerate, are occasionally heard. Sometimes these substitutions derive from sectional customs and sometimes from carelessness. In one rather extreme form of substitution, heard in substandard speech, [aɪ] is replaced with [ə], so that we may hear the expression [ðæts hwʌt əm ′goʊnə du) for *That's what I'm going to do.*

EXERCISES

1. Repeat the following words over and over:

Initial		Medial		Final	
I	idle	cries	ride	tie	sigh
I'll	idea	sighs	might	rye	pie
eye	ivy	lies	rhyme	shy	why
aye	item	bright	time	my	nigh
ice	ire	fight	slight	high	die

2. Enunciate the following sentences clearly:

1. Trial by fright is the idea of the totalitarians.
2. Tired eyelids upon tired eyes is my plight.
3. "Tiger, tiger, burning bright," is a line from a poem by Blake.
4. "Higher still and higher," and "Like a cloud of fire," are lines written by Shelley.
5. "My suit you denied," "This lost love of mine," and "Drink one cup of wine," are not my lines.

3. Practice the following selections:

1.   In winter I get up at night
      And dress by yellow candle-light.
      In summer, quite the other way,
      I have to go to bed by day.

2.   How fleet is a glance of the mind!
         Compared with the speed of its flight,
      The tempest itself lags behind,
         And the swift-winged arrows of light.

3.   She was a form of life and light,
      That seen, became a part of sight;
      And rose, wherever I turn'd my eye,
      The morning star of memory.

4.   In this college
      Useful knowledge
         Everywhere one finds,
      And already,
      Growing steady,
         We've enlarged our minds.

THE DIPHTHONG [aʊ]

[aʊ] is the vowel combination heard in the words *now* [naʊ]
and *town* [taʊn]—at least it should be heard in these words. Its
diacritical mark is *ou*. It is made by quickly gliding from [a]
to [ʊ] while emitting the sound.

The first element in this diphthong is sometimes written [ɑ]
instead of [a]. This is a normal and acceptable substitution, for
both [a] and [ɑ] are relaxed and open vowels and closely related.
In general, [ɑʊ] is heard more frequently in Eastern speech,
and [aʊ] in General American, but both [ɑʊ] and [aʊ] are in
good standing throughout the country as a whole.

FAULTS AND DANGERS

1. Probably no vowel combination in our language is so
frequently mispronounced as this one. The most common sub-

stitution is [æ] for [a] as the first element in the blend. Thus [aʊ] becomes [æʊ] (or sometimes even the triphthong [æʊə]), so that *now* [naʊ], *about* [ə'baʊt], *town* [taʊn], etc., become [næʊ], [ə'bæʊt], [tæʊn], or worse. This substitution, although widespread and quite common throughout the country, is not considered acceptable by careful speakers. Students who wish to improve their speech should labor to overcome this fault, however deep-seated it may be.

2. One variation of the [æʊ] habit is nasalization so that the tone takes on a tense and "metallic" quality which is extremely displeasing to the ears of most cultured persons. This fault is most pronounced in words which bring the nasal consonants close to the [aʊ], as in *now, town, down, noun*, etc.

3. Sometimes, in careless or slangy speech, the second element of the diphthong is dropped entirely, so that [aʊ] becomes the simple vowel [a] or [ɑ]. Thus the question *How are you doing?* becomes something like [hɑ jə 'duən].

EXERCISES

1. Repeat the following words over and over:

Initial		Medial		Final	
our	ounce	round	about	allow	how
hour	outing	mound	town	bough	now
ouch	outlet	sound	clown	prow	endow
out	outer	pounce	flower	plow	lowbrow
owl	outline	trounce	shower	thou	powwow

2. Enunciate the following sentences clearly:
   1. How now brown cow?
   2. When you doubt, shout your doubt from the housetop.
   3. Around, around, flew each sweet sound.
   4. The owl looked down with his great round eyes.
   5. —a kingly cedar green with boughs
      Goes down with a great shout upon the hills.

3. Students who have difficulty with their [aʊ] sounds, particularly those in whom the [æʊ] habit is deeply ingrained from long use,

should do intensive drilling on vowel combinations in which careful distinctions are required, as for example these:

a. Repeat over and over [æ-a-ʊ, æ-a-ʊ, æ-a-ʊ].
b. Drill on words which include these sounds, as *at, I* and *look* [æt-aɪ-lʊk, æt-aɪ-lʊk, æt-aɪ-lʊk].

4. Practice the following selections:

1.   Till like one in slumber bound,
          Borne to ocean, I float down, around,
          Into a sea profound of everlasting sound.

2.   There for my lady's bower
                Built I the lofty tower,
                Which to this very hour,
                   Stands looking seaward.

3.   There is a silence where has been no sound,
      There is a silence where no sound may be,
         In the cold grave—under the deep, deep sea,
         Or in wide desert where no life is found,
      Which has been mute, and still must sleep profound.

4.   The thrush sings high on the topmost bough,—
      Low, louder, low again; and now
      He has changed his tree,—you know not how,
         For you saw no flitting wing.

THE DIPHTHONG [ɔɪ]

[ɔɪ] is the diphthong found in words like *boy* [bɔɪ], *coin* [kɔɪn], *noise* [nɔɪz], etc. (diacritical mark, *oi*). As indicated by the symbol [ɔɪ], it is a blend of the vowels [ɔ] and [ɪ]. It is made by adjusting the articulators for [ɔ], then, while the sound is being emitted, quickly gliding to [ɪ].

Faults and Dangers

In uneducated speech and in some regional speech, we occasionally hear various substitutions, such as [ɝ] or [aɪ] for the first element in this diphthong, so that the word *oil*, for example, is pronounced [ɜ·l] or [aɪl]. In general, however, no special difficulties or hazards are presented by this vowel combination.

EXERCISES

1. Repeat the following words over and **over**:

Initial	Medial		Final	
oil	boil	sirloin	boy	employ
oiler	soil	turmoil	Roy	enjoy
oilcloth	recoil	poignant	ahoy	destroy
oyster	noise	rejoice	toy	annoy
ointment	choice	flamboyant	decoy	deploy

2. Enunciate the following sentences clearly:
  1. He made a special point of loyally caring for his poinsettias.
  2. Year after year beheld the patient toil
     That built that lustrous coil.
  3. Ne'er a peevish boy
     Would break the bowl from which he drank in joy.
  4. Made to tread the mills of toil
     Up and down in ceaseless moil.
  5. The devil hath not, in all his quiver's choice,
     An arrow for the heart like a sweet voice.
  6. What kind of a noise annoys an oyster?

The diphthongs [eɪ], [ou], and [ju] are analyzed in conjunction with the initial vowel of each on pages 226, 243, and 237.

Strong and Weak Forms of Words

Words and syllables have strong and weak forms, depending on the emphasis which is given to them, and on their relationship to other words and syllables that surround them. In order to have rhythm and flowing quality in our speech, it is essential that main words be given greater prominence and that less important ones be submerged.

This process of changing words from a strong to a weak form, or vice versa, is largely a matter of changing the nature of the vowel sounds. Reducing a vowel from its strong (or normal) form to a weak form consists in changing it usually to the so-called neutral vowel [ə], but sometimes to another vowel, such as [ɪ] or [ʊ]; in some cases, the vowel sound is eliminated altogether, as will be explained a little later.

Many well-meaning persons, striving to improve their speech habits and not knowing that words "properly" can and do have weak forms, undertake to use strong pronunciation at all times. The result is an impression of labored overniceness and affectation.

As a first step in correcting this fault, students need to know something about the effect of stress upon pronunciation.

To make meaning clear, it is necessary that the meaning-carrying words stand out. That is, they must be *stressed*, by giving them greater *force* or *time*, or by using some other device which gives them emphasis. But if some words are to be stressed, other words must be unstressed, for when everything is stressed nothing is stressed, nothing stands out.

Take, for instance, the sentence, "Better a discontented Socrates than a contented pig." It is obvious that some of these words carry more meaning than others. The meaningful words are *better, discontented, Socrates, contented,* and *pig.* These carry the thought, whereas the two *a*'s, and to some degree the *than,* merely provide connective tissue. But that is not a typical sentence, for it is much more compact than most sentences, and hence a higher than normal percentage of the words require special stress. Look at another sentence which has a larger component of "filler": "When did you say that you were going on your vacation?" Here *when, say, going,* and *vacation* are the thought-laden words and require the most stress; the rest of the words, being of subordinate importance, will naturally receive less emphasis.

In general, articles, prepositions, conjunctions, etc., are unstressed; nouns and verbs are usually stressed; and pronouns, adjectives, and adverbs may or may not be stressed, depending

on circumstances. In the sentence, "That is the man," the pronoun *that*—a word which in other connections might be quite
insignificant—might assume major importance, depending
upon the meaning.

But the point here is this: Many words and syllables when
unstressed are pronounced differently from when they are
stressed. For example, the word *that* in the sentence just given
could be pronounced [ðæt], with the vowel sounding like the
one in *cat* [kæt]. But in the sentence, "When did you say that you
were going on your vacation?" the *that* would be pronounced
[ðət], with the [æ] changing to the so-called neutral vowel (ə),
or schwa. Also, *your* would probably be contracted to *y'r* [jɚ].
Phonetically, the sentence would be written about like this:
[hwɛn dɪd ju seɪ ðət ju wɚ goɪŋ ɑn jɚ ve'keʃən]?

Again, look at the articles *a* and *the*. Seldom in connected
speech is either of these words pronounced in the strong form [eɪ]
or [ði]. This occurs only when the words stand alone or for some
reason are to receive special stress. Usually the *a* is pronounced
[ə], as in the sentence, "A merry heart doeth good like a medicine" [ə 'mɛrɪ hɑrt 'duɪθ gʊd laɪk ə 'mɛdəsən]. And *the* is almost
always pronounced either [ðə] before a consonant, or [ðɪ] before
a vowel, as in the sentence, *The man ate the apple* [ðə mæn eɪt ðɪ
æpəl].

Some such change in pronunciation occurs with many words
and syllables, according to whether they stand in an emphatic
or an unemphatic position. Let us look at another example.
Notice the word *he* in the sentence, "Will he go with you?" In
this sentence, if *he* is of major importance it will be pronounced
[hi]. But if the answer to the question is, "All I know is, he said
he would go," the word *said* becomes the word of major importance and *he* is subordinate. Therefore, in this case, *he* would
be unstressed and would sound more like [hɪ]. Also the word
would would probably be contracted to *w'd* or just *'d*. Phonetically, this sentence would be written something like this:
[ɔl aɪ nou ɪz, hɪ sɛd ɪd go].

This change in pronunciation from strong to weak forms is not an evidence of careless or slovenly pronunciation; it is perfectly right and proper. It is the only way our language can have rhythm, an easy flowing quality, and meaning. And if the diction student would avoid sounding stilted and artificial, if he would use our language "correctly" in connected speech, he must learn the difference between strong and weak forms in connected speech.

In addition to the words already cited, the list below contains other words which are commonly used in a weak form. The second column shows them as they are pronounced in isolation and in accented syllables; the third column, as they are frequently pronounced in connected speech.

Word	Strong Form	Weak Forms
am	[æm]	[m]
an	[æn]	[ən], [n]
and	[ænd]	[ənd], [nd], [n]
as	[æz]	[əz], [z]
at	[æt]	[ət]
but	[bʌt]	[bət], [bt]
can	[kæn]	[kən], [kn]
could	[kʊd]	[kəd], [kd]
for	[fɔr]	[fɚ]
from	[frʌm]	[frəm]
has	[hæz]	[həz], [əz], [z]
her	[hɝ]	[ɚ]
his	[hɪz]	[ɪz]
is	[ɪz]	[z]
nor	[nɔr]	[nɚ]
of	[ɒv], [ʌv]	[əv]
or	[ɔr]	[ɚ]
shall	[ʃæl]	[ʃəl], [ʃl]
she	[ʃi]	[ʃɪ]
than	[ðæn]	[ðən]
to	[tu]	[tə], [t]
you	[ju]	[jʊ]

EXERCISES

1. Omission of one or more sounds sometimes occurs in the following words. Pronounce them "correctly" but with the appearance of easy naturalness.

belong	interesting	pumpkin
candidate	Italy	regular
cemetery	laboratory	superintendent
chocolate	library	suppose
couldn't	mirror	surprise
diamond	municipal	temperature
dictionary	particular	understand
figure	perhaps	usual
generally	poem	violent
geography	poinsettia	when
government	police	which
governor	privilege	why
intellectual	probably	wouldn't

2. Addition of sounds is rather common in the following words. Work with them as in Exercise 1.

across	elm	often
athlete	evening	parliament
athletics	film	pincers
attacked	grievous	salmon
column	height	statistics
draw	idea	subtle
drowned	law	sword

3. Substitution of sounds sometimes occurs in the following words (as for example when the radio announcer of a football game shouted that the rooters of one of the teams were "jubulant," and later that the players were covered with "prespiration"). For a few of the words we cannot apply the terms *right* or *wrong* because there is a choice; in these cases, decide which pronunciation is preferable in your cultural environment.

accept	experiment	larynx
accessories	futile	percolator
almond	genuine	persist
apparatus	gesture	perspiration
breeches	get	prelude
catch	guarantee	presentation
character	hearth	pronunciation
children	hero	ration
coupon	heroine	relevant
creek	horizon	spontaneity
culinary	hundred	status
cupola	instead	substantiate
data	iodine	syrup
discretion	irrelevant	tedious
docile	jubilant	vigilant

4. Accent is often a problem in the following words. Look them up in the dictionary, and when there is a choice decide which pronunciation is preferable in your community and cultural surroundings. Observe that in many of the words the vowel in the last syllable is properly [ə].

abdomen	comparable	irrefutable
acclimated	contractor	pretense
admirable	despicable	program
adult	dirigible	recess
allies	divan	research
Arab	exquisite	resources
aspirant	finance	robust
assiduity	grimace	romance
autopsy	hospitable	vagary
cement	inquiry	vehement

5. Distinguish between the pronunciations of the following pairs of words. Use them in connected speech, in phrases and sentences like: "*Our* hearts, *our* hopes, *are* all with thee," and "*Are* you *or* *are* you not going?"

accept—except	affect—effect
adapt—adopt	amplitude—aptitude

are—our	line—lion
access—excess	lose—loose
Arthur—author	Mongol—mongrel
ascent—accent	morning—mourning
climatic—climactic	our—or
coating—quoting	pictures—pitchers
comprise—compromise	practical—practicable
consecrate—confiscate	precedence—precedents
consolation—consultation	proceed—precede
detect—detest	respectively—respectfully
disillusion—dissolution	sense—cents
distrait—distraught	sex—sects
exit—exist	sins—since
exult—exalt	statue—statute
garnered—garnished	turbid—turgid
hurtle—hurdle	vocation—vacation
immorality—immortality	wandered—wondered

6. Most of the following words are quite common, but they are frequently mispronounced. Look up their correct pronunciation. Observe that in some of them (as in *education* and *blackguard*) a certain amount of "elision" or "assimilation" is called for. Don't guess at the pronunciation. Make sure.

actually	cynosure	longevity
amateur	deaf	mischievous
Arctic	decade	neither
Arkansas	education	ocean
bade	either	pianist
been	envelope	piano
blackguard	era	precious
bouquet	err	pretty
brochure	forehead	quay
capsule	gesture	quixotic
chasm	Himalaya	route
charivari	Illinois	schism
chiropodist	Italian	sugar
comptroller	lichen	tomato
corps	literature	zoölogical

Part Two USING

THE VOICE

X ✳ Voice as Part of a Unified Personality

Now we come to the very heart of voice training. Every other phase of our development must rest upon the foundation principles laid down in this chapter.

A human being is a complex organism composed of many elements. Each of these elements has an important bearing on each of the others, and on the personality as a whole. In thinking of the voice we should never think of it as something separate and distinct from the rest of the person. It is part of the whole being. What the individual thinks, what he feels—yes, even what he eats—all have a direct and positive relationship to his voice, not only to what his voice says but also to how he says it.

Suppose you are walking down the street behind two young ladies and overhear part of their conversation. One says to the other, "He was a swell, elegant fella"—just that sentence, nothing more. Already, no doubt, you have formed your judgment of the thought processes of this young lady. And the chances are that your estimate was formed—quite unconsciously—as much by the quality, pitch, rate, and emphasis in her voice as by the revealing remark. Rightly or wrongly, justifiably or unjustifiably, we all are inclined to base our judgments on such slender shreds of evidence. Why? Because through years of experience we have found that, by and large, what comes out of a person's mouth in the form of words and phrases is a pretty good index of what is inside.

Two young men were talking. One asked the other, "Do you know ———?" (naming a third young man). Instantly, the man being questioned assumed a pose; he pursed his mouth precisely, lifted his hand in a gesture of exaggerated elegance, pushed his questioner's shoulder daintily, and in a high-pitched and overinflected voice replied, "Why, of course, silly!" Whole volumes were said in those gestures and exaggerated inflections.

These illustrations simply emphasize the ancient maxim: "Speech is a mirror of the soul: as a man speaks, so is he."

Therefore, although for purposes of analysis we divide this chapter into four sections—thought, mental imagery, emotion, and physical action in relation to voice—we must never lose sight of the fact that each of these is part of a whole. Voice is a manifestation of personality; ideally it should be a manifestation of *unified* and *integrated* personality.

Thought and Voice

The voice reports whether we are thinking or only half-thinking, especially if we are only half-thinking. Shallowness and superficiality of thought reflect themselves in the way the voice behaves. If we are guilty, our voices give us away. The superficial thinking of many persons shows even in ordinary conversation. This is especially true of the very loquacious. Shakespeare condemns one of his characters for this fault:

> Gratiano speaks an infinite deal of nothing, more than any man in Venice. His reasons are as two grains of wheat hid in two bushels of chaff: you shall seek all day before you find them: and when you have them, they are not worth the search.

The voices of such conversational bores are likely to be as dull as their words.

Unfortunately, the converse of this observation is not always true. Sometimes a man will disclose, possibly through his writings, that he is possessed of a rich and even scintillating thought life; but when he speaks he uses a voice as dull and colorless as a cowbell. In such cases other personality factors are likely to have entered the picture—excessive timidity, perhaps, or an exaggerated fear of exhibitionism—so that there is no free channel of expression from the inner man through his voice. Then the only remedy is a program of correction by means of a study of speech techniques and drill.

But this is the exceptional case. With most of us, the need is for sharpened perceptions, deeper insight, greater understanding, and, along with these, a freeing of the instruments of expression—in this case, the voice. It is in the various kinds of public speaking and public reading that shallowness and superficiality of thinking, as reflected in the voice, become most objectionable.

THOUGHT CONTENT IN PUBLIC SPEECH

The late Senator Borah, considered by many to be the best speaker of his day in the Senate, once said: "The first qualification of the orator is that he be master of his subject. The second is that the subject be master of him."

This two-sided principle constitutes the foundation rock of effective speech. In an effort to convey thought by voice, the first factor of importance is to have the thought. It is like the old recipe for rabbit pie—the first requirement is to get the rabbit.

Unfortunately, a great many people think of speech training as dealing primarily, if not exclusively, with the mechanics of speech: how one should stand, what he should do with his hands, how he should manipulate his voice to get certain effects, and so forth. This emphasis on the mechanics—the externals—of speech is probably not nearly so much the practice of speech teachers as it is the opinion of individuals looking in from the outside, persons who have had little or no actual experience with speech training.

But the fact is that most speech teachers *are* more or less guilty of this emphasis on surface training. Study of techniques is much easier than trying to improve thought processes. About the hardest job in the whole educative process is to teach students to think. Thinking is hard work. It is much easier to hunt for handy rules of conduct on the platform, to look for oratorical tricks which will spare us the necessity of thinking.

And yet, deep down inside of us, all of us, students and teachers alike, know that a public speaker who relies upon the graces of "eloquence" (in the narrow and superficial meaning of that word) as a substitute for something that needs to be said is headed for failure. Carlyle referred to this type of public address as "wind-eloquence," and said: "Speak not, I passionately entreat thee, 'till thy thought have silently matured itself." And William Jennings Bryan, widely recognized as one of America's most eloquent speakers, put it this way: "A speaker is eloquent in proportion as he knows what he is talking about and means what he says." In saying this, Bryan was not disparaging speech techniques. On the contrary, he himself was a most diligent student of platform skills. What he was doing was putting first things first. And so must we all. The fact that we study voice techniques must not blind us to the primacy of *thought* as the root soil of voice quality.

Yet public speakers constantly fail to make this principle a living moving part of their speaking practice. Student speakers talk on subjects which they only half understand. And experienced speakers talk on subjects which they have discussed so often that the material has become commonplace and trite to them. They roll off the words with little conscious attention to their true significance. As someone has remarked, "They turn on their mouths like faucets and go away and leave them running."

A speech should be the fine flower of a lot of plant growth that has preceded it. This kind of thought growth requires *time*—time for concentration, time for intense mental application. One person will go through an entire art gallery in two hours; another will take a day or a week to study one picture. The first carries away a jumble of vague impressions; the other perhaps finds the inner meaning of one picture and understands it.

Without such maturing of thought the voice is bound to be shallow and colorless. When the mind is dull the voice will be likewise.

It is not, however, in conversation or in public speaking that the voice behaves most objectionably. That doubtful distinction belongs to another classification.

THOUGHT CONTENT IN PUBLIC READING

It is in the various kinds of public reading that the voice is most frequently guilty of the faults we have been discussing. It is here that the voice becomes unbelievably bad—unbelievably in the sense that it is hard to understand how intelligent people can permit their voices to be so boresome. We find this kind of reading in secretaries' reports, in papers read at conventions, in radio speeches, and in most other situations in which people read publicly. The painful fact is that extremely few persons untrained in reading skills can read interestingly; hence most public reading is insufferably dull.

The principal reason for this dullness is the fact that most persons read not ideas, but words. Words are not thoughts; they are the "skins" of thoughts. To read acceptably a person has to go beneath the skin; he has to dig down where the thoughts are.

Most of us can recall the reading which took place in the early grades of our school career. "I-see-a-cat. The-cat-is-on-the-fence." Little or no inflection! All the words given equal force, equal time, and equal pitch! That was reading at its worst. And the trouble arose primarily from the fact that the reader was so busy trying to identify the words and pronounce them that he had little time to think of what they meant.

In some degree the same thing occurs when we are grown, when we read without having a body of meaning back of our words. Try this simple experiment.

Go to your library and find a scientific book. Open it to a difficult passage. Ask a member of your family or a friend who is unacquainted with the passage to read a paragraph or two aloud; listen to his voice as he does so. Note how the voice halts and stumbles as he struggles with the thought. Or, if he ignores the thought, how his voice flows along, flat and dull, quite devoid of expressiveness. Now have him study the passage until it begins to take on significance. Discuss the meaning of the passage with him. Then ask him to read it again. Note the variations in pitch and rate. Note the countless little changes in emphasis. As he increasingly grasps the full meaning, his voice becomes more and more expressive. Lack of understanding, partial understanding, and complete understanding all reflect themselves in the reader's tones.

Now let us devote ourselves to some exercises designed to correct the vocal dullness which comes as a result of mental lassitude. We shall begin with the worst offender, the reading voice!

In general, the method of procedure should be twofold: first *get* the meaning, then *give* the meaning. And since much of the material in succeeding chapters is devoted to techniques for giving meaning, we shall here concentrate chiefly upon the problem of extracting meaning, the only delivery technique consciously attempted at this time being an intensified effort to break down restraints and let the voice respond to our heightened thought processes.

METHOD OF LITERATURE ANALYSIS

Here is a suggested procedure for extracting the meaning from a passage of literature.

1. Read the passage through rapidly. Look for the central idea of the piece. In this first reading skip over any involved

phrases or sentences that you find difficult to grasp; leave them for future study. Your whole effort just now is to get the author's general thought. This step in the study plan should not cause any trouble, for much school training in recent years has been devoted to the development of skill in rapid reading. Perhaps too much, for in the effort to prepare students to take advantage of the vast stores of literature available today, some teachers have deëmphasized the important skill of careful analytical reading.

When you have finished this reading, stop and think. Think of what the whole thing means.

2. Now read it again, more slowly, more carefully. Study the individual phrases. Look up the meaning of all obscure words. Don't guess at them, be sure! Observe the logic of the progression from phrase to phrase; see whether there is genuine cohesion of phrases, or only a weak and tenuous linkage. Hold the ideas before you one at a time and analyze them.

3. The third step is an intensification of the second. Give diligent attention to details. Look into each separate idea with the most penetrating insight you can command. Read challengingly. Do not be a drifter with the tide. Buffet the current of thought a little. Explore the depth of the stream. Take your time! This is intensive rather than extensive reading. Don't try to hurry the process.

4. Now read the passage again for enjoyment. If, after your analysis and your challenge, you still can find truth and beauty in the selection, give yourself over to it. Your enjoyment should be heightened; your appreciation should be intensified. And, in consequence, your oral reading should be more discriminating, and more interesting.

Suppose we try the suggested procedure for literature analysis on a little poem by George Meredith that is usually considered a "toughie" to understand.

1. First, we'll read the poem over rapidly to get the general idea. Here it is:

IS LOVE DIVINE?

Ask, Is Love Divine?
Voices all are *ay.*
Question for the sign:
Would we through our years
Love forego,
Quit of scars and tears?
Ah, but no, no, no!

Hmm! Well! Chances are that the first reading didn't produce a great deal of meaning. The poet seems to be talking about love. But there's nothing unusual about that; most poets do. But how did he get onto that theme of scars and tears? What do they have to do with it? Better read it again!

2. That first sentence is clear enough; the poet is asking whethet or not love is divine. But what does he mean by *divine?* That word, we see by the dictionary, has several meanings. Here's one that seems to fit; let's adopt it temporarily: "proceeding from God."[1] All right then, Meredith seems to be inquiring whether or not love comes from God.

Voices! What does he mean by *voices?* Here's another word with many meanings. But the one that seems most applicable is: "Any sound likened to vocal utterance: *the voice of the wind."* Meredith must mean, then, that all the voices of nature say—what? What is the meaning of that *ay?* We go to the dictionary again and find that there are a series of *ay's* and *aye's,* the two spellings being used interchangeably, at least in part of the meanings. This is strange. Here is a word whose meaning is determined not by the spelling as in *beech* (a hardwood timber tree) versus *beach* (the shore of the sea or of a lake) but by the pronunciation. Both *aye* and *ay* may be pronounced [eɪ], and when so pronounced they mean "ever, always" (an archaic meaning, but that wouldn't stop a poet). Also, both *aye* and *ay* may be pronounced [aɪ], and when so pronounced they mean *yes.* It must be, then, that Meredith is answering his question with an affirmative: voices of nature all say *yes, love is divine!*

Now, we're getting somewhere. But what about that next line:

[1] This definition and the ones following are taken from *The American College Dictionary,* Text Edition, Harper & Brothers, 1948.

Question for the sign? The individual words are clear enough, but together they don't mean much. But wait a minute! What is that colon doing at the end of the line? Let's see. We remember that a colon is often used after an introductory statement to indicate that an explanation follows. Must be that Meredith is saying: *"Do you want proof? All right, I'll give it to you. And here it is:"* Now we'll be on the lookout for his proof that love comes from God. If he can prove that in the four short lines remaining in the poem, he's good.

Those next two lines are simple enough: *Would we be willing to get along without love?* But the following line isn't so clear. What does he mean by *quit?* The dictionary gives as one meaning: *"released from obligation, penalty."* So now we have it: *Would we be willing to give up love, if by so doing we could be free of the penalties that love entails?*

The final line is a negation, made emphatic by three repetitions of the word *no.*

3. As the meaning has unfolded during our work with the second step, no doubt we have exercised our mental challenge. We have decided whether or not we think the poet has proved his case, and whether or not we agree with him. But we may want to spend a little more time musing over the implications of those "scars and tears." We may think of the sickness, accidents, and even death that have come to persons we have loved. Because of our love for the afflicted ones, we suffered—scars and tears. We may reflect upon the "sweet sorrow" that has come to us from lovers' quarrels—scars and tears. We may reluctantly dwell upon the perfidy of a friend whom we had come to love and trust—scars and tears. But we may decide that in spite of the sorrow and the suffering we will cling to love, along with Meredith, and along with that other poet who said, "Tis better to have loved and lost than never to have loved at all."

4. Now read it again, for artistic enjoyment. Enjoy the poet's skill in saying so much in so few words. Enjoy his architectural craftsmanship in building so symmetrical a structure from such carefully chiseled building blocks.

And enjoy it, perhaps, because the poet has said what you believe to be true and would like to have said yourself if you possessed the skill.

Even though you believe that you have the author's meaning, you may feel that you lack the oral reading ability necessary to "put over" so concentrated a message. Your trepidation probably will be especially acute when you look at those three *no*'s in the above poem. You may wonder whether you should run them off quickly as you might answer an absurd request of a child, or give each one a slow and measured emphasis, or build each one upon the other in an ascending crescendo of force and volume. Well, try them all! There is no one right way! Practice them over and over; give your voice a chance to experiment. Some of our best actors have stated that they have practiced certain lines in some of their plays as many as a thousand—ten thousand—times in an effort to have their voices express what they felt was in the lines.

EXERCISES IN THOUGHT AND VOICE RELATIONSHIPS

1. The following brief excerpts from poems and prose poems, although out of context, are worthy of study in their own right. Each exemplifies the poet's flashing insight and power of concise expression. Be sure you grasp the author's full meaning, and add your own reaction to his concept, before you attempt to read the lines aloud.

   1.   Wilt thou not open thy heart to know
        What rainbows teach, and sunsets show!

   2.   What is this life if, full of care,
        We have no time to stand and stare!

   3.   The Devil was sick—the Devil a monk would be;
        The Devil was well—the devil a monk was he![2]

   4.   Eternal Spirit of the chainless mind!
        Brightest in dungeons, Liberty! thou art,
        For there thy habitation is the heart—

---

[2] Do not overlook the significance of the change to a small *d* in *devil* in the second line, thus making the word simply part of a slang phrase.

5.   Beauty is truth, truth beauty—That is all
        Ye know on earth, and all ye need to know.

6.   I warmed my both hands against the fire of Life;
        It sinks, and I am ready to depart.

7.   And Thought leapt out to wed with Thought,
        Ere Thought could wed with Speech.

8. Some books are to be tasted, others to be swallowed, and
   some few to be chewed and digested.

9. Life is a narrow vale between the cold and barren peaks of
   two eternities.

10.   . . . in this batter'd Caravanserai
         Whose Portals are alternate Night and Day.[3]

2. There is good vocal drill in trying to present the full significance
of such balanced expressions as the following:

1.   I come to bury Caesar, not to praise him.

2.   The evil that men do lives after them;
        The good is oft interred with their bones.

3. Destroy our cities and leave our broad farms and cities will
   spring up anew—Destroy our farms and grass will grow in the
   streets of every city.

4.   Oh, East is East, and West is West,
        And never the twain shall meet.

5.   As you are old and reverend, you should be wise.

6.   Striving to better, oft we mar what's well.

7. We live in deeds, not years; in thoughts, not breaths;
   In feelings, not in figures on a dial.

8. You have been brave, but not brutal; confident, but not
   arrogant; and you have welded the tremendous military

[3] Observe the similarity in the philosophical concepts of this and the preceding
selection. Also note the significance of the word *caravanserai* (or *caravansary*) in
this context, i.e., a sort of inn, a brief stopping place for a caravan as it comes
out of the desert and goes back into the desert.

potential of this country into a great fighting machine without
having sacrificed the rights of the individual.[4]

9. The machine can free man or enslave him; it can make of
this world something resembling a paradise or a purgatory.
Men have it within their power to achieve a security hitherto
dreamed of only by philosophers, or they may go the way of
the dinosaurs, actually disappearing from the earth because
they fail to develop the social and political intelligence to
adjust to the world their mechanical intelligence has created.
Right now the outcome is doubtful and the issue hangs in
balance.[5]

3. Study the following poem. First, read it perfunctorily, as a task
to be performed without enthusiasm—read it as the secretary
usually reads the minutes of the last meeting. Then study it to
understand Browning's philosophy of death. Feel the surging
courage—the daring to face death as he had faced life, chest forward, head high, undaunted by the dread specter. Now read it
aloud; give your voice over to the thought and feeling of it.

PROSPICE

Fear death?—to feel the fog in my throat,
    The mist in my face,
When the snows begin, and the blasts denote
    I am nearing the place,
The power of the night, the press of the storm,
    The post of the foe;
Where he stands, the Arch Fear in a visible form,
    Yet the strong man must go:
For the journey is done and the summit attained,
    And the barriers fall,
Though the battle's to fight ere the guerdon be gained,
    The reward of it all.
I was ever a fighter, so—one fight more,
    The best and the last!

[4] Part of Henry L. Stimson's farewell address to his military leaders on his
retirement as Secretary of War in 1945.
[5] From William G. Carleton, "Freedom and the Social Sciences," *Vital Speeches,*
December, 1946

I would hate that death bandaged my eyes, and forebore,
   And bade me creep past.
No! let me taste the whole of it, fare like my peers,
   The heroes of old,
Bear the brunt, in a minute pay glad life's arrears
   Of pain, darkness, and cold.
For sudden the worst turns the best to the brave,
   The black minute's at end,
And the elements' rage, the fiend-voices that rave,
   Shall dwindle, shall blend,
Shall change, shall become first a peace out of pain,
   Then a light, then thy breast,
O thou soul of my soul! I shall clasp thee again,
   And with God be the rest!   —ROBERT BROWNING

4. Figure out the meaning of the following poem. The mental
pictures Mrs. Browning presents are as clear as spring water, but
her *meaning* bears closer resemblance to the turbid river she
describes in the poem. Quite obviously she wants to impress a
message; but what is it? Do you consider it possible that she
deliberately made the message somewhat obscure, on the theory
that we appreciate most those things which we have to struggle
hardest to get? Look closely at the last stanza for the key thought.
   After you have the thought, see if you can give it vocally.

A MUSICAL INSTRUMENT

What was he doing, the great god Pan,
   Down in the reeds by the river?
Spreading ruin and scattering ban,
Splashing and paddling with hoofs of a goat,
And breaking the golden lilies afloat
   With the dragon-fly on the river?

He tore out a reed, the great god Pan,
   From the deep cool bed of the river:
The limpid water turbidly ran,
And the broken lilies a-dying lay,
And the dragon-fly had fled away,
   Ere he brought it out of the river.

High on the shore sat the great god Pan,
　　While turbidly flow'd the river;
And hack'd and hew'd as a great god can,
With his hard bleak steel at the patient reed,
Till there was not a sign of a leaf indeed
　　To prove it fresh from the river.

He cut it short, did the great god Pan,
　　(How tall it stood in the river!)
Then drew the pith, like the heart of a man,
Steadily from the outside ring.
And notch'd the poor dry empty thing
　　In holes, as he sat by the river.

"This is the way," laugh'd the great god Pan,
　　(Laugh'd while he sat by the river),
"The only way, since gods began
To make sweet music, they could succeed."
Then, dropping his mouth to a hole in the reed,
　　He blew in power by the river.

Sweet, sweet, sweet, O Pan!
　　Piercing sweet by the river!
Blinding sweet, O great god Pan!
The sun on the hill forgot to die,
And the lilies revived and the dragon-fly
　　Came back to dream on the river.

Yet half a beast is the great god Pan,
　　To laugh as he sits by the river,
Making a poet out of a man:
The true gods sigh for the cost and pain—
For the reed which grows never more again
　　As a reed with the reeds in the river.

　　　　　　　—ELIZABETH BARRETT BROWNING

5. In the following selection, distinguish between a hazy grasp of
the general meaning and complete realization of all the sig-

nificant implications. Express the detailed meanings in your voice shadings.

From PRELUDE TO THE VISION OF SIR LAUNFAL

And what is so rare as a day in June?
   Then, if ever, come perfect days;
Then Heaven tries earth if it be in tune,
   And over it softly her warm ear lays;
Whether we look, or whether we listen,
We hear life murmur, or see it glisten;
Every clod feels a stir of might,
   An instinct within it that reaches and towers,
And, groping blindly above it for light,
   Climbs to a soul in grass and flowers;
The flush of life may well be seen
   Thrilling back over hills and valleys;
The cowslip startles in meadows green,
   The buttercup catches the sun in its chalice,
And there's never a leaf nor a blade too mean
   To be some happy creature's palace;
The little bird sits at his door in the sun,
   Atilt like a blossom among the leaves,
And lets his illumined being o'errun
   With the deluge of summer it receives;
His mate feels the eggs beneath her wings,
And the heart in her dumb breast flutters and sings;
He sings to the wide world, and she to her nest,—
In the nice ear of Nature which song is the best?
                  —JAMES RUSSELL LOWELL

6. In this exercise you will find two contrasting attitudes toward old age, each expressed by a major poet. Studying the two together will help you to appreciate the full implication of each. After you are thoroughly conversant with both poems, read them aloud. Read each so well that you do full justice to the author's meaning. But in reading the poem which comes closer to your own belief about old age, give it the added emphasis that will show your agreement with it.

1.   *From* RABBI BEN EZRA

Grow old along with me!
The best is yet to be,
The last of life, for which the first was made:
Our times are in his hand
Who saith, "A whole I planned,
Youth shows but half; trust God: see all, nor be afraid!"

· · · · · ·

Therefore I summon age
To grant youth's heritage,
Life's struggle having so far reached its term:
Thence shall I pass, approved
A man, for aye removed
From the developed brute; a god though in the germ.

· · · · · ·

Youth ended, I shall try
My gain or loss thereby;
Leave the fire ashes, what survives is gold:
And I shall weigh the same,
Give life its praise or blame:
Young, all lay in dispute; I shall know, being old.

· · · · · ·

So, still within this life,
Though lifted o'er its strife,
Let me discern, compare, pronounce at last,
"This rage was right i' the main,
That acquiescence vain:
The Future I may face now I have proved the Past."
                                          —ROBERT BROWNING

2.   GROWING OLD

What is it to grow old?
Is it to lose the glory of the form,
The luster of the eye?
Is it for beauty to forego the wreath?
—Yes, but not this alone.

Is it to feel our strength—
Not our bloom only, but our strength—decay?
Is it to feel each limb
Grow stiffer, every function less exact,
Each nerve more loosely strung?

Yes, this, and more; but not,
Ah! 'tis not what in youth we dreamed 'twould be.
'Tis not to have our life
Mellowed and softened as with sunset-glow—
A golden day's decline.

'Tis not to see the world
As from a height, with rapt prophetic eyes,
And heart profoundly stirred;
And weep, and feel the fullness of the past,
The years that are no more.

It is to spend long days,
And not once feel that we were ever young;
It is to add, immured
In the hot prison of the present, month
To month with weary pain.

It is to suffer this,
And feel but half, and feebly, what we feel.
Deep in our hidden heart
Festers the dull remembrance of a change,
But no emotion—none.

It is—last stage of all—
When we are frozen up within, and quite
The phantom of ourselves,
To hear the world applaud the hollow ghost,
Which blamed the living man.

—MATTHEW ARNOLD

7. The following exercise is similar to Exercise 6, except that the theme pertains to personal habits of industry, and the medium is prose instead of poetry.

1.   *From* AN APOLOGY FOR IDLERS

It is certain that much may be judiciously argued in favor of diligence; only there is something to be said against it, and that is what, on the present occasion, I have to say. . . .

I have attended a good many lectures in my time. I still remember that the spinning of a top is a case of Kinetic Stability. I still remember that Emphyteusis is not a disease, nor Stillicide a crime. But though I would not willingly part with such scraps of science, I do not set the same store by them as by certain other odds and ends that I came by in the open street while I was playing truant. . . .

Suffice it to say this: if a lad does not learn in the streets, it is because he has no faculty of learning. Nor is the truant always in the streets, for if he prefers, he may go out by the gardened suburbs into the country. He may pitch on some tuft of lilacs over a burn, and smoke estimable pipes to the tune of the water on the stones. A bird will sing in the thicket. And there he may fall into a vein of kindly thought, and see things in a new perspective. Why, if this be not education, what is? We may conceive Mr. Worldly Wiseman accosting such a one, and the conversation that should thereupon ensue:

"How now, young fellow, what doest thou here?"

"Truly, sir, I take mine ease."

"Is not this the hour of the class? And should'st thou not be plying thy Book with diligence, to the end thou mayest obtain knowledge?"

"Nay, but thus also I follow after Learning, by your leave."

"Learning, quotha! After what fashion, I pray thee? Is it mathematics?"

"No, to be sure."

"Is it metaphysics?"

"Nor that."

"Is it some language?"

"Nay, it is no language."

"Is it a trade?"

"Nor a trade neither."

"Why, then, what is't?"

"Indeed, sir . . . I lie here, by this water, to learn by root-of-heart a lesson which my master teaches me to call Peace, or Contentment." . . .

Look at one of your industrious fellows for a moment, I beseech you. He sows hurry and reaps indigestion; he puts a vast deal of activity out to interest, and receives a large measure of nervous derangement in return. Either he absents himself entirely from all fellowship, and lives a recluse in a garret, with carpet slippers and a leaden inkpot; or he comes among people swiftly and bitterly, in a contraction of his whole nervous system, to discharge some temper before he returns to work. I do not care how much or how well he works, this fellow is an evil feature in other people's lives. They would be happier if he were dead.

—ROBERT LOUIS STEVENSON

2.   *From* HOW TO LIVE ON TWENTY-FOUR HOURS A DAY[6]

. . . It has been said that time is money. That proverb understates the case. Time is a great deal more than money. If you have time you can obtain money—usually. But though you have the wealth of a cloak-room attendant at the Carlton Hotel, you cannot buy yourself a minute more time than I have, or the cat by the fire has. . . .

. . . The supply of time is truly a daily miracle, an affair genuinely astonishing when one examines it. You wake up in the morning and lo! your purse is magically filled with twenty-four hours of the unmanufactured tissue of the universe of your life! It is yours. It is the most precious of possessions. A highly singular commodity, showered upon you in a manner as singular as the commodity itself!

For remark! No one can take it from you. It is unstealable. And no one receives either more or less than you receive. . . .

You have to live on this twenty-four hours of daily time. Out of

[6] Arnold Bennett, *How to Live on Twenty-Four Hours a Day*, George H. Doran Company, 1910.

it you have to spin health, pleasure, money, content, respect, and the evolution of your immortal soul. Its right use, its most effective use, is a matter of the highest urgency and of the most thrilling actuality. . . . Strange that the newspapers, so enterprising and up-to-date as they are, are not full of "How to live on a given income of time" instead of "How to live on a given income of money!" . . .

[Mr. Bennett continues his seventy-five-page essay by outlining a program of study and self-improvement designed to prevent one from being an idler. The following paragraphs dealing with the study of literature are typical of his let-us-then-be-up-and-doing philosophy.]

. . . I have two general suggestions of a certain importance. The first is to define the direction and scope of your efforts. Choose a limited period, or a limited subject, or a single author. Say to yourself: "I will know something about the French Revolution, or the rise of railways, or the works of John Keats." And during a given period, to be settled beforehand, confine yourself to your choice. . . .

The second suggestion is to think as well as to read. I know people who read and read, and for all the good it does them they might just as well cut bread-and-butter. They take to reading as better men take to drink. They fly through the shires of literature on a motor-car, their sole object being motion. They will tell you how many books they have read in a year.

Unless you give at least forty-five minutes to careful, fatiguing reflection (it is an awful bore at first) upon what you are reading, your ninety minutes of a night are chiefly wasted. . . .

—Arnold Bennett

Mental Imagery and Voice

In large measure it is man's power to imagine which distinguishes him from the lower animals. To be sure, animals may have some of this power too. Who can say that it is not the mental picture of a fragrant bundle of clover hay that causes a horse to hurry faster when he turns toward home? Or the sensuous recollection of a luscious bone that makes a dog dig up a long-buried treasure? But whatever visualizing ability the lower animals have or do not have, we human beings flatter ourselves that we have it to a much greater degree.

Indeed, the ability to visualize is one of the really important steps in the thinking process. In the field of problem solving it is indispensable. If, for example, we are deliberating upon the probable outcome of a given line of action, how do we think the problem through? Do we not try to project ourselves into the future and *visualize* what the result will be? Do we not try the plan out mentally before we put it to the test of action? We do if we want to keep out of trouble! Those who fail to do so are the fools who rush in where angels fear to tread.

Certainly from the standpoint of voice study the ability to visualize is of paramount importance. Individuals who have sluggish minds with small power of imagery are likely to have dull and colorless voices.

Quintilian, two thousand years ago, realized the value of mental imagery:

. . . images by which the presentation of absent objects are so distinctly represented to the mind that we seem to see them with our eyes and to have them before us. Whoever shall best conceive such images will have the greatest power in moving the feelings. . . . If I am to make a complaint that a man has been murdered, shall I not bring before my eyes everything that is likely to have happened when the murder occurred? Shall not the assassin suddenly sally forth? Shall not the other tremble, cry out, supplicate, or flee? Shall I not behold the one striking, the other falling? Shall not the blood, the paleness, and the last gasp of the expiring victim, present itself fully to my mental view? Hence will result that power . . . which seems not so much to narrate as to exhibit; and our feelings will be moved not less strongly than if we were actually present at the affair of which we are speaking.[7]

If the voice student has any hope of stirring up images in the minds of his auditors, he must first see the images in his own mind.

Fortunately, it is possible to increase our ability to visualize.

[7] *Quintilian's Institutes of Oratory,* Bohn's Classical Library, George Bell & Sons, 1887, Vol. I, p. 427.

By knowing how to visualize and by exercising the skill, we can greatly increase our power to imagine (which means, to form a mental image).

First, let us consider the *how* of visualizing. If we examine the methods of some of the masters of the written and spoken word, we shall see how they endeavor to stir up mental images in others, and, by inference, we shall know something about how they see things in their own minds. Analysis will show us that these noted writers and speakers employ three special tools: (1) skillful use of the *specific* as contrasted with the *general*, (2) skillful use of the *concrete* as contrasted with the *abstract*, and (3) skillful choice of *significant details*.

THE SPECIFIC

When trained speakers and writers seek to create emotional responses, they lean heavily upon the specific; they shun the general. Pictures that stir the mind are of individuals, not of classes. A speaker, for example, who is appealing for contributions to the Community Chest will bring more pocketbooks out of hiding by picturing an old man digging for scraps of food in a garbage pail back of a restaurant, or a child carrying a paper bag of stones to school so that her playmates will not discover she has no lunch to carry, or a sick baby whose mother has no medicine to give it, not even money to buy milk—than by giving statistics of the number of poor in the community.

THE CONCRETE

Artists in the use of words know that emotions are stirred by sense imagery. They know that people respond best to—because they are most profoundly moved by—those things which they can *see, hear, touch, taste, smell,* and the psychologists now tell us that we have many additional sense perceptions. Amateurs, on the other hand, are likely to rely upon vague abstractions.

SIGNIFICANT DETAILS

A creator of mental images cannot give all the details of a picture. His skill in description lies in his ability to point out significant details. Note that it is details that he deals with. He builds up a whole picture in our minds by showing us parts—significant parts. For example, if he wants us to see a particular man, there is no use to tell us that the man has two eyes; but if the man has only one eye, that is a distinguishing feature, and therefore significant. Furthermore, if this creator of pictures is especially clever, he will strive to present details with which we already have had some experience. For example, if he wants to describe some strange wild animal he has encountered in his explorations, he will describe aspects of the animal which compare with animals we know about—snout like a hog, fur like a dog, hoofs like a cow, etc. For he knows that that sort of mental process is the only way we have of grasping any new concept.

As the student develops power to intensify his imaginative grasp of mental pictures, he goes far toward developing a corresponding richness, depth, and "tone color" in his voice.

In working on the following exercises and practice selections, we should strive to follow Quintilian's injunction not to narrate, but to exhibit. Let us have as our goal the development of a power of imagination like Amruzail's, described in the following lines:

> When Amruzail describes what he has seen,
> Speaking of lands and flocks and hilltops green,
> Such magic in his voice and language lies
> That all his hearers' ears are turned to eyes.

EXERCISES IN MENTAL IMAGERY AND VOICE RELATIONSHIPS

1. In the following excerpts, observe the skill with which the authors support their general statements by giving significant details that create mental images. Use them as vocal exercises, attempting

to turn your auditors' "ears into eyes." First, you have to see the
pictures clearly yourself, and then express them orally.

1. In the following paragraph, note how Garland uses the senses
   of sight, hearing, smell, and temperature to support his statement about a corn field:

> A corn field in July is a sultry place. The soil is hot and
> dry, the wind comes across the lazily-murmuring leaves laden
> with a warm, sickening smell drawn from the rapidly grow-
> ing broad-flung banners of the corn. The sun, nearly
> vertical, drops a flood of dazzling light upon the field over
> which the cool shadows run, only to make the heat seem
> more intense.

2. In "Tam o'Shanter," the Scottish poet Burns exemplifies the
   abstract thought of the ephemeral nature of pleasures thus:

> But pleasures are like poppies spread,
> You seize the flow'r, its bloom is shed!
> Or like the snow-falls in the river,
> A moment white—then melts for ever;
> Or like the borealis race,
> That flit ere you can point their place;
> Or like the rainbow's lovely form
> Evanishing amid the storm.—

3. Note how few details Keats uses to create the desired picture
   in the following stanza:

> I met a lady in the meads,
>   Full beautiful—a faery's child;
> Her hair was long, her foot was light,
>   And her eyes were wild.

4. Here's another quick picture made up of significant details:

> On a little mound, Napoleon
>   Stood on our storming-day:
> With neck out-thrust, you fancy how,
>   Legs wide, arms lock'd behind,
> As if to balance the prone brow
>   Oppressive with its mind.

5. And here is another rapidly drawn picture from the same Browning poem, this one involving action. Note how few details are needed:

> Out 'twixt the battery smokes there flew
> A rider, bound on bound
> Full galloping; or bridle drew
> Until he reached the mound.

6. See how quickly Sandburg creates a picture of a particular city:

> Hog Butcher for the world,
> Stormy, husky, brawling,
> City of the Big Shoulders.

7. Observe how another author, Bryant, creates a mood by presenting a few image-stirring details:

> . . . approach thy grave
> Like one who wraps the drapery of his couch
> About him, and lies down to pleasant dreams.

2. Prepare and deliver (if not to your classmates, at least to the chairs in your room) a two-minute talk on living only a bread-and-butter sort of existence, in contrast to devoting part of one's life to esthetic satisfactions. Vivify your talk by using the following ancient Persian proverb for your text:

> If thou hast two pennies, spend one for bread.
> With the other, buy hyacinths for thy soul.

3. Do the same with one of the following adages, or any other hackneyed saying that appeals to you:

> A stitch in time saves nine.
> All that glitters is not gold.
> The more haste, the less speed.
> Rome was not built in a day.
> The pot calls the kettle black.
> Spare your breath to cool your porridge.
> What cannot be cured must be endured.

4. In the following selection the ancient Greek dramatist Aeschylus is exhibiting a barren, mole-like type of existence. Study it for meaning and for mental imagery. Then express the thought vocally:

> First of all, though they had eyes to see, they saw to no avail; they had ears, but understood not; but, like to shapes in dreams, throughout their length of days, without purpose they wrought all things in confusion. Knowledge had they neither of houses built of bricks and turned to face the sun, nor yet of work in wood; but dwelt beneath the ground like swarming ants, in sunless caves. They had no sign either of winter or of flowery spring or of fruitful summer, whereon they could depend.[8]

5. Re-create mentally the pictures in the following stirring attack on capital punishment; then let your aroused feelings reflect themselves in your voice:

> A man, a convict, a sentenced wretch, is dragged, on a certain morning, to one of our public squares. There he finds the scaffold! He shudders, he struggles, he refuses to die. He is young yet—only twenty-nine. Ah! I know what you will say—'He is a murderer!' But hear me. Two officers seize him. His hands, his feet, are tied. He throws off the two officers. A frightful struggle ensues. His feet, bound as they are, become entangled in the ladder. He uses the scaffold against the scaffold! The struggle is prolonged. Horror seizes on the crowd. The officers—sweat and shame on their brows,—pale, panting, terrified . . . strive savagely. The victim clings to the scaffold, and shrieks for pardon. His clothes are torn,—his shoulders bloody,—still he resists. At length, after three-quarters of an hour of this monstrous effort, of this spectacle without a name, of this agony,—agony for all, be it understood,—agony for the assembled spectators as well as for the condemned man—after this age of anguish, Gentlemen of the Jury, they take back the poor wretch to his prison.
>
> The People breathe again. The People, naturally merciful,

[8] *Prometheus Bound*, Herbert Weir Smith translation, Loeb Classical Library.

hope that the man will be spared. But no,—the guillotine,
though vanquished, remains standing. There it frowns all day,
in the midst of a sickened population. And at night, the officers,
reinforced, drag forth the wretch again, so bound that he is but
an inert weight,—they drag him forth, haggard, bloody, weeping, pleading, howling for life,—calling upon God, calling
upon his father and mother,—for like a very child had this
man become in the prospect of death—they drag him forth to
execution. He is hoisted on the scaffold, and his head falls!—
And then through every conscience runs a shudder.

—VICTOR HUGO

6. Here are pictures in a different mood from that of Hugo's stern
   message. Catch the spirit of a child's imagination as pictured in
   Stevenson's charming poem, then try it orally.

WHERE GO THE BOATS?

Dark brown is the river,
    Golden is the sand,
It flows along forever,
    With trees on every hand.

Green leaves a-floating,
    Castles on the foam,
Boats of mine a-boating—
    Where will all come home?

On goes the river
    And out past the mill,
Away down the valley,
    Away down the hill.

Away down the river,
    A hundred miles or more,
Other little children
    Shall bring my boats ashore.

7. A good vocal exercise is contained in the following example of sense imagery used to create different moods, found in the writing of a noted and beloved war correspondent:

MOMENTS IN THE NORTH AFRICAN CAMPAIGN[9]

It was one time when nobody wanted to do anything about the weather. It was perfect. The rains were over. The cold was gone. Everything was green, and flowers sparkled over the countryside. The sun was up early and bright, and it was a blessing after all the dreary months of wet and wind. It was like June in Virginia. . . . The sun beamed down between the trees, and occasional bees buzzed around with that midwestern summer drone that to me is synonymous with lazy days. That apricot grove was one of the most peaceful places I had ever known, and I found myself lying for hours outside my tent, flat on my back in the grass, reveling in the evil knowledge that I was shirking my work, the war, and everything else. . . .

We had been at the new camp about an hour and were still setting up our tents when German planes appeared overhead. We stopped our work to watch them. It was the usual display of darting planes, with the conglomerate sounds of ack-ack on the ground and in the sky. Suddenly we realized one of the planes was diving straight at us, and we made a mad scramble for foxholes. . . .

We lay there in the hole, face down, as the plane came smack overhead with a terrible roar. We were all drawn up inside, waiting for the blow. Explosions around us were shatteringly loud, and yet when it was all over we couldn't find any bomb holes or anybody hurt. But we could find a lot of nervous people. . . .

We went to bed in our tents. A near-by farmyard was full of dogs and they began a howling that lasted all night. The roll of artillery was constant. It never stopped for twenty-four hours. Once in a while there were nearer shots which might have been German patrols, or might not. We lay uneasily on our cots. Sleep wouldn't come. . . .

One of the dogs suddenly broke into a frenzied barking and

[9] Ernie Pyle, *Here Is Your War*, Henry Holt and Company, Inc., 1943.

went tearing through our little camp as if chasing a demon.
My mind seemed to lose all sense of proportion, and I got
jumpy and mad at myself.

Concussion ghosts, traveling in waves, touched our tent walls
and made them quiver. Ghosts were shaking the ground ever
so lightly. Ghosts were stirring the dogs to hysteria. Ghosts
were wandering in the sky peering for us cringing in our hide-
outs. Ghosts were everywhere, and their hordes were multiply-
ing as every hour added its production of new battlefield dead.

—ERNIE PYLE

8. Imagine yourself on some quiet hidden lake, far from the paths
of mankind; dwell upon the auditory images presented by Tennyson in the following poem. When you have given yourself over
completely to the mood of it, let your voice try to express the
feeling. Imagine your own voice sounding pure and clear like a
bugle note, across the calm lake.

BUGLE SONG

The splendour falls on castle walls
   And snowy summits old in story:
The long light shakes across the lakes,
   And the wild cataract leaps in glory.
Blow, bugle, blow, set the wild echoes flying,
Blow, bugle; answer, echoes, dying, dying, dying.

O hark, O hear! how thin and clear,
   And thinner, clearer, farther going!
O sweet and far from cliff and scar
   The horns of Elfland faintly blowing!
Blow, let us hear the purple glens replying:
Blow, bugle; answer, echoes, dying, dying, dying.

O love, they die in yon rich sky,
   They faint on hill or field or river:
Our echoes roll from soul to soul,
   And grow forever and forever.
Blow, bugle, blow, set the wild echoes flying.
And answer, echoes, answer, dying, dying, dying.

—ALFRED, LORD TENNYSON

9. Here is a group of short selections presenting different types of imagery. In practicing them, bear in mind that mental concentration is more important than conscious voice manipulation. It is essential to see the details of the pictures, not merely to be satisfied with total impressions.

1.   A WISH

Mine be a cot beside the hill;
A bee-hive's hum shall soothe my ear;
A willowy brook that turns a mill,
With many a fall shall linger near.

The swallow, oft, beneath my thatch
Shall twitter from her clay-built nest;
Oft shall the pilgrim lift the latch,
And share my meal, a welcome guest.

Around my ivied porch shall spring
Each fragrant flower that drinks the dew;
And Lucy, at her wheel, shall sing
In russet gown and apron blue.

The village church among the trees,
Where first our marriage vows were given,
With merry peals shall swell the breeze
And point with taper spire to Heaven.

—SAMUEL ROGERS

2.   I waited in the little sunny room:
The cool breeze waves the window lace, at play,
The white rose on the porch was all in bloom,
And out upon the bay,
I watched the wheeling sea-birds go and come.

—EDWARD ROWLAND SILL

3. CASSIUS: Why, man, he doth bestride the narrow world
Like a Colossus, and we petty men
Walk under his huge legs, and peep about

To find ourselves dishonorable graves.
Men at some time are masters of their fates;
The fault, dear Brutus, is not in our stars,
But in ourselves, that we are underlings.
Brutus and Caesar: what should be in that "Caesar"?
Why should that name be sounded more than yours?
Write them together, yours is as fair a name;
Sound them, it doth become the mouth as well;
Weigh them, it is as heavy; conjure with 'em,
"Brutus" will start a spirit as soon as "Caesar."
Now, in the names of all the gods at once,
Upon what meat doth this our Caesar feed,
That he is grown so great?

—SHAKESPEARE

4. If upon this earth we ever have a glimpse of heaven, it is when
we pass a home in winter, at night, and through the windows,
the curtains drawn aside, we see the family about the pleasant
hearth; the old lady knitting, the cat playing with the yarn, the
children wishing they had as many dolls or dollars or knives
or something as there are sparks going out to join the roaring
blast; the father reading and smoking, and the clouds rising
like incense from the altar of domestic joy. I never pass such a
house without feeling that I have received a benediction.

—ROBERT G. INGERSOLL

5. A ship lost at sea for many days suddenly sighted a friendly
vessel. From the mast of the unfortunate vessel was seen the
signal: 'Water, water; we die of thirst!' The answer from the
friendly vessel at once came back: 'Cast down your bucket
where you are.' A second time the distressed signal, 'Water,
water; send us water,' ran up from the distressed vessel, and
was answered: 'Cast down your bucket where you are.' And a
third and a fourth signal for water was answered: 'Cast down
your bucket where you are.' The captain of the distressed
vessel, at last heeding the injunction, cast down his bucket,
and it came up full of fresh, sparkling water from the mouth
of the Amazon river.

To those of my race who depend on bettering their condition in a foreign land, or who underestimate the importance of cultivating friendly relations with the Southern white man, who is their next door neighbor, I would say: 'Cast down your bucket where you are.'

—Booker T. Washington

6. I remember, I remember
The house where I was born,
The little window where the sun
Came peeping in at morn;
He never came a wink too soon
Nor brought too long a day;
But now, I often wish the night
Had borne my breath away.

I remember, I remember
The roses, red and white,
The violets, and the lily-cups—
Those flowers made of light!
The lilacs where the robin built,
And where my brother set
The laburnum on his birthday,—
The tree is living yet.

I remember, I remember
Where I was used to swing—
And thought the air must rush as fresh
To swallows on the wing;
My spirit flew in feathers then
That is so heavy now,
And summer pools could hardly cool
The fever on my brow.

I remember, I remember
The fir trees dark and high;
I used to think their slender tops
Were close against the sky:

It was a childish ignorance,
But now 'tis little joy
To know I'm farther off from Heaven
Than when I was a boy.

—Thomas Hood

7. At length, the sexton, hearing from without
The tumult of the knocking and the shout,
And thinking thieves were in the house of prayer,
Came with his lantern, asking, "Who is there?"
Half choked with rage, King Robert fiercely said,
"Open: 'tis I, the King! Art thou afraid?"
The frightened sexton, muttering, with a curse,
"This is some drunken vagabond, or worse!"
Turned the great key and flung the portal wide;
A man rushed by him at a single stride,
Haggard, half naked, without hat or cloak,
Who neither turned, nor looked at him, nor spoke,
But leaped into the blackness of the night,
And vanished like a specter from his sight.

—Henry W. Longfellow

10. The final practice selection in this section is an excerpt from a campaign address by the late President Roosevelt. Note how he gives the image-stirring details of a single incident to advance his argument. Endeavor to incorporate into your voice some of the rich expressiveness which Roosevelt had in such full measure.

I shall tell you what sold me on old age insurance—old age pensions. Not so long ago—about ten years—I received a great shock. I had been away from my home town of Hyde Park during the winter time and when I came back I found that a tragedy had occurred. I had had an old farm neighbor, who had been a splendid fellow—Supervisor of his town, Highway Commissioner of his town, one of the best of our citizens. Before I had left, around Christmas time, I had seen the old man, who was eighty-nine, his old brother, who was eighty-seven, his other brother, who was eighty-five, and his 'kid' sister, who was eighty-three.

They were living on a farm; I knew it was mortgaged to the hilt; but I assumed that everything was all right, for they still had a couple of cows and a few chickens. But when I came back in the spring, I found that in the severe winter that followed there had been a heavy fall of snow, and one of the old brothers had fallen down on his way out to the barn to milk the cows, and had perished in the snow drift. The town authorities had come along and had taken the two old men and had put them into the county poorhouse, and they had taken the old lady and had sent her down, for want of a better place, to the insane asylum although she was not insane but just old.

That sold me on the idea of trying to keep homes intact for old people.

—FRANKLIN D. ROOSEVELT

Emotion and Voice

For many years the question has been debated whether or not an actor feels the emotion he portrays. Articles and books have been written on both sides of the argument. Many prominent stage people say "Yes," but about as many say "No."

It undoubtedly is true that actors cannot feel the *full extent* of the emotion they depict; the constant repetition of the play, week after week, and sometimes year after year, would be too much of a drain on their emotional resources. This is especially true in some of the great tragedies.

Furthermore, it is doubtful whether an actor could safely depend upon feeling just the right degree of sorrow every time he reproduced a sorrowful line, or be sure of feeling hilarious whenever he came to a line that required laughter, or hate, even to the point of murder, whenever the script called for it. No, the actor must substitute some degree of artistic technique for intense emotional experience on the stage.

Nevertheless, the work of even a master artist would be a

cold and lifeless exhibition were he devoid of emotional response. It is a case, probably, of memorized emotions only partially revived—something like Wordsworth's definition of poetry: "Passion recollected in tranquillity." It would seem that the actor must identify himself with the emotion, understanding it so deeply and sympathetically that he can portray it realistically *with the aid of a trained technique.*

Caruso said that the requisites for a great singer are "a big chest, a big mouth, ninety percent memory, ten percent intelligence, lots of hard work, and something in the heart."

Public Speakers Must Feel What They Say

In the case of the public speaker there is practically universal agreement on this point. From antiquity down to the present day we find the same testimony. Said Socrates, "Let him that would move the world first move himself." Cicero expressed the same thought in these words:

> Nor is it possible for the hearer to grieve, or hate, or fear, or to be moved to commiseration and tears, unless the emotions which the speaker wishes to communicate are deeply impressed upon himself, and stamped on his own bosom with characters of fire.

Senator Albert J. Beveridge, one of the great speakers of the early part of this century, had the same idea in mind when he laid down the fundamental rule for speakers, "Never say anything from the platform that you do not believe." It is what Emerson meant in his essay on eloquence when he said, "The eloquent man is he who is no beautiful speaker, but who is inwardly and desperately drunk with a certain belief."

Public speech, like everyday speech, is neither all emotion nor all thought. It is a judicious blending of the two. Among the better speakers today the trend is toward more emphasis on thought. The speaker aims not so much to give his listeners an emotional spree as to give them something to think about. And yet this tendency, carried to an extreme, results in a dry-as-dust discussion, lacking in human interest and devoid of the appeal which moves people to desired action.

VOICE QUALITY RESPONDS TO EMOTIONAL STATES

Man's emotional nature is exceedingly complex. To attempt to explain the exact neurological process by which voice quality is caused to change in response to our changing emotional states would serve no useful purpose in this textbook. Students desiring to investigate this field will find statements of the current thinking of research students along these lines in speech books by Curry, Gray and Wise, Judson and Weaver, and others; in general textbooks on physiology and psychology; and specifically in the treatise by the Harvard Medical School's noted physiologist, Walter B. Cannon.[10]

Suffice it for our present purposes to say that the central nervous system and the autonomic nervous system, acting together, stimulate the muscles of the speech mechanism in such a way that voice quality is altered to reflect the emotions we feel. Irrespective of how much or how little we know about the physiological process, the fact is obvious. We all know how our voices, if uncontrolled, tend to rise and grow thin when we are excited, and to deepen and take on a somber coloring in moments of grief. These are the grosser, more obvious changes; minor variations of vocal quality are constantly taking place. Many of these smaller changes are subliminal; that is, they are below the threshold of consciousness. We are not aware of the delicate shadings, and perhaps the persons listening to us are likewise unconscious of them; but the voice modulations are having their effect just the same. And these subtle voice changes that we unconsciously hear help to make up our judgments and to determine our courses of action.

[10] Robert Curry, *The Mechanism of the Human Voice*, Longmans, Green & Co., 1940; G. W. Gray and C. M. Wise, *The Bases of Speech*, Harper & Brothers, rev. ed., 1946; L. S. Judson and A. T. Weaver, *Voice Science*, Appleton-Century-Crofts, Inc., 1941; Walter B. Cannon, *Bodily Changes in Pain, Hunger, Fear, and Rage*, Appleton-Century-Crofts, Inc., 1920.

Again we cite ancient Rome's greatest orator to emphasize how long this fundamental truth has been recognized. Cicero once said: "Every emotion of the mind has from nature its own peculiar look, tone, and gesture; and the whole frame of man, and his whole countenance, and the variations of his voice, sound like strings in a musical instrument, just as they are moved by the affections of the mind." And again, "Never, I assure you, have I endeavored to excite in the judges the emotions of grief, commiseration, envy or hatred, without becoming sensibly touched myself with the passion I wished to communicate to them."

EMOTION HAS UNIVERSAL APPEAL

Emotion is basic and universal. It exists in every stratum of human life. The savage exhibits it in his ceremonial dances, and Einstein, who is credited with having the most profound intellect in the world today, exhibits it in his violin. Not only human beings but animals feel and express fear, hate, and love, and refinements of these emotions. A six-weeks-old puppy responds to an accidental injury with a cry expressive of pain; it grunts with satisfaction after a hearty meal; it whines in excited demonstration of affection; it growls when someone approaches too near the bone it is gnawing. Not only that, but it understands and responds to the emotional quality of its master's voice. It may not understand the meaning of the words, but it is quick to interpret and to respond to the tone quality. Babies likewise have enormous power of self-expression long before they know the meaning of words. They cannot tell you that a pin is pricking them but they can tell you that they are in pain. They cannot call explicitly for a bottle of milk but they can tell you that they are hungry, and they can express their satisfaction in coos and gurgles.

To a surprising degree, voice is the mirror of feelings. "Out of the heart the mouth speaketh," and it is also true that out of the "heart" the mouth gets its expressiveness.

Emotion Must Be Controlled

Close as the relationship is, however, between emotion and voice, the emotion must at all times be controlled. Extreme emotions master us. They are essentially chaotic in nature. Refusing to be used for either intellectual or practical purposes, they lead to confusion and awkwardness. In some of his early studies on the effect of emotion upon human action Charles Darwin analyzed the effect of rage thus: "The paralyzed lips refuse to obey the will, and the voice sticks in the throat; or it is rendered loud, harsh, and discordant." This devastating type of uncontrolled feeling must be brought into subjection to the higher thought processes or the voice will be injuriously affected. Overanxiety, extreme excitement, rage, fear, and other accentuated forms of emotionalism do not make for a pleasantly controlled voice.

Stage Fright

Closely related to this uncontrolled emotionalism is a malady which affects not only voice quality but the rest of the personality as well—stage fright. The shaking knees, dry tongue, irregular pulse, spasmodic breathing, and fluttering stomach that accompany this strange affliction are caused largely by overtenseness, which in turn is the result of too much emotionalism. Back of the hyperemotionalism and overtension there may be several causative factors: realization that you are inadequately prepared on the subject, lack of confidence in your command of speech techniques, overeagerness to excel, and a mingling of many other factors.[11]

In this connection we should note that platform artists and teachers of singing and speaking have long recognized that a reasonable degree of nervousness is a valuable asset before a performance. This anticipatory nervousness is nature's condi-

[11] Students interested in learning about the neurological processes that cause all these strange bodily changes which we label *stage fright* should consult D. E. Watkins and H. M. Karr, *Stage Fright and What to Do About It,* Expression Co., 1940.

tioner. It lifts us above the commonplace and stimulates us to do our best. Persons entirely lacking in this nervousness are likely to be dull and sluggish. Someone has quipped that this nervousness "is the price one has to pay for being a race horse instead of a cow."

An additional suggestion pertaining to stage fright will be discussed in the section on physical action and voice (page 329).

CONTROLLED EMOTION PROVIDES A VALUABLE STIMULUS

Robert S. Woodworth, the psychologist, describes the relationship between thought and emotion as follows:

The difference between emotional and unemotional activity . . . depends on the degree to which the individual keeps his head, that is on the degree to which his brainy life . . . dominates his whole activity. If he completely loses his head, his sensations become a diffused mass of feeling, and his set for overt activity becomes a blind struggle. If he only partially loses his head, he throws himself with abandon into overactivity; while still remaining somewhat observant, his movements are vigorous, or even rather violent, and his sensations are mostly a feeling mass. If he completely keeps his head and remains cool and calculating in the midst of his activity, he is able to take advantage of all the breaks of luck, but his movements may lack something in energy, and he loses the relish of the experience.[12]

Bobby Jones recognized the application of this same principle in golf:

I used to think that if I could suppress a feeling of nervousness when starting out to play a match, I could then play a better and more thoughtful game. I have since come to think that the man who goes placidly on his way is often the easiest fellow to beat, for it is only the high-strung temperament that rises above its own ability to meet a great occasion.[13]

[12] R. S. Woodworth, *Psychology*, Henry Holt & Company, 1929, pp. 308-309.
[13] Robert T. Jones, *Bobby Jones on Golf*, New Metropolitan Fiction Co., 1937, p. 66.

The famous pianist, Anton Rubinstein, had a similar experience on the concert platform. Usually he was extremely nervous before an opening number, manifesting great agitation as he paced up and down behind the scenes. After making a tour of America in which he appeared 250 times in a short period, sometimes as often as twice a day, he said that giving so many concerts allayed his nervousness, but thereby made an automaton of him.

Emotionalism is a useful servant, a superb voice conditioner when controlled, a Frankenstein when unleashed. A student probably had something like this in mind when he said, "Be soaked up in your subject, but not washed out by it."

Sincerity of Paramount Importance

Before we finish our consideration of emotion and its basic relationship to voice, we must deal specifically with one emotion which is of primary importance in voice work—sincerity. This word, like many others in our language, has a host of meanings; as it relates to the voice, however, it means *genuineness, honesty, unaffectedness, earnestness*. Speech that lacks this quality comes close to being immoral. People are quick to sense insincerity in speech, and they resent it intensely. No tricks of oratory can substitute for sincerity. Indeed, as Daniel Webster, one of America's greatest orators, once said, "Studied contrivances of speech shock and disgust men."[14]

To be sure, sincerity is not all that is needed to make an effective speaker. That fact was demonstrated in the famous political campaign waged by Franklin D. Roosevelt and Wendell Willkie. As has often been remarked, Willkie was sincere, and his genuine sincerity won him many supporters. But his public speaking voice was poor, or at least he forced it to such a degree during the campaign that it sounded harsh and unappealing; and in consequence he suffered in his competition

---

[14] In his lecture, "Adams and Jefferson."

with the masterful Roosevelt. Roosevelt, too, had sincerity, *plus* a persuasive voice and other speech skills.

There was another Roosevelt who likewise was characterized by a high degree of vocal sincerity. President "Teddy" Roosevelt was the epitome of sincerity, on and off the platform, and this quality provided one of the sources of his leadership.

Another great American possessed sincerity in an unprecedented degree. Listen to the description of Abraham Lincoln by a young journalist (Henry Villard, son-in-law of the abolitionist William Lloyd Garrison) who observed and reported the famous debates between Lincoln and Stephen A. Douglas:

> As far as all external conditions were concerned, there was nothing in favor of Lincoln. He had a lean, lank, indescribably gawky figure, an odd-featured, wrinkled, inexpressive, and altogether uncomely face. He used singularly awkward, almost absurd, up and down and sidewise movements of his body to give emphasis to his arguments. His voice was naturally good, but he frequently raised it to an unnatural pitch. Yet the unprejudiced mind felt at once that, while there was on the one side a skillful dialectician and debater arguing a wrong and weak cause, there was on the other a thoroughly earnest and truthful man, inspired by sound convictions in consonance with the true spirit of American institutions. . . . Putting prejudices to one side, no one can see Mr. Lincoln without recognizing in him a man of immense power and force of character and natural talent. He seems so sincere, so conscientious, so earnest, so simple-hearted, that one cannot help liking him. . . . He seems tremendously rough and tremendously honest and earnest. . . .[15]

The voice student cannot afford to neglect this vital characteristic of personality and of voice. He should not attempt to substitute any vocal tricks for genuine honesty of feeling.

Our objective in the exercises which follow should be to cultivate strong, true feeling, and then let the voice respond with honest sincerity.

[15] Henry Villard, *Lincoln on the Eve of '61*, edited by Harold G. and Oswald Garrison Villard, Alfred A. Knopf, 1941, pp. 3, 4.

EXERCISES IN EMOTION AND VOICE RELATIONSHIPS

1. Try this little experiment in imaginative feeling and note its effect on the voice: Think of yourself as being tired, completely exhausted. In your mind, say to yourself over and over, "I'm tired; very, very tired." Feel the muscles of your throat and jaw begin to relax and to get "set" for the appropriate tone quality. The response is involuntary, almost irresistible. It is this muscular response to emotional states which helps marvelously to enrich the voice quality.

2. Try to squeeze the last drop of emotion from these sentences:

    1. Oh, World, I cannot hold thee close enough!

    2. On with the dance! Let joy be unconfined!

    3. Each age is a dream that is dying, or one that is coming to birth.

    4. Ye blocks, ye stones, ye worse than senseless things!

    5. Methought I heard a voice cry, "Sleep no more!
       Macbeth doth murder sleep . . .
       Macbeth shall sleep no more!"

    6.   Alone, alone, all, all, alone,
                 Alone on a wide, wide sea!

    7.   It matters not how straight the gate,
               How charged with punishment the scroll,
             I am the master of my fate;
               I am the captain of my soul.

    8.   Great God! I'd rather be
         A pagan suckled in a creed outworn,
         So might I, standing on this pleasant lea,
         Have glimpses that would make me less forlorn.

    9.   Fool! All that is, at all,
         Lasts ever, past recall;
         Earth changes, but thy soul and God stand sure;
         What entered into thee,
         That was, is, and shall be:
         Time's wheel runs back or stops: Potter and clay
              endure.

10.   Ne'er saw I, never felt, a calm so deep!
            The river glideth at his own sweet will;
            Dear God! the very houses seem asleep.

11.   Hurrah! hurrah! the west wind comes freshening
                down the bay!
            The rising sails are filling, give way, my lads, give
                way!

3. In the following poem you will find moods within a mood; that
   is, three distinct emotional states are incorporated within the
   dominant emotion. They are like the three acts of a drama. Find
   the changing moods and depict them in your voice.

THE THREE FISHERS

Three fishers went sailing out into the West,
Out into the West as the sun went down;
Each thought on the woman who loved him the best;
    And the children stood watching them out of the town;
For men must work, and women must weep,
And there's little to earn, and many to keep,
    Though the harbour bar be moaning.

Three wives sat up in the light-house tower,
    And they trimm'd the lamps as the sun went down;
They look'd at the squall, and they look'd at the shower,
    And the night rack came rolling up ragged and brown!
But men must work, and women must weep,
Though storms be sudden, and waters deep,
    And the harbour bar be moaning.

Three corpses lay out on the shining sands
    In the morning gleam as the tide went down,
And the women are weeping and wringing their hands
    For those who will never come back to the town;
For men must work, and women must weep,
And the sooner it's over, the sooner to sleep—
    And good-bye to the bar and its moaning.
                                        —CHARLES KINGSLEY

4. Here Corporal Walter J. Slatoff, an American soldier in Germany, epitomizes the tragedy of war in a letter to his son. Do not try to read it aloud until you have thought and felt yourself into the mood the soldier must have had when he wrote the letter.

My Son:

War is more terrible than all the words of men can say; more terrible than a man's mind can comprehend.

It is the corpse of a friend; one moment ago a living human being with thoughts, hopes, and a future—just exactly like yourself—now nothing.

It is the eyes of men after battle, like muddy water, lightless.

It is cities—labor of generations lost—now dusty piles of broken stones and splintered wood—dead.

It is the total pain of a hundred million parted loved ones—some for always.

It is the impossibility of planning a future; uncertainty that mocks every hoping dream.

Remember! It is the reality of these things—not the words.

It is the sound of an exploding shell; a moment's silence, then the searing scream "MEDIC" passed urgently from throat to throat.

It is the groans and the pain of the wounded, and the expressions on their faces.

It is the sound of new soldiers crying before battle; the louder sound of their silence afterwards.

It is the filth and itching and hunger; the endless body discomfort; the feeling like an animal; the fatigue so deep that to die would be good.

It is battle, which is confusion, fear, hate, death, misery and much more.

The reality—not the words. Remember!

It is the evil sickening knowledge that sooner or later the law of averages will catch up with each soldier, the horrible hope that it will take the form of a wound, not maiming or death.

It is boys of 19 who might be in the schoolroom or flirting in the park; husbands who might be telling their wives of a raise—tender and happy-eyed; fathers who might be teaching their sons to throw a ball—bright with pride. It is these men, mouths and insides ugly with fear and hate, driving a bayonet into other men's bodies.

It is "battle fatigue," a nice name for having taken more than the brain and heart can stand, and taking refuge in a shadowy unreal world.

It is the maimed coming home; dreading pity, dreading failure, dreading life.

It is many million precious years of human lives lost; and the watching of the loss, day by day, month by month, year by year, until hope is an ugly sneering thing.

Remember! Remember and multiply these things by the largest number you know. Then repeat them over and over again until they are alive and burning in your mind.

Remember! Remember what we are talking about. Not words; not soldiers; but human beings just exactly like yourself.

And when it is in your mind so strongly that you can never forget; then seek how you can best keep the peace. Work at this hard with every tool of thought and love you have. Do not rest until you can say to every man who ever died for man's happiness: "You did not die in vain."[16]

5. For lovers of the sea, here are two poems which will help give expression to this sentiment:

1.   SEA-FEVER[17]

I must go down to the seas again, to the lonely sea and
    the sky,
And all I ask is a tall ship and a star to steer her by,
And the wheel's kick and the wind's song and the
    white sail's shaking,
And a grey mist on the sea's face and a grey dawn
    breaking.

[16] From the *American Observer*, September 24, 1945.
[17] From John Masefield, *Selected Poems*, copyright 1938 by John Masefield and used with The Macmillan Company's permission.

I must go down to the seas again, for the call of the
    running tide
Is a wild call and a clear call that may not be denied;
And all I ask is a windy day with the white clouds
    flying,
And the flung spray and the blown spume, and the
    sea-gulls crying.

I must go down to the seas again, to the vagrant gypsy
    life,
To the gull's way, and the whale's way, where the
    wind's like a whetted knife,
And all I ask is a merry yarn from a laughing
    fellow-rover,
And a quiet sleep and a sweet dream when the long
    trick's over.

—JOHN MASEFIELD

2.
THE SEA

The sea! the sea! the open sea!
The blue, the fresh, the ever free!
Without a mark, without a bound,
It runneth the earth's wide regions round;
It plays with the clouds; it mocks the skies;
Or like a cradled creature lies.

I'm on the sea! I'm on the sea!
I am where I would ever be;
With the blue above and the blue below,
And silence wheresoe'er I go;
If a storm should come and awake the deep,
What matter? I shall ride and sleep.

I love, O how I love to ride
On the fierce, foaming, bursting tide,
When every mad wave drowns the moon
Or whistles aloft his tempest tune,
And tells how goeth the world below,
And why the sou'west blasts do blow.

—BRYAN WALLER PROCTER

6. Here are three poems pertaining to duty. Before undertaking to read them aloud, analyze them briefly. Wordsworth's and Browning's poems are entirely serious. The fact that the third poem treats the theme playfully should not blind us to the sublime truth of the Wordsworth and Browning poems. Approach them in the spirit that the authors intended.

1.   *From* ODE TO DUTY

Stern Daughter of the Voice of God!
O Duty! if that name thou love
Who art a light to guide, a rod
To check the erring, and reprove;
Thou, who art victory and law
When empty terrors overawe,
From vain temptations dost set free,
And calm'st the weary strife of frail humanity!

. . . . . .

Stern Lawgiver! yet thou dost wear
The Godhead's most benignant grace;
Nor know we anything so fair
As is the smile upon thy face:
Flowers laugh before thee on their beds,
And fragrance in thy footing treads;
Thou dost preserve the stars from wrong;
And the most ancient heavens, through thee, are fresh
    and strong.

To humbler functions, awful Power!
I call thee: I myself commend
Unto thy guidance from this hour;
O let my weakness have an end!
Give unto me, made lowly wise,
The spirit of self-sacrifice;
The confidence of reason give;
And in the light of Truth thy bondman let me live!
                              —WILLIAM WORDSWORTH

2.   DUTY

The sweetest lives are those to duty wed,
Whose deeds, both great and small,
Are close-knit strands of an unbroken thread,
Whose love ennobles all.
The world may sound no trumpet, ring no bells;
The book of life the shining record tells.
Thy love shall chant its own beatitudes,
After its own life-working. A child's kiss
Set on thy singing lips shall make thee glad;
A poor man served by thee shall make thee rich;
A sick man helped by thee shall make thee strong;
Thou shalt be served thyself by every sense
Of service thou renderest.

—ROBERT BROWNING

3. Ogden Nash is chiefly known as a writer of humorous verse.
Several features of the following poem should be noted, in
preparation for its oral delivery:

Note the "coined" words, and show by your voice inflection
that you recognize them for what they are: such words as,
"abominously" and "forbiddinger." The deliberate misspell-
ings for rhyming effect (like "Ortumn" for Autumn), and the
highly unique grammatical constructions have to be treated
with a light and whimsical touch or they become absurd. The
poem will be enriched for you, and for your listeners, if you
appreciate the literary allusions in the piece. There are direct
allusions to passages in Greek mythology, the Bible, Emerson,
the short stories of the popular English writer, P. G. Wodehouse, and one of Coleridge's poems. See if you can locate
them.

KIND OF AN ODE TO DUTY[18]

O Duty,
Why hast thou not the visage of a sweetie or a cutie?

. . . .

[18] From *I'm a Stranger Here Myself,* copyright 1938, by Ogden Nash; by permission of Little, Brown & Co.

Why glitter thy spectacles so ominously?
Why art thou clad so abominously?
Why art thou so different from Venus?
And why do thou and I have so few interests mutually
in common between us?
Why art thou fifty percent martyr
And fifty-one percent Tartar?
Why is it thy unfortunate wont
To attract people by calling on them either to leave
undone the deeds they like, or to do the deeds
they don't?
Why art thou so like an April post-mortem
Or something that died in the Ortumn?
Above all, why dost thou continue to hound me?
Why art thou always albatrossly hanging round me?
Thou so ubiquitous,
And I so iniquitous.
I seem to be the one person in the world thou art
perpetually preaching at who or to who;
Whatever looks like fun, there are thou standing
between me and it, calling yoo-hoo.
O Duty, Duty!
How noble a man should I be, hadst thou the visage
of a sweetie or cutie!

. . . .

But as it is thou art so much forbiddinger than a
Wodehouse hero's forbiddingest aunt,
That in the words of the poet, When Duty whispers
low, Thou must, this erstwhile youth replies, I
just can't.

—Ogden Nash

7. Here is a group of selections which are rather pessimistic in tone,
followed in the next exercise by selections in a more optimistic
vein. Study the two groups together to get the contrast. In fair-
ness to the authors, we should say that some of these excerpts are
taken out of context and do not express the spirit of the poem or
article as a whole. They do, however, serve our purpose here.

1.
  We are not sure of sorrow,
     And joy was never sure;
  Today will die tomorrow;
     Time stoops to no man's lure;
  And love, grown faint and fretful,
  With lips but half regretful
  Sighs, and with eyes forgetful
     Weeps that no loves endure.
                  —ALGERNON CHARLES SWINBURNE

2.
  This is the curse of life! that not
  A nobler, calmer train
  Of wiser thoughts and feelings blot
  Our passions from our brain:

  But each day brings its petty dust
  Our soon-choked souls to fill,
  And we forget because we must
  And not because we will.
                  —MATTHEW ARNOLD

3.
  Milton! thou shouldst be living at this hour:
  England hath need of thee: she is a fen
  Of stagnant waters: altar, sword, and pen,
  Fireside, the heroic wealth of hall and bower
  Have forfeited their ancient English dower
  Of inward happiness. We are selfish men:
  Oh! raise us up, return to us again,
  And give us manners, virtue, freedom, power.
                  —WILLIAM WORDSWORTH

4. Vanity of vanities, saith the preacher; all is vanity.

5.
  My soul is weary of my life;
  I will give free course to my complaint;
  I will speak in the bitterness of my soul.

6.   Come, fill the Cup, and in the fire of Spring
          Your Winter-garment of Repentance fling:
          The Bird of Time has but a little way
          To flutter—and the Bird is on the Wing.

            .   .   .   .   .   .

          O threats of Hell and Hopes of Paradise!
          One thing at least is certain—*This* Life flies;
          One thing is certain and the rest is Lies—
          The Flower that once has blown for ever dies.

            .   .   .   .   .   .

          And that inverted Bowl they call the sky,
          Whereunder crawling cooped we live and die,
          Lift not your hands to *It* for help—for It
          As impotently moves as you or I.

                                —Edward Fitzgerald

7.   Oppress'd with grief, oppress'd with care,
          A burden more than I can bear,
            I sit me down and sigh:
          O life! thou art a galling load,
          Along a rough, a weary road,
            To wretches such as I!
          Dim backward as I cast my view,
            What sick'ning scenes appear!
          What sorrows yet may pierce me through
            Too justly I may fear!

                                  —Robert Burns

8.   Blow, blow, thou winter wind,
           Thou art not so unkind
             As man's ingratitude;
           Thy tooth is not so keen,
           Because thou art not seen,
             Although thy breath be rude.

Freeze, freeze, thou bitter sky,
That dost not bite so nigh
   As benefits forgot;
Though thou the waters warp,
Thy sting is not so sharp
   As friend remember'd not.

           —SHAKESPEARE

9.   OFT IN THE STILLY NIGHT

Oft, in the stilly night,
  Ere Slumber's chain has bound me,
Fond Memory brings the light
  Of other days around me:
    The smiles, the tears,
    Of boyhood's years,
  The words of love then spoken;
    The eyes that shone,
    Now dimmed and gone,
  The cheerful hearts now broken!
Thus, in the stilly night,
  Ere Slumber's chain has bound me,
Sad Memory brings the light
  Of other days around me.

When I remember all
  The friends so linked together
I've seen around me fall,
  Like leaves in wintry weather,
    I feel like one
    Who treads alone
  Some banquet-hall deserted,
    Whose lights are fled,
    Whose garlands dead,
  And all but him departed!
Thus, in the stilly night,
  Ere Slumber's chain has bound me.
Sad Memory brings the light
  Of other days around me.

           —THOMAS MOORE

8. These selections are in a different vein from those in the preceding group. Study the two groups together.

1.   A merry heart is a good medicine:
              But a broken spirit drieth up the bones.

2.   A LOVER AND HIS LASS

It was a lover and his lass,
   With a hey, and a ho, and a hey nonino,
That o'er the green corn-field did pass
    In the spring time, the only pretty ring time,
    When birds do sing, hey ding a ding, ding;
Sweet lovers love the spring.

This carol they began that hour,
   With a hey, and a ho, and a hey nonino,
How that a life was but a flower
    In the spring time, the only pretty ring time,
    When birds do sing, hey ding a ding, ding;
Sweet lovers love the spring.

And therefore take the present time,
   With a hey, and a ho, and a hey nonino,
For love is crowned with the prime
    In the spring time, the only pretty ring time,
    When birds to sing, hey ding a ding, ding;
Sweet lovers love the spring.

—SHAKESPEARE

3.   For, lo, the winter is past,
          The rain is over and gone;
     The flowers appear on the earth;
       The time of the singing of birds is come,
    And the voice of the turtle is heard in our land;
    The fig tree putteth forth her green figs,
       And the vines with the tender grape
       Give a good smell.

—THE BIBLE

4. Oh, the wild joys of living! the leaping from rock up
      to rock,
   The strong rending of boughs from the fir-tree, the
      cool silver shock
   Of the plunge in a pool's living water, the hunt of the
      bear,
   And the sultriness showing the lion is couched in his
      lair.
   And the meal, the rich dates yellowed over with gold
      dust divine,
   And the locust-flesh steeped in the pitcher, the full
      draft of wine,
   And the sleep in the dried river-channel where
      bulrushes tell
   That the water was wont to go warbling so softly and
      well.
   How good is man's life, the mere living! How fit to
      employ
   All the heart and the soul and the senses forever in joy!

   —ROBERT BROWNING

5. Joy comes, grief goes, we know not how;
   Everything is happy now,
      Everything is upward striving;
   'T is as easy now for the heart to be true
   As for grass to be green or skies to be blue,—
      'T is the natural way of living:
   Who knows whither the clouds have fled?
      In the unscarred heaven they leave no wake;
   And the eyes forget the tears they have shed,
      The heart forgets its sorrow and ache;
   The soul partakes the season's youth,
      And the sulphurous rifts of passion and woe
   Lie deep 'neath a silence pure and smooth,
      Like burnt-out craters healed with snow.

   —JAMES RUSSELL LOWELL

6.   BARTER[19]

> Life has loveliness to sell,
> All beautiful and splendid things,
> Blue waves whitened on a cliff,
>   Soaring fire that sways and sings,
> And children's faces looking up
> Holding wonder like a cup.
>
> Life has loveliness to sell,
> Music like a curve of gold,
> Scent of pine trees in the rain,
>   Eyes that love you, arms that fold,
> And for your spirit's still delight,
> Holy thoughts that star the night.
>
> Spend all you have for loveliness,
> Buy it and never count the cost;
> For one white singing hour of peace
>   Count many a year of strife well lost,
> And for a breath of ecstasy
> Give all you have been or could be.
>
> —SARA TEASDALE

7.   TO A SKYLARK

> Hail to thee, blithe spirit!
>   Bird thou never wert,
> That from heaven, or near it,
>   Pourest thy full heart
> In profuse strains of unpremeditated art.
>
> Higher still and higher
>   From the earth thou springest
> Like a cloud of fire;
>   The blue deep thou wingest,
> And singing still dost soar, and soaring ever singest.

[19] From Sara Teasdale, *Collected Poems,* copyright 1937 by The Macmillan Company and used with their permission.

In the golden light'ning
  Of the sunken sun,
O'er which clouds are bright'ning,
  Thou dost float and run;
Like an unbodied joy whose race is just begun.

The pale purple even
  Melts around thy flight;
Like a star of heaven,
  In the broad daylight
Thou art unseen,—but yet I hear thy shrill delight,

    · · · · · ·

Better than all measures
  Of delightful sound—
Better than all treasures
  That in books are found—
Thy skill to poet were, thou scorner of the ground!

Teach me half the gladness
  That thy brain must know,
Such harmonious madness
  From my lips would flow,
The world would listen then—as I am listening now.

                               —PERCY BYSSHE SHELLEY

9. Here is a poem which combines both of the moods in the selections in Exercises 7 and 8. Note how the author has contrasted
the gayety symbolized by Romany with the somber war-like spirit
symbolized by Rome. Stanzas 1 and 3 are light and joyous, stanzas
2 and 4 are heavy and depressing. Both moods are united in
stanza 5.

FROM ROMANY TO ROME[20]

Upon the road to Romany
  It's stay, friend, stay!
There's lots o' love and lots o' time,
  To linger on the way;

[20] Reprinted by special permission of the author.

Poppies for the twilight,
Roses for the noon,
It's happy goes as lucky goes
To Romany in June.

But on the road to Rome—oh
It's march, man, march!
The dust is on the chariot wheels,
The sere is on the larch;
Helmets and javelins
And bridles flecked with foam,—
The flowers are dead, the world's ahead
Upon the road to Rome.

Upon the road to Romany,
It's sing, boys, sing!
Tho rag and pack be on our back
We'll whistle at the King.
Wine is in the sunshine
Madness in the moon,
And de'il may care the road we fare
To Romany in June.

But on the road to Rome,—ah
It's fight, man, fight!
Footman and horseman
Treading left and right
Camp-fires and watch-fires
Ruddying the gloam—
The fields are gray and worn away
Along the road to Rome.

Along the road to Rome, alas!
The glorious dust is whirled,
Strong hearts are fierce to see
The City of the World;
Yet footfall or bugle-call
Or thunder as ye will,
Upon the road to Romany,
The birds are calling still.   —WALLACE IRWIN

10. A sense of mystery is a mood. To interpret it vocally requires a sensitive understanding. Both of the poems included here create this air of mystery. You may consider them as allegorical, or you may accept them at face value, just for their haunting sense of mystery. But in any case, before you attempt to read them aloud, be sure that you know the meaning of all the words and that you see the pictures.

1.   *From* ULALUME

The skies they were ashen and sober;
    The leaves they were crispèd and sere—
    The leaves they were withering and sere:
It was night in the lonesome October
    Of my most immemorial year;
It was hard by the dim lake of Auber,
    In the misty mid region of Weir—
It was down by the dank tarn of Auber,
    In the ghoul-haunted woodland of Weir.

      . . . .

Then my heart it grew ashen and sober
    As the leaves that were crispèd and sere—
    As the leaves that were withering and sere;
And I cried: "It was surely October
    On *this* very night of last year
    That I journeyed—I journeyed down here!—
    That I brought a dread burden down here—
    On this night of all nights in the year,
    Ah, what demon has tempted me here?
Well I know, now, this dim lake of Auber—
    This misty mid region of Weir—
Well I know, now, this dank tarn of Auber,
    This ghoul-haunted woodland of Weir."
                —EDGAR ALLAN POE

2.   THE LISTENERS[21]

"Is there anybody there?" said the Traveller
    Knocking on the moonlit door;
And his horse in the silence champed the grasses
    Of the forest's ferny floor.
And a bird flew up out of the turret,
    Above the Traveller's head:
And he smote upon the door again a second time;
    "Is there anybody there?" he said.
But no one descended to the Traveller;
    No head from the leaf-fringed sill
Leaned over and looked into his grey eyes,
    Where he stood perplexed and still.
But only a host of phantom listeners
    That dwelt in the lone house then
Stood listening in the quiet of the moonlight
    To that voice from the world of men:
Stood thronging the faint moonbeams on the dark stair,
    That goes down to the empty hall,
Hearkening in an air stirred and shaken
    By the lonely Traveller's call.
And he felt in his heart their strangeness,
    Their stillness answering his cry,
While his horse moved, cropping the dark turf,
    'Neath the starred and leafy sky;
For he suddenly smote on the door, even
    Louder, and lifted his head:—
"Tell them I came, and no one answered,
    That I kept my word," he said.
Never the least stir made the listeners,
    Though every word he spake
Fell echoing through the shadowiness of the still house,
    From the one man left awake:

Ay, they heard his foot upon the stirrup,
   And the sound of iron on stone,
And how the silence surged softly backward,
   When the plunging hoofs were gone.

                        —WALTER DE LA MARE

11. The two strongly emotional poems which follow were forged as weapons to fight social evils—one, child labor; the other, the sweatshop. They aided in achieving needed reforms in England, somewhat as did Harriet Beecher Stowe's *Uncle Tom's Cabin* in our country. To do them justice, you'll have to feel yourself into the spirit of a crusader, remembering that the millennium has not yet arrived in either of these fields.

1.   *From* THE CRY OF THE CHILDREN

Do ye hear the children weeping, O my brothers,
   Ere the sorrow comes with years?
They are leaning their young heads against their mothers,—
   And *that* cannot stop their tears.
The young lambs are bleating in the meadows;
   The young birds are chirping in the nest;
The young fawns are playing with the shadows;
   The young flowers are blowing toward the west—
But the young, young children, O my brothers,
   They are weeping bitterly!
They are weeping in the playtime of the others,
   In the country of the free.

                . . . .

"For oh," say the children, "we are weary,
   And we cannot run or leap—
If we cared for any meadows, it were merely
   To drop down in them and sleep.
Our knees tremble sorely in the stooping—
   We fall upon our faces, trying to go;
And, underneath our heavy eyelids drooping,
   The reddest flower would look as pale as snow.

For, all day, we drag our burden tiring,
  Through the coal-dark, underground—
Or, all day, we drive the wheels of iron
  In the factories, round and round.

"For, all day, the wheels are droning, turning,—
  Their wind comes in our faces,—
Till our hearts turn,—our heads, with pulses burning,
  And the walls turn in their places—
Turns the sky in the high window blank and reeling—
  Turns the long light that drops adown the wall—
Turn the black flies that crawl along the ceiling—
  All are turning, all the day, and we with all.—
And, all day, the iron wheels are droning;
  And sometimes we could pray,
'O ye wheels' (breaking out in a mad moaning),
  'Stop! be silent for today!' "

. . . . . .

Now tell the poor young children, O my brothers,
  To look up to Him and pray—
So the blesséd One, who blesseth all the others,
  Will bless them another day.
They answer, "Who is God that He should hear us,
  While the rushing of the iron wheels is stirred?
When we sob aloud, the human creatures near us
  Pass by, hearing not, or answer not a word!
And *we* hear not (for the wheels in their resounding)
  Strangers speaking at the door:
Is it likely God, with angels singing round Him,
  Hears our weeping any more? . . ."

. . . . . .

They look up, with their pale and sunken faces,
  And their look is dread to see,
For they mind you of their angels in high places,
  With eyes turned on Deity:—
"How long," they say, "how long, O cruel nation,
  Will you stand, to move the world, on a child's heart,

Stifle down with a mailéd heel its palpitation,
    And tread onward to your throne amid the mart?
Our blood splashes upward, O gold-heaper,
    And your purple shows your path,
But the child's sob in the silence curses deeper
    Than the strong man in his wrath!"

                  —ELIZABETH BARRETT BROWNING

2.   *From* SONG OF THE SHIRT

    With fingers weary and worn,
        With eyelids heavy and red,
  A woman sat in unwomanly rags,
        Plying her needle and thread—
           Stitch! stitch! stitch!
  In poverty, hunger, and dirt,
        And still with a voice of dolorous pitch
  She sang the "Song of the Shirt!"

  "Work! work! work!
        While the cock is crowing aloof!
  And work—work—work,
        Till the stars shine through the roof!
  It's Oh! to be a slave
        Along with the barbarous Turk,
  Where woman has never a soul to save,
        If this is Christian work!

  "Work—work—work
        Till the brain begins to swim;
  Work—work—work
        Till the eyes are heavy and dim.
  Seam, and gusset, and band,
        Band, and gusset, and seam,
  Till over the buttons I fall asleep,
        And sew them on in a dream!

                '   '   '   ·   ·   ·   ·

"Work—work—work!
   My labor never flags;
And what are its wages? A bed of straw,
   A crust of bread—and rags.
That shatter'd roof—and this naked floor—
   A table—a broken chair—
And a wall so blank, my shadow I thank
   For sometimes falling there.

"Work—work—work!
   From weary chime to chime,
Work—work—work—
   As prisoners work for crime!
Band, and gusset, and seam,
Seam, and gusset, and band,
Till the heart is sick, and the brain benumb'd.
   As well as the weary hand."

. . . . . .

With fingers weary and worn,
   With eyelids heavy and red,
A woman sat in unwomanly rags,
   Plying her needle and thread—
     Stitch! stitch! stitch!
   In poverty, hunger, and dirt,
And still with a voice of dolorous pitch,
Would that its tone could reach the rich!
   She sang this "Song of the Shirt!"
           —THOMAS HOOD

Physical Action and Voice

Aesop, in one of his fables, tells of the hand and mouth which went on strike, refusing to feed the stomach. They said, "We do all the work and the stomach gets all the benefit." But straightway, when they stopped feeding the stomach, they began to grow feeble. Similarly, if you pat a dog on the head it is his tail that wags, and if a man bumps his elbow it's his mouth that says "ouch." This interdependence of the different parts of the body is recognized by everyone. But it is not always realized that there is a similarly close relationship between voice quality and bodily actions.

In the preceding section we saw how the tones of the voice automatically respond to emotional states. These emotional states in turn are vitally affected by the condition of the body. A widely accepted explanation of the nature of emotions is called the James-Lange theory[22] and is based on the principle that emotion does not precede but follows physical change (for example, we do not feel happy and then laugh, but rather we laugh and then feel happy). Proponents of this theory direct our attention to this fact: If there is a sharp explosion close to us, we do not stop to find out whether or not we are afraid before we take action. We respond automatically to the stimulus—we jump. Only afterward do we tremble, shake, and feel the other sensations of fear. We sometimes have a similar reaction in case of a "narrow squeak" in traffic; it is only after we have swung the steering wheel violently or tramped on the brakes—after the danger is all past—that we become conscious of the fear sensation. But it does not matter at all whether or not you accept the James-Lange theory; the important point is that body, emotions, and voice are all bound up together, that what we feel and what we do—with our bodies and with our voices—are so closely related that it is next to impossible to tell which precedes and which follows. This fact has a significant bearing upon voice training.

Civilized Society Emphasizes Physical Restraint

Civilization places a heavy hand on our physical activities. From the time Mother first says, "Now, Johnny, see if you can't sit still; for goodness sake, quit wiggling," up through the restraint of a school desk, and later a business desk, the whole process is a repression of activity. In this it is easy to go to excess.

[22] William James, *Psychology, Briefer Course,* Henry Holt & Company, 1930, pp. 375-380.

Some people, indeed, have been toned down so far that there is justification for the undertaker's advertisement, "Why walk around half dead, when I'll bury you for $40?"

Physical lifelessness reflects itself in vocal lifelessness. It begets voices which make everything sound commonplace, uninteresting. Probably the best corrective for this vocal condition is for its possessor to eat more spinach, play more tennis, or climb more mountains. Physical inhibitions are like a dam which holds back vocal expressiveness; when the dam is broken down, a flood of fresh new vocal life appears.

This is not an argument for wild arm waving, desk pounding, and other forms of exhibitionism, but rather an appeal for common-sense recognition of the fact that an uninhibited body is necessary for vital, colorful voice quality. Action, of course, should not be put on like a coat; it should come from within. What is needed is a degree of abandonment, a self-surrender, a breaking away of barriers. Better than special tricks and manipulations of the voice is a sense of coördination between mind and voice. And one helpful way to achieve this coördination is to release the bodily tensions.

STAGE FRIGHT AND PHYSICAL ACTION

Before an audience rigidity becomes most conspicuous—rigidity through fear. We have mentioned this condition previously under its widely accepted name, stage fright—a condition so common that it is practically universal. Like young love, nearly everyone who gets it thinks that he has it in an especially aggravated form denied to all others. Actually it is very doubtful if anyone is free of stage fright the first time he goes before an audience, or is ever entirely free from it—that is, if he is any good as a speaker. Anyone possessed of so phlegmatic a temperament that he does not feel any fear of an audience, or at least a wholesome respect for it, is bound to give an uninspiring talk.

An explanation of the physical immobility which accompanies stage fright may be found in our biological development. Our primitive forefathers undoubtedly had many experiences in which their safety depended on remaining quiet. The sudden cracking of a twig, the fierce growl of an animal, a glimpse of some crouching predatory beast must frequently have prompted the response of instant and complete immobility. Thus they were able to escape observation, and consequent death, by a reaction in many cases as serviceable as flight. So, through a long process of selection and adaptation man developed this natural method of protection. The response is observable today in many lower animals, particularly the rabbit, deer, and partridge. Confronted with a sudden danger, they show an instant reaction of either flight or immobility. In the latter case they "freeze" into a tense motionlessness and, aided by protective coloration, merge into the background and become practically indistinguishable. So man is inclined to respond to some of his most trying emergencies.

It is unfortunate that just when a person wants to be at his best, when he most needs the qualities of strength and leadership, he is likely to get "scared stiff." Faced with a new situation, especially a new situation which involves a sea of faces, many of us want nothing quite so much as to merge into the background and become as inconspicuous as possible. We develop the scared-rabbit complex. Fearful of making a wrong motion, we make no motion at all. Fearful that our voices will get out of control, we hold them rigidly in check. A sort of panic takes possession of us and transforms us into lifelessness. Our bodies become so tense that they tremble at the knees, our faces are as expressionless as Chinese masks, and our voices as colorless and flavorless as the mud pies of our childhood.

The "Natural" Cure for Stage Fright. Let it be understood by every novice that it is not natural for a normal person to be rigid and motionless on the platform unless he is throttled by fear. The best corrective for the distressful condition called stage fright is to do something. A definite action will usually break the spell of the emotional complex. Many a person has survived those first moments of his talk—when stage fright functions most virulently—by taking a few firm steps across the platform, writing on the blackboard, taking a drink of water, deliberately moving his notes from one side of the reading desk to the other, producing a picture or other object to show the audience—doing anything that requires action.

Physical activity, of course, is not the only "cure" for stage fright. Among other remedies are thorough preparation; deep, rhythmical breathing; a proper attitude toward the audience, thinking of them as friends; a realization that a speech is not a strange, abnormal activity but simply enlarged conversation; and, most important of all, an urgent desire to convey a message, a fire of enthusiasm so great that it burns away timidity and self-consciousness. But for the majority of amateur speakers, the starting point of corrective therapy for stage fright is breaking down physical restraints.

There is still another phase of this close relationship between physical action and the trammeling fears that make us vocally ineffective: the important fact that we can *act* confident, regardless of how we feel. No matter how our stomachs tremble and quake we can control the outward manifestations of nervousness, keep our bodies from "running away." Even though our mouths go dry and our upper lips are wet with sweat, we can make our bodies stand up and look reasonably well poised. And even though our hands and knees continue to tremble a little, we can make ourselves look and act reasonably confident. All of us have had occasions when we've had to act confident— when we applied for that job, when we were presented for the first time to our best girl's mother and father, when we were sent to the principal's office for disciplining. And probably we all have learned the salutary effect of bodily self-mastery upon our voices; if we haven't, it is high time that we did.

Anyone who appears frequently before the public is bound to have nerve-racking experiences which would destroy all his

leadership potentialities if he were not master of his body and
his voice.

Bob Trout, a radio announcer whose line of duty brought
him into frequent contact with Franklin D. Roosevelt, has
described how the President encountered one of these nerve-
testing experiences:

> Once, as I was describing to Columbia's radio audience the ap-
> proach of the President up the ramp to the speakers' platform at
> one of the largest political rallies of all, the braces on his legs gave
> way—and he fell; the pages of his manuscript were scattered. They
> were picked up by willing hands, and hurriedly handed back to the
> President, who by that time had been seated—now within view . . .
> of many thousands. He put the pages together again as best he could
> in the few moments before he was introduced; the manuscript was
> damp, crumpled, and spattered with mud. It was a tense moment,
> but Mr. Roosevelt did not falter. Only a handful of the thousands
> in the stadium that night had the faintest idea that anything at all
> had gone wrong; that was the night the President—in a strong and
> confident voice, proclaimed: "This generation of Americans has a
> rendezvous with destiny."
>
> Many will remember that broadcast speech, delivered at Franklin
> Field, in Philadelphia, at the end of the Democratic Convention
> of 1936. It was the President's acceptance speech, for a second term
> nomination; and if he had allowed the accident to upset him . . .
> the political history of this nation might have been changed. . . .
>
> Customarily, his [Roosevelt's] hands shook, as he stood before the
> crowds which gathered so often in so many cities and villages; but
> there was no tremor in his voice. It was calm and confident . . .
> when, a few minutes after he became President of the United States,
> he told the millions, waiting by their radios so anxiously: "The only
> thing we have to fear is fear itself."[23]

AMATEUR SPEAKERS USUALLY SHOW TOO MUCH RESTRAINT

Urged to put some life into their speeches, novices remon-
strate that it is not natural for them to wave their arms about.

---

[23] *Franklin D. Roosevelt, a Memorial*, Pocket Books, Inc., 1945, pp. 16, 17.

And in a sense they are right; it is not natural for them to use their bodies when they are dominated by fear. They will not admit that timidity has caused their repression; in fact they probably do not realize that they are being abnormally restrained and stiff. Their rationalization is, "There's nothing in this speech to get excited about." And so they continue being wooden-faced and wooden-voiced on the platform. The same persons talking on the same subjects to their intimate friends, provided that they are interested in these subjects, will inject plenty of life into what they say. The fact is that the artificial restraints of the speech situation have robbed them of all spontaneity, all color, all vitality.

NORMAL PHYSICAL ACTION UNNOTICED BY THE AUDIENCE

When a speaker is making a successful speech, very few of his auditors realize whether he is using any gestures or not. Action is so intimate a part of speech that most people never notice it. Of course, such physical powerhouses as Mussolini, Hitler, and New York's dynamic late mayor, Fiorello La Guardia, sometimes get their action out in front of their words. But in most speakers the action is never noticed unless it is either absent or grossly overdone or inept. Even the most vigorous physical action often goes completely unnoticed if it fits in with the thought and emotion being expressed.

Early in the depression of the 1930's, the author took a group of students to hear Senator Robert M. La Follette, Jr., speak. The Senator was advocating huge expenditures by the federal government to help industry lift itself out of the depression— to prime the pump of industry, as he called it. To illustrate the pump-priming activity, he told about his boyhood task of priming the old farm pump, at the same time dramatically pumping the old pump handle. The action was so broad that under other circumstances it might have been branded as the worst sort of "hamminess." But before the thousands in that enormous auditorium, and on that emotion-fraught occasion, the elaborate gestures were entirely appropriate. Not one of the students considered the physical action extreme; indeed, few of them had taken any special notice of it.

Following the publication of Darwin's *Origin of Species*, Herbert Spencer, noted English philosopher, made an extensive study of the way our bodies behave under the stress of emotions. In reporting his findings he stressed the constant relationship between degree of emotion and extent of the physical action in speech. Mild feelings, he said, are accompanied by mild physical actions; intense feelings, by intense physical actions. If the emotion is light, only the small muscles of the body, notably those around the eyes and the mouth, will be affected; but as the emotion grows in intensity, the larger muscle groups (legs, arms, trunk) begin to respond. When the gross body movements occur without the preceding smaller muscular responses, we instinctively feel that something is amiss. What we have then is an exhibition of "sawing the air," or "tearing a passion to tatters." Spencer called attention to the obvious fact that a body, especially a face, that is devoid of action signifies lack of feeling.

It is not necessary to go back to Spencer or Darwin or anyone else to be convinced of the normalcy of bodily action. Proof is everywhere at hand. All that is necessary is to observe any group in conversation, that is, any group in which interest has carried the conversation beyond commonplaces about the weather. Even in the most reserved and dignified groups, faces light up expressively, shoulders are shrugged, heads are nodded in emphasis. The investigator usually does not have to go beyond his own body to prove this fact. Let him but watch himself when he gets deeply interested in any discussion and he will find that his body is actively engaged in helping him talk—that is, any place but on the public platform; there, likely as not, his body is as stiff as a board.

Need for Physical Action by the Young Speaker

There are really two good reasons why the speaker should free himself of abnormal physical restraints. One is the effect upon the audience, the other is the effect upon the speaker himself.

As to the effect upon the audience, it is well known that a scowl may be more expressive than a spoken paragraph, a smile than a whole speech. In well-trained actors we see this type of bodily movement carried to the acme of perfection; the lifting of an eyebrow, the twitching of a lip, the clenching of a fist may provide the key to an essential bit of characterization. See how well Shakespeare observed these physical manifestations in the italicized lines of the following quotation:

> In peace there's nothing so becomes a man,
> As modest stillness and humility;
> But when the blast of war blows in our ears,
> Then imitate the action of the tiger;
> *Stiffen the sinews, summon up the blood,*
> *Then lend the eye a terrible aspect;*
> *Now set the teeth and stretch the nostrils wide,*
> *Hold hard the breath, and bind up every spirit*
> *To its full height!* On, on, you noblest English!

But far more important, particularly from the standpoint of overcoming expressionless and colorless voice, is the effect of physical action upon the speaker himself. The point to remember is that free, uninhibited physical action helps mightily in bringing vocal expressiveness.

EXERCISES IN PHYSICAL ACTION

Many students will try to rationalize themselves out of doing these exercises. And the sad part of it is that these students are the very ones who need these exercises most. Timid people, excessively modest and retiring people, overly sensitive people—these are the ones who most dislike to do anything demonstrative. And of course they are the very ones who will profit most from getting out of their shells.

To such timid souls we can only say that your salvation lies in your own hands. Be sure of this: If you have a strong desire not to do these exercises, that in itself is the best proof that you need them. Don't be too fearful of losing your dignity. Even the austere and scholarly Ralph Waldo Emerson recognized that mere physical vigor has an important place in effective speech, as made clear in his essay, "Eloquence."

1. Do the following actions and others of your own devising, with imaginary implements:

   1. Split wood.

   2. Throw a baseball.

   3. Grasp your sword, pull it from its scabbard, and hold it aloft.

   4. Fight a duel.

   5. Throw corn to the chickens.

   6. Scatter grass seed.

2. Do the following exercises before a large mirror if possible:

   1. Stand on one foot and swing the other, back and forth, from side to side, keeping the body erect and well balanced.

   2. With widespread arms, welcome a large audience.

   3. Invite the audience to rise and sing.

   4. Give a warm smile and an extended hand of greeting to that person in the mirror. Try to get him to warm up to you in friendliness.

   5. Shake your fist and scowl.

   6. Shake your arms and hands vigorously until they are loose and wabbly.

   7. Swing your arms back and forth while carrying on an imaginary conversation.

3. Give yourself over to the following passages with abandon. Replace repression with freedom. Let your imagination have full sway.

   1. Imagine you are Macbeth:

      Lay on, MacDuff, and damn'd be him who first cries, "Hold, enough!"

   2. Imagine you are Othello:

      Now, by heaven,
      My blood begins my safer guides to rule.

   3. Imagine you are Marmion defying Douglas:

      And 'twere not for thy hoary beard,
      Such hand as Marmion's had not spared
      To cleave the Douglas head!

   4. Imagine you are Lorenzo:

      Sit, Jessica. Look how the floor of heaven
      Is thick inlaid with patines of bright gold.

   5. Imagine you are Spartacus trying to foment an uprising among the gladiators:

      If ye be beasts, then stand there like fat oxen, waiting for the butcher's knife.

   6. Imagine you are Mark Antony striving to quiet the restless throng:

      "Friends!"

      (You get very little response; the crowd keeps milling around. You try again.)

      "Romans!"

      (A few of the excited crowd listen, but the confusion is still great. You make your strongest appeal, with vigor and power.)

      "Countrymen!"

      (You have their attention now, and you continue.)

      "Lend me your ears!"

7. Imagine you are Warren trying to hearten your soldiers at Bunker Hill:

> Stand! The ground's your own, my braves!
> Will ye give it up to slaves?

8. Imagine yourself Patrick Henry before the Virginia House of Burgesses:

> "I know not what course others may take, but as for me, give me liberty or give me death!"

9. Imagine you are Lord Chatham before the English House of Lords during the American Revolution:

> "If I were an American, as I am an Englishman, while a foreign troop were landed in my country, I would never lay down my arms, never, *never*, NEVER!"

4. Here is a good selection to induce physical release. Feel the courage and vitality of the old adventurer, Ulysses. Although old, he keeps thinking back to his earlier exploits (remember the one-eyed Cyclops, Circe, Scylla and Charybdis!) and he longs for one more adventure. He calls his old comrades around him and says:

> There lies the port; the vessel puffs her sail:
> There gloom the dark, broad seas. My mariners,
> Souls that have toil'd, and wrought, and thought, with me—
> That ever with a frolic welcome took
> The thunder and the sunshine, and opposed
> Free hearts, free foreheads—you and I are old;
> Old age hath yet his honour and his toil;
> Death closes all: but something ere the end,
> Some work of noble note, may yet be done,
> Not unbecoming men that strove with gods.
> The lights begin to twinkle from the rocks:
> The long day wanes: the slow moon climbs: the deep
> Moans round with many voices. Come, my friends,
> 'Tis not too late to seek a newer world.
> Push off, and sitting well in order smite
> The sounding furrows; for my purpose holds
> To sail beyond the sunset, and the baths

Of all the western stars, until I die.
It may be that the gulfs will wash us down:
It may be we shall touch the Happy Isles,
And see the great Achilles, whom we knew.
Though much is taken, much abides; and though
We are not now that strength which in old days
Moved earth and heaven, that which we are, we are—
One equal temper of heroic hearts,
Made weak by time and fate, but strong in will
To strive, to seek, to find, and not to yield.

—ALFRED, LORD TENNYSON

5. Below is part of a speech which should stir your emotional and physical reflexes. In 1837, when pro- and anti-slavery feeling was approaching the climax which resulted in the Civil War, an event occurred which brought the brilliant orator, Wendell Phillips, into the public eye. Twenty-six years old and recently graduated from Harvard Law School, Phillips attended a public indignation meeting in Faneuil Hall that was called to denounce a pro-slavery mob which had destroyed the printing press of an abolitionist editor, Elijah P. Lovejoy, in Alton, Illinois. Feeling was especially strong because in attempting to defend his press Lovejoy had lost his life. One speaker, Attorney General Austin, opposed the resolution about to be passed; he accused Lovejoy of being a troublemaker and said that he "died as the fool dieth." He also compared the mob to the Boston citizens who destroyed the British tea at the Boston Tea Party. Phillips sprang to the platform:

Mr. Chairman . . . I hope I shall be permitted to express my surprise at the sentiments of the last speaker, surprise not only at such sentiments from such a man, but at the applause they have received within these walls. A comparison has been drawn between the events of the Revolution and the tragedy at Alton . . . and we have heard the mob at Alton, the drunken murderers of Lovejoy, compared to those patriot fathers who threw the tea overboard. . . .

Sir, when I heard the gentleman lay down the principles which place the murderers of Alton side by side with Otis and Hancock, with Quincy and Adams (*pointing to their pictures on the wall*),

I thought those pictured lips would have broken into voice to rebuke the recreant American, the slanderer of the dead.

The gentleman says Lovejoy was presumptuous and imprudent, he "died as the fool dieth." . . . Imprudent to defend the liberty of the press! Why? Because the defense was unsuccessful? Does success gild crime into patriotism, and the want of it change heroic self-devotion into imprudence? Was Hampden imprudent when he drew the sword and threw away the scabbard? Yet he, judged by that single hour, was unsuccessful. After a short exile the race he hated sat again upon the throne.

Imagine yourself present when the first news of Bunker Hill battle reached a New England town. The tale would have run thus: "The patriots are routed, the redcoats victorious, Warren lies dead upon the field." With what scorn would that Tory have been received who should have charged Warren with imprudence, who should have said that bred as a physician, he was "out of place" in the battle, and "died as a fool dieth." . . .

Presumptuous to assert the freedom of the press upon American ground? . . . Who invents this libel on his country? It is the very thing which entitles Lovejoy to greater praise. The disputed right which provoked the Revolution—taxation without representation —is far beneath that for which he died. As much as thought is better than money, so much is the cause in which Lovejoy died nobler than a mere question of taxes. James Otis thundered in this hall when the king did but touch his pocket. Imagine if you can his indignant eloquence had England offered to put a gag upon his lips.

6. Following are parts of two speeches by American Indians. Catch the spirit of strength and simple dignity which pervades their words, and let it motivate your spirit and body.

1.   A RED MAN LOOKS AT THE WHITE MAN'S RELIGION

Friends and Brothers:—You say that you are sent to instruct us how to worship the Great Spirit agreeably to His mind; and, if we do not take hold of the religion which you white people teach, we shall be unhappy hereafter. You say that you are right and we are lost. How do we know this to be true? We understand that your religion is written in a Book. If it was intended for us, as well as you, why has not the Great Spirit given to us, and not only to us, but why did not the Great Spirit give to our forefathers the knowledge of that Book, with the means of understanding it rightly? We only know what you tell us about it. How shall we know when to believe, being so often deceived by the white people?

Brother, you say that there is but one way to worship and serve the Great Spirit. If there is but one religion, why do you white people differ so much about it? Why not all agreed, as you can all read the Book?

Brother, we do not understand these things. We are told that your religion was given to your forefathers and has been handed down from father to son. We also have a religion which was given to our forefathers and has been handed down to us, their children. We worship in that way. It teaches us to be thankful for all the favors we receive, to love each other, and to be united. We never quarrel about religion.

Brother, the Great Spirit had made us all, but He has made a great difference between His white and His red children. He has given us different complexions and different customs. . . . Since He has made so great a difference between us in other things, why may we not conclude that He has given us a different religion according to our understanding? The Great Spirit does right. He knows what is best for his children; we are satisfied.

Brother, we do not wish to destroy your religion or take it from you. We only want to enjoy our own. . . .

Brother, we are told that you have been preaching to the white people in this place. These people are our neighbors. We are acquainted with them. We will wait a little while and see what effect your preaching has upon them. If we find it does them good, makes them honest, and less disposed to cheat Indians, we will then consider again of what you have said.

—RED JACKET

2.   BLACK HAWK SURRENDERS

You have taken me prisoner, with all my warriors. I am much grieved; for I expected, if I did not defeat you, to hold out much longer, and give you more trouble, before I surrendered. I tried hard to bring you into ambush, but your last general understood Indian fighting. I determined to rush on you, and fight you face to face. I fought hard. But your guns were well aimed. The bullets flew like birds in the air, and whizzed by our ears like the wind through the trees in winter. My warriors fell around me; it began to look dismal.

I saw my evil day at hand. The sun rose dim on us in the morning, and at night it sank in a dark cloud, and looked like a ball of fire. That was the last sun that shone on Black Hawk. His heart is dead, and no longer beats quick in his bosom. He is now a prisoner of the white men; they will do with him as they wish. But he can stand torture, and is not afraid of death. He is no coward. Black Hawk is an Indian. He has done nothing for which an Indian ought to be ashamed. He has fought for his countrymen, against white men, who came, year after year, to cheat them and take away their lands. . . .

The spirits of our fathers arose, and spoke to us to avenge our wrongs or die. We set up the war-whoop, and dug up the tomahawk; our knives were ready and the heart of Black Hawk swelled high in his bosom, when he led his warriors to battle. He is satisfied. He will go to the world of spirits contented. He has done his duty. His father will meet him there and commend him.

Black Hawk is a true Indian, and disdains to cry like a woman. He feels for his wife, his children, and his friends. But he does not care for himself. He cares for the Nation and the Indians. They will suffer. He laments their fate. Farewell, my Nation! Black Hawk tried to save you, and avenge your wrongs. He drank the blood of some of the whites. He has been taken prisoner, and his plans are crushed. He can do no more. He is near his end. His sun is setting and he will rise no more. Farewell to Black Hawk.

7. The following scene may be read by a young man and a young woman or by a single individual reading both parts.

If one person takes both parts, a certain principle of voice control should be kept in mind: A boy should not attempt to imitate a woman's voice by forcing his pitch up into the falsetto range, nor should a girl imitate a man by pushing her voice down into an unnatural guttural. There should be no imitation at all. If the boy simply lightens his voice a little, i.e., uses a little less volume and a slightly higher pitch, in its natural quality, he is likely to get the desired contrast. And if the girl relaxes her throat and lets her natural voice sink a little lower in pitch, she too is likely to get the contrast she desires. At any rate, there must be no imitation of someone else's tone; that kind of straining is injurious to the student's voice, and it sounds artificial to the audience.

MACBETH. I have done the deed. Didst thou not hear a noise?
LADY M. I heard the owl scream and the crickets cry.
  Did not you speak?
MACBETH.   When?
LADY M.   Now.
MACBETH.   As I descended?
LADY M. Ay.
MACBETH. Hark!
  Who lies i' the second chamber?
LADY M.   Donalbain.
MACBETH (*Looking on his hands*). This is a sorry sight.
LADY M. A foolish thought to say a sorry sight.
MACBETH. There's one did laugh in 's sleep, and one cried
          "Murder!"
  That they did wake each other: I stood and heard them;
  But they did say their prayers, and address'd them
  Again to sleep.
LADY M.   There are two lodg'd together.
MACBETH. One cried "God bless us!" and "Amen" the other,
  As they had seen me with these hangman's hands.
  Listening their fear, I could not say "Amen,"
  When they did say "God bless us!"
LADY M.   Consider it not so deeply.
MACBETH. But wherefore could not I pronounce "Amen"?
  I had most need of blessing, and "Amen"
  Stuck in my throat.
LADY M.   These deeds must not be thought
  After these ways; so, it will make us mad.
MACBETH. Methought I heard a voice cry "Sleep no more!
  Macbeth does murder sleep"—the innocent sleep,
  Sleep that knits up the ravell'd sleave of care,

The death of each day's life, sore labour's bath,
Balm of hurt minds, great nature's second course,
Chief nourisher in life's feast,—

LADY M.   What do you mean?

MACBETH.   Still it cried "Sleep no more!" to all the house:
"Glamis hath murder'd sleep, and therefore Cawdor
Shall sleep no more; Macbeth shall sleep no more."

LADY M.   Who was it that thus cried? Why, worthy thane,
You do unbend your noble strength, to think
So brainsickly of things. Go get some water,
And wash this filthy witness from your hand.
Why did you bring these daggers from the place?
They must lie there; go carry them, and smear
The sleepy grooms with blood.

MACBETH.   I'll go no more.
I am afraid to think what I have done;
Look on't again I dare not.

LADY M.   Infirm of purpose!
Give me the daggers. The sleeping and the dead
Are but as pictures; 'tis the eye of childhood
That fears a painted devil. If he do bleed,
I'll gild the faces of the grooms withal,
For it must seem their guilt.

(Exit. Knocking within.)

MACBETH.   Whence is that knocking?
How is't with me, when every noise appals me?
What hands are here? Ha! they pluck out mine eyes.
Will all great Neptune's ocean wash this blood
Clean from my hand? No, this my hand will rather
The multitudinous seas incarnadine,
Making the green one red.

(Enter LADY MACBETH.*)*

LADY M.   My hands are of your color; but I shame
To wear a heart so white. *(Knocking within.)* I hear a knocking
At the south entry: retire we to our chamber.
A little water clears us of this deed:
How easy is it, then! Your constancy
Hath left you unattended. Hark! more knocking.
Get on your nightgown, lest occasion call us,

And show us to be watchers. Be not lost
So poorly in your thoughts.
MACBETH. To know my deed, 'twere best not know myself.
(Knocking within.)
Wake Duncan with thy knocking! I would thou couldst!
—WILLIAM SHAKESPEARE

8. Here are several selections of various types, each calling for a considerable degree of physical participation. Not all of them are in the Give-me-liberty-or-give-me-death mood. Some are quite mild, and one or two are even mildly humorous; but in all of them, the voice will be more expressive if the person presenting them is free from body stiffness. Most of them are best adapted to the informal touch. This does not mean sloppy speech, but speech that is not stilted or "speechy" in tone.

1. During the past few decades there has been a steady movement in American life toward greater and greater informality. Take men's clothes, for instance. Men have discarded waistcoats, hats, garters, undershirts, and are frequently discovered wearing their neckties (and such neckties!) at half-mast. It is increasingly difficult for them, apparently, to put on a dinner coat, even with a soft shirt, and only on the rarest occasions can they be persuaded to cope with a white tie. It may be remarked parenthetically that when they do achieve that peak of grandeur, however much they may have complained earlier, they do have a look of rather smug self-satisfaction. And although we still follow the custom of the male members of a wedding party wearing morning coats, these morning coats are far more often than not rented—except in the case of the fathers of the bridal couple. Why own a costume that you'll wear only when you're a bridegroom or an usher?

A more striking and far more regrettable example of the trend of the past 25 years or so is the rumpus room, or whatever the current term is for that party room where your friends can enjoy themselves freely without breaking your really good furniture and burning holes in the rugs. A pretty idea, very very pretty. Another pretty one is the bar in the living room. Convenient though it is (a table is pretty convenient too) there is something less than distinguished in the notion that in order to make your friends feel really at home you contrive to give the impression that they're in a café.

There's no need to belabor this point: the use of first names at first sight; the barbecue, no matter how elaborate, served on paper plates; the assumption that the more highbrow your guests, the more will they warm to music that originated in Basin Street; the reluctance of modern novelists to concern themselves with "nice people"; the peasant influence in dress and décor; the systematic exposure of that most mysterious and unromantic section of woman's anatomy, the midriff; and the idea that almost straight alcohol in sufficient quantity will make everybody very democratic and cordial and happy—all these current phenomena are so familiar that they hardly need mention. . . .

We're wondering if possibly the time isn't ripe to suggest to the public elegance as a concept, a state of mind. It's a moot question whether good taste as such can be taught through editorial or advertising pressures. Good taste demands an independence of mind and an assurance that not everybody is capable of. But the public taste can certainly be steered in new and different directions by these same pressures. It seems to us quite possible to put over the idea, for instance, that the best party is not necessarily the one where the most alcohol is consumed and the greatest number of cigarette stubs litter the floor. . . .

We have been emphasizing America's contributions to culture; we have been pointing with pride to the indigenous, or vernacular, culture that has grown out of the needs and ambitions of an expanding, machinery-conscious society. And while this is an interesting and an honorable thing to do— that is, not to be ashamed of what we have made—it is a limiting and chauvinistic thing as well. It is no way for a people who has suddenly come into a position of preëminence in the world to behave.

We should be through with revolt against puritanism just for the sake of revolt. We should be through with the cult of youth . . . because we're really quite grown-up now, and we have grown to be a man, not a rowdy kid trying to show how

independent he is. We can relax. The world knows we're
here, all right. We don't have to put on a cocktail apron, and
plaster our initials on everything in sight to be noticed.[24]

—AGNES ROGERS

2.   *From* LOCHINVAR

So boldly he entered the Netherby Hall,
Among bride's-men, and kinsmen, and brothers, and
    all:
Then spoke the bride's father, his hand on his sword
(For the poor craven bridegroom said never a word),
"O come ye in peace here, or come ye in war,
Or to dance at our bridal, young Lord Lochinvar?"—

"I long wooed your daughter, my suit you denied;—
Love swells like the Solway, but ebbs like its tide!
And now am I come, with this lost love of mine,
To lead but one measure, drink one cup of wine;
There are maidens in Scotland more lovely by far,
That would gladly be bride to the young Lochinvar."

The bride kissed the goblet: the knight took it up.
He quaffed off the wine, and he threw down the cup.
She looked down to blush, and she looked up to sigh,
With a smile on her lips, and a tear in her eye.
He took her soft hand, ere her mother could bar,—
"Now tread we a measure!" said young Lochinvar.

            .   .   .   .

One touch to her hand, and one word in her ear,
When they reached the hall door, and the charger
    stood near;
So light to the croupe the fair lady he swung!
So light to the saddle before her he sprung!
"She is won! we are gone, over bank, bush, and scaur:
They'll have fleet steeds that follow," quoth young
    Lochinvar.

[24] From Agnes Rogers, "Elegance Is Not Undemocratic," *Vital Speeches,* December, 1949.

There was mounting 'mong Graemes of the Netherby
   clan:
Forsters, Fenwicks, and Musgraves, they rode and they
   ran;
There was racing and chasing on Canobie Lee,
But the lost bride of Netherby ne'er did they see.
       . . . .

                         —SIR WALTER SCOTT

3. MACBETH.   Is this a dagger which I see before me,
   The handle toward my hand? Come, let me clutch thee.
   I have thee not, and yet I see thee still.
   Art thou not, fatal vision, sensible
   To feeling as to sight? Or art thou but
   A dagger of the mind, a false creation,
   Proceeding from the heat-oppressed brain?
   I see thee yet, in form as palpable
   As this which now I draw.
   Thou marshall'st me the way that I was going;
   And such an instrument I was to use.
   Mine eyes are made the fools o' the other senses,
   Or else worth all the rest. I see thee still;
   And on thy blade and dudgeon gouts of blood,
   Which was not so before. There's no such thing;
   It is the bloody business which informs
   Thus to mine eyes. . . .

                         —SHAKESPEARE

4. The whole fury and might of the enemy must very soon be
turned on us. Hitler knows that he will have to break us in
this Island or lose the war. If we can stand up to him all
Europe may be free, and the life of the world may move
forward into broad, sunlit uplands. But if we fail, then the
whole world, including the United States, and all that we
have known and cared for, will sink into the abyss of a new
Dark Age made more sinister, and perhaps more prolonged,
by the lights of a perverted science.
   Let us therefore brace ourselves to our duty and so bear

ourselves that, if the British Commonwealth and Empire last for a thousand years, men will still say, "This was their finest hour."[25]

—WINSTON CHURCHILL

5. Deep sleep had fallen on the destined victim, and on all beneath his roof. A healthful old man to whom sleep was sweet, the first sound slumbers of the night held him in their soft but strong embrace. The assassin enters, through the window, already prepared, into an unoccupied apartment. With noiseless foot he paces the lonely hall, half lighted by the moon. He winds up the ascent of the stairs and reaches the door of the chamber. Of this he moves the lock, by soft and continued pressure, till it turns on its hinges without noise, and he enters, and beholds his victim before him. The room is uncommonly open to the admission of light. The face of the innocent sleeper is turned from the murderer, and the beams of the moon, resting on the grey locks of his aged temple, show him where to strike. The fatal blow is given and the victim passes without a struggle or a motion, from the repose of sleep to the repose of death! It is the assassin's purpose to make sure work; and he plies the dagger, though it is obvious that life has been destroyed by the blow of the bludgeon. He even raises the aged arm, that he may not fail in his aim at the heart, and replaces it again over the wounds of the poniard. To finish the picture, he explores the wrist for the pulse! He feels for it and ascertains that it beats no longer! It is accomplished. The deed is done. He retreats, retraces his steps to the window; passes out through it as he came in and escapes. The secret is his own and it is safe! Ah, gentlemen, that was a dreadful mistake.

—DANIEL WEBSTER

[25] Winston Churchill, *Their Finest Hour*, Houghton Mifflin Company, 1949.

XI ✳ *Achieving Vocal Expressiveness: Rate*

Monotony

Many voices are monotonous, some to the point of boredom. Almost anyone can readily detect the fault in others, even though he may be a bit slow in recognizing his own shortcomings in this respect.

Some voices are monotonous even in ordinary conversation. But this fault is most inexcusable among public speakers. An audience is practically defenseless against a boresome speaker. Courtesy demands that the long-suffering members of the audience sit and take it. Of the many crimes committed in the name of public speech, certainly among the worst is the crime of being dull.

Although dull speaking may result from uninteresting material as well as from lifeless presentation, most persons who are invited to make speeches today are chosen because they are known to have something worth saying. Unfortunately, however, the restraints, fears, and inhibitions of the platform scare many speakers literally stiff. And stiffness means monotony.

But platform stiffness—stage fright—is not the sole cause of monotonous speech delivery. Monotony may equally well come from too much confidence. Professional speechmakers of one kind and another, including political spellbinders, sometimes develop extremely unpleasant speech faults. Occasionally they

become victims of their own high-sounding eloquence, permitting their voices to rise and fall in recurrent patterns of
slides and dips and swoops, until the singsong cadence has a
soporific effect upon their own minds as well as upon their
auditors'. They give every evidence of having gone to sleep on
their feet. This is monotony at its worst.

Vocal monotony is sure death to attention. When a speaker
smothers his thoughts in wearisome patterns of sameness, the
hearer loses both his power and his desire to attend. And when
the listener's attention is lost, the speaker might as well stop
talking, no matter how well prepared he is, no matter how vital
his message.

It is well for a speaker to realize that audience interest is
unstable. There is a constant leakage of attention, a thousand
thoughts clamoring for a place in the auditor's consciousness.
At the first suggestion of monotony one listener thinks back to
a recent business deal, another looks ahead to tomorrow's golf
game, another thinks of the physical discomfort of the hard
bench or stifling heat. New stimulation must constantly be
provided to reclaim flagging attention. Part of this stimulation
naturally has to come from fresh and interesting material; but
in no small degree it comes from lively and expressive changes
in the speaker's voice.

The purpose of this chapter is to point out ways to remedy
monotony. As a first step in this process let us look at some of
the influences that produce monotony.

Causes of Vocal Monotony

One frequent cause of voice monotony is a *rigid, unresponsive voice mechanism.* That is, the muscles in and around the
larynx are too tense to permit the voice to respond to the
person's thoughts and feelings. This condition may be temporary, the result of an attack of stage fright, timidity, anxiety, or
other emotional stress; or it may be habitual, the result of
persistent nervous tensions.

Another cause of monotony is *poor health,* or possibly just the absence of abounding good health. The weakness may come from a temporary exhaustion or illness, or it may be a manifestation of a long-standing ailment, such as anemia.

Mental flabbiness is another cause. If the mind is slow and dull, the voice also is likely to be flat and dull. So too if the mind is simply lazy. Vocal expressiveness is dependent upon clear and vigorous thinking.

Physical inertness, like mental inertness, is a common cause of vocal monotony. Whether the inactivity of the body results from physical laziness or from restraints induced by social fears and platform inhibitions, the results are likely to be similar—a monotonous voice. But of these two causes of bodily immobility, the latter is more common. Our social fears—actually our fear of doing something which will cause us to lose dignity— put a heavy restraint upon our bodies and our voices.

Excessive modesty sometimes causes vocal monotony. A highly sensitive person, through perfectly laudable motives, may develop a disagreeable uniformity in his speech. His desire to avoid being too aggressive, too domineering, in his relationship with his fellows leads him to the other extreme. To shun any suggestion of high-pressure salesmanship for his ideas, he habitually restrains his voice so rigidly that it becomes fixed in a habit of dullness. His very strength has become a weakness. That is, his sensitive understanding of other people's thoughts and feelings, which might have made his voice unusually expressive, has instead, because of excessive modesty, caused him to hide his natural voice, much as he might use a mask to hide the expression of his face. In consequence, his speech has about the same degree of animation and color as a dripping faucet.

Defective hearing takes its toll of vocal expressiveness. The totally deaf are understandably prone to vocal monotony. Not so readily recognized is the fact that many persons have vocal defects attributable to *partial* deafness. Children learn to speak by imitation, which depends upon hearing; when hearing is defective, the speech patterns are pretty sure to suffer. Even with adults, hearing provides the models for speaking; when we hear imperfectly there are likely to be imperfections in our speaking. These imperfections often take the form of monotony. Even when a person's hearing apparatus is normal he may never have heard his voice as others hear it. Possibly he never really has listened to it. To hear one's own voice with discriminating ears requires a special kind of cultivated listening.

These are not the sole causes of vocal monotony, but they are among the most common. These and the other causes deprive us of our rightful heritage—a really useful vocal instrument. The human voice has possibilities of portraying the finest shades of thought and feeling, but we permit habits of rigidity and unresponsiveness to grow on us until we are completely enslaved by monotony. This priceless possession, our ability to communicate with others, is only half developed, half utilized.

REMEDIES FOR MONOTONY

Three principles are fundamental to any program of corrective therapy.

1. *An Earnest Desire to Correct the Fault.* The first step toward redemption is a conviction of sin. He who would overcome the sin of monotony must first come to the mourner's bench. He must really hunger and thirst for the righteousness of a flexible and responsive voice. The necessity for recognition of one's own guilt is illustrated by an anecdote attributed to the famous preacher and lecturer, Henry Ward Beecher. When asked by a young preacher what to do when members of his congregation went to sleep, Beecher replied: "I'll tell you what I do. I have reinstated the *beadle* of the old Pilgrim church. I have instructed him to have ready a long pointed stick, and if he sees a member of my congregation nodding he is to slip up quietly and jab . . . me."

2. *An Understanding of the Laws of Habit Formation.* Monotony is a habit. Habits are changed not by knowing but

by doing. Simply knowing what is required avails little. He who seriously undertakes to overcome monotony must make up his mind to do some hard work. He must drill, over and over again, until a new set of habits is established. And drilling takes a lot of determination, a lot of stick-to-itiveness.

3. *A Realization That Normally a Harmonious Coördination Between Nerve Centers and Voice Musculature Is More Effective Than Mechanical Manipulation of the Voice.* As has constantly been stressed, the biggest help in overcoming monotony is to have ideas that you really want to express, then break down the barriers and let the voice go. If we see clearly enough and feel deeply enough, the normal voice will respond with appropriate shadings and inflections if not artificially restrained. The great need is to increase the internal pressures, to build hotter fires of thought and feeling; and then cultivate a state of muscular tonicity in and around the speech mechanism so that the voice can respond. As we have repeatedly emphasized, when monotony is caused by excessive tension in and around the larynx, the obvious corrective is to work for relaxation, both for the body as a whole and for the speech mechanism in particular. Specific directives and exercises for the achievement of relaxation were given in Chapter IV.

When monotony is caused by lack of physical vitality, the remedy lies in a program of general health building. Without some degree of good health it is difficult for a person to have any liveliness or enthusiasm in his voice. And we cannot get away from the truth of Emerson's observation that "nothing great was ever achieved without enthusiasm."

When monotony is associated with emotional repressions resulting from excessive modesty, the best cure is a wholesome dose of self-respect. Somehow the individual must build up his own ego. An aid to accomplishing this is an understanding of the qualities of leadership, some of the most fundamental of which are vitality, enthusiasm, and belief in oneself. Fear caused by a sense of insufficiency makes the voice weak and dry.

When monotony results from inadequate hearing, the therapy calls for working directly with the hearing. Two steps in the corrective procedure are indicated: the first when the poor hearing is caused by a defect in the auditory mechanism, the other when it is caused by bad listening habits. Young children should have periodic checkups by competent specialists to insure that their hearing is not impaired. Adults likewise will do well to remember that an aggravated case of monotony may indicate a hearing deficiency that requires the services of a physician or surgeon.

With most people the need is not so much for medical attention as for ear training. If we would free our voices from old habits of monotony we must learn to listen with discriminating ears. A great aid to this, as already mentioned, is to make records of our voices and listen to them.

When, as is so often the case, monotony bears a direct and close relationship to total bodily immobility, the urgent need is to cultivate physical freedom, along the lines outlined in the preceding chapter and further developed in the chapter on force.

Rate of Speaking

VARIETY IN RATE

A distinguishing feature of animated conversation is its interesting variety in rate. As the subject under discussion shifts and turns, so does the rate of speech. As indifference changes to interest, and interest to excitement, or as the mood alters from gaiety to sobriety, the rate swings from slow to fast, from quick acceleration to deliberate retardation, and to sudden stops.

In contrast to this lively variation, most memorized speeches are fearfully monotonous in rate. The words come in a uniform pattern, equal in duration and equal in spacing—a sure mark of the speech given by rote. Even untrained observers know that there is something lacking in spontaneity and brand the speech as "canned." Everyone detects it, and nearly everyone detests it. This same tiresome regularity often characterizes the mechanical speech of book agents and magazine salesmen who "work their way through college" by ringing doorbells and trying to project their sales argument through reluctantly opened doors. So, too, it sometimes marks the college professor's oft-repeated lecture, the information clerk's bored response to a question, the child's recitation at Children's Day exercises, and the professional guide's dull harangue.

But words committed to memory are not always measured out with the uniformity of link sausages. On the contrary, some of the most emotion-stirring words are memorized. The great dramas would die overnight if actors gave the sublime words of the drama monotonous rendition, and the actors would pass into oblivion too. But a Sarah Bernhardt, a Beerbohm Tree, a Julia Marlowe, an E. H. Sothern, and any other actor whose name lives on, would scorn to speak in that fashion. No matter if they gave the same play six days a week for a dozen years, the words would never be uttered in droning uniformity. Instead, they will be given new life and new meaning at every rendition.

So it is with a really good public speaker. To be sure, he is not likely to use exactly the same words again and again as the actor does, but he frequently expresses the same sentiments; some notable speakers memorize and give certain portions of their speeches verbatim. But they keep the words fresh, vital, and far removed from any suggestion of monotony.

What is the difference? Why do some memorized words acquire a dreadful monotony, and others pulse with the breath of life? One answer concerns this matter of rate. The good speaker re-creates the meaning of the words at every rendition. He relives the thought, and thus unconsciously gives the words the varied rate which characterizes fresh and sparkling conversation. But the actor, as we noted earlier, may substitute a certain degree of artistic skill to create a semblance of spontaneity. He has learned through careful analysis how to alter rate and the other factors of emphasis so that his words sound as if they were bubbling forth free and unrehearsed.

Mere variation in rate, however, is not sufficient. Variation might become simply choppiness, which could be even more annoying than uniformity. Therefore it is obvious that we must acquaint ourselves with the nature of normal, true-to-life variations, to be able to distinguish between rate changes which indicate thoughtful speaking and those which merely indicate a sort of verbal St. Vitus's dance.

TEMPO

How fast should I talk? How slow? If you are a student of speech you probably have asked these questions at one time or another. But no one can give you an exact answer. One hundred words a minute is obviously a slow rate of speech, whereas 225 words a minute is fast. Except in unusual circumstances you should not risk going much above or below these limits. But this information is not of great help, for such limits afford extremely wide variation.

We know that there are good speakers who talk fast, and good speakers who talk slowly. Some well-known broadcasters and sports announcers talk with the speed of machine guns and yet are considered effective speakers. On the other hand, Winston Churchill, like the late President Roosevelt, speaks with great deliberateness and allows plenty of time for the import of his words to sink in.

No strict rules can be applied. In the final analysis you have to discover for yourself your own optimum rate—the rate at which you speak most effectively in terms of the response desired from your listeners. By experimentation and observation you can develop a sensitive appreciation of time values which will make your speech most productive of results. Certain broad guiding principles can be laid down to assist you in finding your own best rate.

By and large, young and inexperienced speakers are inclined to talk too fast. Often they talk in a sort of breathless hurry which not only is hard to listen to, but also is injurious to their voices. Much poor tonal quality results from long habits of talking too fast. Especially if the rapid speech is characterized by a sense of hurry and excitement, it is likely that the speech mechanism is too tense for good tone production.

From the standpoint of the auditors, too, the speech of most amateur speakers is likely to be too fast. In one respect their talk is like restaurants located along the railroad right-of-way. The traveler leaves the train and settles down to enjoy his meal. But there is an atmosphere of hurry around him; he lacks time to enjoy any one dish. And at last the whistle blows, calling him away from a half-eaten or too hastily eaten meal. Similarly, the speaker often rushes his auditors away from the ideas he has presented.

In general, public speech needs to be slower than ordinary conversation in order that the entire audience may both hear and understand. Sound has a peculiar property, in that it tends to become jumbled as it travels through space. In a large auditorium or outdoor assembly, words become indistinguishable unless set apart by proper spacing. For this mechanical reason, the rate must be slow enough to insure adequate hearing. In general, the larger the audience the slower the speech must be in order to be heard clearly. Equally important is the fact that audiences think slowly. The larger the group, the more the independence of each member is submerged in the mass. Individuals do not feel the same degree of responsibility to pay attention; minds are relaxed and lazy. Thoughts from the platform must be uttered slowly enough so that the hearer will not have to hurry to catch up with them. An audience that is hurried too much gives up and lets the speaker go on without it, mentally speaking.

At the other extreme, of course, is too slow and ponderous a rate. The mechanically measured, artificially and exaggeratedly deliberate speech of some of the old-time spellbinders is as fatal to attention as the breakneck speed of the most stage-frightened tyro.

RATE OF SPEAKING DEPENDS UPON THE NATURE OF THE MA-
TERIAL

Obviously some subjects lend themselves to a faster rate than other subjects. Material that is exciting requires, and in normal conversation is given, a rapid rate of utterance; material which provokes sadness and sorrow calls for a slow rate. Gaiety and joyousness are given the same rate as grief and somberness only under the stress of an unnatural strain, such as stage fright perhaps, or by a voice made unresponsive by years of bad speech habits.

Likewise, in public speech, material which is heavy, involved, or unfamiliar to the audience naturally calls for a slower rate than that which is old, familiar, and well understood. For the former, the judicious speaker deliberately slows down and gives his hearers plenty of time to think around his subject; for the latter he may go along with considerable speed.

BEGIN A SPEECH SLOWLY

The beginning of a speech should usually be fairly slow and deliberate, with plenty of pauses. The audience requires a little time to get accustomed to you and your way of speaking. They will hear and understand better after they have become familiar with your voice and diction; then you can safely speed up a little. Furthermore, at the beginning your subject is strange; your theme is likely to be foreign to their present chain of thought; therefore their attention is diffused. Don't shift into high at once. Give them time to adjust themselves to your line of thought, and you will get better attention.

Phrasing

LENGTH OF PHRASES

What about phrasing? How long is a well-turned phrase? There is no categorical answer to this question. We are dealing with an art, not a science; and an art leaves plenty of room for the individual's creative tastes. The dictionary definition indicates how variable phrases are: "A word or group of spoken words which the mind focuses on momentarily as a meaningful unit and which is preceded and followed by pauses."[1] A phrase, then, may be a single word, just one word, or it may be "a group of words." How many words in a group? Two? Ten? Twenty? Nobody knows. It all depends.

Does that mean that the length of the phrases in spoken discourse doesn't matter? Far from it! There is a world of difference between good phrasing and poor phrasing. Consider the following example, a fairly typical case of poor phrasing: The author meets periodically with a university committee whose members are invariably restless and give every evidence of being eager to get away. This is not because the matters under consideration are uninteresting; on the contrary, they are often very important to the welfare of the members of the group, and therefore of great potential interest. The restlessness is chargeable to just one thing: the chairman's poor phrasing. Possibly as a result of nervousness—for university professors and chairmen of committees do get nervous, you know, just as young college students do—this chairman fails to coördinate his breathing with his phrasing. Habitually he talks without pausing until he runs out of breath, then he gasps and starts over again and keeps going until need for more oxygen causes him to gasp again. This process is repeated until the committee members are gasping with him. It becomes difficult to listen to what the man is saying, because of the united effort to help him get enough breath.

Let us look at another example. Some wag has devised the following bit of wisdom:

> Advice to the lean: don't eat fast.
> Advice to the fat: don't eat! fast!

[1] *The American College Dictionary*, Text Edition, Harper & Brothers.

Now suppose you reversed the phrasing, advising the lean, "Don't eat! fast!" If your advice were followed, you might have an anemic underfed invalid on your hands.

Not only can meaning be altered by a change in phrasing, it can be falsified or completely destroyed. Consider the following case in point: In the little poem, "Cupid Swallowed," by Leigh Hunt (p. 147), the following lines occur:

> What, of all things, midst the heap,
> Should I light on, fast asleep,
> But the little desperate elf—
> The tiny traitor—Love, himself!

The narrator is saying that while twining a crown of roses he encountered the little elf, Love. Then for emphasis he uses the reflexive pronoun *himself*, as one might say, *He looked like the old devil himself*. But when students reading the poem include both *Love* and *himself* in one phrase, as they frequently do, the lines sound as if the reference were to someone who had a bad case of self-admiration. There is a lot of difference between *Love himself* and *Love/himself*.

It is in reading poetry that college students are most likely to make such mistakes in phrasing. They often seem to have the impression that phrases should always coincide with lines, and that therefore the reader should pause at the end of every line. This is illustrated by another two lines in the same poem. The poem starts:

> T'other day, as I was twining
> Roses for a crown to dine in. . . .

Again and again students phrase these lines thus:

> T'other day as I was twining/
> Roses for a crown to dine in/

The slightest attention to thought grouping will make clear the need for combining *twining* and *roses*, so that the phrase will read *as I was twining roses/*.

Look for a minute at a poem that expresses a more serious sentiment, Milton's sonnet "On His Blindness." Note the following lines:

> And that one talent which is death to hide
> Lodged with me useless, though my soul more bent
> To serve therewith my Maker, and present
> My true account, lest he returning chide . . .

What a mess we would make of the meaning if we phrased thus:

> . . . though my soul more bent/
> To serve therewith my Maker and present/
> My true account/ . . .

The meaning Milton intended obviously is:

> . . . though my soul/ more bent to serve therewith my Maker/
> and present my true account/ . . .

Two lines from Wordsworth's "She Was a Phantom of Delight" illustrate the same point:

> But all things else about her drawn
> From May-time and the cheerful dawn . . .

A phrase being a group of "words which the mind focuses on momentarily as a meaningful unit," it is obvious that if we would give any sense of logical meaning to a listener we must disregard the line endings. Therefore the phrasing would be:

> But all things else about her/ drawn from May-time/
> and the cheerful dawn/ . . .

Hence, we may draw a rule, or rather a principle, for rules are too narrow and restrictive to be applicable to artistic endeavor: *In reading poetry, if the thought is important we should disregard line endings, rhyming, and any other factor which interferes with proper phrasing.*

In the above principle, the qualifying phrase *if the thought is important* must be included, because sometimes the poet is striving to create a mood rather than to impart a thought, in which case the rhythmical beat is much more important than the thought grouping. This is the case in many of Poe's rhythmical poems, like "Annabel Lee."

But not all poor phrasing is associated with the oral reading of poetry. Almost equally bad is phrasing based upon the notion that the oral reader of prose should always follow the punctuation. Intelligent reading is impossible unless the reader realizes that punctuation in writing does not apply to speech. In the first place, it is not necessary to pause at every punctuation mark. For example, in the phrase, "Now, if I were in your place . . . ," we normally would not pause after *now*. Furthermore, the punctuation marks in written discourse are usually spaced much too far apart for good oral phrasing. If the oral reader phrases his reading according to the punctuation in his material, he is bound to try to express in one group and one breath long complex clauses which are clearly beyond his breath capacity, and just as clearly beyond the capacity of his hearers' minds to focus on as meaningful units.

The punctuation of the printed page has become conventionalized. You will note that the definition of phrasing on page 362 refers to speech. The dictionary also has a whole series of definitions for writing, based on grammatical rules. These rules are designed to aid the eye, so that the mind can grasp the units of meaning quickly and easily. Sometimes punctuation for the ear (the pause) is synonymous with this eye punctuation; but sometimes—in fact usually—punctuation for the ear is entirely different.

That brings us to another principle regarding phrasing for voice and speech: *The speaker or reader has to make his own phrasing as he goes along, according to the needs of the occasion.* Phrasing for speech cannot be standardized. Identical words, spoken in different surroundings and with different attendant circumstances, may call for entirely different phrasing. Let us look at some of the conditions which influence the length of spoken phrases.

1. The Breath Control of the Speaker. No speaker should ever let himself get involved in a phrase that is long enough to make him sound "run down."

2. Articulative Ability of the Speaker. If the speaker has the slightest difficulty in carving out his words with complete clarity, he must compensate by using shorter phrases to aid his auditors in easy hearing.

3. The Audience's Familiarity or Lack of Familiarity with the Subject Matter. Unfamiliar material has to be spoken in much shorter phrases, to give the hearers time to make the desired associations of the new ideas.

4. Acoustic Properties of the Auditorium. Reverberations from broad expanses of smooth barren walls, or, if out of doors, the noise of the wind in the trees, the horns of passing automobiles, the whistle from a passing train, and so forth, make short phrases absolutely mandatory.

5. Desire of the Speaker to Emphasize His Words. No trained speaker would think of using twelve or fifteen words in a phrase if he really wanted to drive home a significant thought. For example, can you imagine a speaker who "knows his stuff" putting into one long phrase a sentence like the following?

I cannot emphasize too strongly our need to stop and think before we jump into this thing.

His phrasing would be more like this:

I cannot emphasize too strongly/ our need to stop/ and think/ before we jump into this thing.

6. The Size of the Audience. The author once heard Theodore Roosevelt address a huge audience in Chicago before the days of public-address systems. His phrasing was about as follows:

Materially/ we must strive/ to secure/ a broader/ economic/ opportunity/ for all men,/ so that each/ shall have/ a better chance/ to show/ the stuff/ of which/ he/ is made.

Old-time circus announcers had to make their phrases even shorter than that. Almost every syllable was a separate phrase:

La/dies/ and gen/tle/men./ You/ will now/ see/ the/ greatest/ sen/sa/tion/ of/ the age,/ the/ death/ defying/ slide/ for life.

People today sometimes hear phrasing similar to this in city railroad stations, even with public-address systems, because reverberations from the marble walls would make the announcer's words indistinguishable if he did not use these short phrases. Also, many of us have used phrasing of this nature when shouting to a companion across a distance.

In contrast to this short phrasing, the modern conference-room speech addressed to a comparatively small audience in a room which has good acoustics, would perhaps be phrased something like this excerpt from one of the speeches of the late Edward A. Filene:

Leadership,/ therefore,/ must pass to other hands./ And just now/ it is rapidly passing to economic illiterates/ whose hearts/ at any rate/ seem to respond to the needs of the masses/ however incapable their hands may be./ One man gains upwards of twenty million followers/ by promising $200 a month/ to everybody/ as a reward for becoming sixty years of age.

An essential part of general voice training is to learn to see words in group relationships. If we fail to see these word-group relationships and to transmit them by means of our voices, we throw an unnecessary burden upon our auditors, a burden that it is extremely unlikely they will assume, that is, the task of sorting out our words into their proper units, to make our thought clear.

Phrasing will be discussed later in this section (as well as elsewhere in the book), for it has a significant bearing on every phase of *rate*.

TIMING FOR DRAMATIC EFFECT

What is timing? What does it have to do with voice training? The dictionary definition is helpful: Timing is "the act of adjusting one's tempo of reading and movement for dramatic effect."[2] A striking example of thus adjusting the tempo occurred in a recent stage play. Otto Kruger, the well-known actor, was taking the part of an attorney who became involved in numerous intrigues. Gradually the threat of exposure began to prey upon his mind. As he became more and more enmeshed in the web of his own machinations, he engaged increasingly in morbid introspections. Finally, seeing no way out but self-destruction, he prepared to hurl himself from the window of his office. All this time, as the psychological study grew more and more intense, the action of the play was slowed down in tempo, thus accentuating the actor's mental frustration and bewilderment. Just as Kruger was on the point of plunging through the window, the door was thrown open and a brash, fast-talking news reporter rushed in. Excitedly he reported certain facts which cleared the atmosphere and lifted Kruger's despondency. His manner changed. His movements quickened. His utterances became short, quick, abrupt. All the action was speeded up. The play began to zip and hum. The whole tempo was suddenly changed from slow to fast with striking dramatic effect.

In the golf swing, experts tell us that good timing consists of starting the swing slowly and rhythmically, gradually accelerating the speed of the club until at the exact instant of impact with the golf ball the head of the club is traveling at maximum speed. To begin the swing fast and gradually lose speed, so that some of the power is lost before the moment of impact, is poor timing. Grantland Rice, one of the foremost names in sports, says about timing: "All great champions have it! It is the one thing a *would-be* lacks. . . . Watch a great golfer, a great pitcher,

[2] *Ibid.*

and you will see that the essence of their superiority is timing."[3]

Good comedians look upon timing as one of their chief stocks in trade. Without it many of their best jokes would fall flat. Jack Benny, who has a fine sense of timing, skillfully utilizes timing in the way he interjects his famous *hmmm* at the exact psychological instant to get the maximum effect.

In voice work, good timing indicates the trained and efficient speaker. Mechanical rules cannot be laid down to govern it. It must be achieved through practice—practice and the development of a sensitive appreciation of thought values and audience relationships.

In Walt Whitman's poem "O Captain! My Captain!" which appears toward the end of the next chapter, consider the mastery of timing required to show the contrast between

> Exult O shores, and ring O bells!

and the lines which immediately follow:

> But I, with mournful tread,
> Walk the deck my Captain lies,
> Fallen cold and dead.

SOUNDING SPONTANEOUS

How can I make a memorized speech sound spontaneous? One answer to this question is: Use a conversational rate. (*Pitch, force,* and *voice quality* also enter in; but for the moment we are concentrating on rate.) Conversation has a broken rate. Normally, if a person is thinking his ideas out as he goes along, he has to pause occasionally to find just the word he wants. Not only that, but the thoughtful person will often pause long enough to test mentally the sound of a phrase before giving it utterance. Then, perhaps, as his mind grasps a phrase which expresses his thought to his complete satisfaction, he utters it with quick, emphatic force, only to pause again the next instant

[3] *Colliers*, June 18, 1936, p. 81.

and feel his way cautiously, even hesitatingly, through another area of his developing thought. We have come to associate this uneven pace with normal conversation. Hence, when we hear words measured out with the regularity of a metronome we suspect the speaker either of lacking in thought or of serving us warmed-over ideas.

What we want is to learn how to make the mental food we propose to dish up appear to be freshly cooked, even though it is warmed over. To do this we'll have to study the ingredients with considerable care. The two chief ingredients of rate are *duration of tone (quantity)* and *duration of the interval between tones (pause)*. That is, not only the speech sounds, but the spaces between the sounds, require different amounts of time.

Take for example the following ejaculation: *"What! Why I never heard of such a thing!"* The vowel sound in *"What"* is prolonged markedly, as is also the vowel sound in *"heard."* Most of the other syllables are hurried over; being comparatively unimportant, they do not require any great duration for emphasis. The same kind of variation occurs in the spacing between words. After *"What"* there would usually be a prolonged pause, and possibly a shorter one after *"heard."* Hence the sentence, if written to show rate changes, would appear about as follows: *Wh-a-a-t!—Why I never h-e-a-r-d—of such a thing!*

Since skill in the use of these two elements of rate will help to determine whether or not we are able to read a selection to make it sound fresh and unrehearsed, it will be worth our while to analyze them in more detail.

Quantity

Quantity refers to the amount of time given to individual sounds. On the whole, as we have seen in our study of articulation, vowels inherently have longer duration than consonants. Vowels, however, differ in the amount of time they require. In their short form ([æ] as in *cat,* [ɛ] as in *get,* [ɪ] as in *it,* [ɑ] as in *hot,* [ʌ] as in *cut*) they take less time than in their long form

⟨[eɪ] as in *ate*, [i] as in *me*, [aɪ] as in *high*, [ou] as in *go*, [u] as in *tune*).

Furthermore, although consonants, on the whole, take less time than vowels, there is considerable difference in the time they require. Fricatives, glides, nasals, and semivowels need more time for utterance than do the plosives. (See Chapter VIII.)

Likewise, as we have seen, stressed syllables in words require more time than do unstressed syllables. Take, for instance, the word we just used, *inherently*. Note how much more time is given to the stressed syllable -*her*- than to the other syllables. So it is with words like *con*-stant-ly, in-*quis*-i-tive, or-*nate*, *dai*-sies, *ro*-ses, *vi*-o-lets, and so forth.

In a similar fashion, certain words in a phrase or sentence require more time than other words. In general, nouns, verbs, adjectives, and adverbs naturally call for more quantity than prepositions, articles, conjunctions, and the like. Such words as *the, a, or, but, and,* and *as* ordinarily play only a minor role in trasmitting thought, and serve their purpose best if touched lightly—but distinctly—and hurried over.

A nice sense of discrimination between inherently long and inherently short sounds is essential for cultured speech. If we fail to give sufficient quantity to sounds which are rightfully prolonged, our diction is unpleasantly staccato, or "clipped." On the other hand, if we give undue quantity to sounds which should be short, our diction is tediously slow and draggy or pedantic.

The above facts pertaining to quantity are pretty well standardized, determined by rules of grammar and phonetics. But there is another area in which there are no rules. That is the field of individual attitudes, where you differ from everybody else. In this area each individual determines for himself how much quantity to use. Here quantity becomes an extremely important phase of emphasis.

Consider the sentence, "It was a cold day." The individual

may hold the vowel sound in *cold* almost at will; within limits, the longer he holds it, the colder he represents the day to be. Notice how quickly the comparatively unimportant words *it, was,* and *a* may be passed over. They receive only the shortest time required to make them distinct. Quantity is given only to the last two words, and particularly to the qualifying word *cold*.

Syllables, words, phrases, and sentences which the speaker considers important he may emphasize by means of the quantity of time he gives them. In radio speech, where extreme changes in force are to be avoided because of the danger of blasting the auditors' ears, this prolongation of sounds is one of the most effective means of emphasis.

Note the emphasis added by prolonging the italicized syllables in the following:

> What do *you* think we should do now?
> What's the *good* of all this?
> Grant me just this *one* favor.
> No place to *hide!*
> She was *old,* and *gray,* and *wrinkled.*

But it is in reading poetry that the skillful use of quantity becomes most effective. A good poet is adept in using sonorous and melodious vowels in accented (prolonged) syllables to help create the effect he is striving for. Poetry should be read aloud to make these sound effects evident. If read silently, it is imperative that the reader hear, by auditory imagery, the sound of the vowels. In well-constructed poetry there is always a close relationship between the quantity of time given to the various syllables, and the meaning of the lines. If this association is lacking, the poetry is not good. For example, if short sounds are used to express sentiments of solemnity, the effect is missed, as it is also if long sounds are used to portray gaiety and liveliness. Note how effectively quantity is employed to carry both meaning and feeling in the following excerpts:

1. The road was a ribbon of moonlight over the purple moor,
   And the highwayman came riding, riding, riding,
   The highwayman came riding, up to the old inn door.

2. This is the forest primeval. The murmuring pines and the
      hemlocks,
   Bearded with moss, and in garments green, indistinct in the
      twilight,
   Stand like Druids of eld . . .

3. Maid of Athens, ere we part,
   Give, oh, give me back my heart!

To test the value of quantity as a means of enriching the
oral reading of poetry, hold the italicized words in the lines
below beyond the normal time; just for this one time, as an
exercise, really draw them out.

1.
   I *love* thee, I love but *thee*,
   With a love that shall not *die*
   Till the *sun* grows *cold*,
   And the *stars* are *old*,
   And the *leaves* of the *Judgment Book unfold*.

2.
      For *frantic boast* and *foolish word*,
      Thy *mercy* on thy *people*, Lord!
      Amen.

3.
   They rowed her in across the *rolling foam*,
   The *cruel crawling foam,*
   The *cruel hungry* foam.

4.
   I like a *church;* I like a *cowl;*
   I like a prophet of the *soul;*
   And on my heart monastic *aisles*
   Fall like *sweet strains*, or *pensive smiles.*

Pause

Long ago, a great speaker and a great writer about speech named Cicero said, "There is an art in silence, and there is an eloquence in it too." In similar vein an ancient proverb says, "Speech is silvern; silence is golden"; to which James A. Winans, a modern writer on speech, adds, "And silence is never more golden than in the midst of speech."[4]

Sometimes it seems that a speaker has to become both experienced and skillful before he learns that there is art and eloquence in a judicious bit of silence.

Trained actors use the pause with tremendous dramatic effect. Great speakers drive home their strongest points by pausing for emphasis. But most beginners appear to be obsessed with the fear that their audiences will walk out on them if they stop talking for even half a minute. Pauses seem so terribly long and frightening!

Lack of confidence, however, is not the only cause for failure to use pauses. Another cause is lack of thought. For example, when a speech student is reading Shakespeare's dramatic scene in which Macbeth challenges Macduff, and he reads it all in one phrase, thus:

> Damned be him that first cries hold enough

as if Macbeth were talking about some kind of eating contest or drinking bout, the student's mind is clearly not on what he is saying. And that is by no means a far-fetched example of typical oral reading and memoriter speaking.

Still another reason for the absence of effective pauses is that the student does not know how to pause. That is, he is so accustomed to speaking automatically, without any conscious thought of how normal, habitual speech really sounds, that when he faces a new and nervously tense situation he does not have command of the techniques necessary for making his

---

[4] James A. Winans, *Public Speaking*, Appleton-Century-Crofts, Inc., rev. ed., 1922.

speech appear natural. Pauses sound unnatural. They are louder to his ears than speech, so he carefully shuns them. Tell him to talk slower and he is likely to respond—providing he slows up at all—by dragging out all the words in a slow and painful monotony.

PAUSE AND EMPHASIS

Let us look at a few of the specific things pauses can accomplish by way of emphasis.

1. *They can indicate major thought transitions.* As chapter and paragraph indentations in printing and writing call attention to changes of thought, so deliberate, meaningful speech stops can make evident the rounding out of one idea and the shifting to another one.

Look for a minute at part of the speech on football given by the famous football coach, the late Knute Rockne, before the Chicago Executives' Club.

When my good friend, Coach Thistlewaite, or any other high-grade man in the coaching profession, looks over his squad in the fall trying to get tangible evidence as to whom he shall place on the first eleven, what does he look for?

The first thing he looks for is brains . . . [followed by about 300 words on the need for intelligence in players].

Another thing the coach will insist upon from his men is concentration. Brains are no good if they rattle . . . [followed by about 100 words on this theme].

The third thing we insist on is hard work . . . [followed by about 150 words on the importance of hard work].

A man with Rockne's shrewd knowledge of practical psychology would hardly have jumped from one to another of these steps in his theme development without pauses to mark the transitions. For that matter, knowing as he did how to talk to people—his teams, and other people too—so that they would respond the way he wanted them to, it is certain that he would not have asked the question *What does he look for?* without pausing a good long time to be sure that his listeners were answering it mentally, before he proceeded to answer it verbally.

Transitional phrases like the following cry for deliberate, meaningful pauses, somewhat as indicated:

1. However—in spite of all that we have just said—the future—holds the light of promise.
2. But, that—is only one side of the picture.—Let us—for a few minutes—look at the other side.
3. That—in brief summary—gives you the heart—of Hayne's argument.—Now—listen to what Webster—said in reply—.

2. *Pauses can give added significance to names of people and places.* Frequently an inexperienced speaker will literally bury the name of the poem he is going to recite, the title of the book he wants you to read, even the name of the person he is introducing. These names, titles, subjects, places are perfectly familiar to him; what he fails to realize is that they are not familiar to his listeners, and therefore need to be made especially distinct. Pauses rightly placed could relieve auditors of the uncertainty and the sense of dissatisfaction and frustration which such uncertainty induces.

Notice how the master of ceremonies on a radio or television program builds up his guest artists. Usually it is something like this:

And—look who's h-e-r-e—GEORGE—AND GRACIE A-L-L-E-N!

3. *Pauses can make an important idea stand out.* As a background of white paint emphasizes the colored letters on a billboard sign, so silence spaces can outline in bold relief a thought the speaker wishes to emphasize. Or, to change the figure of speech, an abrupt stop and deliberate silence just before an important idea will prepare the hearers as plowing prepares a field for planting seed; making an extended pause after the idea is like giving the seed time to germinate in the ground.

Daniel Webster, defending his state from an attack by Hayne in the Senate, used the following words. Imagine how flat they would have sounded without pauses, somewhat as indicated.

Mr. President,—I shall enter on no encomium upon Massachusetts—she needs none.—There she is—behold her—and judge for yourselves.

Consider the following two Beatitudes; how much more meaningful they become when solemn pauses are used, instead of being chanted as they so frequently are:

Blessed are the meek—for they—shall inherit—the earth.
Blessed are the merciful—for they—shall obtain—mercy.

4. *Pauses can sharpen humor.* A meaningful pause just before the point of a joke can heighten the comic effect immeasurably. Many a potentially good story is ruined by the storyteller's rushing at and over his climax.

Consider the added punch given the following by using a pause as indicated:

Bernard Shaw, it was reported, was standing on the sidelines at a social function, looking bored. A friend asked, "Aren't you enjoying yourself?" Shaw replied, "Yes I am—but that's the only thing I'm enjoying."

Another example illustrative of a possible whimsical turn which may be given a phrase by means of a pause, is the following sentence from Ruskin's essay on the fly:

He steps out of the way of your hand, and alights on the back of it.

Note how the whimsy is heightened by inserting a pause, thus:

He steps out of the way of your hand, and—alights on the back of it.

Perhaps better than either of the above examples of building up humorous effects through pauses is the following:

The late Dr. P. S. Henson was once engaged for a Chautauqua lecture on the subject of "Fools." He was introduced by Bishop

John H. Vincent with the remark: "Ladies and Gentlemen, we are now to have a lecture on 'Fools' by one of the most distinguished—." There was a long pause, the inflection of the Bishop's voice indicated he had finished. The audience howled with delight. When they had subsided, the Bishop concluded, "men of Chicago." Dr. Henson in no way perturbed began his speech with: "Ladies and Gentlemen, I am not so great a fool as Bishop Vincent—" here he paused pointedly before adding "— would have you think."[5]

5. *Pauses can help to make reading sound conversational.* One reason reading is often so dull is perhaps the format of the printed page—lines the same length, letters the same height, words on the same level, all the printing in the same degree of blackness, sentences packed in rows like sardines in a can. Every suggestion urges the reader to hurry along. How different these printed symbols of speech are from the ups and downs, the shading and coloring, and especially the speeding up and the slowing down of animated, thoughtful conversation! If there is a bit of advice the oral reader needs more often than any other, it is: S l o w   d o w n! if you have any hope of giving your hearers the full flavor of what you are reading, p a u s e and give them time to think! If you have any hope of having your reading sound like talk, p a u s e and give *yourself* time to think!

The two excerpts which follow are marked with pauses to indicate how they might be read. Naturally, we wouldn't all read them the same way, any more than we would talk them the same way. But, at least, this is one way to read them so they do not sound like chanting.

I think—by far the most important bill—in our whole code—is that for the—diffusion of knowledge—among the people—.

In a great crisis—it is thinking—so as to make others think—feeling—so as to make others feel—which tips the orator's tongue—with fire—that lights—as well as burns—.

[5] *Coronet,* April, 1945.

PAUSE VERSUS HESITATION

All the preceding discussion refers to deliberate, meaningful pauses for emphasis. Careful distinction must be made between pause and hesitation. Pause is strength; hesitation is weakness. And do not think that the audience does not recognize the difference. Even if the dreadful *ah's* and *uh's* that so often accompany hesitation are absent, the shifting eye and general air of indecision give it away.

Pause to let the idea sink into the audience's mind! Pause to choose the fitting word to dress the idea for expression! But avoid those *er-* and *um-*bedecked hesitations. Get the idea so well in mind that the thoughts are there ready to be given fiesh. Hesitation will lose the audience; judicious pauses will hold them to the speech.

PAUSES SHOULD NOT BE MECHANICAL

"O'erstep not the Modesty of Nature" is another way of saying what we have said more than once before, and will say again; for this observance will bear frequent repetition. It applies not only to this discussion of Rate, but to Pitch and Force which are considered later, and with equal cogency to every other phase of voice development. In other words, let the spirit dominate the flesh.

To vary the rate does not mean to introduce artificial and continued irregularities. Sudden spurts and ponderous pauses may easily be overdone, and they will be overdone if they are mechanical.

An Experiment in Controlling Rate by Mental Concentration

The close relationship between mental concentration and rate of speaking may be demonstrated by the following experiment: Read aloud in an offhand, indifferent manner Tennyson's little poem, "Flower in the Crannied Wall." As you read, carefully observe your own voice and its rate of speech.

> Flower in the crannied wall,
> I pluck you out of the crannies,
> I hold you here, root and all, in my hand,
> Little flower—but *if* I could understand
> What you are, root and all, and all in all,
> I should know what God and man is.

Now really study the poem. Picture in your mind a flower growing out of a crack in some crumbling old rock wall. Let your mind dwell for a bit on the marvelous characteristics of the growing plant, its power to push a rock apart with the prodigious strength of its slender roots.

When you have created that picture, let your thoughts turn to the next image, a man stepping up and nonchalantly plucking the flower out of the wall. Get the picture: man, the lord of creation, strong, dominating, ruthless; the little flower so unimportant and so feeble that it can offer no resistance when the man plucks it out of its home. There is deliberate significance in the choice of the word "pluck"; it suggests indifference, almost contemptuousness. From the flower's point of view there might be some dignity about being gathered, but not "plucked"; that's sheer effrontery.

The next idea makes that cumulative: "I hold you here, root and all, in my hand, little flower." The whole life process of the plant is lying helpless there in his hand. Big man, lord of creation; little, insignificant flower lying bruised and helpless in his hand.

But the next thought shows a change in mood, a change so deep, so fundamental, that it is colossal in its mental and emotional scope. "But *if* I could understand what you are." That word "understand" has a world of meaning. There is nothing superficial about it. Understanding is deep; it is something more than a glib recital of the botanical names of the parts of the flower, something more than scientifically classifying it. To *understand* is to know what force makes the seed apparently die and then begin a new life; to know what power makes it grow into a chrysanthemum instead of a daisy; to know whence come its color and its fragrance. To know this would be to unlock the door to complete understanding, to unravel the master knot of human fate.

The next line gives this thought cumulative significance: "What you are, root and all, and all in all." Then comes the unfolding of the whole poem, "I should know what God and man is." God and man *is*. Plural subject, singular verb! Shame on Tennyson; a grammatical error! Or maybe it was just poetic license. Not at all! The word was deliberately chosen and there's no poetic license about it. In the choice of that word lies the key to Tennyson's religious philosophy. God and man *is*. To Tennyson, God and man are one.

Now read the poem again, thinking these thoughts, seeing these mental images, dwelling on these philosophizings. The rate will necessarily be slow—not the slow drawling of the phlegmatic mind, but the deliberateness, the prolonged pauses of the thinking person. Such a reading would perhaps be something like the following, though of course each individual will interpret according to his own past experience and his own mental habits, and there will be no absolute uniformity:

Flower—in the crannied wall,—I pluck you—out of the crannies, —I hold you here,—root and all—in my hand.—Little flower—but *if* I could understand—what you are—root and all,—and all in all, —I should know—what God and man is.

EXERCISES AND SELECTIONS FOR PRACTICE

1. Contrast the general tempo of the two following selections:

1.

PIPPA PASSES

The year's at the spring
And day's at the morn;
Morning's at seven;
The hillside's dew-pearled;

The lark's on the wing;
The snail's on the thorn:
God's in his heaven—
All's right with the world!

—Robert Browning

2.   Tomorrow, and tomorrow, and tomorrow,
     Creeps in this petty pace from day to day
     To the last syllable of recorded time;
     And all our yesterdays have lighted fools
     The way to dusty death. Out, out, brief candle!
     Life's but a walking shadow, a poor player
     That struts and frets his hour upon the stage
     And then is heard no more. It is a tale
     Told by an idiot, full of sound and fury,
     Signifying nothing.

—Shakespeare

2. Phrasing is a special problem in the following group of selections.
Experiment with different types of phrasing in your effort to get
across the greatest meaning.

1.   On either side the river lie
          Long fields of barley and of rye . . .

2.   This City now doth, like a garment, wear
       The beauty of the morning; silent, bare,
       Ships, towers, domes, theatres, and temples lie
       Open upon the fields, and to the sky;
       All bright and glittering in the smokeless air. . . .
       Ne'er saw I, never felt, a calm so deep!

—William Wordsworth

3. If to do were as easy as to know what were good to do, chapels
had been churches, and poor men's cottages princes' palaces.
It is a good divine that follows his own instructions: I can
easier teach twenty what were good to be done, than be one of
the twenty to follow mine own teaching. The brain may de-

vise laws for the blood, but a hot temper leaps o'er a cold decree: such a hare is madness the youth, to skip o'er the meshes of good counsel the cripple.

—SHAKESPEARE

4. Turn to "The Cry of the Children" (p. 326) and study it from the standpoint of phrasing.

3. Give full quantity to the italicized syllables in these sentences:

1. It was *ro*ses, *ro*ses all the way.
2. *Get*ting and *spend*ing, we lay *waste* our *powers.*
3. The *sea* is *calm* tonight.
4. Where are the *songs* of *Spring?*
5. I love not *man* the *less,* but *Nature more.*
6. Lord God of *Hosts,* be with us *yet,* lest we *forget,* lest we *forget!*
7. If *music* be the food of *love, play on!*
8. *Arm! Arm!* it is the *cannon's* opening roar.
9. *Drink* to me *only* with thine *eyes.*
10. They rowed her in across the *cruel, crawling foam.*
11. I was *wea*ry and ill at *ease.*
12. Sail *on,* and *on,* and *on!*

4. In the following tribute paid to the University of Oxford Library by King James (as reported in *The Anatomy of Melancholy* by Robert Burton), give enough *quantity* to the meaning-carrying words to express the high regard which King James evidently felt.

If I were not a King, I would be an University man; and if it were so that I must be a prisoner, if I might have my wish, I would desire to have no other prison than that Library, and to be chained together with so many good Authors and dead Masters. So sweet is the delight of study, the more learning they have, (as he that hath a Dropsy, the more he drinks the thirstier he is), the more they covet to learn.

5. Insert long, meaningful pauses where you think they will do the most good in each of the following sentences:

1. The villainy you teach me, I will execute.
2. Gentlemen, this means war.

3. Fear death? to feel the fog in my throat? the mist in my face?
4. But hush! hark! a deep sound strikes like a rising knell!
5. Youth is like summer morn, age like winter weather.
6. The quality of mercy blesses him that gives and him that takes.
7. And damned be him that first cries, *Hold, enough!*
8. For me, there is something almost shocking in the realization that, though many millions have been voluntarily donated for research in cancer of the individual body, nothing similar has been done with respect to the most malignant cancer of the world body, war.

—Dwight D. Eisenhower

9. Never in the field of human conflict was so much owed by so many to so few.

—Winston Churchill

10. In all my fifty years of public service I have never seen a document so crowded with infamous falsehoods and distortions.

—Cordell Hull

11. . . . Shall we now contaminate our fingers with base bribes,
And sell the mighty space of our large honors
For so much trash as may be grasped—thus?

—Shakespeare

6. In reading the following selection you will heighten the effect if you make the pauses sharp, abrupt, clear cut; but be sure to hold them long enough to let your listeners get the pictures.

THE GATE

Scene I

A gate.
Two lovers.
A father mad.
The hour is late.
Two hearts are glad.

Scene II

A growl.
A leap.
A nip.
A tear.
A cry.
A sigh.
And then—
A swear.

Scene III

A gate.
No lovers.
A father glad.
A dog triumphant.
A maiden sad.

Epilogue

If it took two hours to say good-night,
It served him right if the dog did bite.

—BESSIE CAHN

7. The pauses in the following poem, although definite and prolonged, are blended in with the words. The selection, in musical
terminology, should be *legato*, in contrast to the *staccato* of the
preceding selection. Try to achieve a flowing quality which will
carry through your pauses. And observe that those breakers are
ocean waves, not ripples in the bathtub.

Break, break, break,
  On thy cold gray stones, O Sea!
And I would that my tongue could utter
  The thoughts that arise in me.

O, well for the fisherman's boy,
  That he shouts with his sister at play!
O, well for the sailor lad,
  That he sings in his boat on the bay!

And the stately ships go on
  To their haven under the hill;
But O for the touch of a vanish'd hand,
  And the sound of a voice that is still!

Break, break, break,
  At the foot of thy crags, O Sea!
But the tender grace of a day that is dead
  Will never come back to me.

—ALFRED, LORD TENNYSON

8. The following picture of a distraught mind affords abundant opportunity to test your skill at timing, along with the changing moods:

Dead, long dead,
Long dead!
And my heart is a handful of dust,
And the wheels go over my head,
And my bones are shaken with pain,
For into a shallow grave they are thrust,
Only a yard beneath the street.
And the hoofs of the horses beat, beat,
The hoofs of the horses beat,
Beat into my scalp and my brain,
With never an end to the stream of passing feet,
Driving, hurrying, marrying, burying,
Clamour and rumble, and ringing and clatter;
And here beneath it is all as bad,
For I thought the dead had peace, but it is not so;
To have no peace in the grave, is that not sad?
But up and down and to and fro,
Ever about me the dead men go;
And then to hear a dead man chatter
Is enough to drive one mad.

—ALFRED, LORD TENNYSON

9. Below are a group of selections in varying moods and tempo. In the slow-moving, thoughtful ones use plenty of quantity and pauses. A beautiful poem should be sipped like a delicious bev-

erage, not gulped like a dose of castor oil. Even in the faster-moving poem by Franklin P. Adams, "To Chloris," do not go so fast that your hearers lose the clever nuances. Use pauses, but of the staccato type; they will give the illusion of speed, even though they are fairly long.

1. WAITING

Serene, I fold my hands and wait,
    Nor care for wind, nor tide, nor sea;
I rave no more 'gainst time or fate,
    For, lo! my own shall come to me.

I stay my haste, I make delays,
    For what avails this eager pace?
I stand amid the eternal ways,
    And what is mine shall know my face.

Asleep, awake, by night or day,
    The friends I seek are seeking me;
No wind can drive my bark astray,
    Nor change the tide of destiny. . . .
                    —JOHN BURROUGHS

2. ON HIS BLINDNESS

When I consider how my light is spent
Ere half my days, in this dark world and wide
And that one talent which is death to hide
Lodged with me useless, though my soul more bent
To serve therewith my Maker, and present
My true account, lest he returning chide,
"Doth God exact day-labor, light denied?"
I fondly ask. But Patience, to prevent
That murmur, soon replies, "God doth not need
Either man's work or his own gifts. Who best
Bear his mild yoke, they serve him best. His state
Is kingly: thousands at his bidding speed,
And post o'er land and ocean without rest;
They also serve who only stand and wait."
                    —JOHN MILTON

3.   THE RAINY DAY

The day is cold, and dark, and dreary;
It rains, and the wind is never weary;
The vine still clings to the mouldering wall,
But at every gust the dead leaves fall,
    And the day is dark and dreary.

My life is cold, and dark, and dreary;
It rains, and the wind is never weary;
My thoughts still cling to the mouldering Past,
But the hopes of youth fall thick in the blast,
    And the days are dark and dreary.

Be still, sad heart! and cease repining;
Behind the clouds is the sun still shining;
Thy fate is the common fate of all,
Into each life some rain must fall,
    Some days must be dark and dreary.
                        —HENRY WADSWORTH LONGFELLOW

4.   TO CHLORIS[6]

Your conduct, naughty Chloris, is
Not just exactly Horace's
    Ideal of a lady
    At the shady
        Time of life;

You mustn't throw your soul away
On foolishness, like Pholoe—
    Her days are folly-laden—
    She's a maiden,
        You're a wife.

[6] Translated from Horace by Franklin P. Adams. Reprinted by permission of
the author.

Your daughter, with propriety,
May look for male society,
  Do one thing and another
  In which mother
    Shouldn't mix;

But revels Bacchanalian
Are—or should be—quite alien
  To you a married person,
  Something worse'n
    Forty-six!

Yes, Chloris, you cut up too much,
You love the dance and cup too much.
  Your years are quickly flitting;
  To your knitting
    Right about!

Forget the incidental things
That keep you from parental things
  The World, the Flesh, the Devil,
  On the level
    Cut 'em out!

—F.P.A.

5. FORTUNE'S WHEEL

Turn, Fortune, turn thy wheel, and lower the proud;
Turn thy wild wheel through sunshine, storm, and cloud;
Thy wheel and thee we neither love nor hate.

Turn, Fortune, turn thy wheel with smile or frown;
With that wild wheel we go not up or down;
Our hoard is little, but our hearts are great.

Smile and we smile, the lords of many lands;
Frown and we smile, the lords of our own hands;
For man is man and master of his fate.

—ALFRED, LORD TENNYSON

6.   CURFEW

I

Solemnly, mournfully,
   Dealing its dole,
The Curfew Bell
   Is beginning to toll.

Cover the embers,
   And put out the light;
Toil comes with the morning,
   And rest with the night.

Dark grow the windows,
   And quenched is the fire;
Sound fades into silence,—
   All footsteps retire.

No voice in the chambers,
   No sound in the hall!
Sleep and oblivion
   Reign over all!

II

The book is completed,
   And closed, like the day;
And the hand that has written it
   Lays it away.

Dim grow its fancies;
   Forgotten they lie;
Like coals in the ashes,
   They darken and die.

Song sinks into silence,
   The story is told,
The windows are darkened,
   The hearth-stone is cold.

> Darker and darker
> The black shadows fall;
> Sleep and oblivion
> Reign over all.
> —HENRY WADSWORTH LONGFELLOW

7.   WHENCE COMETH MY HELP[7]

I must go up to the mountains,
   To that star-drenched silent place,
To the primal balm of their wise old calm
   And the freedom of wind-swept space.

Oh the valley is golden and throbbing
   With the turbulent clamor of life!
There is virile power in each crowded hour
   And the stinging joy of strife.

But I must go up where the mountains
   In blue-green surges roll,
Sweeping to me from infinity
   The quiet that heals the soul.

I learn new faith in my brother;
   Alone on the mountain height.
I catch the gleam of his age-old dream
   As he struggles from clod to the light.

I know in the hush of the mountains
   The shelter of holy wings,
While shy thoughts creep through the silence deep
   Into the word that sings.
Oh the valley is vibrant and golden,
   But the mountains are still and fair.
There is sovereign balm in their infinite calm
   And I meet God walking there.
                    —ETHELEAN TYSON GAW

[7] Reprinted by permission of the author.

8.   *From* THE OLD CLOCK ON THE STAIRS

    Somewhat back from the village street
    Stands the old-fashioned country-seat.
    Across its antique portico
    Tall poplar-trees their shadows throw;
    And from its station in the hall
    An ancient timepiece says to all,—
        "Forever—never!
        Never—forever!"

    Half-way up the stairs it stands,
    And points and beckons with its hands
    From its case of massive oak,
    Like a monk, who, under his cloak,
    Crosses himself, and sighs, alas!
    With sorrowful voice to all who pass,—
        "Forever—never!
        Never—forever!"

    By day its voice is low and light;
    But in the silent dead of night,
    Distinct as a passing footstep's fall,
    It echoes along the vacant hall,
    Along the ceiling, along the floor,
    And seems to say, at each chamber-door,—
        "Forever—never!
        Never—forever!"

          . . . . . .

    In that mansion used to be
    Free-hearted Hospitality;
    His great fires up the chimney roared;
    The stranger feasted at his board;
    But, like the skeleton at the feast,
    That warning timepiece never ceased,—
        "Forever—never!
        Never—forever!"

From that chamber, clothed in white,
The bride came forth on her wedding night;
There, in that silent room below,
The dead lay in his shroud of snow;
And in the hush that followed the prayer,
Was heard the old clock on the stair,—
    "Forever—never!
    Never—forever!"

. . . .

All are scattered now and fled,
Some are married, some are dead;
And when I ask, with throbs of pain,
"Ah! when shall they all meet again?"
As in the day long since gone by,
The ancient timepiece makes reply,—
    "Forever—never!
    Never—forever!"
                —HENRY WADSWORTH LONGFELLOW

XII * Achieving Vocal Expressiveness: Pitch

Pitch is the relative height or depth of a tone. If we were talking in musical terms, pitch would refer to the position of a given note on the musical scale.

As explained in the discussion of the physiology of the vocal mechanism, pitch is determined by the vibration rate of the vocal bands; the faster the rate of vibration the higher the pitch, and vice versa. In turn, the rate of vibration is determined by the tautness or laxness of the bands in relation to their length, thickness, and density. The tauter the bands the faster they vibrate in response to a given degree of pressure by the exhaled breath stream.

Pitch Variety Essential

In our effort to achieve expressiveness in the speaking voice, few things are of more importance than developing skill in the use of pitch variations. Pitch is more effective than either rate or force in expressing delicate shades of meaning. Modulations of quality, rate, and force are more closely related to total emotional states; pitch variation is primarily the instrument of fine thought discriminations. Consequently its wise use indicates a high order of mental development.

However, while it is true that pitch is essentially the instrument of thought expression, it also plays a role in the expression of emotion. As a matter of fact, no one is capable of establishing a clear line of distinction between thinking and feeling. And it cannot be denied that the pitch of the voice is related to the person's feelings. If the voice is free and uninhibited, excitement will produce a heightened pitch, and sorrow a lowered pitch, almost as inevitably as the rising and setting of the sun produce daylight and darkness.

An idea of the significance of pitch in achieving vocal expressiveness can readily be gained by listening to the mechanical voice produced by the artificial larynx described on page 30. The inability of this mechanism to produce changes in pitch is the chief explanation of its difference from the normal voice, for its voice *quality* is a surprisingly accurate imitation of the human voice.

An approximation of this dead level of pitch is sometimes heard in the voices of the deaf and near-deaf. Although they seldom if ever display complete mono-pitch, their voices are often so restricted in range as to give that impression.

The flat voice is employed by certain comedians—notably Ned Sparks, and to some extent Groucho Marx—as a vehicle for their particular type of humor. Often it is accompanied by a facial expression of bored disgust. With these comedians, the flat, hard voice becomes a trademark.

In contrast to these unusual types, the expressive conversational voice is delightfully flexible. Never monotonous, never rigid, never tiresome, it is always changing pitch to suit the fine shades of meaning in the speaker's thought development.

And that brings us again to our frequently repeated observation, that sluggish minds with small power of imagery will naturally be characterized by sluggish and inexpressive voices. Dull minds make dull speaking, in pitch monotony, as well as in rate monotony, force monotony, and quality monotony. On the other hand, the person who has an active mind, a vivid power of imagery, and keeps his mind on what he is saying, should have an interesting and expressive pitch variety, provided he is free from artificial restraints. To acquire the kind of pitch control which is necessary to carry the speech student through all the emotion-fraught occasions he is likely to meet, there is no alternative to "holding the mirror up to nature" and thoroughly familiarizing himself with just how pitch functions in the transmission of thought and feeling.

Optimum Pitch

Each voice has a pitch level at which it functions best. This does not mean that there is any one note to which a voice should cling in order to be at its best. But there is a sort of general pitch level at which a voice can be used with least strain and effort, and at which its quality is most pleasing. To speak again in musical terminology, one man's voice performs best in the baritone range, another's in the tenor range; one woman's in the contralto range, another's in the soprano. In speech students, this most favorable speaking pitch level is called the *optimum pitch.*

Optimum pitch for a given voice is determined by the length and thickness of the vocal cords, the size and shape of the resonance chambers, and other physical considerations, much as a violin, violoncello, viola, and bass viol, although similar in design, are constructed to produce their best tones in different pitch ranges.

Obviously, the pitch level at which an individual habitually talks may or may not be his optimum pitch, according to whether he uses or does not use his speech mechanism to the best advantage. All sorts of pitch faults can develop and become fixed in habit, so that the person habitually talks above or below his optimum pitch. One important objective of voice training is to help the individual in determining his optimum pitch and in establishing the habit of using it.

How to Determine Optimum Pitch

One way of finding your best speaking pitch is as follows: If you are musically inclined, you may use the piano to advantage;

or, if not musical yourself, perhaps you can persuade a musically-minded friend to help you. Sing up and down the scale (*do, re, mi, fa, so, la, si, do*) to test the upper and lower limits which you can sing without strain. Find the middle note between these extremes. The tone about one-third below this mid-point should be close to your optimum pitch. That is, if your easy singing range is two octaves, which is a good range for a normally flexible voice, you will be able to sing from the lowest *do* up to the second *do* above, thus: *do re mi fa so la si, do re mi fa so la si do.* The mid-point will be *si* at the top of the first octave, or *do* at the beginning of the second octave. The second note below this will be either *so* or *la*, about two-thirds of the way up in the first octave. After repeated trials, you should be able to determine which of these two notes—or possibly another note near it, for this is not a scientific formula—comes easiest to your voice. On this note your voice should ring out most clearly, freely, and comfortably. This note you should work to establish as sort of a base, from which your voice fluctuates upward and downward as you talk, and to which it returns as a pigeon comes home to its roost.

Another method of determining optimum pitch involves reading aloud. If singing tends to tighten your throat and introduces an element of strain into your voice, it is better to skip the exercise outlined above. However, a piano and a musical friend may still be useful in helping you locate your optimum pitch, thus: While you read aloud some of the practice selections below, have this friend "accompany" you by gently touching the keys of the piano. It is best, during this exercise, to read in a fairly level voice, pitched in the general neighborhood where you consider your optimum pitch to be. Meanwhile, your "accompanist" will locate the average pitch of your voice. Then, have him strike the next lower note in the scale, while you let your voice drop to that level and continue reading in a mono-pitch. If this note seems too low for voice comfort, have him strike the next note above the pitch you have been using. Continue to experiment in this fashion until you locate the pitch at which your voice functions easiest and best. It may take quite a lot of testing before you find the right key, especially if you have been using your voice improperly for a long time. In general, more people habitually talk above their best pitch than below it. Often a student finds that he can lower his average pitch two or three tones, or even more, without strain, and discovers that his tone quality is improved thereby.

As suggested, it is better to read on, or fairly near, a monopitch, until you are sure that you have established your optimum. Then, when you are definitely sure of your best pitch, begin to let your voice fluctuate normally. Better still, begin working to extend the range (of fluctuations) up and down the scale—but more about this later.

A third method of determining optimum pitch is designed for those who avoid things musical. This method consists merely in emitting open-throated groans: *o-o-o-h-h, a-a-a-h-h, h-o-o h-u-m,* etc. Toward the end of the groans let your voice trail off into a lower pitch range. Repeat several times, then follow the groans by repeating some of the practice lines below.

It will be noted that most of these lines are in somber mood. They were deliberately chosen to meet the needs of the majority of students. As was said, most students need to lower their pitch a little to find their optimum; and somber thoughts, rather than gay ones, are conducive to lowered pitch. Read them on the pitch level established by your funnel-throated groan.

1.   The mountains look on Marathon,
               And Marathon looks on the sea;
           And musing there an hour alone,
               I dreamed that Greece might still be free.

2. Night is the time to weep,
   To wet with unseen tears
   Those graves of memory where sleep
   The joys of other years.

3. Man wants but little here below,
   Nor wants that little long.

4. How can ye chant, ye little birds,
   And I so full of care?

5. Lo, all our pomp of yesterday
   Is one with Nineveh and Tyre.

6. A thing of beauty is a joy forever;
   Its loveliness increases; it will never
   Pass into nothingness.

7. I pray that our Heavenly Father may assuage the anguish of your bereavement and leave you only the cherished memory of the loved and lost, and the solemn pride that must be yours to have laid so costly a sacrifice upon the altar of freedom.
   —ABRAHAM LINCOLN, "Letter to Mrs. Bixby"

Lowering the Pitch

For many, perhaps most, who set out to improve their voices, the chief goal is lowered pitch. Within certain limits this is a thoroughly commendable purpose. It is true, as we said above, that most persons habitually talk in a higher pitch than they need to, a pitch too high to produce their best tonal quality. That seems to be part of the price we have to pay for living in a society where hurry, strife, and nervous tensions are rife, where little relaxed and leisurely living is to be found. These stresses and strains of daily life take their toll of our voices, especially in the form of heightened pitch. So far as our objective in voice training is to learn to counteract these adverse influences and to educate our voices to utilize the pitch level intended by nature, we are headed in the right direction.

Any attempt to force the voice to lower levels will result only in throaty, unmusical sounds. To "choke" the voice down, as some people do, is unnatural and strained; it not only robs the voice of its flexibility, but often results in permanent injury.

Physiologically, the right method of lowering the pitch has two principal aspects: (1) relaxing the extrinsic muscles of the larynx which interfere with the free, unhampered vibration of the vocal cords, as explained in Chapter IV; and (2) learning to use effectively the resonance chambers which reinforce our deeper tones, as explained in Chapter VII. In our effort to achieve a lower voice, let us once more look briefly at these two fundamental aspects of voice training.

Utilizing the Full Swing of the Vocal Cords

Principally, the utilization of the full swing of the vocal cords consists in relaxing the muscles of the lower jaw and the other swallowing muscles. It involves letting the voice drop to lower notes through increased relaxation, never by forcing it down. Hence all the exercises given in Chapter IV for releasing tension in the throat and jaw—yawning, head rolling, gentle massage, the cultivation of a calm frame of mind, and so forth. At this time we add only one further suggestion, which was touched upon in the preceding chapter: Before starting to talk, stop and think. Deliberately place your voice at the new pitch level (probably lower than your habitual pitch) which you established by the experiment on optimum pitch. Learn to talk more deliberately. Utilize pauses to help you achieve this lower pitch. And don't become impatient. Let nature take its course, and don't try to hurry the process.

Using Resonance to Amplify the Lower Notes

Principally, resonance helps by enlarging the pharynx, or, in other words, opening the throat. Everything else being equal, large resonating chambers (especially longer and deeper in contrast to wider and shallower chambers) resonate deeper overtones. To accomplish this enlarging of the pharynx, the muscles in its walls must be relaxed. These muscles are used in masticating food, in pushing food and drink along toward the esophagus, and in swallowing. When these muscles are constricted they make the pharynx smaller. On the other hand, the yawning, the head rolling, and all the other exercises to relax these muscles tend to make the pharynx larger. To refresh your mind about this place your fingers lightly on your larynx and begin a yawn. Note how the Adam's apple is drawn down, thus elongating the pharynx and preparing it for resonating the deeper overtones.

At this time add one more resonance exercise to those you are already using. Certain actors, notably the late E. E. Clive, who had such unusual depth and fullness in his voice that he was frequently cast as a dignified judge on the bench, have testified to the results achieved by talking or reading aloud daily with a one-inch cork held between the teeth. You can test this by placing two fingers one upon the other between your teeth, and talking. It does seem to open the throat and lower the tone somewhat, and it definitely increases the volume—another proof of the fact that effective resonance requires an open mouth. However, it also tires the throat muscles, and should therefore be used with discretion.

Before launching a program of voice lowering, two other facts should be borne in mind.

1. Feeling can be portrayed as truly and effectively by tones in the middle and higher register as by those that come from the cellar. After all, the secret of a pleasant, expressive voice lies not so much in excessive depth as in round, full, vibrant tones. When the tones are full and round, we are scarcely conscious of their pitch level; it is mainly the thin high tones that we dislike. Who will say that a basso profundo sings more beautifully than a tenor? Tones compounded of many harmoniously adjusted overtones are agreeable at any pitch level, in both speaking and singing. The question is not how low, but how pleasant and how expressive.

2. One bad pitch fault is holding the pitch too low, lower

than the voice's efficiency level. Such voices are bound to be rigid and expressionless. And almost inevitably these artificially low tones are associated with harsh, unpleasant voice quality.

Pitch Range

Sometimes a well-endowed and well-trained singer uses a range up to three octaves. Recently a South American singer, Yma Sumac, far exceeded this limitation. One music critic, reporting one of her concerts, said: "For the first few bars . . . [she] rumbled roundly at the bottom of contralto range. Then, to their astonishment, she soared effortlessly up a full four octaves, and began trilling like a canary at the top of coloratura."[1]

The average voice, while not capable of anything like Miss Sumac's achievement, can master a variation of from one and one-half to two octaves. In spite of this capability, many persons confine their speaking voices to a range of half an octave, or even less. But speech students should realize that one way to add to their vocal expressiveness is to increase their functional pitch range. Let us, therefore, analyze the available means of accomplishing this.

There are three ways of varying pitch: *key*, *inflection*, and *step*.

KEY

Key is the general height or depth of the voice in expressing a given sentiment. In reading aloud, for instance, the key would be the predominant pitch level of a selection. With a good speaker, it varies markedly according to the spirit of the occasion. Obviously, no proficient reader would key his voice the same for one of Ogden Nash's humorous poems as for Hamlet's soliloquy. Between these extremes there are many gradations of key. The better control a student has over his voice, the better he adjusts his key to the needs of the moment.

[1] *Time*, August 28, 1950, p. 58.

This is equally true in conversation, oral reading, or public speaking. In the exercises at the end of this chapter the student will find opportunity to test his skill in the use of key.

INFLECTION

Inflection, or *slide*, means change in pitch *on* the tone. The voice slides or glides up and down the scale to express changing thoughts and to express the speaker's attitude toward what he is saying—in other words, to emphasize. In general, upward slides express questions, indecision, or incomplete thoughts; downward slides express complete thoughts and positive emphasis; the double slide, or circumflex,—up and down, or down and up—expresses uncertainty, irony, or double meaning. For example, the question, *Will you go with me?* naturally ends with a definite upward slide, thus / .

The declaration, *I won't go; and that's final,* naturally ends with a downward slide, thus \ .

The expression of surprised incredulity, *What! (Why you don't mean it)* naturally has a double slide, down and up thus \/ .

In such a tongue-in-cheek statement as *The atomic bomb is the fine flower of twenty centuries of Christian teaching,* on the words *flower, Christian,* and *teaching* there might be slides down and up and down, thus \ ∧. (However, when we get into the field of cynicism, irony, and various other kinds of double talk, there is little standardization, except this: All voices are likely to use in this type of expression some form of the circumflex, or, as it is sometimes called, the "wave" accent. A clever comedian becomes especially skillful in its use; often he makes a joke just by the inflection twist he gets into his voice. In the practice exercises for pitch, the student will find a series of sentences with a humorous or whimsical turn, upon which he can practice his use of the circumflex.)

In conversational speech, not only are there slides at the ends of sentences and on especially significant words but slides occur on practically all words. Almost never does the voice remain on a level for the duration of a single word. Consider for instance the simple declarative sentence, *I am going to buy a new suit of clothes.* It might at first appear, on only casually listening, that all the words except the last one are uttered on a level pitch, but that is not the case. Close analysis discloses that all the words except the last one are given with upward slides, thus /////////\. If any appreciable number of these words were given in level pitch, the statement would sound like singing or chanting, not talk.

The slides which constantly occur in the speaking voice are usually short. In a matter-of-fact statement such as *The man was riding a horse,* the slides are frequent but not very long—perhaps about like this:

If, on the other hand, the speaker is trying to explain something, the slides are longer and more pronounced. Note the need for longer slides in the following:

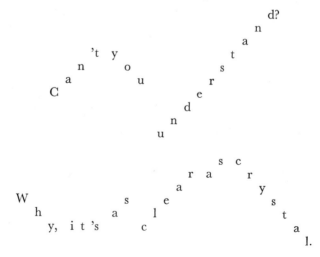

Inflection Differences Between Emotional and Nonemotional Speech. To the question, "Which requires more slides, emotional or nonemotional speech?" most students would answer, "Emotional." But they would be wrong, as a little observation will disclose. Such elevated passages as the following require very few slides:

> The Lord is my shepherd, I shall not want,
> He maketh me to lie down in green pastures,
> He restoreth my soul.
>
> Lift up your head, oh ye gates,
> And be ye lift up, ye everlasting doors,
> And the King of Glory shall come in.

To express these deeply emotional sentiments in the frequent short slides of ordinary conversation would be to remove them from the serenity of the temple to the give-and-take of the market place.

Such highly emotional literature approaches the smooth, sustained pitch of poetry and song. But when a minister announces on Sunday morning—as he sometimes does—a board meeting or a chicken dinner in the same level tones in which he reads the Scripture lesson, the effect is ludicrous. It is not hard to understand why he does this. He has used an emotional type of speech so much of the time that it has become part of his standard equipment. We label it the "ministerial voice." (Morticians, librarians, auctioneers, salesmen, newsboys, college debaters, and many others are likely to develop occupation-labeled voices if they aren't careful.) However, if the minister read the Lord's Prayer or the Twenty-Third Psalm in the short, quick slides of ordinary conversation, he would sound even more ridiculous.

Try this out for yourself with, for example, the first sentence from the Twenty-Third Psalm. Read it first with the inflection with which you might announce your intention of going to a football game. Analysis of your pitch will show that you talk somewhat like this:

The Lord is my shepherd; I shall not want.

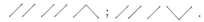

No doubt you will instantly recognize the incongruous nature of these inflections for such sacred thoughts. Now try it in the level tones which the effective preacher uses for such passages. You will find your voice goes more like this:

The inflections in emotional prose or poetry are fewer in number than they are in conversation, but they are longer and more sweeping. In such a sentence as the one below, one way to make *slaves* really unpleasant is to utter the word with a long downward slide. All else being equal, the longer the slide the more detestable is the idea of slavery. The sentence would be charted somewhat as follows:

You are slaves; gross, ignoble slaves.

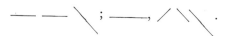

The short, quick slides of ordinary matter-of-fact speech are not adequate.

Most poetry is emotional in nature. Therefore it usually does not call for the quick, short slides of conversational speech. However, poetry differs. Some of it is more emotional, and some of it more thought-laden. That in which thought predominates naturally calls for more slides; that in which feeling predominates calls for fewer slides, but often longer, more sweeping ones. Read the following brief selections, paying careful attention to the number and nature of slides required. Note that Lowell's thought-laden lines require many more slides, with sharper, more abrupt changes, than Whitman's highly emotional ones. The slides in the latter selection, however, although fewer in number, are not shorter; indeed, they may profitably be considerably longer.

> New occasions teach new duties; Time makes ancient
>   good uncouth;
> They must upward still, and onward, who would keep
>   abreast of truth.
> —JAMES RUSSELL LOWELL

> But O heart! heart! heart!
> O the bleeding drops of red,
> Where on the deck my captain lies,
> Fallen cold and dead.
> —WALT WHITMAN

The student who wishes to develop his voice to the point where he can really express strong, deep feeling when occasion demands it must cultivate the ability to use long, sweeping slides. This is one way to make his voice expressive. Just how expressive these long slides can be may be observed by listening to recordings made by fine actors—such, for example, as *Macbeth* recorded by Maurice Evans and Judith Anderson.

STEP

Step is the third way of varying pitch. It means the changing of pitch *between* words or syllables. Inflection involves changes of pitch *on* the sound; step changes it *between* sounds.

The singer ordinarily steps from one note to another, and holds the voice level on each note, thus:

$$mi$$
$$re$$
$$do$$

Only rarely does he use slides to get from one note to another.

The speaker, on the other hand, ordinarily combines slides and steps in a series of constant fluctuations. Thus, in a declarative sentence such as the following, there would be fairly wide variations both in inflection and step:

I will never yield.

The need for step in the oral reading of poetry is illustrated by the following lines:

> Break, break, break,
>   On thy cold, grey stones, O sea!

Probably they would go somewhat like this:

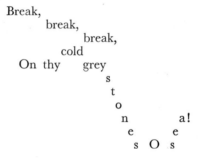

In general, matter-of-fact material calls for many short steps just as it calls for many short slides. The greater the need for emphasis (that is, the expression of personal attitudes, which means feeling) the greater the tendency to use fewer steps but to make those few much greater in extent. For example, such a strong statement as,

> You act like a pack of wolves!

would probably be expressed somewhat like this:

Whereas a simple declarative sentence of no great feeling, such as:

> I went over to my neighbor to borrow a wrench

would be more like this:

Here, then, is still another effective way for the student to extend his range, and thereby make his voice more expressive. Exercises for practice are provided at the end of the chapter.

Pitch Faults

In our discussion of pitch we considered several faults, such as narrow pitch range, holding the pitch too low, and strained high pitch. Two other pitch faults are distinctive enough, and common enough, to deserve special mention. These are (1) excessive pitch variation and (2) pitch patterns.

EXCESSIVE PITCH VARIATION, ESPECIALLY IN THE UPPER LEVELS

Excessive variation in pitch, at the opposite extreme from droning, suggests childishness, talking down, the overemphasis of the effeminate man, the attention-getting tricks of the flapper, and the "eager beaver's" efforts to ingratiate himself. It is an offense against good taste. The corrective lies in working on material that requires strength and power in its rendition, such as some of the selections and exercises provided in the next chapter. Also, this type of overinflection is usually associated with a weak, thin tonal quality. Building breath control and resonance will aid in this respect.

PITCH PATTERNS

Pitch patterns are the special fault of the old-time spellbinder. This fault represents oratory at its worst. Sometimes the pattern consists of starting every sentence on a high key and trailing off at the end. Sometimes it is characterized by a swelling in the middle of the sentence, with a submerged and hard-to-hear beginning and end. But most often it is recognized by the upward curve and suspended note at sentence endings (note Gabriel Heatter's "There's good news tonight"). Whatever the pattern, for the true addict it is always present. Such an individual should be punished by being made to listen to some of his own voice recordings. Thorough drilling in thinking and feeling in relation to voice should also work wonders.

EXERCISES AND SELECTIONS FOR PRACTICE

1. Say the word "mood." Establish your optimum pitch by repeating the word on different levels, with relaxed throat and jaw. Then read the following lines of poetry, clinging pretty close to a mono-pitch at your optimum level.

> 'Tis the last rose of summer,
>   Left blooming alone;
> All her lovely companions
>   Are faded and gone;
> No flower of her kindred,
>   No rose-bud is nigh,
> To reflect back her blushes
>   Or give sigh for sigh.
>
>   —THOMAS MOORE

2. As an exercise in extending the range of your voice, find a note close to your optimum pitch. Sing that note (using an open-throated *ah* throughout the exercise), the note a half step below it, and go back to the starting note. Then start the exercise a half tone higher, and repeat a half tone higher still. And so on up the scale as far as you can go in comfort. Then start a half tone lower, and so on down the scale. Do not go either up or down beyond the limits of good voice quality. In other words, don't strain.

3. Read the following poem as an exercise in step. There are plenty of slides in it, too, but pay special attention to the steps. Extend them beyond your customary limits. Chart your pitch variations on paper, using flat lines and curved lines as required to help you get the picture of what your voice is doing.

REQUIEM

Under the wide and starry sky,
Dig the grave and let me lie.
Glad did I live and gladly die,
And I laid me down with a will.

This be the verse you grave for me:
Here he lies where he longed to be;
Home is the sailor, home from sea,
And the hunter home from the hill.
                          —ROBERT LOUIS STEVENSON

4. By inflection, try to give the following meanings to the question, "Is that so?"

  1. Pleased surprise.
  2. Indifference ("What about it?")
  3. Very serious doubt.
  4. Cynical attitude ("Oh, yeah?")
  5. Pugnacious ("Do you want to make something of it?").

5. Experiment with two possible interpretations of Lady Macbeth's answer:

MACBETH.   If we should fail?
LADY M.   We fail!
  But screw your courage to the sticking place and we'll not fail.

Judith Anderson, as Lady Macbeth, gives the *We* a circumflex accent, with the obvious intent of setting Macbeth and herself apart from the "common herd"; she gives *fail* a long upward slide, as if disgusted that Macbeth would for a single minute entertain the thought of failure. On the next lines her inflections seem to say, "If you'll just buck up a little, there's not a chance that we'll fail."

Other actresses have used other inflections and thereby put entirely different meaning into the words, as for example, touching the *we* lightly, quickly, and on a level pitch, but giving *fail* a long downward slide, as if fatalistically accepting the possibility of failure—something of a *so what?* attitude. This interpretation is naturally followed on the next lines by inflections which seem to say, *But if you'll do your part . . . etc.*

6. See if you can give the following meanings to the phrase "Good morning." It is not necessary to make the inflections arbitrarily. Get the mood and the voice will respond.

   1. Grudging acknowledgment.
   2. Surprise to see your friend around so early.
   3. Perfunctory task, a duty.
   4. Greeting from habit, without feeling.
   5. Preoccupied greeting, mind deeply engrossed elsewhere.
   6. Restrained dislike.
   7. Great pleasure in the greeting.

7. Read the following selections, putting special pitch emphasis on the italicized words; then try emphasizing different words:

   1.   Why so *pale* and *wan,* fond lover?
      Prithee, why so *pale?*
      Will, when looking *well* can't move her,
      Looking *ill* prevail?
      Prithee, why so *pale?*

   2.   *What,* is the *jay* more *precious* than the *lark,*
      Because his *feathers* are more *beautiful?*
      Or is the *adder* better than the *eel,*
      Because his *painted skin* contents the *eye?*

   3.   Shall I *wasting* in *despair,*
      Die, because a woman's *fair?*
      Or make *pale* my *cheeks* with care,
      'Cause another's *rosy* are?
      Be she *fairer* than the *day,*
      Or the *flowery meads* of *May!*
        If she be not *so* to *me,*
      What care *I* how *fair* she be?

8. Say this limerick by the noted poet, Oliver Wendell Holmes. Use pause and phrasing as well as inflection to bring out the pun in the last line.

The Reverend Henry Ward Beecher
Called a hen a most elegant creature.
The hen, just for that,
Laid an egg in his hat—
And thus did the hen reward Beecher.

9. The following poem affords an opportunity to depict climax through use of pitch. Observe the arrangement of Time's ravages: *weary, sad, health, wealth,* and *growing old.* That order is not accidental; it suggests cumulative intensity of feeling. Show that climax, as well as the punch in the last line. Wide steps will help you put it over.

RONDEAU

Jenny kiss'd me when we met,
Jumping from the chair she sat in;
Time, you thief, who love to get
Sweets into your list, put that in.
Say I'm weary, say I'm sad,
Say that health and wealth have missed me,
Say I'm growing old, but add,
Jenny kissed me.

—LEIGH HUNT

10. If you will study the following poem, somewhat as you did Tennyson's "Flower," on page 380, you will find an infinite amount of meaning compacted into a few lines: not only the major comparison between the external world and the human being, but minor comparisons between night and day, and mind and soul. To express it all, your voice will need a good command of slide and step.

THE NIGHT HAS A THOUSAND EYES[2]

The night has a thousand eyes,
And the day but one;
Yet the light of the bright world dies
With the dying sun.

[2] Reprinted by permission.

The mind has a thousand eyes,
And the heart but one;
Yet the light of a whole life dies
When love is done.

—Francis Bourdillon

11. See what you can do with the whimsy and satire in the following sentences, using pauses, steps, and inflections on and around the key words:

   1.   For the sin ye do by two and two,
          Ye must pay for one by one.

   2. We hardly find any person of good sense save those who agree with us.

   3.   You spat on me on Wednesday last . . .
          Another time you called me dog.
          And for these courtesies, I'll lend
          You thus much moneys.

   4. I never thrust my nose into other men's porridge. It is no bread and butter of mine; every man for himself, and God for all of us.

   5. I have a good deal of sympathy for the proposal of Barrett Wendell of Harvard that every American citizen should receive the Bachelor's degree at birth.

   6.   There are worser ills to face
          Than foemen in the fray;
          And many a man has fought because—
          He feared to run away.

   7.   My friends, in course of time,
          We shall be civilized!
          We are going to live in cities!
          We are going to fight in wars!

   8.   Behold the mighty Dinosaur . . .
          The creature had two sets of brains—
          One in his head (the usual place),

The other in his spinal base.
Thus he could reason *a priori*
As well as *a posteriori*.[3]

9. I used to think that Eve talked too much. But after all these years I find I am wrong. I would rather live outside the Garden of Eden with her than inside the Garden without her. Wheresoever is Eve, there also is Eden.

10. Just then, with a wink and a sly normal lurch,
The owl very gravely got down from his perch,
Walked round, and regarded his fault-finding critic
(Who thought he was stuffed) with a glance analytic.

12. Use definite steps to establish the contrasts in age in the following selections:

1. Crabbèd Age and Youth
Cannot live together:
Youth is full of pleasance,
Age is full of care,
Youth like summer morn,
Age like winter weather,
Youth like summer brave,
Age like winter bare:
Youth is full of sport
Age's breath is short,
Youth is nimble, Age is lame:
Youth is hot and bold,
Age is weak and cold,
Youth is wild, and Age is tame:—
Age, I do abhor thee,
Youth, I do adore thee;
O, my love, my Love is young!
Age, I do defy thee—
O sweet shepherd, hie thee,
For methinks thou stay'st too long.
—SHAKESPEARE

[3] By Bert Leston Taylor. Reprinted by permission of the *Chicago Tribune*.

2. All the world's a stage,
   And all the men and women merely players.
   They have their exits and their entrances,
   And one man in his time plays many parts,
   His acts being seven ages. At first the infant,
   Mewling and puking in the nurse's arms.
   And then the whining schoolboy, with his satchel
   And shining morning face, creeping like snail
   Unwillingly to school. And then the lover,
   Sighing like furnace, with a woeful ballad
   Made to his mistress' eyebrow: Then a soldier,
   Full of strange oaths, and bearded like the pard,
   Jealous in honour, sudden, and quick in quarrel,
   Seeking the bubble reputation
   Even in the cannon's mouth. And then the justice,
   In fair round belly with good capon lined,
   With eyes severe and beard of formal cut,
   Full of wise saws and modern instances;
   And so he plays his part. The sixth age shifts
   Into the lean and slipper'd pantaloon,
   With spectacles on nose and pouch on side;
   His youthful hose, well saved, a world too wide
   For his shrunk shank; and his big manly voice,
   Turning again toward childish treble, pipes
   And whistles in his sound. Last scene of all,
   That ends this strange eventful history,
   Is second childishness and mere oblivion,
   Sans teeth, sans eyes, sans taste, sans everything.
   —SHAKESPEARE

13. As an exercise, exaggerate the length of the slides in the follow-
    ing selection, especially on such words as "slaves."

    Friends: Ye know too well
    The story of our thraldom;—we are slaves!
    The bright sun rises to his course, and lights
    A race of slaves! He sets, and his last beam
    Falls on a slave!—not such as, swept along
    By the full tide of power, the conqueror leads

To crimson glory and undying fame;
But base, ignoble slaves—slaves to a horde
Of petty tyrants, feudal despots, lords,
Rich in some dozen paltry villages—
Strong in some hundred spearmen—only great
In that strange spell, a name!
                              —MARY RUSSELL MITFORD

14. A classic example of the effective use of circumflex accent to give words a double meaning is Mark Antony's play upon the word *honourable,* using changing intonations, first to placate Brutus and the other plotters, then gradually to inflame the mob against the plotters. Try Antony's technique in your own inflections. (And don't forget your pauses. A significant pause just before that last *honourable* will give it added punch.)

The noble Brutus
Hath told you Caesar was ambitious;
If it were so, it was a grievous fault,
And grievously hath Caesar answer'd it.
Here, under leave of Brutus, and the rest—
For Brutus is an honourable man;
So are they all, all honourable men—
Come I to speak in Caesar's funeral.
He was my friend, faithful and just to me;
But Brutus says he was ambitious,
And Brutus is an honourable man.
He hath brought many captives home to Rome,
Whose ransoms did the general coffers fill;
Did this in Caesar seem ambitious?
When that the poor have cried, Caesar hath wept;
Ambition should be made of sterner stuff:
Yet Brutus says he was ambitious,
And Brutus is an honourable man.
You all did see that on the Lupercal
I thrice presented him a kingly crown,
Which he did thrice refuse. Was this ambition?
Yet Brutus says he was ambitious,
And, sure, he is an honourable man.

I speak not to disprove what Brutus spoke,
But here I am to speak what I do know.
You all did love him once, not without cause;
What cause withholds you then to mourn for him?
O judgment! thou art fled to brutish beasts,
And men have lost their reason. Bear with me;
My heart is in the coffin there with Caesar,
And I must pause, till it come back to me.

—SHAKESPEARE

15. The next selection will gain in significance if the reader gives each of the two characters a definite pitch. This pitch placement should be done not arbitrarily, but by feeling the part. Try to let the voice drop a little for the man's part and rise a little for the woman's part. A slight distinction gained in this fashion is better than a wide contrast achieved by choking the voice down or forcing it up to a falsetto.

ROSALIND. Why, how now, Orlando! where have you been all this while? You a lover! And you serve me such another trick, never come in my sight more.

ORLANDO. My fair Rosalind, I come within an hour of my promise.

ROSALIND. Break an hour's promise in love! He that will divide a minute into a thousand parts and break but a part of the thousandth part of a minute in the affairs of love, it may be said of him that Cupid hath clapped him o' the shoulder, but I'll warrant him heart-whole.

ORLANDO. Pardon me, dear Rosalind.

ROSALIND. Nay, and you be so tardy, come no more in my sight: I had as lief be wooed of a snail.

ORLANDO. Of a snail?

ROSALIND. Ay, of a snail; for though he comes slowly, he carries his house on his head. Come, woo me, woo me, for now I am in a holiday humor and like enough to consent. What would you say to me now, and I were your very very Rosalind?

ORLANDO. I would kiss before I spoke.

—SHAKESPEARE

16. Have fun with the following selection and let your voice show that you are having fun:

THE CATERPILLAR[4]

I find among the poems of Schiller
No mention of the caterpillar,
Nor can I find one anywhere
In Petrarch or in Baudelaire,
So here I sit in extra session
To give my personal impression.
The caterpillar, as it's called,
Is often hairy, seldom bald;
It looks as if it never shaves;
When as it walks, it walks in waves;
And from the cradle to the chrysalis
It's utterly speechless, songless, whistleless.

—OGDEN NASH

17. This group of selections demands expressive slides to express special shades of meaning.

1. JULIET. 'Tis but thy name that is my enemy;—
Thou art thyself though, not a Montague.
What's Montague? It is not hand, nor foot,
Nor arm, nor face, nor any other part
Belonging to a man. O, be some other name!
What's in a name? That which we call a rose,
By any other name would smell as sweet;
So Romeo would, were he not Romeo call'd,
Retain that dear perfection which he owes
Without that title. Romeo, doff thy name;
And for that name, which is no part of thee,
Take all myself.

—SHAKESPEARE

2. IAGO. Ha! I like not that.
OTHELLO. What dost thou say?

[4] Copyright 1949 by The Curtis Publishing Co. Reprinted by permission of the author.

IAGO.   Nothing, my lord; or if—I know not what.

OTHELLO.   Was not that Cassio parted from my wife?

IAGO.   Cassio, my lord? No, sure, I cannot think
That he would steal away so guilty-like,
Seeing you coming. . . .

IAGO.   My noble lord,—

OTHELLO.   What dost thou say, Iago?

IAGO.   Did Michael Cassio, when you woo'd my lady,
Know of your love?

OTHELLO.   He did, from first to last; why dost thou ask?

IAGO.   But for a satisfaction of my thought;
No further harm.

OTHELLO.   Why of thy thought, Iago?

IAGO.   I did not think he had been acquainted with her.

OTHELLO.   O, yes; and went between us very oft.

IAGO.   Indeed!

OTHELLO.   Indeed! ay, indeed; discern'st thou aught in that?
Is he not honest?

IAGO.   Honest, my lord?

OTHELLO.   Honest! ay, honest.

IAGO.   My lord, for aught I know.

OTHELLO.   What dost thou think?

IAGO.   Think, my lord!

OTHELLO.   Think, my lord!
By heavens, he echoes me,
As if there were some monster in his thought
Too hideous to be shown.

—SHAKESPEARE

3.   "AH, ARE YOU DIGGING ON MY GRAVE?"[5]

"Ah, are you digging on my grave
My beloved one?—planting rue?"
—"No; yesterday he went to wed
One of the brightest wealth has bred.
'It cannot hurt her now,' he said,
'That I should not be true.' "

[5] From Thomas Hardy, *Collected Poems*, copyright 1931 by The Macmillan
Company and used with the publishers' permission.

"Then who is digging on my grave?
My nearest dearest kin?"
—"Ah, no; they sit and think, 'What use!
What good will planting flowers produce?
No tendance of her mound can loose
Her spirit from Death's gin.' "

"But some one digs upon my grave?
My enemy?—prodding sly?"
—"Nay; when she heard you had passed the Gate
That shuts on all flesh soon or late,
She thought you no more worth her hate,
And cares not where you lie."

"Then, who is digging on my grave?
Say—since I have not guessed!"
—"O it is I, my mistress dear,
Your little dog, who still lives near,
And much I hope my movements here
Have not disturbed your rest?"

"Ah, yes! *You* dig upon my grave . . .
Why flashed it not on me
That one true friend was left behind!
What feeling do we ever find
To equal among human kind
A dog's fidelity!"

"Mistress, I dug upon your grave
To bury a bone, in case
I should be hungry near this spot
When passing on my daily trot.
I am sorry, but I quite forgot
It was your resting place."

—Thomas Hardy

18. The following selections, being sad or somber, naturally induce
the elongated pharynx which resonates the deeper tones. Be
sure that your throat (and your mouth, too) is relaxed and open.

1. O, now, forever
    Farewell the tranquil mind! farewell content!
    Farewell the plumed troop, and the big wars,
    That make ambition virtue! O, farewell!
    Farewell the neighing steed, and the shrill trump,
    The spirit-stirring drum, and the ear-piercing fife,
    The royal banner, and all quality,
    Pride, pomp, and circumstance of glorious war!
    And O you mortal engines, whose rude throats
    The immortal Jove's dread clamours counterfeit,
    Farewell! Othello's occupation's gone.

    —SHAKESPEARE

2. Vanity of vanities, saith the Preacher, vanity of vanities, all is vanity. What profit hath man of all his labour wherein he laboureth under the sun?

    One generation goeth, and another generation cometh: and the earth abideth for ever. The sun also ariseth, and the sun goeth down, and hasteth to his place where he ariseth. The wind goeth toward the south, and turneth about unto the north; it turneth about continually in its course, and the wind returneth again to its circuits. All the rivers run into the sea, yet the sea is not full: unto the place whither the rivers go, thither they go again.

    All things are full of weariness, man cannot utter it: the eye is not satisfied with seeing, nor the ear filled with hearing.

    That which hath been is that which shall be; and that which hath been done is that which shall be done: and there is no new thing under the sun. Is there a thing whereof men say, See, this is new? It hath been already, in the ages which were before us.

    There is no remembrance of the former generations; neither shall there be any remembrance of the latter generations that are to come after.

    —ECCLESIASTES

3.   O CAPTAIN! MY CAPTAIN!

O Captain! my Captain! our fearful trip is done,
The ship has weathered every rack, the prize we sought
    is won,
The port is near, the bells I hear, the people all
    exulting,
While follow eyes the steady keel, the vessel grim and
    daring;
    But O heart! heart! heart!
      O the bleeding drops of red,
    Where on the deck my Captain lies,
      Fallen cold and dead.

O Captain! my Captain! rise up and hear the bells;
Rise up—for you the flag is flung—for you the bugle
    trills,
For you bouquets and ribboned wreaths—for you the
    shores a-crowding,
For you they call, the swaying mass, their eager faces
    turning;
    Here, Captain! dear father!
      This arm beneath your head!
    It is some dream that on the deck
      You've fallen cold and dead.

My Captain does not answer, his lips are pale and still,
My father does not feel my arm, he has no pulse nor
    will,
The ship is anchored safe and sound, its voyage closed
    and done,
From fearful trip the victor ship comes in with object
    won;
    Exult O shores, and ring O bells!
      But I, with mournful tread,
    Walk the deck my Captain lies,
      Fallen cold and dead.
                                —WALT WHITMAN

4.   THAT MEN MIGHT BE FREE[6]

This is perhaps the grimmest, and surely the holiest, task we have faced since D-day. Here before us lie the bodies of comrades and friends. Men who until yesterday or last week laughed with us, joked with us, trained with us. Men who were on the same ships with us, and went over the sides with us, as we prepared to hit the beaches of this island. Men who fought with us, and feared with us. Somewhere in this plot of ground there may lie the man who could have discovered the cure for cancer. Under one of these Christian crosses, or beneath a Jewish Star of David, there may rest now a man who was destined to be a great prophet; to find the way, perhaps, for all to live in plenty, with poverty and hardship for none. Now they lie here silently in this sacred soil, and we gather to consecrate this earth in their memory. . . .

Here lie men who loved America because their ancestors generations ago helped in her founding, and other men who loved her with equal passion because they themselves or their own fathers escaped from oppression to her blessed shores. Here lie officers and men, Negroes and whites, rich men and poor—together. Here are Protestants, Catholics, and Jews—together. Here no man prefers another because of his faith or despises him because of his color. Here there are no quotas of how many from each group are admitted or allowed. Among these men there is no discrimination; no prejudices; no hatreds. Theirs is the highest and purest democracy.

We promise that when once again men seek profit at your expense, we shall remember how you looked when we placed you, reverently, lovingly in the ground.

Thus do we memorialize those who, having ceased living with us, now live within us. Thus do we consecrate the living to carry on the struggle they began. Too much blood has gone into this soil for us to let it lie barren. Too much pain and heartache have fertilized the earth on which we stand.

[6] From *Vital Speeches*, December 15, 1945. Speech delivered on the occasion of the dedication of the Fifth Marine Division Cemetery, Iwo Jima, March, 1945.

We here solemnly swear: This shall not be in vain. Out of this, and from the suffering and sorrow of those who mourn this, shall come—we promise—the birth of a new freedom for the sons of men everywhere. Amen.

—CHAPLIN ROLAND B. GITTELSOHN

19. The following excerpts, one from an epic poem and the other from a dramatic scene, call for a combination of the frequent slides of animated conversation, and the more sweeping slides and longer steps of emotional passages.

1. THE LEPER

"Room for the leper! Room!" and as he came
The cry passed on. "Room for the leper! Room!"
And aside they stood—
Matron, and child, and pitiless manhood—all
Who met him on the way—and let him pass.
And onward through the open gate he came,
A leper, with ashes on his brow.
Sackcloth about his loins, and on his lip
A covering—stepping painfully and slow,
And with difficult utterance, like one
Whose heart is with an iron nerve put down,
Crying, "Unclean! Unclean!"
    For Helon was a leper.

Day was breaking,
When at the altar of the temple stood
The holy priest of God. The incense lamp
Burned with a struggling light, and a low chant
Swelled through the hollow arches of the roof,
Like an articulate wail; and there, alone,
Wasted to ghastly thinness, Helon knelt.
The echoes of the melancholy strain
Died in the distant aisles, and he rose up,
Struggling with weakness; and bowed down his head
Unto the sprinkled ashes, and put off
His costly raiment for the leper's garb,

And with the sackcloth round him, and his lip
Hid in the loathsome covering, stood still,
   Waiting to hear his doom:

"Depart! depart, O child
Of Israel, from the temple of thy God!
For He has smote thee with his chastening rod,
   And to the desert wild,
From all thou lov'st, away thy feet must flee,
That from thy plague His people may be free."
               —NATHANIEL P. WILLIS

2.   *From* IF I WERE KING[7]

In the Fir Cone Tavern a merry group was gathered, drinking and dicing. The door swung noisily open and a strange figure entered, a man of middle height, spare and slight. His face was bronzed by sun and wind, his dark hair long and unkempt, his eyes bright and quick. . . . He was dressed in faded finery. His ruined cloak was tilted by a long sword and in his leathern belt a vellum-bound book of verse kept company with a dagger. It was François Villon, scholar, poet, drinker, sworder, good at pen, point, and pitcher.

He poised for a moment on the threshold in a fantastic attitude of salutation ere he slammed the door behind him and strode forward to meet his friends.

"Well, Hearts of Gold, how are ye? Did ye miss me, lads?"

Every man thrust his own mug towards Master François, beseeching him to drink of it.

"What can a man do but drink when France is going to the devil, with the Burgundian camped on the fields where I played in childhood, and a nincompoop sits on the throne and lets them besiege his city?"

"No doubt, you could do better than the King if you wore the King's shoes," cried one [King Louis, disguised as one of the revelers].

[7] *If I Were King*, by Justin Huntly McCarthy. Reprinted by permission of Harper & Brothers.

"If I could not do better than Louis-do-Nothing, Louis-Dare-Nothing, may my lips never again touch wine."

"Our François has made a rhyme of it, how he would carry himself if he wore the King's shoes," shouted another.

"Has he, indeed?" said Louis. "May we not hear it, Master Poet?"

"You may; you shall; for 'tis a true song, though it would cost me my neck if it came to the King's ears, very likely."

With a shout Villon sprang to his feet, draped his tattered cloak closely about him, struck a commanding attitude, and began to recite with great solemnity:

> All French folks, whereso'er ye be,
> Who love your country, soil and sand
> From Paris to the Breton sea,
> And back again to Norman strand,
> Forsooth ye seem a silly band,
> Sheep without shepherd, left to chance.
> Far otherwise our Fatherland
> If Villon were the King of France!

> The figure on the throne you see
> Is nothing but a puppet, planned
> To wear the regal bravery
> Of silken coat and gilded wand.
> Not so we Frenchmen understand
> The Lord of lion's heart and glance,
> And such a one would take command,
> If Villon were the King of France!
> —JUSTIN HUNTLY McCARTHY

XIII * Achieving Vocal Expressiveness: Force

The third and last means of achieving vocal expressiveness which we shall consider is variation in the degree of *force*.

There are several other terms which express the same idea, such as amplitude, energy, intensity, loudness and volume. These terms are alike in that they have some relationship to the degree of loudness of the tone. But they lack a good deal of being exact synonyms, as has been explained. (See Chapter VI.) The reason we have chosen the term *force* is that at this time we are not primarily interested in the extent of the swing of the vocal cords (amplitude), or the violence with which the vibrator is activated (energy), or the strength with which the sound waves strike the ear (intensity), or even the impression of richness and fullness of tone (volume). That is, we are not concerned with any one of these exclusively. Rather, we are concerned with all of them, plus something else—the something people mean when they speak of a "forceful personality."

Force, then, in the sense in which the term is used here, implies several things when effectively employed as a means of achieving vocal expressiveness:

1. The speaker initiates his tones with enough energy to suggest a strong and thoroughly alive personality.

2. He makes his tones loud enough to be heard without strain or effort on the part of his listeners.

3. He uses sufficient volume—combination of fundamentals and overtones—so that his voice has a satisfying fullness, even in its low and quiet tones.

4. He adjusts his use of energy and loudness to the needs of the occasion.

5. He uses vocal force as a means of emphasis to indicate his personal attitudes and to exert the desired influence over others.

For the student to acquire command of force in these various areas requires that he approach the study in an intelligent, thoughtful, and analytical spirit. While vocal force does not lend itself to the portrayal of as fine shades of meaning as does pitch, because on the whole it is more an instrument of total emotional attitudes than of intellectual discriminations, it does provide a revealing cue to the speaker's personality. People instinctively judge a person according to the sensitivity, or lack of it, he displays in adjusting his degree of vocal force to the occasion.

"Big" Voice Not Necessary

It is not possible for everyone to acquire the stentorian tones of a Webster, an O'Connell, or a Demosthenes, nor is it necessary. Science through the medium of the public-address system has obviated the necessity for the shouting which was required of those who harangued huge gatherings in past generations. Today a speaker can address himself to a microphone in his ordinary tones and be heard with equal distinctness in all parts of a large auditorium or outdoor assemblage.

But more important to us is the fact that the average man is seldom called upon to meet such occasions. Most of our speaking is done in the conference room, in committees, in business groups, in fraternal or religious gatherings—usually in comparatively small assemblies. To be sure, this is not always the case. Great public meetings where thousands gather to hear a speaker are still held, and probably always will be. It is likewise true that these meetings are not always equipped with modern address systems. But the exceptions do not alter the fact that most speeches today are made before smaller groups, where thunderous volume is quite unnecessary.

The ambitious young speaker need not be disheartened because he does not have the voice attributed to O'Connell by Wendell Phillips: ". . . a voice that careened across the Atlantic like a thunderstorm, bounced off the Rocky Mountains, and then reverberated and re-echoed back to London." He may be satisfied with something less than this in the way of volume and still hope to be effective as a speaker in the present century. It is not necessary, even, that he be able to shout down the roar of the ocean waves, as Demosthenes could.

Queen Victoria was not complimenting Gladstone when she said, "Whenever he talks to me I feel as if I were an assembly." Modern audiences will not be coerced through sound and fury. They resent, and rightly so, the impression that they are being bombarded with sheer noise. Sweet reasonableness of tone is infinitely more persuasive than mere shouting. Most educated and cultured people today would join with the Duke in *As You Like It*, when he gently reprimands the blustering Orlando: "Your gentleness shall force, more than your force move us to gentleness." And many an audience would join with Hamlet in his remark: "Oh, it offends me to the soul to hear a robustious, periwig-pated fellow tear a passion to tatters. . . ."

However, it should be noted that Hamlet did not conclude this diatribe against "dumb show and noise" without another admonition, equally important: "Be not too tame neither!"

Nothing that has been said against bombast should be construed as a defense of a weak voice and lifeless tones. Most young speakers are in greater need of the injunction, "Be not too tame" than of a warning against vehemence. In our era of urban culture, repression is the vogue. From their earliest years children are taught to be restrained. "Hush! Don't make so much noise! Be quiet!" These are the phrases that constitute most of their early vocal training. The usual result is an exaggerated sense of restraint. In consequence, the majority of young speakers are too greatly inhibited in both voice and body to be truly effective. Restrictions drilled into them in youth, coupled with the fear constriction which almost invariably accompanies early appearances upon the platform, are usually sufficient to make these inexperienced speakers far too quiet.

And nowhere is the admonition to avoid being too tame more needed than around "ivied halls of learning." Where so much emphasis is placed upon withholding judgment until all the facts are in—a condition which in many fields never arrives—it is perfectly natural that great importance should be attached to emotional restraint, so that the quiet, often over-hushed voice becomes a virtue. In consequence, for the professor who spends all his life in this atmosphere, the quiet voice may be a positive asset. It may be—although it is refreshing even in this atmosphere occasionally to find an academic man who lets his voice out in natural unrestrained exuberance. And often it is to such as he that the "plums" of recognition around the campus are handed.

For most people in most situations, command of a considerable degree of vocal force to be used with discretion and judgment is an asset greatly to be desired. Easy, effortless hearing by the man in the farthest corner of the room is imperative, if that man's attention is to be held; to accomplish this, the student must cultivate adequate volume. Not only this, but he must strive for a voice that denotes vitality, energy, and force of personality—sufficient vocal power to express strong feelings when occasion demands. These qualities are as essential in the small group as in the large. There are times, indeed, when a full, vibrant voice, well controlled, is an indispensable aid to leadership; it is necessary to dominate certain situations.

DEGREE OF FORCE TO USE

Hamlet said to the players, "Let your own discretion be your tutor." And yet Hamlet must have thought that their discretion could be improved, or at least awakened by a little judicious pricking, or why would he have troubled to talk to them about the desirable amount of force to use?

There is no doubt that our judgment with respect to the use of vocal force can be improved by heeding certain principles. Let us summarize some of these principles which should influence our "discretion" in the use of vocal force.

1. There is the obvious fact that conflicting noises—the rumble of traffic, coughing, flapping curtains, and so forth—must be overcome; an obvious fact, yet one frequently ignored by inexperienced and indifferent speakers.

2. The size of the audience, acoustic properties of the auditorium, and similar considerations constitute another obvious but not always observed factor which should influence our judgment. Discretion and good taste should instruct the speaker regarding his responsibility for keeping all his audience awake. To do this, he must first of all make them hear.

3. The nature of the audience has a bearing. As mentioned above, in a college community quiet speaking is the vogue; in certain other circles, however, especially among people who do not hear much public speaking and are therefore unskilled in listening, a strong, virile tone pays much bigger dividends. Indeed, some audiences consider noise practically tantamount to eloquence, and a quiet voice a badge of weakness or indicative of lack of sureness. Without doubt, Hitler and Mussolini derived a large share of their great influence from their vocal force.

4. The nature of the subject being discussed and the type of occasion must not be ignored. For extreme examples which will demonstrate the point, consider the difference in the vocal force requirements of a funeral eulogy and a Fourth of July whoop-it-up.

5. The limitations of the speaker's vocal powers constitute a significant factor. If one can use good strong tones without pushing and straining, that is one thing; for a person to attempt to use loud tones when his effort results only in red-faced squawks and squeals is another thing entirely. If you have conscientiously practiced vocal exercises in phonation, respiration, and resonation, you have launched upon a program which ultimately will help to meet the demand of leadership in this respect.

6. A fundamental and obvious consideration is the inherent difference in speech sounds themselves. On the whole, the vowels naturally call for more volume than do the consonants. Likewise, voiced consonants require more volume than do the unvoiced ones; note the difference between *p* and *b* sounds, between *w* and *wh*, between *th* in *thin* and *th* in *the*. This matter has been discussed at some length in the chapters on articulation.

In all these areas some public speakers and some conversationalists come perilously close to a dead level of sameness.

CONVERSATIONAL SPEECH REQUIRES VARIETY IN VOCAL FORCE

Monotony may be of the full-voiced, leather-lunged type or it may be of the frail and mouselike variety, or it may be, and usually is, of the innocuous, medium-range, commonplace type, which, in the words of Holy Writ, being neither hot nor cold, is fit only to be spewed out of the mouth. Any degree of force, if too long sustained, becomes an invitation to mental drowsiness on the part of the auditor.

Political haranguers and Fourth of July spellbinders who maintain the same degree of bombastic force throughout their long "efforts," and mild professors who drone on through hour-long lectures, alike forget the interest-destroying effect of monotony in force. Continuous sledge-hammer blows fray the nerves, and continuous soothing strokes lull to pleasant slumber. Both fail in their objective: to hold the eager attention of an audience.

Types of Vocal Force

There are three types of vocal force which we should understand in order to make the most efficient use of our voices. They are the *expulsive*, the *explosive*, and the *effusive*.

EXPULSIVE FORCE

Expulsive force is that used in animated conversation. It is characterized by frequent changes in degree, with strokes of emphasis on important words and syllables, and quietness for unimportant ones. This is the type to which we are most accustomed—so much so, in fact, that we scarcely notice that there are constant changes in it. A little conscious attention to anyone's lively conversation, however, will make clear the frequent and rather pronounced changes. We hear it clearly exemplified in such conversation bits around the campus as the following:

Just *WHERE* do you think *YOU'RE* going?

What did *YOU* get in that test? I got a B.

She *SAID* she was going to wear her *FOR*mal. But not *ME*: **I'm** going to wear an after*NOON* dress.

EXPLOSIVE FORCE

Explosive force is more extreme. As its name implies, it is more emotional in nature. Important words and syllables are emphasized by an abrupt application of force—really shouts of emphasis. This is the vehicle of strong emotions. It is not adaptable to polite and dignified occasions. Used to excess, it readily becomes jangling to the nerves. But under proper conditions, and in proper proportions, it is undeniably useful; it often stirs a lethargic audience to attention when all other devices fail. And there are times when no other kind of force gives adequate release to the speaker's feelings.

Explosive force is adaptable to such emotion-charged expressions as:

STAND! the GROUND'S your OWN, my BRAVES!

CHARGE, Chester, CHARGE! ON, Stanley, ON!

THIS is no time for deBATE. This is the time for ACtion.

Effusive Force

Effusive force is the smooth, regular flow of certain types of poetical speech. It expresses calmness, serenity, submissiveness. Also, rightly used, it may suggest assured competence on the part of the speaker—an effective antidote to jangled nerves and hysteria. Likewise it may suggest weakness and old age. It may be either loud or soft as the sentiment requires. But it seldom changes abruptly from loud to soft, or vice versa. Changes are made gradually, and by long sweeping gradations. It is sustained force. Its chief use is in poetry, poetic prose, and highly emotionalized expression of the calm, placid variety.

Effusive force is the natural form for expressing such smooth-flowing lines as the following:

Roll on, thou deep and dark blue ocean, roll!

The day is cold, and dark, and dreary.

O, my love is like a red, red rose.

Sometimes oratory, in its most elevated moments, approaches the rolling, wavelike, effusive form of poetry. Churchill is inclined to use a good deal of it in rendering such lines as these: "If the British Commonwealth and Empire last for a thousand years, men will say, 'This was their finest hour.'"

Faults in Vocal Force

Let us quickly review some of the worst faults, and some of the most common ones, in the use of vocal force.

First, there is that altogether too common fault which has already been mentioned many times but which must be called to our attention again and again: *monotony*. Remember, neither the muted murmurings of a lazy brook nor the ceaseless clatter of a riveting machine will suffice as a speech technique. There must be an interesting and stimulating variety.

A too quiet voice suggests weakness, a feeling of insufficiency on the part of the speaker. If the voice has that artificially hushed tone sometimes affected by overly nice people, the suggestion is one of insincerity.

The *too loud voice* suggests superficiality and a lack of sensitivity. If overused to an extreme degree, it suggests boorish stupidity.

But of all the faults and dangers connected with vocal force, perhaps the one most in need of emphasis is the danger of achieving vocal force in the wrong way, that is, by strain upon the vocal cords. One type of such strain is sufficiently common to deserve special attention at this time. It is the *glottal shock* mentioned earlier.

When a vigorous attack upon the tone is made by tensely pinching the vocal cords together and holding them thus while the flow of outgoing breath is dammed up back of them, and then hitting the syllable by a hard explosion of breath through the tensed cords, injury to the cords is likely to result. The student may get this feeling of strong glottal closure and explosion in coughing, hiccuping, or sneezing. If used habitually, this kind of vocal attack may result in harsh, guttural tones, or it may bring about a permanent raucous quality.

In contrast to this wrong method of attack is the ability of the trained singer to hold the flow of breath back of his closed lips and then release it on a strongly initiated tone. Thus he gives body to the tone without any strain on the vocal cords. Such a line as "Blow the man down, sailor, blow the man down" will illustrate.

The speaker may gain the same kind of vigorous attack in the following:

The gentlemen may cry Peace, Peace! But there is no peace.

Time Is Required to Develop Vocal Power

Young speakers, in their effort to achieve big voice, often rush ahead too fast, and in their zeal to get quick results they succeed only in straining their voice mechanisms. Volume that is accomplished by means of a tense and strained throat is bought at too great a price. Whatever increase there is in vocal power must be achieved without strain.

Vocal force gained through constriction of the throat sounds artificial. It is harsh and metallic, unpleasant to the ear. Its use is often accompanied by a monotonous pitch. It is rigid and inflexible, causing the voice to break and to wear out.

Before volume or force is ever attempted, it is essential that the habit of producing tones correctly be firmly established. As Lawrence Tibbett says: "A good tone will never be obtained by merely strengthening a bad one."[1]

Only when the tone is rightly produced can the voice be strengthened and volume increased by practice. This takes time. Strong volume cannot be gained in a day. Great singers take years of practice to build adequate volume. Speakers likewise must be willing to work and wait. Hurry not only means waste, it may mean ruin.

But again we repeat, volume can be achieved; and it can be achieved without danger of strain, of artificiality, or of harshness or rigidity. The necessary steps have been outlined here in Chapters IV, V, and VII: (1) Make all tones at all times with a relaxed throat. (2) Develop habits of correct breathing, and through continuous practice acquire an adequate breath supply for tone support. (3) Initiate the tone by the abdominal muscles, not by the throat muscles; that is, have the propulsive power come from the abdominal muscles. (4) Get the tone forward where it can surge and reverberate through the resonance chambers.

[1] Lawrence Tibbett, *Etude*, August, 1935, p. 458.

Touch

Touch is the refined and artistic use of degrees of force. It implies a nice sense of values. It recognizes the effectiveness of quiet intensity when not carried to excess, which is the point where monotony begins. It likewise recognizes the power of strong voice when emotional content justifies it, but never that incessant pounding that offends good taste and exhausts the ears.

Not all ideas in an address are of equal importance, nor are all words in a sentence. Any reasonably good conversationalist varies the force of his tones according to his meaning. Unimportant words are properly subordinated. Likewise, certain complete sentences stand out in bold relief, when the thought or emotion demands emphasis. But all too often this pleasant and interesting variation is suppressed into a dead level of monotonous mediocrity, with no lights and shadows, no hills and valleys, no relief.

Emphasis can be gained by force after quietness, and by quietness after force. The lull after the storm is as impressive as the sudden thunder after clear weather.

Give emphasis where emphasis is due. Cultivate, even on the platform, a sense of touch comparable to the variety in vocal force which characterizes brilliant, scintillating conversation.

EXERCISES AND SELECTIONS FOR PRACTICE

1. Emphasize the indicated words and syllables by added force:
   1. I want YOU to do it.
   2. Never DARken my DOORway again!
   3. What NEW KNAVery has he been up to?
   4. Let it RAIN; let it POUR.
   5. Isn't a DOLLAR enOUGH?

2. In the following sentences, stress the indicated word and note the changing meanings:
   1. *I* said he was a scoundrel.

2. I SAID he was a scoundrel.
3. I said HE was a scoundrel.
4. I said he WAS a scoundrel.
5. I said he was a SCOUNDREL.

3. Study the following selection. Hunt for the key words and underscore them. Now read the selection aloud, emphasizing the underscored words with added force and subordinating those that are not underscored. Give the latter only such force as is necessary for distinctness. Do this solely as an exercise and for practice. To follow such a plan in actual speaking might make your speech sound mechanical.

The man who enjoys marching in line and file to the strains of martial music falls below my contempt; he received his great brain by mistake—the spinal cord would have been amply sufficient. This heroism at command, this senseless violence, this accursed bombast of patriotism—how intensely I despise them![2]

—ALBERT EINSTEIN

4. Try the effusive form of force on the following lines:
1. Death and sorrow will be the companions of our journey; hardship our garment; constancy and valor our only shield.

—WINSTON CHURCHILL

2. Long live also the forward march of the common people in all the lands toward their just and true inheritance, and toward the broader and fuller age.

—WINSTON CHURCHILL

3. And in the dark hours of this day—and through dark days that may be yet to come—we will know that the vast majority of the members of the human race are on our side. Many of them are fighting with us. All of them are praying with us. For, in representing our cause, we represent theirs as well— our hope and their hope for liberty under God.

—FRANKLIN DELANO ROOSEVELT

[2] *Forum*, March, 1936.

5. Use expulsive force in the following sentences:

1. Together with other free peoples, we are now fighting to maintain our right to live among our world neighbors in freedom, in common decency, without fear of assault.

—FRANKLIN DELANO ROOSEVELT

2. If I were to tell you the story of Washington, I should take it from your hearts—you who think no marble white enough on which to carve the name of the Father of his Country.

—WENDELL PHILLIPS

3. War is like a fire. You cannot win a fire, but you can prevent a fire.

—GENERAL OMAR BRADLEY

4. We have now reached the point where we cannot have war and civilization too.

—ROBERT M. HUTCHINS

5. The road to victory, the guarantee of victory is to be found in one word—ships; and a second word—ships; and a third word—ships.

—DAVID LLOYD GEORGE

6. We've learned how to destroy, but not how to create; how to waste, but not how to build; how to kill men, but not how to save them; how to die, but seldom how to live.

—GENERAL OMAR BRADLEY

6. Experiment with a combination of effusive and expulsive force as they seem to be indicated in the following bits of poetry:

1.   Day after day, day after day,
         We stuck,—nor breath nor motion;
         As idle as a painted ship
         Upon a painted ocean.

         Water, water, everywhere,
         And all the boards did shrink;
         Water, water, everywhere,
         Nor any drop to drink. . . .

About, about, in reel and rout,
The deathfires danced at night;
The water, like a witch's oils,
Burnt green, and blue, and white.
                              —SAMUEL TAYLOR COLERIDGE

2.   Then welcome each rebuff
        That turns earth's smoothness rough,
        Each sting that bids nor sit nor stand but go!
                              —ROBERT BROWNING

3.   Over the cobbles he clattered and clashed in
           the dark inn-yard,
     And he tapped with his whip on the shutters,
           but all was locked and barred;
     He whistled a tune at the window, and who should
           be waiting there
     But the landlord's black-eyed daughter,
           Bess, the landlord's daughter,
     Plaiting a dark red love-knot into her long
           black hair.
                              —ALFRED NOYES[3]

4.   Bowed by the weight of centuries, he leans
     Upon his hoe and gazes on the ground,
     The emptiness of ages in his face,
     And on his back the burden of the world.
     Who made him dead to rapture and despair,
     A thing that grieves not and that never hopes,
     Stolid and stunned, a brother to the ox?
     Who loosened and let down this brutal jaw?
     Whose was the hand that slanted back this brow?
     Whose breath blew out the light within this brain?
     Is this the thing the Lord God made and gave
     To have dominion over sea and land?
                              —EDWIN MARKHAM[4]

[3] Reprinted by permission of the publishers, J. B. Lippincott Company, from *Collected Poems in One Volume*, by Alfred Noyes. Copyright, 1906, 1934, 1947, by Alfred Noyes.
[4] Reprinted by permission of Virgil Markham.

7. When you are sure you are making tones correctly and without strain, practice the following sentences, and others of your own devising, using considerable force:

1. You can drive that rock from its base easier than you can drive me from this platform.
2. I defy the whole mob of you.
3. The District Attorney says, "Crime must go!"
   The Chief of Police says, "Crime must go!"
   The Governor says, "Crime must go!"
   But it's up to you to make it go!
4. Let wind be shrill,
   Let waves roll high,
   I fear not wave nor wind.
5. I am in earnest; I will not equivocate; I will not excuse; I will not retreat a single inch; and I will be heard.
6. I will sit down now, but the time will come
   when you will hear me.

8. Shout the following lines with a well-rounded tone, and be sure that there is no strain in the voice. Get the power from your abdominal muscles. Treat your throat like an open funnel.

1. Charge! Charge! It's too late to retreat!
2. I call to you with all my voice!
3. Ship ahoy! Ship ahoy! (as if you were calling to a passing ship.)
4. Strawberries, tomatoes, potatoes! (as if you were a vegetable vendor.)
5. Charcoal, charcoal, charcoal! (Call out this word over and over in a chanting cadence, as if you were an old-time charcoal vendor.)
6. F-O-R-ward MARCH!
   Com-pan-y HALT!
   A-bout FACE!
   ONE, two, three, four; ONE, two, three, four!

9. Do this exercise in voice projection without strain. Have some of your classmates coöperate with you in talking across a considerable distance. Divide your group and have them face each other at some distance. Then have them engage in a series of questions and answers, speaking slowly and distinctly, and with sufficient

volume to be heard easily. Project the tone out of your well-opened mouth. (Find a spot for this exercise where you will not disturb the neighbors or arouse the police.) Such questions as the following, together with the appropriate answers, will do:

Can you hear me easily when I talk like this?

How did you come to school this morning?

Do you have satisfactory transportation?

Do you know anyone who has achieved prominence simply by means of a strong voice?

Which do you think sounds louder, a high-pitched or a low-pitched tone that has the same degree of intensity?

Do two squealing pigs sound twice as loud as one pig? (The answer is no; only about twenty percent louder.)

10. The following selections provide good practice for those addicted to bombast and sustained force.

1.   A PETITION TO TIME

Touch us gently, Time!
    Let us glide adown thy stream
Gently—as we sometimes glide
    Through a quiet dream.
Humble voyagers are we,
Husband, wife and children three—
    (One is lost—an angel, fled
    To the azure overhead!)

Touch us gently, Time!
    We've not proud nor soaring wings,
Our ambitions, our content,
    Lies in simple things.
Humble voyagers are we
O'er Life's dim, unsounded sea,
Seeking only some calm clime:
Touch us gently, gentle Time!

              —BRYAN WALLER PROCTER

2. How sweet the moonlight sleeps upon this bank!
    Here will we sit, and let the sounds of music
    Creep in our ears; soft stillness and the night
    Become the touches of sweet harmony.
    Sit, Jessica; look how the floor of heaven
    Is thick inlaid with patines of bright gold;
    There's not the smallest orb which thou behold'st,
    But in his motion like an angel sings,
    Still quiring to the young-eyed cherubins;
    Such harmony is in immortal souls,
    But whilst this muddy vesture of decay
    Doth grossly close it in, we cannot hear it . . .

    —SHAKESPEARE

3.   OUT IN THE FIELDS

        The little cares that fretted me,
            I lost them yesterday
        Among the fields above the seas,
            Among the winds at play,
        Among the lowing of the herds,
            The rustling of the trees,
        Among the singing of the birds,
            The humming of the bees.
        The foolish fears of what might happen,—
            I cast them all away
        Among the clover-scented grass,
            Among the new-mown hay;
        Among the husking of the corn,
            Where drowsy poppies nod,
        Where ill thoughts die and good are born,
            Out in the fields with God.

                        —ELIZABETH BARRETT BROWNING

11. The following selections are good practice material for those who lack strength and volume:

1. Think you a little din can daunt mine ears?
   Have I not in my time heard lions roar?
   Have I not heard the sea, puff'd up with winds,
   Rage like an angry boar chafed with sweat?
   Have I not heard great ordnance in the field,
   And heaven's artillery thunder in the skies?
   Have I not in a pitch'd battle heard
   Loud 'larums, neighing steeds, and trumpets' clang?
   And do you tell me of a woman's tongue,
   That gives not half so great a blow to hear
   As will a chestnut in a farmer's fire?
   Tush, tush! fear boys with bugs.

   —SHAKESPEARE

2. Blow, winds, and crack your cheeks! rage! blow!
   You cataracts and hurricanoes, spout
   Till you have drench'd our steeples, drown'd the cocks!
   You sulphurous and thought-executing fires,
   Vaunt-couriers of oak-cleaving thunderbolts,
   Singe my white head! And thou, all-shaking thunder,
   Strike flat the thick rotundity o' the world!
   Crack nature's moulds, all germens spill at once,
   That make ingrateful man! . . .
   Rumble thy bellyful! Spit, fire! spout, rain!
   Nor rain, wind, thunder, fire, are my daughters:
   I tax not you, you elements, with unkindness;
   I never gave you kingdom, call'd you children,
   You owe me no subscription: then let fall
   Your horrible pleasure; here I stand, your slave,
   A poor, infirm, weak, and despis'd old man;
   But yet I call you servile ministers,
   That will with two pernicious daughters join
   Your high engender'd battles 'gainst a head
   So old and white as this. O! O! 'tis foul!

   —SHAKESPEARE

3. Ye crags and peaks, I'm with you once again!
   I hold to you the hands you first beheld,
   To show they still are free. Methinks I hear
   A spirit in your echoes answer me,
   And bid your tenant welcome to his home
   Again! O, sacred forms, how proud you look!
   How high you lift your heads into the sky!
   How huge you are! how mighty and how free!
   Ye are the things that tower, that shine, whose smile
   Makes glad, whose frown is terrible, whose forms,
   Robed or unrobed, do all the impress wear
   Of awe divine. Ye guards of liberty!
   I'm with you once again!—I call to you
   With all my voice! I hold my hands to you
   To show they still are free. I rush to you,
   As though I could embrace you!

   —SHERIDAN KNOWLES

4. Wherefore rejoice? What conquest brings he home?
   What tributaries follow him to Rome
   To grace in captive bonds his chariot-wheels?
   You blocks, you stones, you worse than senseless things!
   O you hard hearts, you cruel men of Rome,
   Knew you not Pompey? Many a time and oft
   Have you climbed up to walls and battlements,
   To towers and windows, yea, to chimney-tops,
   Your infants in your arms, and there have sat
   The live-long day, with patient expectation
   To see great Pompey pass the streets of Rome:
   And when you saw his chariot but appear,
   Have you not made an universal shout,
   That Tiber trembled underneath her banks,
   To hear the replication of your sounds
   Made in her concave shores?
   And do you now put on your best attire?
   And do you now cull out a holiday?
   And do you now strew flowers in his way
   That comes in triumph over Pompey's blood?
   Be gone!

Run to your houses, fall upon your knees,
Pray to the gods to intermit the plague
That needs must light on this ingratitude.

—SHAKESPEARE

5. Awake! Awake!
Ring the alarum bell! Murder and treason!
Banquo and Donalbain! Malcolm! awake!
Shake off this drowsy sleep, death's counterfeit,
And look on death itself! up, up, and see
The great doom's image! Malcolm! Banquo!
As from your graves rise up, and walk like sprites,
To countenance this horror! Ring the bell!

—SHAKESPEARE

6. Out of the North the wild news came,
Far flashing on its wings of flame,
Swift as the boreal light which flies
At midnight through the startled skies.
And there was tumult in the air,
    The fife's shrill note, the drum's loud beat,
And through the wide land everywhere
    The answering tread of hurrying feet;
While the first oath of Freedom's gun
Came on the blast from Lexington;
And Concord roused, no longer tame,
Forgot her old baptismal name,
Made bare her patriot arm of power,
And swelled the discord of the hour.
And there the startling drum and fife
Fired the living with fiercer life;
While overheard, with wild increase,
Forgetting its ancient toll of peace,
    The great bell swung as ne'er before:
It seemed as it would never cease;
And every word its ardor flung
From off its jubilant iron tongue
    Was "War! War! WAR!"

--THOMAS B. READ

7.   The train from out the castle drew,
     But Marmion stopped to bid adieu:—
     . . . "Part we in friendship from your land,
     And noble Earl, receive my hand."—
     But Douglas round him drew his cloak,
     Folded his arms, and thus he spoke:—
     "My manors, halls, and bowers shall still
     Be open, at my sovereign's will,
     To each one whom he lists, howe'er
     Unmeet to be the owner's peer.
     My castles are my king's alone
     From turret to foundation-stone,—
     The hand of Douglas is his own;
     And never shall in friendly grasp
     The hand of such as Marmion clasp."—

     Burned Marmion's swarthy cheek like fire,
     And shook his very frame for ire,
         And—"This to me!" he said,—
     "An 't were not for thy hoary beard,
     Such hand as Marmion's had not spared
     To cleave the Douglas' head!
     And first, I tell thee, haughty Peer,
     He who does England's message here,
     Although the meanest in her state,
     May well, proud Angus, be thy mate:
     And, Douglas, more I tell thee here,
         Even in thy pitch of pride,
     Here in thy hold, thy vassals near,—
     Nay, never look upon your lord,
     And lay your hands upon your sword,—
         I tell thee, thou'rt defied!
     And if thou said'st I am not peer
     To any lord in Scotland here,
     Lowland or Highland, far or near,
     Lord Angus, thou hast lied!"—

                                        —SIR WALTER SCOTT

8. I believe in the doctrine of peace; but men must have liberty before there can come abiding peace. When has a battle for humanity and liberty ever been won except by force? What barricade of wrong, injustice, and oppression has ever been carried except by force?

Force compelled the signature of unwilling royalty to the great Magna Charta; force put life into the Declaration of Independence and made effective the Emancipation Proclamation; force waved the flag of revolution over Bunker Hill and marked the snows of Valley Forge with blood-stained feet; force held the broken line of Shiloh, climbed the flame-swept hill at Chattanooga, and stormed the clouds on Lookout Heights; force marched with Sheridan in the Valley of the Shenandoah, and gave Grant victory at Appomattox; force saved the Union, kept the stars in the flag, made "niggers" men. The time for God's force has come again.

—JOHN M. THURSTON

12. The following selections, although somewhat varied in mood, in general are strong and vigorous. However, they are not of the bombastic type like the preceding group. In these there is the mingling of thought and feeling which characterizes much sincere, animated speech. They provide opportunity for the variety in force which is desirable for all of us to master. Do not, however, depend upon force alone for your emphasis; use pause, quantity, and inflection.

1. Our future belongs to us Americans.

It is for us to design it; for us to build it.

In that building of it we shall prove that our faith is strong enough to survive the most fearsome storms that have ever swept over the earth.

In the days and months and years to come, we shall be making history—hewing out a new shape for the future. And we shall make very sure that that future of ours bears the likeness of liberty.

Always the heart and the soul of our country will be the heart and the soul of the common man—the men and women who never have ceased to believe in democracy, who never have ceased to love their families, their homes and their country.

The spirit of the common man is the spirit of peace and good will. It is the spirit of God. And in His faith is the strength of all America. . . .

I pledge you, I pledge myself, to a new deal for the American people. Let us all here assembled constitute ourselves prophets of a new order of competence and of courage. This is more than a political campaign: it is a call to arms. Give me your help, not to win votes alone, but to win in this crusade to restore America to its own people.

—FRANKLIN DELANO ROOSEVELT

2. There was a sound of revelry by night,
    And Belgium's capital had gathered then
Her beauty and her chivalry, and bright
    The lamps shone o'er fair women and brave men.
    A thousand hearts beat happily; and when
Music arose with its voluptuous swell,
    Soft eyes looked love to eyes which spake again,
And all went merry as a marriage bell;
But hush! hark! a deep sound strikes like a rising knell.

Did you not hear it?—No: 'twas but the wind,
    Or the car rattling o'er the stony street;
On with the dance! Let joy be unconfined;
    No sleep till morn, when youth and pleasure meet
    To chase the glowing hours with flying feet—
But, hark!—that heavy sound breaks in once more,
    As if the clouds its echo would repeat
And nearer, clearer, deadlier than before!
Arm! Arm! it is—it is the cannon's opening roar.

Ah! then and there was hurrying to and fro,
    And gathering tears, and tremblings of distress,
And cheeks all pale, which but an hour ago
    Blush'd at the praise of their own loveliness;
    And there were sudden partings, such as press

The life from out young hearts, and choking sighs
   Which ne'er might be repeated: who could guess
If ever more should meet those mutual eyes,
Since upon night so sweet such awful morn could rise!

And there was mounting in hot haste; the steed,
   The mustering squadron, and the clattering car
Went pouring forward with impetuous speed,
   And swiftly forming in the ranks of war;
   And the deep thunder, peal on peal afar;
And, near, the beat of the alarming drum
   Roused up the soldier ere the morning star:
While thronged the citizens with terror dumb,
—Or whispering with white lips, "The foe! they come!
   they come!"
              —George Gordon, Lord Byron

3. The man who is content to let politics go from bad to worse,
jesting at the corruption of politicians, the man who is content to see the maladministration of justice without an
immediate and resolute effort to reform it, is shirking his
duty and is preparing the way for infinite woe in the future.
Hard, brutal indifference to the right, and an equally brutal
shortsightedness as to the inevitable results of corruption and
injustice, are baleful beyond measure; and yet they are characteristic of a great many Americans who consider themselves
perfectly respectable, and who are considered thriving, prosperous men by their easy-going fellow-citizens.
              —Theodore Roosevelt

4.   CONSERVATION IN OUR NATIONAL PARKS[5]

   The American people are lucky in having enough men
with liberal minds and keen foresight in our Government—
particularly since the days of Teddy Roosevelt—to do something about the conservation of our natural resources.
   But what is conservation and what difference does it make?

[5] A student speech.

Who cares? Well I care, and so does anyone else who has seen—really seen—one of our great National parks; for example, Sequoia National Park.

Sequoia, famous for its redwood trees! Trees that reach hundreds of feet into the air! Trees so wide that it takes fifteen men holding hands to completely encircle one of their trunks! So big that more than twenty five-room houses can be made from the lumber in one tree! So old that a thousand years before Christ was born they were feeling the warm rays of the sun reflecting from their green leaves and reddish branches! So magnificent that a person has to view their beauty to appreciate what nature has created!

Anyone who has climbed to the top of Morro Rock in the Sequoias cares about conservation. Morro Rock, standing several hundred feet high and perched on top of a hill, can be climbed by almost any surefooted visitor. And what a view! Thousands and thousands of redwood trees pointing toward the sky! And in the background mountains, beautiful mountains, with their snow-capped peaks reaching toward heaven!

But what is that over there? What is that piece of dry, barren land doing in so magnificent a picture? Let's see now, it could have happened from a fire started by a bolt of lightning. It could have happened from a fire started by a carelessly thrown cigarette. But it also could have happened from an axe biting into the thick reddish bark of a redwood. The responsibility could lie on a lumberman yelling "TIMBERRRR," as another magnificent beauty, a tall redwood, crashes to the ground; crashes with a deafening roar that pierces the silence of a calm and serene forest.

And what of the man who ordered those axes and saws to dig into those trees? He wasn't thinking of you or me. He wasn't thinking of California, or of the centuries that it takes to grow one of those trees. He was thinking of this (*holding up a dollar bill*)!

But exploitation does not stop with trees. Exploitation knows no boundaries. You who have been to the Hetch Hetchy district in Yosemite know what I mean. You who have seen the white foaming waterfalls and the blue rivers that once were there, now penned behind a concrete dam. A dam that has stolen the surging power of the rivers and the roaring strength of the waterfalls, and taken away the homes of the wildlife! A dam that supplies a distant city with a little water and a little power that could easily have been obtained elsewhere! A dam constructed for this (*showing the dollar bill*).

Anyone who has visited Grand Teton National Park and camped by Jenny Lake knows what I mean. A lake that is perfectly calm, with not a ripple to mar the smooth surface of the water. And what a beautiful sky-blue water it is, surrounded by mountains that soar thousands of feet into the sky, snow-crowned and magnificent! The mirrored imagery of the lake is indescribable. A spectator cannot tell where the real mountains end and the images in the lake begin. But just a few miles from this sight is Jackson Hole, not a National Park but under the control of the Federal Government. Jackson Hole is not a place where visitors can enjoy themselves as they drink in the loveliness of nature, because it has been exploited. Powerful men have lobbied Congress to stop conservation laws from protecting Jackson Hole. Men whose land and cattle interests have caused them to block all the National Park bills that would have made this beauty spot available to all the people. And all because of this (*showing the dollar bill*)!

As one who has seen these parks, and also seen what selfish interests can do, I beg you . . . do all you can to protect and save our National parks.

—Harold Haig Kassarjian

13. Engage in some voice exercises of your own creation. Here are some suggestions:

1. Prepare a short, impassioned talk vehemently condemning some entrenched wrong in your community. Get off by yourself and deliver the talk to an imaginary audience. Don't be afraid to overdo in this practice session. Pull out all the stops and GIVE.

2. Dramatize in your own words emotional scenes from stage or movie plays you have seen. Act them out with plenty of gusto, and give your voice free rein.

3. Impersonate, in your own words, characters from literature: Dickens's old Scrooge and Tiny Tim; Stevenson's Dr. Jekyll and Mr. Hyde; Shakespeare's Shylock, Sir Toby Belch, Touchstone, etc.

4. Burlesque the mannerisms and vocal expressions of odd "characters" you have known.

5. Mimic the actions and vocal antics of a spoiled child you have seen engage in tantrums of anger, stubbornness, coaxing, and whining.

6. Mimic various animals—dog, cat, rooster, cow; the tiger's snarl, the lion's roar, etc.[6]

[6] David Ross, well-known radio announcer, told the author that he had found this method most helpful in keeping his voice "elastic." But if you use this exercise, be conscious at all times that it is simply an exercise. There should not be, and there need not be, any carry-over of such vocal gymnastics into your actual speaking.

XIV ✳ *Speech Rhythm and Melody*

Rhythm is defined as "movement or procedure with uniform recurrence of a beat, accent, or the like."

Melody is defined as "musical sounds in agreeable succession or arrangement; an air or tune."

Speech rhythm and melody, then, considered somewhat as a unit, involve the use of accented and unaccented syllables in an arrangement which produces an agreeable effect upon the auditors' ears. They include making artistic—but not arty—use of the elements of emphasis, particularly *rate* and *pitch*.

This rhythmical flow of esthetically pleasing speech sounds is opposed at one extreme to the spasmodic jerks and jolts of crude and undisciplined speech, and at the other extreme to the level, flat-as-a-table-top progression of speech sounds in indolent and indifferent speech.

Also, lest there be misunderstanding, we hasten to state that by speech rhythm and melody we do not mean the regular metrical structure which we find in poetry; this will be made clear a little later. And obviously we do not mean the chanting cadence, the periodic upward swoops and downward glides of certain political speechmakers and radio commentators, for surely no one in his right senses would advocate this. Perhaps we can best explain what we *do* mean by looking at examples of harmonious rhythm in other phases of life.

RHYTHM IN NATURE

Rhythmical movement is common throughout nature. There is something basic and fundamental about it. Nature uses it as one of her chief devices for making life smooth and harmonious. The alternation of night and day, of dusk and dawn, of winter and summer, are examples of nature's use of rhythmical patterns; so, too, are the ebb and flow of ocean tides, the northward and southward migration of birds, the opening of young flower buds and the falling of old flower petals. We develop rhythmical patterns in our eating and sleeping, our working and resting; and as we grow older we find ourselves more and more dependent upon the rhythm of these patterns to keep us well and happy.

Primitive people are strongly influenced by rhythm in its various forms. Peasants in some countries time their work to a swinging rhythm. Laborers at the great docks along the Mississippi lift bales of hay or cotton and toss them aboard the barges to the accompaniment of a rhythmical chant. Often this is extemporized rhythm, created spontaneously. Such an instance occurred when two laborers were lifting a bale of wire; it slipped and fell, striking one man's bare toe. His immediate response was a reproach to the bale in the form of "O, you debbil, you." His companion laughingly repeated it. Then they joined in saying it together, and this time it took on the form of a rhythmical chant. For hours afterward they were lifting and swinging the bales to the same chant, with the effort of the swing coming on the word, "debbil."

An American poet has pictured the rhythmical sway of American Indian squaws in a tribal dance, thus:

> Shuffle to the left, shuffle to the left,
> Shuffle, shuffle, shuffle to the left, to the left.
> Fat squaws, lean squaws, gliding in a row,
> Grunting, wheezing, laughing as they go.[1]

Unconsciously and instinctively, many of the responses of more civilized people are rhythmical: beating time with the

[1] From "Squaw Dance" in *The Collected Poems of Lew Sarett.* Copyright, 1920, 1941, by Henry Holt and Company, Inc. Copyright, 1948, by Lew Sarett.

hands, thumping with the fingers, tapping the foot, nodding the head. Likewise, both educated and uneducated enjoy the rhythm of the dance, of the patter of the rain, of the singing of a babbling brook.

All our life seems pleasanter and easier when rhythm is present. A rhythmical stride makes walking easier, and also pleasanter to behold. Dish washing and wood chopping are less onerous tasks when done in rhythm. A well-timed rhythm brings joy to the golfer, the swimmer, the runner.

Rhythm and Melody in Poetry

Melodic rhythm is the special tool of the poet. The regular recurrence of accented and unaccented syllables is essential to him. When the modern poets—imagists, impressionists, and so forth—get away from the rhythm of the older poets, their art loses some of its charm for many people.

Children readily respond to the persuasive appeal of melodic rhythm. One of their earliest delights is hearing "Old Mother Hubbard," "Little Boy Blue," "Mary's Little Lamb," and "Pussy in the Well." And there are times when these childhood rhymes delight us in our mature years. Many a work-weary father and care-burdened mother find genuine delight in reading to sleepy children jingles like Eugene Field's "Wynken, Blynken, and Nod."

In general, however, such simple jingles fit only certain of our moods. As we mature in years and in mentality we come to desire more adult types of rhythm in poetry. Poets adjust their rhythmical patterns to the types of readers they wish to reach, to the thoughts they wish to express, and to the moods they wish to create. Observe, for example, the difference between the swift, smooth flow of Robert Browning's story for children, "The Pied Piper of Hamelin," and the irregular rhythm of his mature philosophical study of a primitive crea-ture's religion in "Caliban upon Setebos" (Setebos being Cal-iban's name for God):

1. And out of the house the rats came tumbling,
   Great rats, small rats, lean rats, brawny rats,
   Brown rats, black rats, grey rats, tawny rats,
   Grave old plodders, gay young friskers,
         Fathers, mothers, uncles, cousins,
   Cocking tails and pricking whiskers,
         Families by tens and dozens,
   Brothers, sisters, husbands, wives—
   Followed the Piper for their lives.
   From street to street he piped advancing,
   And step by step they followed dancing.

2. Setebos, Setebos, and Setebos!
   'Thinketh He dwelleth i' the cold o' the moon.
   'Thinketh He made it, with the sun to match,
   But not the stars; the stars came otherwise;
   Only made clouds, winds, meteors, such as that:
   Also this isle, what lives and grows thereon,
   And snaky sea which rounds and ends the same. . . .
   Made all we see, and us, in spite: how else?
   He could not, Himself, make a second self
   To be His mate; as well have made Himself. . . .

Note how this same poet creates a mood with his description of galloping horses in "How They Brought the Good News from Ghent to Aix":

   I sprang to the stirrup, and Joris and he;
   I gallop'd, Dirck gallop'd, we gallop'd all three;
   "Good speed!" cried the watch, as the gate bolts undrew;
   "Speed!" echo'd the wall to us galloping through;
   Behind shut the postern, the lights sank to rest,
   And into the midnight we gallop'd abreast.

Observe how Tennyson uses rhythm to capture the song of "The Brook":

         I chatter over stony ways,
         In little sharps and trebles,
         I bubble into eddying bays,
         I babble on the pebbles.

I wind about, and in and out,
With here a blossom sailing,
And here and there a lusty trout,
And here and there a grayling.

See how Poe uses melodic rhythm to create mood, without much regard for thought or meaning, in "The Raven":

Deep into the darkness peering, long I stood there
wondering, fearing,
Doubting, dreaming dreams no mortals ever dared to
dream before;
But the silence was unbroken, and the stillness gave
no token,
And the only word there spoken was the whispered word
"Lenore!"

It would serve no useful purpose in this book to enter on a detailed study of the metrical structure of poetry. It is important, nevertheless, to note the precise and well-defined units of poetry. These units or "feet" assume patterns of alternating accented and unaccented syllables which have universally recognized names: iambic, trochaic, dactylic, and so forth. After the poet has selected one of these patterns for a particular poem, he clings to it with a considerable degree of consistency. He is not, to be sure, slavishly bound to that one pattern, but on the other hand he does not shift about from one pattern to another without order and plan. The whole structure of a poem is almost mathematically exact and measurable.

Also, while the systematic analysis of these metrical patterns (called *scansion*) has no place in the present study, as a phase of voice training it is desirable for us to appreciate the difference between poetry rhythm and prose rhythm, particularly the prose rhythm of speech, in order to use our voices more pleasingly in various situations and under various conditions.

Prose Rhythm

The rhythm of written prose is much more elusive than that of poetry. It does not follow a metrical scheme. It cannot be measured off into patterned units of so many feet to the line, so many accented and unaccented syllables to the foot. Nevertheless, in spite of its lack of scanable meter, prose designed to stir us emotionally or please us esthetically often has a definite rhythmical flow. Feel the pulse of the following lines from the Bible:

Though I speak with the tongues of men and of angels, and have not charity, I am become as sounding brass or a tinkling cymbal. And though I have the gift of prophecy, and understand all mysteries, and all knowledge; and though I have all faith, so that I could remove mountains, and have not charity, I am nothing.

The difference between poetic rhythm and prose rhythm becomes readily apparent if we mark the regular succession of accented and unaccented syllables in a line or two of poetry (even if they are set up like prose), thus:

The splendor falls on castle walls, and snowy summits old in story

and then attempt to do the same thing to one of the Biblical sentences quoted above. We find it impossible to discern any such sustained pattern of accented and unaccented syllables in the latter.

The great variety of the wave structure in even the most rhythmical prose can be observed in the following literary passages: "The Art of Seeing Things," p. 478), "Daniel Webster" (p. 478), and "Concord River" (p. 477).

Rhythm and Melody in Speech

The melodic rhythm of speech is, on the whole, more akin to prose than to poetry. Generally, it is more subtle, more complex, and subject to more frequent changes in structure than is the rhythm of poetry. Speech rhythm, however, even though it follows no mechanical scanable pattern, does have, at least in its more eloquent moments, a pulse beat that can be felt even though it cannot be analyzed.

Speech rhythm is extremely flexible. It varies according to the individual preferences of speakers, the special requirements of different occasions, and the nature of the subject matter. Let us look at two types of speeches with respect to their rhythmical melody. These two will serve to illustrate the great diversity in the use of rhythmical melody in public speech.

RHYTHM IN INFORMAL PUBLIC ADDRESS

The standard for informal public address is conversation. Therefore the rhythm of this type of public speech is much like conversation. It has the sudden starts and stops, the changes from slow to fast and back to slow again, the long syllables and the short syllables, the long pauses and the short pauses, which characterize conversation. Changes in force, pitch, and rate are applied for emphasis, not for their contribution to any rhythmical pattern.

This is the type of speech in which the speaker is really thinking, and is seeking to stir a thoughtful rather than an emotional response in his auditors. It is commonly called conversational public speaking.

However, we should not infer that there is no rhythm in conversation, or in conversational speaking. An underlying rhythm is present in practically all speech; otherwise speech would be so halting, so broken, as to obscure the meaning. In all normal speech there is enough rhythm to give a certain sweep to the thought. The surges of emphasis cannot be so irregular that they destroy the thought continuity.

RHYTHM IN FORMAL PUBLIC ADDRESS AND ORATORY

People in large groups are especially susceptible to melodic rhythm. Experienced orators realize this, as do playwrights and composers. Part of the tremendous emotional grip of O'Neill's play, *The Emperor Jones*, comes from the mood created by the ceaseless beating of tom-toms in the distance. In the play

Rain, the incessant patter of rain is used for the same purpose. Orators use this means of accomplishing their highest emotional effects; for oratory, dealing with elevated and noble sentiments, is essentially emotional and approaches the rhythmical flow of poetry. Tiberius Gracchus, one of the early Roman orators, went to the extreme of placing a servant just off-stage to play a flute as he talked, to help him achieve a melodic rhythm. (A student responded to this information with the comment that many speakers sound as if they were accompanied by the bazooka.)

Everyone is familiar with the stately rhythm of Lincoln's Gettysburg address: "Four score and seven years ago, our fathers brought forth upon this continent . . ." But this is by no means the only speech in which Lincoln's words rose to lyrical heights. Observe the pulse beat in the two following examples:

1. Fondly do we hope, fervently do we pray, that this scourge of war may speedily pass away. . . .
2. As I would not be a slave, so I would not be a master; this expresses my idea of democracy. Whatever differs from this, to the extent of the difference is no democracy.

One device used by the orator to achieve this rhythm is called *parallel structure,* i.e., the repetition of a phrase in a series of balanced sentences. An often-quoted example of parallel structure is found in the climax of Burke's famous impeachment speech:

Therefore, it is with confidence that, ordered by the Commons of Great Britain, I impeach Warren Hastings of high crimes and misdemeanors. I impeach him in the name of the Commons of Great Britain in Parliament assembled, whose parliamentary trust he has abused. I impeach him in the name of the Commons of Great Britain, whose national character he has dishonored. I impeach him in the name of the people of India, whose laws, right, and liberties he has subverted. . . .

Franklin D. Roosevelt often employed this rhetorical principle to give a rolling surge of emotion to the climactic portions of his speeches, as illustrated by the two examples that follow:

1. I have seen war. I have seen war on land and sea. . . . I have seen the dead in the mud. I have seen cities destroyed. I have seen children starving. I have seen the agonies of mothers and wives. I hate war! I have passed unnumbered hours, I shall pass unnumbered hours, thinking and planning how war may be kept from this nation.

2. Of course we will continue to seek to improve working conditions for the workers of America—to reduce hours over-long, to increase wages that spell starvation, to end the labor of children, to wipe out sweat shops. Of course we will continue every effort to end monopoly in business, to support collective bargaining, to stop unfair competition, to abolish dishonorable trade practices. For all these we have only just begun to fight.

Rhythm in Oratory versus Rhythm in Poetry

As previously mentioned, even in the most rhythmical speech there is no regular meter such as we find in poetry. There is still another difference, a difference which inheres in the purpose of the two types of expression. The poet Shelley said: "A poet is a nightingale, who sits in darkness and sings to cheer his own solitude." The speaker, on the other hand, uses his "sweet sounds" not for himself to enjoy in solitude, and not for others to admire as a work of art, but to make his ideas more appealing and acceptable.

This essential difference constitutes the reason why many students of speech consider the oratory of Robert Ingersoll to be second rate, despite its rhythmical perfection. Indeed, it is in part this mechanical perfection that keeps it from being first rate—this, plus a suggestion of contrived "sweetness" which seems to rob it of the deep sincerity that characterizes great oratory. The following examples of Ingersoll's rhythmical prose illustrate the point:

1. From the voiceless lips of the unreplying dead there comes no word; but in the night of death hope sees a star, and listening love can hear the rustle of a wing.

2. We see them [the soldiers] part with those they love. Some are walking for the last time in quiet, woody places, with the maidens they adore. We hear the whisperings and the sweet vows of eternal love as they lingeringly part forever.

Beautiful as these passages are, and much as we may admire their cadence, they are a kind of prose-poetry rather than great oratory. We find it hard to escape the impression that this speaker is listening admiringly to his own "sweet sounds."

This distinction is made in order to emphasize once more to the young speaker the primary importance of developing a vocal quality of deepest sincerity and honesty; and also to emphasize that even when his emotionalism carries him to the highest points of rolling rhythm, he still should retain in his voice a subtle objectiveness, a reaching out for his auditors, which does not necessarily obtain in the reading of poetry.

How Much Rhythm to Use

The question for the young speaker is not whether or not he should use rhythm in his speech, but rather how much rhythm to use. In reading or reciting poetry he must retain enough of the rhythmical pattern to create the desired mood; at the same time he must break the meter sufficiently to convey the finer nuances of thought. Similarly, in his most thoughtful discussions he must have enough rhythmical continuity to keep his speech from coming apart at the joints, and at the same time he must break the rhythmical flow enough to give evidence that he is thinking of the meaning of his words.

It is not difficult to distinguish between the swift and lilting rhythm of the first three selections below, and the slow measured cadence of the last three.

1.   Marching along, fifty score strong,
              Great-hearted gentlemen, singing this song.

2.   Boots, saddle, to horse and away!
            Rescue my castle before the hot day
            Brightens to blue from its silvery grey,
            Boots, saddle, to horse and away.

3.   For the Colonel's Lady an' Judy O'Grady
            Are sisters under the skin!

4.   The day is cold, and dark, and dreary;
            It rains, and the wind is never weary.

5.   Solemnly, mournfully,
                    Dealing its dole,
                The Curfew Bell
                    Is beginning to toll.

6.   I do not know what I was playing
            Or what I was dreaming then,
            But I struck one chord of music
            Like the sound of a great, "Amen!"

These contrasts in rhythmical sequence are obvious. It is for the finer shades of emotion and thought that the artistic temperament—the soul of the poet—is required. Voice can be effective only when the mind grasps and the heart feels these finer distinctions.

The voice student must develop a "feel" for rhythm. He will gain the desired mastery of it in his own speaking not so much by cold analysis, like a scientist dissecting a flower or a frog, as by experimenting with various types of rhythmical prose and poetry, until he senses what kind and what degree of rhythm are appropriate in his own speaking.

This ability to make fine distinctions in rhythm and melody are of paramount importance for a person who has even a trace of a foreign accent that he wishes to get rid of. Each language has its own melodic pattern, as is readily apparent by listening carefully to foreign speech. In learning a new language, it is often more difficult to learn the new melody than to pronounce the new syllables and words.

The following selections, designed to aid the student in developing a discriminating sense of speech rhythm, are divided into three sections: poems, written prose, and excerpts from speeches. The student should read some from each group, concentrating on the group which best meets his individual needs.

Poems

The poems which follow are in various moods, and on several levels of difficulty. For the student who speaks haltingly, there are swift-moving, easy jingles which should help him to acquire smoothness and lightness; for the plodding speaker there are sprightly poems to help him put lyric quality into his speech; and similarly there are other types of poems to meet other problems.

1.   WYNKEN, BLYNKEN, AND NOD

Wynken, Blynken, and Nod one night
    Sailed off in a wooden shoe,—
Sailed on a river of crystal light
    Into a sea of dew.
"Where are you going, and what do you wish?"
    The old man asked the three.
"We have come to fish for the herring fish
    That live in this beautiful sea;
Nets of silver and gold have we!"
        Said Wynken,
        Blynken,
        And Nod.

The old moon laughed and sang a song,
    As they rocked in the wooden shoe;
And the wind that sped them all night long
    Ruffled the waves of dew.
The little stars were the herring fish
    That lived in that beautiful sea—
"Now cast your nets wherever you wish,—
    Never afeard are we!"

So cried the stars to the fishermen three,
>> Wynken,
>> Blynken,
>> And Nod.

All night long their nets they threw
> To the stars in the twinkling foam,—
Then down from the skies came the wooden shoe,
> Bringing the fishermen home:
'Twas all so pretty a sail, it seemed
> As if it could not be;
And some folk thought 'twas a dream they'd dreamed
> Of sailing that beautiful sea;
But I shall name you the fishermen three:
>> Wynken,
>> Blynken,
>> And Nod.

Wynken and Blynken are two little eyes,
> And Nod is a little head,
And the wooden shoe that sailed the skies
> Is a wee one's trundle-bed;
So shut your eyes while Mother sings
> Of wonderful sights that be,
And you shall see the beautiful things
> As you rock in the misty sea
Where the old shoe rocked the fishermen three:—
>> Wynken,
>> Blynken,
>> And Nod.

—EUGENE FIELD

ANNABEL LEE

2

It was many and many a year ago,
> In a kingdom by the sea,
That a maiden there lived whom you may know
> By the name of Annabel Lee;
And this maiden she lived with no other thought
> Than to love and be loved by me.

I was a child and she was a child,
  In this kingdom by the sea,
But we loved with a love that was more than love—
  I and my Annabel Lee;
With a love that the wingèd seraphs of heaven
  Coveted her and me.

And this is the reason that, long ago,
  In this kingdom by the sea,
A wind blew out of a cloud, chilling
  My beautiful Annabel Lee;
So that her highborn kinsmen came
  And bore her away from me,
To shut her up in a sepulchre
  In this kingdom by the sea.

—EDGAR ALLAN POE

3.   D'ARTAGNAN'S RIDE[2]

Fifty leagues, fifty leagues—and I ridé, and I ride—
Fifty leagues as the black crow flies.
None of the three are by my side . . .
The bay horse reels, and the bay horse dies—
But I ride, and I ride
To Callice.

We were four, we were four—and I ride, and I ride—
We were four, but Porthos lies
God knows where by the highway side . . .
The roan horse reels, and the roan horse dies—
But I ride, and I ride
To Callice.

We were three, we were three—and I ride, and I ride—
We were three, but Aramis lies
Bludgeoned and bound and thrown aside . . .
The dun horse reels, and the dun horse dies—
But I ride, and I ride
To Callice.

[2] Reprinted by permission of the author.

We were two, we were two—and I ride, and I ride—
We were two, but Athos lies
With a lead-crushed rib and a steel-torn side . . .
The black horse reels, and the black horse dies—
But I ride, and I ride
To Callice.

All alone, all alone—and I ride, and I ride—
All alone, and an ambush lies
God knows where by the highway side . . .
The gray horse reels, and the gray horse dies—
But I ride, and I ride
To Callice.
Yes—I ride and I ride and I ride and I ride
And I ride and I ride
To Callice.

—GOUVERNEUR MORRIS

4.   SONG OF THE CHATTAHOOCHEE

Out of the hills of Habersham,
  Down the valleys of Hall,
I hurry amain to reach the plain,
Run the rapid and leap the fall,
Split at the rock and together again,
Accept my bed, or narrow or wide,
And flee from folly on every side
With a lover's pain to attain the plain
  Far from the hills of Habersham,
  Far from the valleys of Hall.

All down the hills of Habersham,
  All through the valleys of Hall,
The rushes cried *Abide, abide!*
The willful waterweeds held me thrall,
The laving laurel turned my tide,
The ferns and the fondling grass said *Stay,*

The dewberry dipped for to work delay,
And the little reeds sighed *Abide, abide,*
 Here in the hills of Habersham,
 Here in the valleys of Hall.

 High o'er the hills of Habersham,
 Veiling the valleys of Hall,
The hickory told me manifold
Fair tales of shade, the poplar tall
Wrought me her shadowy self to hold,
The chestnut, the oak, the walnut, the pine,
Overleaning, with flickering meaning and sign,
Said, *Pass not, so cold, these manifold*
 Deep shades of the hills of Habersham,
 These glades in the valleys of Hall.

 And oft in the hills of Habersham,
 And oft in the valleys of Hall,
The white quartz shone, and the smooth brook-stone
Did bar me of passage with friendly brawl,
And many a luminous jewel lone
—Crystals clear or a-cloud with mist,
Ruby, garnet, and amethyst—
Made lures with the lights of streaming stone
 In the clefts of the hills of Habersham,
 In the beds of the valleys of Hall.

 But oh, not the hills of Habersham,
 And oh, not the valleys of Hall
Avail: I am fain for to water the plain.
Downward the voices of Duty call—
Downward, to toil and be mixed with the main,
The dry fields burn, and the mills are to turn,
And a myriad flowers mortally yearn,
And the lordly main from beyond the plain
 Calls o'er the hills of Habersham,
 Calls through the valleys of Hall.

—SIDNEY LANIER

5.   EL CAMINO REAL[3]

All in the golden weather, forth let us ride today,
You and I together on the King's Highway,
The blue skies above us, and below the shining sea;
There's many a road to travel, but it's this road for me.

It's a long road and sunny, and the fairest in the world.
There are peaks that rise above it in their snowy
      mantles curled.
And it leads from the mountains through a hedge of
      chaparral,
Down to the waters where the sea gulls call.

It's a long road and sunny, it's a long road and old,
And the brown padres made it for the flocks of the fold;
They made it for the sandals of the sinner-folk that
      trod
From the fields in the open to the shelter-house of God.

They made it for the sandals of the sinner-folk of old;
Now the flocks they are scattered and death keeps the
      fold;
But you and I together we will take the road today,
With the breath in our nostrils, on the King's Highway.

We will take the road together through the morning's
      golden glow,
And we'll dream of those who trod it in the mellowed
      long ago;
We will stop at the missions where the sleeping padres
      lay,
And we'll bend a knee above them for their souls' sake
      to pray.

We'll ride through the valleys where the blossom's on
      the tree,
[3] Reprinted by permission.

Through the orchards and the meadows with the bird
    and the bee,
And we'll take the rising hills where the manzanitas
    grow,
Past the gray trails of waterfalls where blue violets
blow.

Old Conquistadores, O brown priests, and all,
Give us your ghosts for company when night begins to
    fall;
There's many a road to travel, but it's this road today,
With the breath of God about us on the King's
    Highway.

—JOHN S. McGROARTY

6.   BEDOUIN SONG

From the Desert I come to thee
    On a stallion shod with fire;
And the winds are left behind
    In the speed of my desire.
Under thy window I stand
    And the midnight hears my cry:
I love thee, I love but thee,
    With a love that shall not die
        Till the sun grows cold,
        And the stars are old,
        And the leaves of the Judgment
        Book unfold!

Look from my window and see
    My passion and my pain;
I lie on the sands below;
    And I faint in thy disdain.
Let the night-winds touch thy brow
    With the heat of my burning sigh,

And melt thee to hear the vow
  Of a love that shall not die
    Till the sun grows cold,
    And the stars are old,
    And the leaves of the Judgment
      Book unfold!

My steps are nightly driven,
  By the fever in my breast,
To hear from thy lattice breathed
  The word that shall give me rest.
Open the door of thy heart,
  And open thy chamber door,
And my kisses shall teach thy lips,
  The love that shall fade no more
    Till the sun grows cold,
    And the stars are old
    And the leaves of the Judgment
      Book unfold!

                          —BAYARD TAYLOR

7.   *From* VAGABOND'S HOUSE[4]

When I have a house—as I sometime may—
I'll suit my fancy in every way.
I'll fill it with things that have caught my eye
In drifting from Iceland to Molokai.
It won't be correct or in period style
But . . . oh, I've thought for a long, long while
Of all the corners and all the nooks,
Of all the bookshelves and all the books,
The great big table, the deep soft chairs
And the Chinese rug at the foot of the stairs,
(It's an old, old rug from far Chow Wan
That a Chinese princess once walked on).

[4] Reprinted by permission of Dodd, Mead & Company from *Vagabond's House* by Don Blanding. Copyright 1928 by Don Blanding.

My house will stand on the side of a hill
By a slow broad river, deep and still,
With a tall lone pine on guard nearby
Where the birds can sing and the storm winds cry.
A flagstone walk with lazy curves
Will lead to the door where a Pan's head serves
As a knocker there like a vibrant drum
To let me know that a friend has come,
And the door will squeak as I swing it wide
To welcome you to the cheer inside.
For I'll have good friends who can sit and chat
Or simply sit, when it comes to that,
By the fireplace where the fir logs blaze
And the smoke rolls up in a weaving haze.
I'll want a wood-box, scarred and rough,
For leaves and bark and odorous stuff
Like resinous knots and cones and gums
To chuck on the flames when winter comes.
And I hope a cricket will stay around
For I love its creaky lonesome sound. . . .

—Don Blanding

8.   *From* THE CREATION[5]
                       (A Negro Sermon)

And God looked around
On all that he had made.
He looked at his sun,
And he looked at his moon,
And he looked at his little stars;
He looked on his world
With all its living things,
And God said: I'm lonely still.

Then God sat down—
On the side of a hill where he could think;
By a deep, wide river he sat down;

[5] From *God's Trombones* by James Weldon Johnson. Copyright 1927 by The Viking Press, Inc. Reprinted by permission of The Viking Press, Inc., New York.

field, where he had a farm as large as half a county. Everyone had heard him on the platform, every boy and girl had seen his picture, the dark brow that looked like Mount Monadnock, the wide-brimmed hat and the knee-high boots, the linsey-woolsey coat and the flowing necktie, the walking stick that was said to be ten feet long. There was something elemental in his composition, something large and lavish. Even his faults were ample. Webster despised the traditional virtues. He spent money in a grand way, borrowing and lending with equal freedom. He was far from sober, or would have been if two tumblers of brandy had been enough to put him under the table. He could be surly enough, when he had his moods of God-Almightiness, or when he wished to insult some sycophant. The thunderclouds would gather on his brow and the lightning flash from his eye, and he would tell a committee that their town was the dullest place on earth. No one could be more truculent, especially in the hay-fever season; but he was always good-natured with the farmers, who liked to think of him as their man. They knew what Webster meant when he said that his oxen were better company than the men in the Senate. They knew all his ways and the names of his guns and animals, as the Jews of old knew the weapons of Nimrod, or Abraham's flocks and herds—his great ram Goliath, his shotguns, "Mrs. Patrick" and "Wilmot Proviso," his trout rod, "Old Killall." They knew he had written the Bunker Hill oration, composed it word by word, with Old Killall in his hand, wading in the Marshfield River. They had heard of his tens of thousands of swine and sheep, his herds of Peruvian llamas and blooded cattle, the hundreds of thousands of trees he had raised from seed. They knew that while his guests were still asleep—the scores of guests who were always visiting Marshfield—he rose at four o'clock and lighted the fires, roused the cocks with his early-morning candles, milked and fed the stock, and chatted in the kitchen with his farm hands, quoting Mr. Virgil, the Roman farmer. And at Marshfield, as everyone knew, his horses were buried in a special graveyard, with all the honors of war, standing upright, with their shoes and halters.

—Van Wyck Brooks

Speech Excerpts

The following excerpts from notable speeches exemplify the pulselike surge which great speakers employ in their most eloquent moments. Do not think that this lyric quality pervades the entire speeches. These passages, in some instances, represent only the climactic portions of much longer addresses. The speakers may have spent thirty, fifty, a hundred minutes talking at or near the conversational level, rising only to these emotional and lyrical heights in the closing minutes of their speeches.

1. I have nothing to offer but blood, toil, tears, and sweat. . . . You ask, what is our policy? I will say, it is to wage war, by sea, land, and air, with all our might and with all the strength that God can give us; to wage war against a monstrous tyranny, never surpassed in the dark, lamentable catalogue of human crime. That is our policy. You ask, what is our aim? I can answer in one word: it is victory, victory at all costs, victory in spite of terror, victory, however long and hard the road may be; for without victory there is no survival.

—WINSTON CHURCHILL

2. We shall not flag or fail. We shall go on to the end. We shall fight in France, we shall fight on the seas and oceans, we shall fight with growing strength in the air, we shall defend our Island, whatever the cost may be. We shall fight on the beaches, we shall fight on the landing grounds, we shall fight in the fields and in the streets, we shall fight in the hills; we shall never surrender, and even if, which I do not for a moment believe, this Island or a large part of it were subjugated and starving, then our empire beyond the seas, armed and guarded by the British Fleet, would carry on the struggle, until, in God's good time, the New World, with all its power and might, steps forth to the rescue and the liberation of the old.

—WINSTON CHURCHILL

3. At four o'clock this morning Hitler attacked and invaded Russia. . . . We have but one aim and one single, irrevocable purpose. We are resolved to destroy Hitler and every vestige of the Nazi

regime. From this nothing will turn us—nothing. We will never parley, we will never negotiate with Hitler or any of his gang. We shall fight him by land, we shall fight him by sea, we shall fight him in the air, until with God's help we have rid the earth of his shadow and liberated its peoples from his yoke. Any man or State who fights on against Nazidom will have our aid. Any man or State who marches with Hitler is our foe.

—WINSTON CHURCHILL

4. While good men sit at home, not knowing that there is anything to be done, nor caring to know; cultivating a feeling that politics are tiresome and dirty, and politicians vulgar bullies and bravoes; half persuaded that a republic is the contemptible rule of a mob, and secretly longing for a splendid and vigorous despotism— then remember, it is not a government mastered by ignorance, it is a government betrayed by intelligence; it is not the victory of the slums, it is the surrender of the schools; it is not that bad men are brave, but that good men are infidels and cowards.

—GEORGE WILLIAM CURTIS

5. We are a nation of many nationalities, many races, many re- ligions—bound together by a single unity, the unity of freedom and equality. Whoever seeks to set one nationality against an- other, seeks to degrade all nationalities. Whoever seeks to set one race against another seeks to enslave all races. Whoever seeks to set one religion against another seeks to destroy all religion. I am fighting for a free America—for a country in which *all* men and women have equal rights to liberty and justice. I am fighting, as I always have fought, for the rights of the little man as well as the big man—for the weak as well as the strong, for those who are helpless as well as for those who can help themselves.

—FRANKLIN D. ROOSEVELT

6. You ought to thank God tonight if, regardless of your years, you are young enough in spirit to dream dreams and see visions— dreams and visions about a greater and finer America that is to be: if you are young enough in spirit to believe that poverty can be greatly lessened: that the disgrace of involuntary unemploy- ment can be wiped out: that class hatreds can be done away with:

that peace at home and peace abroad can be maintained: and that one day a generation may possess this land, blessed beyond anything we now know, blessed with those things—material and spiritual—that make man's life abundant. If this is the fashion of your dreaming then I say: "Hold fast to your dream. America needs it."

—Franklin D. Roosevelt

7. I see a great nation, upon a great continent, blessed with a great wealth of natural resources.

Its 130,000,000 people are at peace among themselves; they are making their country a good neighbor among the nations.

I see a United States which can demonstrate that, under democratic methods of government, national wealth can be translated into a spreading volume of human comforts hitherto unknown—and the lowest standards of living can be raised far above the level of mere subsistence.

But here is the challenge to our democracy: In this nation I see tens of millions of its citizens—a substantial part of its whole population—who at this very moment are denied the greater part of what the very lowest standards of today call the necessities of life.

I see millions of families trying to live on incomes so meager that the pall of family disaster hangs over them day by day.

I see millions whose daily lives in city and on farm continue under conditions labeled indecent by a so-called polite society half a century ago.

I see millions denied education, recreation, and the opportunity to better the lot of themselves and their children.

I see millions lacking the means to buy the products of farm and factory and by their poverty denying work and productiveness to many other millions.

I see one-third of a nation ill-housed, ill-clad, ill-nourished.

But it is not in despair that I paint you that picture. I paint it for you in hope—because the nation, seeing and understanding the injustice of it, proposes to paint it out.

—Franklin D. Roosevelt

8.   GETTYSBURG ADDRESS

Fourscore and seven years ago our fathers brought forth upon this continent a new nation, conceived in liberty, and dedicated to the proposition that all men are created equal. Now we are engaged in a great civil war, testing whether that nation, or any nation so conceived and so dedicated, can long endure. We are met on a great battle-field of that war. We have come to dedicate a portion of that field as a final resting-place for those who here gave their lives that that nation might live. It is altogether fitting and proper that we should do this. But in a larger sense we cannot dedicate, we cannot consecrate, we cannot hallow this ground. The brave men, living and dead, who struggled here have consecrated it far above our power to add or detract. The world will little note, nor long remember, what we say here; but it can never forget what they did here. It is for us, the living, rather to be dedicated here to the unfinished work which they who fought here have thus far so nobly advanced. It is rather for us to be here dedicated to the great task remaining before us, that from these honored dead we take increased devotion to that cause for which they gave the last full measure of devotion—that we here highly resolve that these dead shall not have died in vain —that this nation, under God, shall have a new birth of freedom, and that government of the people, by the people, and for the people shall not perish from the earth.

—ABRAHAM LINCOLN

XV ✳ The Voice in Conversation

This chapter will deal with simple things—simple and fundamental. We will apply to conversation and conversational situations some of the voice principles we have been studying.

To be sure, this is not the first time we have referred to conversation; the term has occurred repeatedly throughout the book. But the references have been somewhat incidental, possibly giving the erroneous impression that we look upon conversation as simply one of many ways in which the speaking voice is used. Conversation deserves better treatment than this. In other words, it is high time we turned the spotlight of our full attention upon this most fundamental and most important of all our vocal activities.

Let us hope that no one will be inclined to sit back and say: "Why, we've engaged in conversation all our lives; what's the use of spending time on that?" If any justification is needed for asking college students in this sophisticated mid-twentieth century to study anything so common as conversation, it is this: In all likelihood it will be at the conversational level that most of you will either make or break your futures. It will be in your everyday talk that you will influence people to want to work with you, plan with you, coöperate with you, or shun you. Therefore, anything that you can do to make your conversational voice work for you instead of against you is certainly worth while. Even though you have been conversing all your life, perhaps you have not been doing so to the best advantage.

484

Like a person who for one reason or another learned to walk in a stiff-legged, jolting, exhausting fashion, but has taken physical training and learned a rhythmical way of putting one foot in front of the other so that walking is now an exhilarating pleasure, you may by concentrated attention discover how to smooth some of the jolts out of your conversation. Certainly there can be no doubt in anybody's mind that many people could profitably devote a great deal of time and attention to polishing their conversational personalities, for certain unfortunate individuals no more than open their mouths in conversation before they rub us the wrong way. Just as surely, other individuals quickly engender a warm, comfortable feeling in us, and a friendly, receptive attitude toward them. The vast majority of us, who are somewhere between these two extremes, can do something to improve our status in this regard if we consider it important enough and work hard enough at the needed reforms.

Stop for a minute or two and think how important a role conversation plays in our way of living. Without some method of communication similar to conversation, not only would our lives be insufferably lonely, but living together would be a virtual impossibility. Our home life, our community life, our national life, our international life, our very civilization, depend upon some way of communicating with one another. And by all odds the most important instrument of communication—the one used dozens of times to every time that any other instrument is used—is the conversational voice.

Conversation versus Public Speaking

Many writers on speech have tried to describe the difference between conversation and public speaking, especially that between conversation and conversational public speaking. Among these writers, no one has analyzed the subject more thoroughly than Winans.[1] Most writers agree with his conclusion that there

[1] James Albert Winans, *Public Speaking*, Appleton-Century-Crofts, 1st ed., 1915.

is no clear-cut differentiation. The first distinction likely to spring to mind—namely, that the public speaker is on a platform whereas the converser is not—cannot be maintained, for sometimes the public speaker speaks from the floor; in fact, this is often the case in discussion groups. The distinction that the public speaker is prepared whereas the converser is not is likewise untenable; sometimes (all too often) a public speaker is not prepared, and conversely sometimes the converser is prepared, particularly if the conversation involves an application for a job, or some other type of talk which may mean bread and butter to him. Nor can the size of the audience be taken as a line of distinction. Occasionally speakers address pitifully small audiences, and occasionally true conversations take place in large groups, as around big family picnic tables, etc. Even the most obvious of all distinctions—that the public speaker does all the talking, whereas the converser engages in an exchange of talk—is not a safe and sure guide. Some audiences heckle the speaker, and thus take an active part in the discussion; and all audiences, if in the desired rapport with the speaker, give him visible signs of their reactions which virtually amount to talking back to him; on the other hand, some conversers come so close to monopolizing the conversation that they practically do all the talking. Finally, there is no real difference between the objectives of the two speakers; both the public speaker and the converser are primarily concerned with the *communication of ideas*, not with an exhibition of their vocal skills. The most that can be said by way of distinction is that usually the speaker is on a platform and the converser is not, usually the public speaker desires to achieve a more specific purpose, usually the public speaker talks to larger groups and does most, or all, of the talking. The inescapable conclusion is that the only real distinction between conversation and conversational public speaking is one of degree rather than of kind.

One more of these "usual" distinctions should claim our

attention; to voice students it is more significant than any of the others. It pertains to the number of times the average person engages in the two activities. Only the most popular speakers make more than three or four speeches a week; even campaigners-for-office seldom make more than three or four speeches a day during the hottest part of their campaigns; probably the average for all college students would be more like three or four speeches a year. But conversations—their number is like unto the drops of water in the ocean. Day in, day out, in sunshine and in cloudy weather, in season and out of season, we converse. In this respect, comparing conversation to public speaking is like comparing the constant dripping of water which will wear away a stone to the rainstorm that washes over the surface of the stone. More than any other influence, the never-ending "drops" of conversation make up our attitudes, our characters, and ultimately the destinies of nations.

To say this is not to discount public speech. Public speech from ancient times to the present has wielded an enormous influence. On numerous occasions it has helped to determine the course of history, as in the National Democratic convention of 1912, when William Jennings Bryan's effective speech virtually took the nomination away from Champ Clark and handed it to Woodrow Wilson. And today, through radio and television, public speaking exerts a greater influence than ever before. Yes, public speech is enormouly important—but conversation is the very breath of our collective life.

Furthermore, conversation is basic. In it the voice student lays the foundation for his public speaking. The habits that he develops day by day, hour by hour, in casual, offhand talks with his fellows, are the habits which will make his voice either effective or ineffective in public speech. He cannot use one kind of voice in everyday talk and another in public talk and still be the "natural" type of public speaker people like to hear. The difference between his public voice and his private voice will have to be a difference in degree, not a difference in kind.

If you have an ambition to become a public speaker, or a radio announcer, or an actor, or even a singer, think of conversation as providing the rootsoil for growing the kind of public voice you hope to acquire. The chances are that the deeper you sink the roots of your public voice into a rich conversation soil, the more satisfactory a plant you will be able to grow.

Formal and Informal Conversation

If you will look back over your conversations of the last few hours, no doubt you will find that some of them were pretty trivial. Even these in all probability served a useful purpose in promoting relaxation, sociability, and mutual understanding. Some of them may have been fairly serious and may possibly have done something to help you form opinions on certain subjects. A few may have been of outstanding significance and have played a part in determining your conduct for years to come.

Similarly, conversations differ in degrees of formality, ranging all the way from the lounging, perfectly-at-ease "bull session" to the polite exchange of social amenities at a formal dinner party. Consider the diverse nature of such conversational occasions as the friendly chat over a "Coke," the conversation of a group of unacquainted students who happen to ride to school together, the difficult getting-acquainted of a boy and his girl's parents, the strained questions and answers which sometimes take place between a student and his college dean, the easy talk among a group of congenial spirits relaxing after a satisfying dinner, the talk of an executive committee of an organization deciding on a course of action, the teacup-balancing polite small talk at a professor's "at home."

Just these few, out of the infinite number of such occasions, convince us at once of the impossibility of finding a handy set of rules that covers the degree of formality or informality suitable. You must develop a "feel" for the right and proper attitude in voice as well as in the rest of your deportment. Good judgment and practice must be your guides.

There are, however, broad general principles which can be applied, and this is where the voice class comes into the picture. The voice class may become a conversation workshop. In it you may analyze and experiment with various principles and thus evaluate their true worth. You may also get some needed practice that will help you start the chain of habits you must establish if you have any hope of improving. We must never forget that merely learning rules and principles relative to voice and speech will do us virtually no good unless we learn them in our habit reflexes. Speech is essentially a habit function.

Desirable Characteristics of the Conversational Voice

FRIENDLINESS

What makes a voice sound friendly is hard to say. There are big voices and little voices that sound friendly. There are strong and weak voices, loud and soft voices, high-pitched and low-pitched voices, men's voices and women's voices, all of which sound friendly and pleasing to us. And in all these classifications there are other voices which sound either coolly indifferent or positively unfriendly. What makes the difference? Undoubtedly, more than anything else it is the inflections in the tones. It is pretty hard to sound friendly with a flat, unvaried tone. Try it and see. See if you can say the sentence "You've always been a good friend to me" so that it sounds meaningful with a flat, inflexible tone! Pretty hard to do, isn't it? If you felt the appropriate emotion, little subtle shifts in pitch undoubtedly crept into your tones to reveal your feelings.

But inflections are not the whole story. Some singers, using sustained notes and shifting from one pitch level to another only by steps, are able to give their listeners a feeling of friendliness by the quality of their tones alone. Those of you who had the good fortune to hear the musical play, *Lost in the Stars*, heard Todd Duncan inject such a tonal quality—not just friendliness but a deep affection—into his song about the little gray house which wasn't much to look at but it was "home."

With long and continuous practice, coupled with a careful and shrewd analysis of tones, you may be able to simulate friendliness without actually feeling it. But why try? How much easier it is to cultivate a feeling of friendliness for people! And how much safer! If you actually feel the friendliness, you will not accidentally slip into the mistakes in quality or inflection which brand your friendliness as make-believe. People are quick to detect spurious friendliness in the voice, and not just educated people. Everybody recognizes it.

CHEERFULNESS

Few people like to associate with a person whose conversational voice habitually expresses unhappiness. The natural reaction is, There's enough trouble in the world without having to listen to his doleful tones. On the other hand, there is a deal of truth in the Biblical proverb, "A merry heart doeth good like a medicine." So does a cheerful voice.

ANIMATION

There is an appeal in the voice that has vitality. To be pleasing, the conversational voice should carry the suggestion that its possessor is thoroughly alive. And for leadership, a quality of vibrant strength is almost a necessity.

RESTFULNESS

While the conversational voice should have vitality, it should not have constant aggressive force. Strained nervous tones are tiring to the listener as well as to the speaker. Instinctively, we try to get away from the voice which continually bears down on us. Conversational tones should be made easily, relaxedly, so that the vocal cords will function properly and thus create their full quota of overtones. When the tones are made in this manner, the conversational voice will sound not only full and round, but restful as well.

FLEXIBILITY

The conversational voice should be adaptable. In order to adjust itself to the seriousness, the levity, the formality, the informality, the need for engendering enthusiasm, the need for allaying fear, and all the other moods which characterize our infinitely varied conversational situations, the conversational voice requires a considerable degree of flexibility.

DISTINCTNESS

Who enjoys conversations interspersed with "What?" "What was that?" "What did you say?" Who wants to engage in conversations that are, more than anything else, mere guessing games about what the other fellow is saying? Who deliberately seeks conversational companions who are too lazy to speak distinctly? The answers are inherent in the questions.

CULTURE

Voices which give the impression of refinement are prized by educated and sensitive people. Not overniceness, not prissyness, but culture. This refinement is desirable not only in the tone itself, but also in the diction. Cultured speech does not admit such slovenly phrases as: "Where d'ju git chur new bus, Hank?" "Wull, whyn'chu say so?" "Aw gwan, don' try t' kid me!"

Undesirable Characteristics in the Conversational Voice

In addition to the negative counterparts of the desirable qualities named above, certain voice characteristics are so repelling that they deserve special mention. Near the top of this list should come the following:

CONDESCENSION

Nothing will more quickly irritate people than having some-one appear to be talking down to them. No one enjoys being branded as inferior. No one likes to have his efforts discredited, his opinions treated with contempt. And unfortunate is the voice which, intentionally or unintentionally, has this effect upon others. Instinctively people know that persons of real worth do not resort to such pretensions. Greatness is simple. Use the conversation workshop to develop tones which show appreciation for those around you, tones which seem to desire to build up your classmates, not to put them in their place.

ARGUMENTATIVENESS

Some voices seem always to have a chip on their shoulders, so to speak. The owners of these voices appear to be positively unhappy if they cannot dominate every conversation by ag-gressive force or smug positiveness.

If, unfortunately, you have acquired an argumentative voice, try this: The next time you have the desire to put a vocal chip on your shoulder, stop and think, "Will any good come from my effort to show the fellow where he's wrong?" Probably not! Well, then, try another approach; for instance, this: "Yes, I can see what you mean, and there's a good deal of truth in what you say. But have you thought of this other angle?" It is not necessary to use just these words, but try to get the quality into your voice which seems to say something like this.

You won't succeed very well, however, unless you get the concept of conversation as a reciprocal business. Think of con-versation as a teeter-totter and be sure to give the other fellow his share of the free rides.

LIFELESSNESS

By lifelessness is meant something more than mere lack of animation. It is a listlessness, a lazy indifference that quickly becomes boresome to listeners. It is the kind of flat, dull voice in which some persons drone out long, pointless family anecdotes. This type of converser often gets in the habit of talking with gum in his mouth, or a pencil, or a pipe. Often, too, he sits with his elbow on chair arm or desk, his hand propping up his chin and his fingers covering part of his lips, thus adding another difficulty in understanding his already muffled and indistinct tones. Often, too, his voice seems to suggest a mind too lazy to concentrate. The tones indicate a mental fuzziness.

HEAVINESS

By heaviness is meant an unvarying solemnity, a constant heavy-as-lead somberness. This voice characterizes the person who takes himself too seriously, who never can give a phrase a light touch. He seems never to be able to get away from the "life is real, life is earnest" mood. The person who possesses this kind of voice should learn that it is possible to be serious without being somber, to be earnest without being heavy. He should use the workshop as a laboratory to practice an occasional lifting of his heavy burden of solemnity, to encourage his voice now and then to try a phrase that has its tongue in its cheek and a twinkle in its eye.

Besides these objectionable characteristics of the conversational voice, there are, of course, all the undesirable tonal qualities which we have discussed from time to time: *thinness, throatiness, nasality*, etc. The conversational workshop offers another opportunity to work for the eradication of these elements which detract from the effective speaking voice.

If you are convinced that the person who can converse readily, pleasingly, and persuasively, has a key which will unlock many a door leading to popularity and success, the conversation workshop should be a productive undertaking.

The importance of frequent and continuous practice until desired habits are established was well stated by the late Fred Stone, star of *The Wizard of Oz, Jack O'Lantern,* and other notable stage hits:

Sometimes I wonder whether any one watching a stage comedian go through an acrobatic routine, burlesquing his own efforts, has the faintest idea of the hours and days, of the weeks and months of gruelling practice that go into the performance. It looks so easy. Yet the hours of hard, unrelenting practice that have gone into perfecting my stunts add up to years.[2]

EXERCISES

1. Set up demonstration conversations at the casual everyday level. For example, have a few (five or six) members of the group seated comfortably at the front of the room. While these students engage in the ordinary small talk of which so much of our conversation consists, one or two of the other students should be designated to act as critics. These critics will work with the instructor in observing, and later reporting on, whether or not the various conversers (1) maintain an easy conversational tone and manner, (2) make contributions to the discussion without usurping more than their share of the time, (3) keep their voices friendly, (4) are distinct without being overprecise, (5) use suitable variations in voice quality, pitch, rate, and force, (6) indicate by voice and manner due respect for the opinions of the other members of the group, (7) are free from annoying mannerisms such as using disjointed melodic patterns, uttering frequent "uh's" and "ah's," indulging in hackneyed and repetitious phrases in the monotonous tones usually used for these phrases.

   As for the grain to be ground in these conversation mills, use the same kernels that you do around the campus: clothes, food, places to eat, athletics, hobbies, jobs, living costs, grades, weekend plans, parties—anything that suits your fancy and is appropriate for discussion in mixed groups.

   In these casual conversations, do not try to channel the topics too definitely. Let them drift where they will. Keep the sessions as free, flexible, and true to life as possible.

2. Arrange conversation situations slightly more purposeful than called for in the preceding exercise. That is, have one or two students prepared to lead a discussion on a certain subject, and

[2] Fred Stone, "Rolling Stone," *Omnibook*, April, 1945, p. 112.

have the group hold to the planned subject with a fair degree of fidelity. Here are possible situations:

1. A student who is prepared to discuss the problem of the growing population throughout the world introduces the subject in an informal way, somewhat as follows: "I was reading an interesting article in Blank Magazine a few days ago. The fellow who wrote it [identifying him] had some unique ideas. See if they make sense to you. . . ."

2. Several students who have read the same book (or seen the same play or heard the same orchestra) discuss its merits and demerits.

3. A group of students inject new life into that hackneyed old subject, the weather, by reading different articles on the causative factors of winds, storms, droughts, and other natural phenomena. Consult *Reader's Guide to Periodical Literature* for articles.

4. A group of "hepcats" discuss their tastes in records.

5. A group of students who have literary inclinations discuss the contrasting philosophy relative to old age in Browning's "Rabbi Ben Ezra" (p. 282) and Arnold's "Growing Old" (p. 282).

3. Have experimental groups work with special situations like the following:

1. One student applies for a job, another acts as employer.

2. Someone introduces to a group a friend from out of the city. (The introducer will be unusual if he pronounces the names so they can be heard.)

3. A student has the unhappy task of calling a friend on the telephone and reporting an automobile accident in which someone close to the friend has been injured.

4. Set up a number of demonstrations like the following. The object is to retain all possible conversational elements with necessary adaptations in rate, force, pitch, etc.

1. Two students begin a conversation on any subject of mutual interest (music, literary tastes, vacation plans, or any other subject they choose). At first they stand or sit close together

and converse in the quiet, relaxed tones commonly used under such circumstances. Next, they move five or six feet apart, and continue their talk, retaining just as much of the easy, relaxed quality as possible but using enough vocal force to be heard without effort. Gradually they move farther apart—ten feet, twenty, the limits of the room. Meanwhile the class carefully observes the necessary adjustments in vocal energy, pitch, rate, articulation, length of pauses and phrases, etc.

2. A student makes a report to a committee. For example, the committee may be considering the desirability of recommending the honor system for the school, and the student may report on his observations of the system in another school. He encourages questions and comments from the committee, but he purposefully clings to his subject and completes his report. He is carefully prepared, but keeps his outline flexible and his voice truly conversational.

3. A student acts as emissary from the class in asking the president of the university for a longer Christmas holiday. He shows proper respect for the president, but presents his case with sincerity and conviction.

4. A student pleads a case before a student jury, defending a fellow student who has been charged with defacing books in the library. The "lawyer" realizes that if the jury has any intimation that he is making a speech he will have small chance of winning his case; hence he converses with them, earnestly and directly.

5. A student presents to his club, fraternity, or class a plan for raising funds for a special purpose. By his voice and manner he does everything in his power to keep his fellows from feeling that he is making a speech *at* them.

5. Plan some group discussions at the conversational level. Do not hesitate to introduce controversial subjects on which the members of the group have firm convictions—including those often-taboo subjects, politics and religion. College students should be able to discuss these subjects without rancor, and with sufficient objectivity to avoid offense. And they should be able to champion

a point of view with enthusiasm and earnestness, without permitting their voices to become acrimonious.

Even though these discussions are kept at the conversational level, it is best to have a chairman appointed; it is his responsibility to see that everyone has a chance to talk and that no one talks more than he should. He also directs the course of the discussion by carefully planned questions. But he does not take sides or uphold any point of view; he remains neutral.

1. Hold a round-table discussion on a subject like: "How can we provide adequate medical care for all the people?"

2. Hold a panel discussion on a subject such as: "Should our school abolish the present grading system and substitute simple pass-fail marks (or vice versa)?"

   The panel acts as a jury to consider the question freely. The discussion is not like a debate; no one should try to argue the other fellow down. The purpose of the panel is to endeavor to focus the group mind on a problem, and if possible get agreement as to a course of action. It is democracy at work. The voice and attitude should be "Come, let us reason together."

3. Hold a symposium-forum. The distinguishing feature of the symposium is that the various participants are assigned specific phases of the subject to cover. After the original presentations, the symposium may be turned into a panel discussion if desired. Subjects suitable for such discussions are:

   (1) What are some of the underlying causes of war? What are some possible cures?

   (2) Some of the issues involved in a forthcoming election.

   (3) An overall view of our city administration (or school administration) presented by various representatives.

Index